The Voice of the Dawn

To David Wattens
with best wishes
+
Thanks for a
wonderful
Conference!

J.M. D—

The
Voice of

University Press
of
New England

Hanover
and
London

Frederick Matthew Wiseman

the Dawn

An Autohistory

of the

Abenaki Nation

University Press of New England, Hanover, NH 03755

Printed in United States of America

5 4 3 2 1

LIBRARY OF CONGRESS CATALOGING-IN-PUBLICATION DATA

Wiseman, Frederick Matthew, 1948–
The voice of the dawn: an autohistory of the Abenaki nation /
by Frederick Matthew Wiseman.
p. cm.
Includes bibliographical references and index.
ISBN 1–58465–058–3 (cloth)—ISBN 1–58465–059–1 (pbk.)
1. Abenaki Indians—History. I. Title.
E99.A13 W45 2000
974.004'973—dc21   00–010361

For Anna

GIVING THANKS

*We are grateful to the powers of the universe. The essence that underlies
and binds everything. From which time and space were created.*

*We are grateful to Grandfather Sun, who created the world.
We are your children.*

*We are grateful to Grandmother Moon, who, with the Sun,
conspired to make human beings. We sing to you every time we see
your crescent; new again in the evening sky.*

*We are grateful to the One Tree, from which humankind came.
It is the road of spirits, connecting all realms of existence.*

We give thanks to the Seven Directions that make up our ordinary world.

*We give thanks to the Great Council Fire; from it comes our law and the
age-old connections to our former foes, who are now our friends.*

*We remember Saint Anne, Matrii Virginii Abnaquaeidd,
she who supported us through the long dark of Genocide.*

*We give thanks to our Elders, for they have seen so much and
share their wisdom of life.*

*We give thanks to our Relatives, the plant and animal people,
and the earth and waters that support us all.*

*We give thanks to our Children, for they are ancestors to
generations yet unborn.*

Medawas, 1998

Contents

PART TWO: THE WAR FOR THE DAWNLAND

Illustrations

Preface

Many passages of the sun ago my grandfather took me to Wazowategok, the River, and said," Grandson, this is the Missisquoi; its waters flow in my veins, and when I die, I will be buried where I can always see the River. The River is in your blood too, and you will come back to it." I know now what he meant, after living in the deserts of the Tahono O'odam, the bayous of the land of the Chitimachas, and the bustle of the city built upon the ruined lodges of the Massachusetts. I now am back in Wôbanakik, the Land of the Dawn, where I can be at peace. I would like to tell you a story, one about my people and their land. The story is a sash woven of many strands of language. The first strand is the remembered wisdom of the Abenaki community. The second strand is our history and that of our relatives, written down by European, Native American, and Euro-American observers. The third strand is what our Mother the Earth has revealed to us through the studies and writings of those who delve in her, the archaeologists and paleoecologists. The fourth strand is my own family history and its stories. The fifth strand is, of course, that which has come to me alone, stories that I create with my own beliefs and visions. The sash story has spiritual guardians, among them white bear, fox, beaver, ash, black bear, and corn, each of whom dictates to me the unique pattern that the sash takes as it is woven. Woven into the sash are many beads, words in the language of the Alnôbak, the Abenaki people. The sash is many generations long, sometimes with many strands and simple pattern and sometimes complex, woven of but a few strands.

Acknowledgments

I would like to thank the following colleagues for their help with bringing this manuscript to fruition: James Petersen of the University of Vermont for his careful evaluation and editing of the manuscript. In correspondence and discussion he was able to "rein me back in" and gently force me to substantiate my arguments when my opinions veered too far from current archaeological canon. Colin Calloway of Dartmouth College for his evaluation of the historical sections and for general discussions that allowed me to refine my ideas of the Contact Period and the eighteenth century, as well as my "voice" in the manuscript. Wayne Newell of the Indian Township School, Indian Township, Maine, and Lt. Governor Ed Bassett and Brian Altavater (Pleasant Point Health Service) of Pleasant Point, Maine, for their continual encouragement and discussions concerning what it is to be a Wabanaki person writing about Wabanaki issues. John Moody of the Winter Center, Sharon, Vermont, for many years of discussions concerning the history and spirit of the Abenaki and how they work together. Jeff Benay of the Governor's Commission on Native American Affairs, Grand Chief Homer St. Francis, and April Rushlow, Acting Chief, Abenaki Nation at Missisquoi, for their careful reading of the post-1970s sections and helping me through the minefield of modern history and factionalism.

I would also like to thank my many students at Johnson State College, who have, over the years, made marvelous materials that figure in some of the illustrations. Aaron York and Taqralik Partridge, who consented to be models for the clothing illustrations. Andrew Lee, a former student, who took many of the photographs found in this work and also made the arrow and dart points. Portions of the research leading to this publication have been supported by the Vermont Council on the Humanities, under a grant from the National Endowment for the Humanities, and a sabbatical leave from Johnson State College, Johnson, Vermont. I would also like to thank April Ossmann of the University Press of New England, who oversaw the conversion of a rough draft into a credible work of scholarship. Finally, I would like to thank my wife, Anna Roy, for her support, encouragement, and assistance in the long travels that were required to find the information and artifacts presented here.

A Note on the Illustrations

There seems to be endless debate of what constitutes Western Abenaki material culture. This confusion was best summed up by an archaeologist several years ago: "I have never seen a postcolonial Abenaki artifact." Almost everyone who attempts to portray "postcontact" Abenaki material garners incessant criticism and controversy. Beginning in 1990, with the "Material

Heritage of Vermont Abenaki" project, funded by the Vermont Council on the Humanities and Johnson State College, I have collected evidence of what the Abenaki past may have looked like. Using this evidence, I have constructed archetypes; models that integrate this evidence into proxemic and ecological systems, much as a museum curator creates a Chippendale period room. These archetypes are described in many ways, as exposition in the text, as well as in the illustrations. I have made, commissioned, or selected a series of drawings, paintings, postcards, and artifact spreads and created scenes to portray my "best guess" as to what the Abenaki dressed in, lived in, and used throughout their long history.

The artifacts shown have been found within or have a provenance from modern Wôbanakik. The reconstructed artifacts have either a Wôbanakik prototype or are from the immediate vicinity. A few are widespread materials available to all indigenous people. Some of the illustrations are loosely based on paintings or drawings held by Euro-American institutions.

Please see pages 253–59 for extended comments on the illustrations.

The Voice of the Dawn

1

Introduction and Methods of Research

Anglo Perceptions of the Abenaki

Robert Berkhofer, in his ground-breaking *The White Man's Indian*, has shown all of us that the image of the First Nations peoples is held firmly in White hands. The image in New England is of basket-making Indian people dressed in beads and buckskins, adrift somewhere in time, unconnected to the present. This "exotic other" is a fluid mixture of the pathetic "disappearing Indian," the counterculture spiritual warrior, and the healer-shamanic elder. The image is used by White people to critique their own society, provide an escape from the stress of modern life, or achieve inner peace and personal growth. Other scholars have contrasted the exotic other with the disheveled, factional, yet vaguely menacing "interior" Abenaki communities and individuals routinely encountered in the news media. The disconnection between these White images of the Indian can be traced to a deeper belief held by modern scholars, politicians, and the public, namely, a failure of Abenaki tribal government as an institution and of tribal sovereignty as a concept. This leads the American community to believe that they are the rightful stewards of our people's archaeology, culture history, land, and genetic material.[1]

In November 1999 the University of Vermont hosted a conference titled "Reflections on Remembering and Forgetting: Revisiting *The Original Vermonters.*" It was attended by over one hundred scholars and First Nations people from the United States and Canada. This excellent and academically ground-breaking conference brought Indians and academics together in interesting ways and tentatively explored the dimensions of native sovereignty in three presentations. However, the title, structure, and nature of the conference was based on the "exterior" qualities of a faded (or "remembered") Indian Vermont as it meets academic Anglo concerns. Modern "interior" issues facing the Vermont native community, including Indian gaming, the role of Indian intellectuals, factionalism, poverty (and its attending social ills), hostility of the judicial and executive branches of Vermont government, border-crossing issues, and a host of other problems were essentially left unexplored. First Nations citizens were expressly invited as "Indian people" to do the opening and closing prayers and to introduce one session. At least two tribal-enrolled Indians with postgraduate degrees presented papers as "experts" in history or the arts, rather than providing an explicit tribal perspective. However, this conference provided an environment where "interior" concerns could be attended to in the halls, among Native peoples, and sometimes even including scholars and organizers. Apologies were made, new external threats and coalitions were explored, and goodwill began to prosper in several venues. So while the conference was overtly focused on the anthropological and ethnohistorical qualities of Vermonters who happened to have Native ancestry, a covert agenda of tribal persistence and sovereignty was brought and pursued by First Nations attendees. Advice and assistance was sought and given for issues ranging from the repatriation of wampum, and the political nature of Vermont's Indian factions and their relation to state recognition, to the Micmacs' struggle with the Canadian government's environmental bureaucracies and the Quebec Abenakis' land claims.

The Abenaki Family Tree and a Little Chauvinism

This lengthy introduction leads me to the philosophy and nature of this book. The twin assumptions of the "exotic other" Abenaki and demise of Abenaki sovereignty will be denounced in this volume. The Abenaki people are the political, spiritual, and cultural heirs in a legal sense, not merely the descendants, of their ancestors. They are a proud and doughty people, with a story as powerful, if not more so, than that of their better-known neighbors. The connection between the "exterior" Paleo-Indian hunter or eighteenth-century warrior defending his homeland and the "interior" Swanton Abenaki citizen dealing with the school board is as vast as time, space, and spirit. This is a view that assumes that we are our ancestors and they are us. Mere genealogical mathematics shows this. Each modern Abenaki citizen has over fifty million ancestors in A.D. 1350, more than the estimated population of North America at the time. The study of the evolution and divergence of our language also indicates that the widespread "proto-Algonquins" of long ago are our linguistic ancestors. Anyone who has ventured into genealogies learns that his pedigree spreads out through space to encompass huge geographic regions. Following this genealogical-geographic lead rather than cultural geography, this book considers regions larger than the anthropologists' "Western Abenaki culture area" as our Wôbanakik in the more distant past.[2]

My scholarly friends will probably disagree with my characterization of such things as the "St. Lawrence Iroquoians" or the discovery of Europe by the Abenakis, yet both of these are based on a monolithic commitment to Abenaki sovereignty, as deep as the scholars' commitment to "Iroquois supremacy" and antidiffusionist paradigms. What would history look like if all North Americans assumed that the Abenaki were a sovereign nation, with control of their past as well as their future? That is the story I wish to present.

The Philosophy of Repatriation

The tradition of Western science is unidirectional from subject (Abenaki elder, archaeological site, industrial raw material) to the collector/researcher to the publisher. From there it goes to the teacher (college professor) or media person (*Nova* scriptwriter) and finally to the multiethnic American community, the ultimate consumer. As viewed by the consumer, this is a process of enrichment. But viewed from the perspective of the elder who has lost legal control of her life story, the backfilled hole that was once a site, or the plant crucified on acid-free paper in some paradichlorobenzined herbarium cabinet, this may seem exploitative to say the least. But repatriation, closing the circle between consumer and subject, is possible. The returning of archaeological remains to Native people is a key foundation of Native-Anglo relationships and a useful beginning to our methodology. Yet it deals with the material world, not the world of information and ideas. My method is to treat archaeology, paleoenvironmental studies, ethnohistory, and the like, as worlds ripe for repatriation into Native control.

This method has been attempted by First Nations scholars. George Sioui's *Amerindian Autohistory* was the first bid in the Northeast to reconfigure the Euro-American database into a native narrative. Sioui attempted to reconcile the Wendat (Huron) spiritual worldview with the facts garnered by archaeologists and historians. As with all pioneering works, it has received some criticism from scholarly communities. In 1995, Daniel Paul published *We Were Not the Savages*, an autohistory of the Micmac people. Using a paradigm of political sovereignty, he inverted many assumptions about Micmac-British roles and relations and applied them to the Canadian Maritimes of the twentieth century. My exposition combines Paul's and Sioui's approaches: a commitment to Abenaki and First Nations spiritual and political sovereignty. So this book is a tool as well as a scholarly publication. The work it must accomplish is to prove that the Abenaki have always been here, not just as a set of transmitted genes or even as a set of dimly remembered stories of the "old days." That is why I cover pre-nineteenth-century history fairly lightly. That has been done, and it serves Abenaki citizenry no useful purpose. Our history is not dead but alive and as full of intrigue, double-cross, and dogged heroism as any historical novel. Modern history and its direct antecedents are the stories that will set us free.

Source Material

The most desirable material is an unmediated Abenaki voice from the past or present. Unfortunately, the Western Abenaki have attracted scanty folkloric inquiry until recently, so there is little seventeenth-, eighteenth- or nineteenth-century voice, and that which exists has been well documented by Colin Calloway's excellent historical researches. Therefore, I have chosen to include a narration from my short life span, material I remember from my family and friends. In that I am fortunate, for my father and grandfather, Ben Gravel, "Monkey" Drew, Ernest Larocque, and other Swantonians of the 1950s and 1960s transmitted much lore of wind and water, long-lost wars, long-winded jokes, and supernatural tales to a boy eager to hear about "what the French and Indians used to do" (fig. 1). This wellspring of remembered lore, some of which is quite clear and some just impressions, represents a personal snapshot of time with roots in the Native past. Since this is my family and personal history, I do not have any qualms about sharing it with another.

Fig. 1. The author in Monkey Drew's boat, 1956. *Wiseman collection.*

Science

Almost as sure as my memory is Quaternary geography, information on the climate, geology, and ecology of the last twelve thousand years. This is reliable information and is not value-laden with regard to Abenaki sovereignty. The biogeographic backdrop of the Abenaki is an easy repatriation, despite the technical jargon.

Archaeology

Archaeology, although similar to Pleistocene geography, is actually a "rat's nest" of problems for repatriation. First is the nature of the material. A first concern is the destructive nature of the archaeological process. An excavation destroys the traces on the earth of our Old Ones and consigns their spirit to the museum shelf or printed page. Our elders believe this disrespectful at best, genocidal at worst. Luckily, almost all modern professional archaeology is of Abenaki sites menaced by stream erosion or by road and utility construction, although some would say it is better to be destroyed by the backhoe than to lie in a museum! Of all remains, archaeologists most covet those interred, or buried. For many Native people, "grave desecration research" produces such contaminated information that its mere contemplation, not to mention use, will affect their health and that of their loved ones. The problem is that some of the ancient Abenakis' greatest material accomplishments are known only through gravesite research. Ignoring this information diminishes the Abenaki in the eyes of people interested in comparing us with other communities, such as the Iroquois. However, since I have a family, I will follow the elders' cautions in the use of specific burial data. A second problem with repatriation of archaeological information lies in the realm of interpretation. Archaeological theory is convoluted and obtuse and changes from one generation of archaeologists to the next. Some theories are less than complimentary to the Abenaki and their ancestors. For example, the Abenaki and their relatives seem to appear as mere "bark eating" brutes living to the west of the civilized Iroquois Confederacy.

"The Iroquois called themselves Ho-de-no-sau-nee ('People of the Longhouse') thus proudly distinguishing themselves from their hunting and foraging neighbors (the 'tree eaters')" (Joseph Campbell, *The Way of the Seeded Earth*, p. 131). Indian role-player Louis Henry Morgan's researches of the 1840s, archaeologist William Richie's seminal *Archaeology of New York State*, Cornell University's and perhaps the D'Arcy McNickle Center's (during Francis Jennings's tenure) "engines" for producing Irocentric anthropologists and ethnohistorians all had influences on this "Iroquois supremacy" belief that remain unexamined. Archaeologists are continually amazed that the Abenaki and their kin are capable of doing anything "advanced." A late-1980s video, "Secrets of the Lost Red Paint People," in the *Nova* series dramatizes this point as archaeologists William Fitzhugh, James Tuck, Bruce Borque, and others have their "socks knocked off" by our ancestors' unaccountably sophisticated art and architecture. These may be merely amusing or interesting to the observer of the human condition, but other controversies, such as the St. Lawrence Iroquoian issue, will certainly emerge as a legal threat to our quest for recognition. More distant controversies, such as the Bering Land Bridge hypothesis, while having a great deal of support from the hard science of Pleistocene geography, is nonetheless anathema to many Native people in that it contradicts their strong assurances of their people's local creation. These are but some of the many issues of interpretation in which we as sovereign Abenaki people may differ from the canon.[3]

Ethnohistory

More imprecise and biased than archaeology in many ways is ethnohistory. Here we look through the lens of the oppressor to gain insight into the life of the oppressed. Only in the explicit records of direct treaty negotiations is the Native voice heard at all, but often it is twisted to favor the recorder. This is poignantly clear in the long misunderstanding between the Maine Abenakis and successive Anglo governments. The Abenakis continually asserted that they had given up no land, whereas the Anglo treaty records clearly state that the land was given over. This led to the Maine land claims controversies of the late 1970s. Sympathetic government officials, often of New France, and clerics such as the Jesuits may have had a neutral or even pro-Abenaki tendency, but institutional and ecclesiastical agendas and biases remain. The problem is that the worldview of the eighteenth-century lieutenant or priest is more similar to that of the twentieth-century historian than it was to the Abenaki citizen he faced across the council fire. This unexamined bias "contaminates" the relevance of the data for repatriation. Sampling this material is problematic, and correcting for implicit assumptions is a dicey task. Even in the realm of ethnohistory, some materials are considered unrecoverably contaminated, such as the issue of Christian conversion or of disease. One elder at our reserve at Odanak, Quebec, said that I must not discuss ancient diseases in this volume, "lest consequences ensue." The mere contemplation of ancient smallpox is enough to bring sickness into the world again.

Probably the major problem is not the materials but the implicit assumption of the failure of tribal sovereignty and government characterizing most of these primary and secondary works. This appears time and again as the historian hits 1800; he becomes vague and unfocused, relying on anecdotes or borrowings from our "non-Abenaki" neighbors to get him to the post-1970 "Abenaki renaissance." The disregarding of this period by academic historians is a threat to our sovereignty, in that it disconnects us from our ancestors. A final suite of problems in data repatriation lies in the recent past, in attempting to reconstruct the last twenty-five years from an often hostile news media that has ridiculed our leadership and quest for recognition. This was particularly vexing for me in writing the last two chapters of this book, for I soon discovered that much of what was written is different from what I or other Abenaki citizens remember.

Pan-Indianism

The last problem lies within the First Nations communities, through an internalized "exotic other" discussed in the first part of the introduction. Self-righteous spiritual pundits abound in Abenaki country, attempting to control the dissemination of what they believe is the spiritual nature of an Abenaki world. I have no problem with anyone's spirituality—it is a personal choice. Indeed, you will be seeing some of my beliefs quite soon! But there is inappropriate evangelism going on, with its concomitant ridiculing of other people's beliefs. Much of this proselytizing but ersatz Abenaki religion seems to be an uneasy decoction of Black Elk Lakota (Sioux) liturgy with a dash of Micmac from Ruth Holmes Whitehead and a pinch of Penobscot from Frank Speck. We are awash in assumed post-Indian names, the owners of which accuse others of not being Indian. This self-destructive nonsense violates the cardinal directive of Abenaki sovereignty. Yet I am writing a book and must discuss spirituality, at least a bit. I treat the spirit world as I believe it would wish to be treated, as part and parcel of creation, a seamless gradient of life and spirit. As my friend Tsonakwa says: "The great secret of the world of men is that the world of spirits exists, and the great secret of the world of spirits is that there are no secrets." In this book, I will separate my personal belief from information that has been repatriated, and yes, I go to Speck and Whitehead; but that is evaluated in light of what I know of Abenaki knowledge and my personal beliefs. I will leave the Mediwiwin lodge, White Buffalo Calf Woman, spirit sweat lodge, and sage smudge to the West, except in the context of diplomatic exchange.[4]

Independence

Traditional scholarly works require extensive citation of statements in a well-defined format. They require source data and permission for illustrative material. The original source material I repatriate was almost certainly taken from the Abenaki and their land without human permission or environmental advocacy (a Guatemala Maya once asked me, "Who speaks for the lake sediments you core for pollen?"). Do we now need to acknowledge or seek permission to get it back under our control? Certainly not! This may be the theoretical basis for data repatriation, but it will diminish the credibility of the book. Since the information I present may be used for purposes other than simple entertainment, citation in some form is necessary. Rather than page citation or footnoting, I will discuss, in the text and in endnotes, my sources of data and ideas, in order to lead the inquisitive scholar back to these wellsprings. Second, legal title to the fiction, stories, and materials illustrated in this work are all held exclusively by me, so there is no problem with external permission from museums or publishers.[5]

Organization and Interpretation

Converting this complex patchwork quilt of information and interpretations into autohistory is relatively simple compared to the amassing of the data. I have found several organizational and methodological principles appropriate to the task. Let me reiterate and expand the underlying assumptions:

1. The Abenaki are the descendants of people who lived in Vermont, New Hampshire, and Western Maine "since time immemorial," as they said in 1766. Therefore I will not question whether the archaeologists' "Laurentian" or "Maritime" Archaic culture is directly ancestral to the Abenaki but accept both. The Abenaki citizens' ancestors occupied an area far greater than the modern "Western Abenaki" area. I therefore feel that I have the right to discuss relatively distant locales and events if relevant to my story.

2. There is unbroken political sovereignty. This may vary from extended family organization (bands) to more complex organizations such as confederacies, but the thread of sovereignty remains, and has *never* been relinquished to any foreign power.

3. An Abenaki ascendancy. We the Abenaki people are not inferior to the Iroquois of any other Native or non-Native group. We excelled and continue to excel in many things and need not be ashamed. So there will be some flag waving on our behalf in the book.

4. There is a gradient of truth. Much of what I tell you here is "scholarly conjecture," true or false depending on your belief in the underlying assumptions. Oral history and personal experience is in the netherworld between fact and fiction—I know that I saw a UFO once, but I can't prove it. If you believe in UFOs, you will agree with me; if not, you won't. Stories are considered fiction, yet they express basic concepts and ideas that are important to a logic or direction of study. But if you believe in the underlying assumptions, they are more than untruths.

5. Questioning the assumptions of past histories and anthropologies when they contradict assumptions 1–4 listed above.

I hope that this long-winded discussion of autohistory and repatriation will let those of you with an academic bent know "where I'm coming from" when I ignore the smallpox epidemic of 1535 or gloss over the bloodshed of the Deerfield Raid or disconnected spirits of the Boucher burials. It is not ignorance or neglect but respect, tinged with a bit of concern for my family. And so to the narrative.

PART I
Before the Darkness

2

The Coming of the Great Animals:
The Years of the Adebaskedon

(13,000 to 10,000 Winters Ago)

It is said among my people that we were created by Ktsi Nwaskw from the ash tree. At that time long ago, Ktsi Nwaskw gave us permission to use Aki, the Earth, and its bounty with care and respect. We renew that permission by ceremony and prayer to assure harmony and balance of the world. The Alnôbak, the Abenaki people, have been in Wôbanakik, our land, since the Frost Monsters withdrew thousands of years ago. Our oldest stories look back to a world ruled by the icy breath of the Monsters and animals large and fierce. Our great hero, known as Pedewadzo, Gluskabe, Odsiodzo, or Koluscap, is called by some spring-bringer. It was he, through spiritual and physical strength, who partly defeated the Monsters, changing the very land into that which is familiar and comfortable. In this book I will use his Eastern name, *Koluscap*, for it is said that using his Western Abenaki name too much bothers him unnecessarily.

KOLUSCAP AND THE FROST MONSTERS

Here camps my story, an old granite rock scoured by ice and covered by hoar-frost and lichen. Koluscap was tired of the cold. It was so cold that people had moved to Nibenakik, where it was warm enough to hunt and fish. He went to find Bezegawan, the Fog. Slowly, tendrils of mist flowed down snow-covered hills, merged and coalesced, and Bezegawan stood before Koluscap. "Why does Ice now cover the earth so much that it bends under its weight?" "Koluscap," said the Fog, "the Frost Monsters in the north have gotten too strong. They blow their icy breath so that Winter is long and the other seasons are so short they cannot melt the ice. The Frost Monsters are powerful and dangerous; if they catch a man, they will eat him alive, consuming him into more ice." Koluscap said, "Grandfather, these creatures do not frighten me, I will go and fight them and make them stop the Ice". "Koluscap," said the Fog, "the Frost Monsters live in Pabonkik, so far to the north that you will need four pairs of ogenak [snowshoes] to reach them." So Koluscap made four wonderful pairs of snowshoes to journey to the village of the Frost Monsters. Koluscap set off across the ice. By the time his first pair of snowshoes fell apart, the icy wind was blowing so hard that his cape flew from his shoulders. By the time his second pair wore out, the wind froze his hair to his neck. By the time the third pair wore out, Koluscap could only crawl through the howling gale.

In time he came to a huge village called Wazoli, palisaded with ice stalagmites and with houses made of snow lit inside by cold blue fire that took away warmth. There he saw the Frost Monsters, with their great toothed and tusked mouths from which came a huge cold gale that froze the world. They were naked. Koluscap said, "You must stop making the world cold. You have forced my people to move far to the south to be able to find game. I will wrestle you each, and if I win, warmth will come to show that I have beaten you." The Monsters were persistent and tricky in wrestling and could not be beaten without killing them, which he did, though it was hard work. After killing many, he said, "Enough, I cannot kill you all." He also thought, "If I kill them all, winter, and the rest that it gives the earth, will not come, and Aki will tire quickly." So he returned home, leaving some of the Frost Monsters alive. That is why we still have winter but not so strong as before, and Frost Monsters still eat the unwary hunter in the dead of winter. Koluscap laboriously slogged back to his lodge beside the lake. Bezegawan rose from the lake said, "Koluscap, you did well to stop the breath of the Monsters, but you did even better to let some live so that my sister the earth can rest." The Alnôbak were again able to live in Wôbanakik, the Land of the Dawn.[1]

Medawas, 1993

The departed ice is the Great White Bear of the North, who has left us to become a series of stars in the night sky to the north of the Spirit Road Alakswsowodi (the Milky Way). But, like the storyteller, the land has not forgotten those times when our Oldest Ones followed retreating ice into Wôbanakik, our ancient land.

Eighteen thousand winters ago, ice lay heavily on the land, so that Aki, the sleeping earth herself, was bent under its weight. In all of Wôbanakik, perhaps only the highest peak of Monademack (Mount Monadnock, New Hampshire) saw the feeble light of the ancient sun. Summer was short and weak, for the icy blast from the north was unremitting. Sixteen thousand winters ago, the ice, perhaps with Koluscap's help, relented. The mile-high glaciers, flesh of the White Bear, stopped their advance and began to melt.

The highest peaks of Kodaakwadso (Mount Washington) and Gawasi-wadso (Mount Kearsage) to the east and Mozeodebe Wadso (Mount Mansfield) and Tawakbedeo Wadso (Camel's Hump) to the west, slowly reappeared above the stagnant ice. Then the Great Bear melted to the northwest at a rate of one thousand feet each year. The glacier-scoured land, bowed under the weight of the millennia-old ice, began to rise. Melt-water filled valleys and hollows choked by chunks of remaining ice, be-coming cold, lifeless lakes shrouded with ice six or seven feet deep. The primordial windswept Bitawbagok (called Lake Vermont by geologists) and Kwinitekwbagok (Lake Hitchcock to geologists) were filled by muddy torrents scouring clay, silt, and rock from the land. These ancient muds and sands now lie four hundred to seven hundred feet above our modern shorelines and can be seen where the Euro-Americans endlessly quarry them for their roads and buildings.

The blockading ice then moved beyond the Valley of the Ktsitegw (St. Lawrence River), and the high cold lakes quickly emptied into the Great Sea, leaving the primordial rivers to cut through old lake bottoms on their way to the sea (fig. 2). After thirty thousand years of sleep in the bosom of the Bear, Wôbanakik was now reborn as a northeastern peninsula between the salt ocean and the salt Champlain Sea.[2] The land and waters were life-less but fertile and full of promise:

ABENAKI DAWN

Great Spirit, let me see the land as it was
when our Old Ones first came to Wôbanakik.
Call forth the Soubagwa, the Great Sea from the east
to let it fill our valleys with its teeming life.
Awaken the Ktsiawaasak, the great animals
from their resting places beneath our hills.
Let me see all of this so I may share it with others.

Medawas, 1994

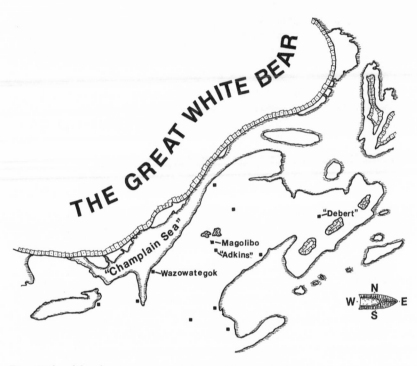

Fig. 2. Wôbanakik and environs, 10,500 winters ago. *Wiseman collection.*

The New Land and Its Life

Twelve thousand winters ago the White Bear and his brethren had dwindled, their melted flesh filling the oceans. The newly risen Great Sea rushed into our glacially depressed landscape, bringing cold salt water to supplant the fresh water of the now depleted Bitawbagok. The lifeless Northwestern Sea rose 250 feet above modern lake levels. A millennium later, mollusks, fish, and sea mammals had turned the quiet waters into a bounteous, productive seascape. We see their remains in the old gray oceanic clays located somewhat inland from Kwinaska (Shelburne Point, Vermont) or along the Wazowategok (Missisquoi River). This pattern of rebirth can still be seen in the glacial inlets of Alaska and Greenland and gives us a contemporary view of this interesting ecological process. (See fig. 2.)

Pollen, the seed of life sacred to us and our neighbors, was entombed in these ancient muds. It tells us that Wôbanakik was bare of trees but for an occasional tiny plant that had gained a foothold on the lifeless rock and silt. As the years grew longer and the summers warmer, seeds of grasses and sedges blew into the hills and plains of Wôbanakik to make a vast carpeted landscape. Mingled with the spreading low grasses and sedges were tiny shrubs such as the *kanosasiz* (dwarf willow, *Salix herbacea*) or tasty *sata* (blueberry, *Vaccinium uliginosum*) and *paksiwimen* (twinberry, *Mitchella repens*). Into this grassy world moved a host of animals unlike any existing today: woolly mammoths with great hairy bodies and curved tusks and herds of shaggy musk oxen, as well as smaller animals such as horses, wolves, and predatory cats.

Although Mozeodebe wadso and its brothers had the same form as they do today, they were only the bones of the earth, scraped clean by the Bear, hosting much ice and snow but few plants and fewer animals. The Wawobadenak, which we now call the Adirondack, White, and Green Mountains, had lingering glaciers that made bowl-shaped scoops (called cirques by Euro-American geologists) on their sides. In the lowlands a cub of the White Bear long remained as a glacier near Wintegok (the Lamoille River). It left a distinctive "kame deposit" adjacent to the Euro-American village of Belvedere, Vermont, to remind us that the land was yet in the waning grip of the Frost Monsters. The earth was new and alive, its spirit strong but hard. In the winter a bone-numbing cold froze the land solid and piled it below drifting snow whipped by gales and blizzards. During the lengthening summers, snow melted on Aki's surface, but the ice below blocked its drainage, making mosquito-infested muskeg.[3]

The Coming of the Alnôbak

This soil holds spoor of our Oldest Ones, who, in thick, fur-lined overgarments over supple woven clothing, moved along ancient seashores from Nibenakik, the south, hunting animals and fish of the ocean and strand. Our bands ranged along the glacial margin far to the east and west of our area—from the Great Sea to the Great Lakes. Tools found near the shores of Bitawbagok were made from stone from the White Mountains, Northern Maine, or from far to the west, toward what are now the Great Lakes. Life revolved around the hunt on sea and shore and the need to survive in this primordial land. Our Oldest Ones lived in highly dispersed groups of families tied together by language and kinship. Since there were few people in any given area, each mobile band reported to others on the distribution and movement of game over vast regions. They followed the marine

life and the herds of upland game in a well-planned yearly cycle, returning to the seasonal camps year after year, for they knew that certain areas
were advantageous. Spring brought smelt and stickleback to their spawning grounds and our nets in cold rivers feeding the sea. Summer camps of
caribou-skin-covered wigwams were placed on the shores of rivers or
lakes, where the wind gave relief from the hordes of mosquitoes and black
flies that had become so common. Nonegonnikon Wazowategok, a marine mammal hunting site on old beach dunes near the modern Euro-
American village of East Highgate, Vermont (fig. 2) tells us of our past
through hearths with fire-cracked boiling stones, the remains of fuel-
wood, and over two hundred tools left by our Old Ones. Spear points, including fifty-five fluted and related points, hide- and plant-processing
scrapers, knives, and polished and drilled soapstone pendants remind us
of our life in the Eldest days. Another site in Maine, called Adkins by archaeologists, has excellent evidence of our earliest architecture. From
these summer camps, small toothed whales, such as the porpoise and beluga, could be hunted by canoe, perhaps of baleen frames covered with
stitched caribou hide. (Fig. 3.)

Our eastern relatives still remember the small, hide-covered boat,
known as the *mozolol*, that may be descended from these early craft. The
beluga whale could be hunted in rivers and estuaries or in the shallows
where it occasionally beached itself. Although the larger *podabak* (fin-
back, humpback, and bowhead whales) were too big and strong to be
hunted, if they became beached, we did not neglect their meat, bone, and
blubber. We still tell stories of when Koluscap, our hero, used to ride the
whales, a remembrance of these times. *Askigwak* (bearded and hooded
seals), as well as walrus, which congregated in droves on the shores, were
hunted between their spring arrival and fall departure. The ringed and
harp seals, year-round denizens of the Northwestern Sea, could be hunted
anytime. Seabirds, fish such as capelin or sculpin, and the little *sisak*
(common clam), such are seen in old muds near Bitawbagok, rounded out
the diet. During the Years of the Adebaskedon the land was bereft of its ice
mantle, and it rose, slowly emptying the ocean northeastward. At first the
sea was unchanged. The life of water and strand was abundant and easily
hunted. As time went on, uplift of the earth's crust made our beloved sea
smaller, more brackish, and less suitable for saltwater plants and animals.

In the fall, our ancestors dispersed to inland hunting camps to harvest the
hide, meat, and fur of upland mammals that were now prime. Their meat
was laced with life- and warmth-giving fats and oils. We ate fat from larger

Fig. 3. Whale hunt on the Champlain Sea, 10,500 winters ago. *Wôbanakik Heritage Center Collections, photograph by Andrew Lee.*

animals to assure the necessary calories for winter survival. Our neighbors to the north still say that the rabbit, or Arctic hare, while fine for summer, did not have enough fat to use during cold—you can starve to death while eating rabbit. An archaeological site in the center of Wôbanakik was probably one of these fall hunting camps. Nonnegonikon Magolibo (known to archaeologists as the Vail site) consisted of a group of shelters with over 1,500 artifacts, including fluted points for big game hunting, animal-processing tools, and distinctive "fluted drills" for making tools and ornaments such as the pendants found at Nonnegonikon Wazowategok. Nearby is evidence of the killing of large game animals. The bone is long returned to our Mother the Earth, but the tools found there must have been used on caribou-sized game or larger. Since there were few staple plants, our diet was mostly meat and hunting our means of livelihood. Small animals and birds, such as the ptarmigan, squirrels, and Arctic hare, could be hunted with snares or even by throwing sticks when obtaining fat was less important.

My grandfather tells me about rabbit hunting in a style that may descend from the tundra-covered plains when Wôbanakik was young.

RABBIT HUNTING STORY

To hunt the rabbit-kind you need only a stick, patience and thanksgiving. If you notice a rabbit as you walk toward it, you see it will first stop eating the grass. As you get closer, it will pull its hind feet under it and crouch, ready to run. As you approach the rabbit closer it will flee, until it is as far from you as when it first noticed you. However, if you do not look directly at the rabbit and spiral slowly inward toward it at an easy walk you can get amazingly close, since the rabbit cannot easily tell how close you are. You can often get so close that you can kill it with a stick!

Frederick W. Wiseman, 1956

Our Oldest Ones moved away from the coldest, most lifeless areas during the winter and returned when conditions were right to harvest the land's and water's bounty. Winter camps were chosen for protection from the coldest drafts that blew from glaciers lingering as little as sixty miles to the northwest. The camps were sturdy hide shelters, and the warmth of the hearth protected us from cold winds. Food and hides could be processed inside, away from the cold. During these times people met to discuss Aki and her bounty, hold celebrations of birth, marriage, and death, and tell stories about life and hopes for the future. They acknowledged the forces of this dawn-land: the teeming life of sea and shore, the great carnivores that fed on them, the sun and earth, and most certainly the winds. They remembered the ceremonies to renew life and to assure balance in this truly new land. They found ways to share their bounty with those less fortunate in the hunt.[4]

Hunting the Ktsiawaasak

The *Ktsiawaasak* (great wild animals) were hunted with respect and ceremony. We asked for the favor of the animals' spirits; otherwise they might have prevented us from finding and harvesting their flesh. We used as much as we could and showed respect for the bones. To hunt small and medium-sized game we used a lightweight javelin, perhaps thrown with the wooden machine called an *atlatl*, or spear thrower (fig. 4). The *atlatl* was a piece of flexible wood with a hook or notch at one end to accept the butt of the javelin. A pair of leather finger loops were tied to the other end with rawhide or sinew. This tool gave our bodies the power to drive a javelin deep into the bodies of medium-sized prey.

The *atlatl* was not for all species of very large game. For mammoths, we used a heavy, two-part lance with removable foreshaft that would separate from a socket in the main shaft, allowing it to remain in the animal rather than work its way out. We carried many foreshafts in a hide quiver. The "repeating lance" had a distinctive stone point (called by Euro-American archaeologists "Clovis" or "Debert"); it was made with a groove along its side (see the compass rose in fig.2 for a drawing of a Clovis point). Its razor-thin cutting edges were blunted at the rear to allow sinew to bind it to the foreshaft. It had a barbed concave base to assure that the foreshaft worked deeper into its body with every movement. Most of these points were made of chert such as that found at quarries at the northern and southern ends of Bitawbagok, though some, such as those of rhyolite from Mount Jasper in the Wawobedanik (White Mountains), were beautiful as well as deadly. Beauty was functional. It honored the animals' spirits with the care taken in making the tools to hunt their flesh. The points were so effective that they were refurbished if they broke or dulled. Good wood for hafting (attaching) these points was hard to come by; few trees were large and straight enough. We had to import *mahlawks* (ash) or *senomozi* (maple) from Nibenakik, the forested South,. Although our ancestors' *atlatl* and two-part spear have disappeared, their stone points remain enfolded in Aki, until She gives them back to us: a gift to remind us of how we came to be.

Each game animal required specific weapons, hunting strategy, and ceremony to assure its continuance as food provider. The *adebaskedon* (mammoth), lord of the Barren Grounds, left us its teeth, tusks, and bones west of Okemo (Mount Holly, Vermont) and east of Mamhlawbagok (Derby, Vermont). These animals lived in rare family herds that were extremely dangerous to hunt, as we remember in our oldest stories. They would stand their ground if attacked or charge with surprising speed to kill the unwary hunter with trunk, tusk, or foot. When setting forth after *adebaskedonak*, we took the repeating lance that could be used with a thrusting motion. We preferred to separate a single mammoth from the family group, although this was hard to do. We could attempt to drive it into a marsh where it could not charge effectively, then try to weaken it by lucky

Fig. 4. Depiction of Paleo-Indian hunter. *Wôbanakik Heritage Center Collection, photograph by Andrew Lee.*

atlatl dart shots or strong lance thrusts. When it was tired, we could kill it with a repeating lance.

The smaller musk ox, hunted in late autumn, was the spirit of steadfast-ness. Like the other *Ktsiawaasak,* musk oxen stayed in a group, quickly forming a tight defiant circle of their hollow horns when we came near. They would hold their ground but not often attack. They could be killed by weakening them with dart shots and killing with a lance.

The lighter and faster *magolibo* (caribou) migrated into Wôbanakik as huge springtime herds that took days to pass. Caribou Mother, spirit of the herds, was honored as the essence of the endless cycle of migration that provided the staple of our ancient lives. Caribou broke into smaller bands in the summer, when we could hunt them. On land, the caribou could be stampeded over a defile, although they were more nimble than the bison our neighbors to the west hunted in a similar way. A swimming caribou could be dispatched from a hide canoe and paddle-dragged to shore. On land, the *atlatl* was the preferred tool of the hunt. In time, caribou became

our most precious resource. Caribou bone is found by archaeologists in direct association with our old tools. Caribou hide provided the best clothing, which could be made flexible, waterproof, and even somewhat insect-
repellent by smoking over a fire smothered in moss. We could even cook
food in bags made of caribou hide (fig. 5). *Ktsiwoboz* (giant elk), bone of
which has been found on an island in Bitawbagok, could be hunted in
their small herds or preferably separated and killed. The giant elk's magnificent antlers were dangerous as well as beautiful. Although the earth has
not yielded their bones in Wôbanakik, there were probably many other
grazers, including horses and camels.

The solitary *ponkiawassos* (polar bear), little brother of the White Bear
of the North, was most human of the great animals. It was extremely dangerous and would often hunt us on or near the ice-blocked Bitawbagok or
Soubagwa. Its speed, endurance, cunning, and resolve made the dart from
the *atlatl* useless; the only hope was the killing lance, and then it was problematic. As the climate began to warm and sea declined, the bear left us to
head north to Pebonkik, where it lives today. It is said that Koluscap himself banished the white bear to the land of ice and rocks because it would
not give up eating humans. Its soul was powerful and, like its body, could
be dangerous; needing special care when the beast was killed. *Ktsiawassos*,
the short-faced bear, was honored for its closeness to humans and for sym-
bolizing the seasons. It could perhaps even understand human speech.

The large cats and wolves were not often hunted. But the big-toothed
ones were great sport to meet since they as often got the hunter as we got
them. It was always an honor to see them. Their teeth, pelts, and claws became important talismans or fetishes. They, along with the great grazers,
were part of our religious world.

The giant thunderbird, known as *Tetraornis* to paleontologists, was honored for its connections to the heavens whence it was returning, even as we
moved into Wôbanakik.

We used a host of chipped stone, wood, and bone processing tools.
Stone and bone knives, side and end scrapers, awls, fluted drills, and grav-
ers separated and slit meat, tendon, and bone to provide food, clothing,
and shelter. Softer soapstone and talc became amulets that captured the
spirit of our people and the ordinary world, to help us in life and death.
These tools remain in Aki, the Earth, lessons in the ways of our ancestors.
Many of our elders believe that it is disrespectful for me to show you actual
artifacts, so I will show you replicated scenes and paintings. For those who
are specifically interested in our ancient stone tools, please refer to Appendix 3 for books, videos, and museums which show collections.[5]

Fig. 5. Wabanaki hunters pursue a woodland caribou by canoe. *Wiseman collection.*

The Beginnings of Gathering

As new plants moved into our land, the Oldest Ones experimented, talked to others from the South who knew about them or remembered when they lived well to the south of the White Bear. The first trees to come, eleven thousand winters ago, were *mskak* (spruce), *kokokhoakw* (fir), *maskwamozi* (birch), and *ossggakw* (poplar). Along the streams grew small *kanosasak* (willows) and *wdopiak* (alders). They were followed by *senomozi* (sugar maple) and *ogmakw* (ash), and the land turned into an open woodland. Wôbanakik looked as does the land of the Cree, our neighbors to the north. We began to know Wôbanakik's fuel woods such as *pobnodageso* (tamarack) and the admirable bark tinder of the white birch. The rare but spreading ash and maple were sought out for *atlatls* and javelin shafts. We lived within spruce and fir construction timbers covered with hides or *wigmask*, lightweight, waterproof birch bark lashed with flexible willow branches or sturdy spruce root.

The Changing of Days

Open conifer forests had arrived in the lowlands. They began ascending the hills, driving the grasses, lichens, and sedges into rapidly constricting habitats that cling precariously to the tops of our highest mountains. With the forests came *kokw* (porcupine); *mozeowoboz* (moose-elk); a smaller, forest-dwelling *Ktsiawaasak* (the mastodon, who has left us a tusk at Richmond, Vermont); *magolibo* (forest caribou), *moz* (moose), *awassos* (black bear), and *pezo* (lynx), as well as the smaller *mateguas* (hare), *meskagoda-gihla* (spruce grouse), and *apanakega* (marten). The marshes had *moskwas* (muskrat) as well as *tamakwa* (beaver), which left gnawed wood from these years near Mozeodebe Wadso (at Stowe, Vermont). The *adebaskedon* and musk-ox became uncommon. However, our ancestors saw little need to change their hunting strategy; the *atlatl* worked fine for the animals of the barren ground as well as the animals of the woodlands. With more plants available, they added berries, leaves, bark, and tubers to a growing inventory of food, medicinal, and industrial plants. Women assumed the role of primary plant harvesters, since plants were closest to our Mother the Earth. But the land continued changing. The great beasts of the uplands, which had been our livelihood, began to depart. Some believed that the weather had changed, causing the food of the great animals to disappear, while others argued that hunting was wasteful and that we, the Alnôbak, were responsible for their departure.

Like the land, the waters were changing. The earth continued to rise, draining our beloved Northwestern Sea and driving the *podabak* (whales) and most of the *akigwak* (seals) to the northeast. By the end of the Years of the Adebaskedon, all that was left of the Sea was the original freshwater Bitawbagok as made by Koluscap. Smaller salt-water plants and animals departed, the last seal leaving well over a century ago. Today only the beach heath, a salt-loving Atlantic coastal plant, clings to the shores of Bitawbagok, lamenting for the ocean that once was. Without its saltwater life, the lake rested. Our eldest ancestors temporarily abandoned the lake and its margins until freshwater fish and marsh plants could move in. Some people followed the emptying saltwater sea northeastward, learning to become even more efficient maritime hunters. Others moved to the changing shorelines of the Great Sea, to continue our maritime lifestyle.[6]

3

The Forest Closes In:
The Years of the Moose

(10,000 to 6,500 Winters Ago)

The open woodlands became threatened by warm forests, the ancient animals died or followed the tundra to the north, to be seen only in dream, spirit, or on the edges of old stories told around our hearth fires. Gone were the grazers of the tundra and woodland and the huge meat eaters that fed on them. By nine thousand winters ago, summers became dry and warm, and the last of the *Ktsiawaasak*, the mastodon, departed. Trees that lost their leaves in winter grew abundantly in Wôbanakik, trees that had large edible seeds such as *pagôn* (butternut) or *watsilmezi* (white oak). But the lowland forests, which had been small and conifer-dominated, now grew one hundred feet high and so dense that in summer little light penetrated to the soil. Few large animals lived there except *magolibo* (woods caribou), *moz* (moose), and *awassos* (bear). Areas that had been dense with game were useless for hunting in the old way. Forest animals were small, swift, and elusive. The fluted point, symbol of our union with the barren ground and open woodland, was replaced with tools that were better suited to the elusive forest game. Even the woods caribou and moose were succeeded by beaver, hare, muskrat, and *mihkua* (squirrel)—animals that could be hunted with a *klahigan*, the wooden deadfall trap. Smaller, lighter *atlatls* shot darts hafted with shorter, wider points, including a type called "Swanton corner notched" after our hunting camp, Wazowategok II, where it was first discovered in the soil. With better weather, more natural resources, and well-adapted tools, we spread out over the changed land and shorelines and prospered.

Life in the Uplands, Lakes, and Marshes

Nonnegonikon Wazowategok II, at John's Bridge (Swanton, Vermont), is an eighth-millennium B.P. hunting and fishing station (see fig. 8 for its location). This spring or fall campsite had a five-meter shelter, the second earliest evidence of Alnôbaiwi (a word meaning "done in an Abenaki way") architecture. Broken stems of javelin points indicate long-ago repair of hunting tools at the site. Quartz "boiling stones" were transferred from the fire to cook in skin or bark vessels full of stew. In time the hot rocks brought the stew to a boil. Graphite found here was probably a pigment used for body paint or artwork, evidence of an Abenaki painting tradition. By the end of the Years of the Moose, we had hamlets with wigwams fifteen feet in diameter at Nonnegonikon Onegigiwizibo (along Otter Creek, Vermont). We also had smaller, seasonal camps on most rivers eight thousand winters ago. One of these, on the Wintegok (Lamoille River, Vermont), yielded ground-stone *atlatl* weights associated with dart points, evidence of increasing sophistication in hunting technology. These sites were strategically situated to fish the river and hunt in the uplands or to move easily up and downstream in canoes.

At such sites we learned how to wrestle the sweet, protein- and fat-rich nutmeats from *pagôn* (butternut). *Sata* (blueberry), *sgueskimenal* (raspberry), *mskikikoiminsal* (wild strawberry), and *pessimenal* (currant), provided sweets to enliven our diet. Bark containers with tight-fitting lids were filled with cooked fruit mixed with maple sweetening. These *maskwaijoal* would be sealed with waxy moose fat, a precursor of our modern paraffin. The containers were hung from the wigwam frame to keep them away from hungry animals and children. Sap of *wins* (black or yellow birch), *maskwaimon* (white birch), *mskwabagas* (red maple), and of course, *senomozi* (sugar maple) gave us longer-lasting sweets. In the early spring moon, some left winter camp to go to the sugar groves. To get the sweet sap, we soon learned that a slash could be made in the bark and a spout of *salon* (sumac) or *saskib* (elderberry) attached at the bottom of the slash. "Quick baskets" from the bark of *anibi* (elm) or birch quickly gathered up and tied at the ends, collected the sap from the dripping spouts. The water in the sap was evaporated by sun-drying or perhaps heating in large bark vessels with boiling stones such as those found at Wazowategok II. The sugar could be stored for later use or to be given as gift. (Fig. 6.)

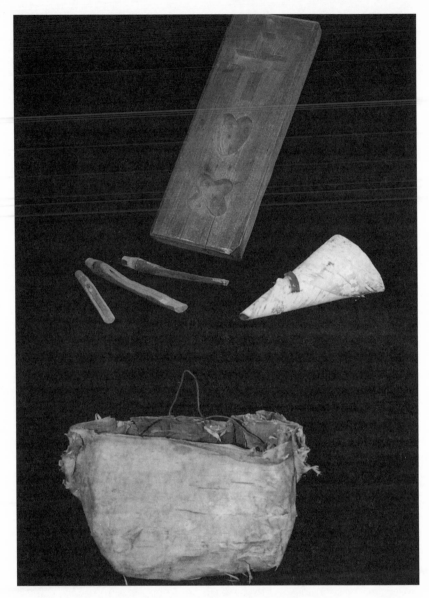

Fig. 6. Traditional and transitional maple sugaring equipment found in Wôbanakik. *Wôbanakik Heritage Center Collection, photograph by Andrew Lee.*

Oak, ash, maple, birch, and later *bagimenakwam* (hickory) became our preferred fuel woods. Tinder was from *wigmask* (birch bark), rendered highly flammable by butulinol and suberin, vegetable alcohols and fats in the bark. The slightly less flammable bark of *mekwisigazo* (red cedar) and *alnizidi* (hemlock) were also used as tinder. Bark of the white birch and probably *anibi* (American elm), *wigbimizi* (basswood), *wawabibibagw* (cottonwood), and *wazimenakuam* (wild cherry root) became our shelter and containers. Roots of spruce and hemlock and inner bark of basswood became our vegetal cordage and lacings. We learned which woods were flexible, like *mahlawks* (ash) and *watsilmezi* (white oak); which species were easy to carve, like *goa* (pine) and *wigbmizi* (basswood); and which were strong and hard, like *bagimenakwam* (hickory) and maple.

Marshes and wetlands, which were more common than now, hosted *tamakwa* (beaver), *moskuas* (muskrat) and other marsh animals. Nonegonnikon wiwinebesaki, our old village site at the modern tourist enclave of Weirs Beach, New Hampshire, has deep, dark middens confirming long use of lake and marsh environments in the central area of Wôbanakik. Wiwinebesaki, Bitawbagok, and their sisters hosted a growing list of freshwater fish: *lapasalod* (yellow perch), *monazigan* (black bass), *kwenoza* (northern pike), and the great fish *maskwenoza* (muskellunge) and *kabassa* (sturgeon). They could be hunted at night from canoes with birchbark torches serving as lures. *Namas* (salmon) and sturgeon especially were hunted by the light of the *maskwaiwagsanigan* (birchbark torch) until it was outlawed by Euro-Americans. Hordes of *gwigwigen* (duck), *ahowago* (brant), *woptegua* (geese), and *pelzak* (passenger pigeons) flew over the marshlands on their annual migration. But the most important animal of the marshes and swamps was *moz*, the moose.

MOOSE HUNTING STORY

(This story differs slightly from the oft-cited Eastern Abenaki version that uses a vocal moose call, a gogelu, which is often seen in coastal Maine antique shops. The dearth of oral calls in Western Abenaki country may support the fact that we often used this technique.)

To hunt a moose by water, you approach the moose by canoe around a peninsula which hides him from you. In this canoe you must have two hunters, the one in the bow, who carries the hunting weapon, and the stern paddler who also calls the moose. When you have paddled silently as close to the moose as possible without being seen, you quietly bring the canoe to a stop. The stern hunter dips the moose call, a Mason jar (or cone of birch bark in the past), into the water. The call is then lifted three feet above the lake and its water carefully poured in such as way that it sounds exactly like a female moose, in heat, urinating. The male moose, hearing this sound, will quickly and foolishly round the peninsula in search of the female. You must quickly kill the moose or, in his rage at being tricked, he may sink the canoe.

"Monkey" Drew, ca. 1955

After killing, game was processed, in camp if possible or at the kill site if the animal was too large to carry or move on a sled. Although men did most of the hunting, women were expected to process the meat, bone, and hide. Moose meat, the most desired food, could be processed in many ways if practice during the nineteenth and twentieth centuries is any guide to the past. One highly esteemed recipe for moose meat involved the following steps: Moose meat was cut into thin strips, then crushed between strips of bark to extract the blood. The pressed meat was smoked until hard over a maple or *wajomozi* (beechwood) fire, then pulverized by grinding, in the manner of the Mexican meat dish *machaca*. The powdered meat was cooked with *menomen* (wild rice) and herbs, then placed in a carefully cleaned deerhide for storage. A related dish was a sausage made with meat, berries, nuts, and fat, placed in moose intestines, then smoked. The marrow of the moose was boiled and skimmed—bark containers filled with the white fatlike food were given as gifts. Moose and caribou hide became our clothing, as well as bear hides and, along the coast, that of seals. Moose- and caribou-hide robes, also used as bedclothes, might have been painted in graphite black; red, and yellow ochre earth colors; or white from shell, bound with fish roe or egg binder. Painted leather also could be appliquéd on with sinew thread sewn with *spoganak* (bone awls) and needles.[1]

Life along the Coasts

Marine resources continued to be important to people in the lower Ktsitegw valley, where beluga whales still congregate. Along the coasts of Soubagwa we began to develop a social and technological adaptation to hunting deep-water mammals and fish—soon to blossom into the so-called

Fig. 7. Dugout canoe, white pine (replica, 1995). *Wôbanakik Heritage Center Collection, photograph by Andrew Lee.*

Maritime Archaic of the Euro-American archaeologist. This was based on woodworking technology allowed by increasingly sophisticated ground-stone tools. We perfected the first specific woodworking tools, such as the "full-channel" gouge and the adze, which were necessary for hollowing out dugout canoes, as well as the whetstones that were required to keep them sharp. The dugout canoe largely supplanted the skin boat because it was more permanent. Smaller, twelve- to twenty-foot dugouts plied our rivers and lakes, while larger, oceangoing vessels began to venture offshore in search of deep-sea fish and oceanic mammal. (Fig. 7.)

The new woodworking tools imply finer implements, such as better *astahigan* (harpoon) shafts. Stone, shell, and bone technology became re-fined and adapted to the points of our harpoons and lances. We developed the "toggling harpoon," a major breakthrough that prevented the harpoon and its lanyard from pulling out of the whale, big fish, or seal after it had been speared. This invention allowed the boats or separate floats to pull on, slow down, and tire our prey so that it could be dispatched with a kill-ing lance. This technology was adapted to freshwater fishing, although the canoes, harpoons, and other implements were smaller. Recently, archaeo-logical sites in the treeless northern reaches of Wôbanakik have given us a somewhat clearer view of our ancestors' use of the coasts over seven thou-sand years ago. This region was fishable only for the summer, but its high productivity made the long seacoast trip worthwhile. Unfortunately, these are often burial sites, and in respect for our ancestors, I must decline to

Fig. 8. Wôbanakik and environs during the Years of the Moose and Log Ships. *Drawn by Frederick Wiseman.*

discuss the burials that they obviously didn't want us to see. However, over the dead, they erected stone mounds, which they *did* wish us to see, giving us a persistent ritual landscape. These mounds were erected in areas of great natural beauty and sweeping vistas, which are so grand in the near-Arctic. (See fig. 8; the L'Anse Amour site contains the best evidence for early mound building.) This implies a distinct aesthetic sense of communion with the land, one not seen before but one that has remained undiminished for seven millennia following. These sites probably also characterize the more southerly areas but are hard to find in heavily forested zones.[2]

4

The Land Becomes Warm:
The Years of the Log Ships

(6,500 to 1000 Winters Ago)

Wôbanakik was warm and moist 6,500 winters ago, for we were entering a deep interglacial period. During this "Climatic Optimum," living was pleasant for the people of the Land of the Dawn (fig. 8). During this age our ancestors developed radical technologies for harvesting and honoring the land and waters. Building on groundstone and ivory technologies developed in the latter part of the Years of the Moose, we created a rich woodworking tradition that lasted many millennia. This had implications for seafaring to hunting. The boundaries of our land were pushed far northward to the Arctic fisheries by our seafaring log ships. Wôbanakik now became intimately connected to a wide world of trading partners far to the south and west. Some may say that this was our "golden age," but we believe that every age of the world is golden, with its own challenges and rewards. Our family and village life became larger and more complex during the Years of the Log Ships, a facet of our life that I'd like to discuss first.

Life in the Ancient Villages

Our villages were located in rich alluvial river valleys, which gave access to lakes or the Great Sea downstream or to the upstream life of hill and mountain. These alluvial valleys later buried many villages, enfolding and sheltering them from inquisitive Euro-Americans (fig. 9). The villages were clusters of wigwams, perhaps arranged about larger council houses

Fig. 9. Kennebec River Valley at Norridgewock, Maine. *Wiseman collection.*

and dance grounds. I do not know of any above-ground evidence of what our ancient houses looked like. I assume that a conical or semiconical wigwam was the type used by families in the Years of the Log Ships. The historic wigwam of Wôbanakik is a cone, a widely distributed and probably archaic dwelling. Postholes of our ancient wigwams are not inconsistent with this type of residence. Each wigwam could hold up to fifteen people, and was probably a conical frame of flexible saplings covered with birch, elm, or softwood bark. The ten- to sixteen-foot-diameter framework used three-inch main posts and smaller horizontal members bound together with basswood, hickory, or elm lashings. Coverings were sewn on with thinner *wadabal* (spruce root ties). Each wigwam had a central hearth to provide light and heat for domestic activities and a central smokehole that could be closed with a flexible mat during foul weather.

To erect the wigwam a "protoframe" was made from two fifteen- to twenty-foot poles laid on the ground in the form of a cross. A third pole was placed in the crotch and the tripod tied together and erected. Accessory poles were laid in the tripod to make a cone-shaped framework. The framework was tied to a horizontal hoop placed at a man's height to strengthen it. Birchbark (or other flexible bark) rolls, about three feet wide, were shingled on and sewed to the framework with spruce root lacings. More logs laid against the outside of the bark held it down in windy weather (fig. 10). A log ladder allowed a child to ascend to the smoke hole and cover it with a bark collar for inclement or winter weather. Poles were laid across the interior hoop for suspending moccasins, bags, and bark containers. Moose sausages, fish, or meat could be smoked by hanging from the crosspiece. A leather or fiber cord could suspend a cut of meat next to the hearth fire for cooking. When the long cord was twisted, the meat revolved as the cord slowly unwound and rewound. A bark paddle slowed down the revolution even more, making rewinding less frequent.

We infrequently built another form of village. Nonnigonikon nuliak, our most northerly ancient fishing outpost in Labrador (see fig. 8), is the remains of twenty-six linear buildings up to ninety meters long! Remaining patterns of rock lines indicate that the buildings were of hide held in place against the earth by lines of boulders. The framework of these buildings in the treeless north was a mystery. Although the edge of the forest was farther north during the Years of the Log Ships, it was still many miles to the south of Nonnigonikon nuliak. The frameworks may have been of driftwood coming from central and southern Wôbanakik or transported in by ship. A second possibility is that of whalebone frames. These "extended buildings" were apartments arranged side by side in the manner of a motel. Easily seen because of the lack of trees, it represents a little studied variety of Alnôbaiwi village. There is slight evidence of life inside the hide buildings, but flakes of chert indicate that stone from a nearby quarry was made into tools brought far to the south in the fall, when Nuliak had to be abandoned.

Furniture was sparse, and little was needed in the wigwams and extended houses. Cattail mats called *anhahkoganal* were woven with basswood wefts after their late summer harvest. These mats provided comfort and privacy. Other furniture consisted of aromatic spruce branches covered with hides and staked to the earth. Covered with soft *oswadagen* (hides tanned with the fur on), these provided comfortable, insulating bedding. The outsides of the buildings could be painted with family crests or decorative symbols.

The cramped wigwams and apartments were but privacy or sleeping areas in the summer, when most activities took place outside. But people often retreated to the dim, smoky interiors during bad weather. During the long winter months our ancestors lived inside, venturing outside for hunting and fuel wood gathering. These were times for productive activity and time for telling stories. The cramped interiors required strict rules for personal and family space. Each person had his or her inviolate space, and one needed to ask permission before entering it. The central hearth was

Fig. 10. Wabanaki cone wigwam. *Wiseman collection.*

communal, but the periphery was private space, not to be violated. Passing before the hearth-fire without permission was bad behavior.

Preparing hides and meat was done in the villages with the old chipped-stone scrapers or the new ground-slate *ulu* crescent knife. Cooking over the fire included roasting, sometimes with the rotisserie, and using heated boiling-stones transferred from the fire to stone, skin, or bark cookpots. Sewing tailored clothing was made possible by eyed needles. We had tailored solid-hide and woven-hide shirts and woven vegetal fiber/animal hair garments. Cordage, basketry, and textiles were made all year round. Woodcarving was perfected during this time but only dimly known through a ten-inch bowl recovered in Quobaug Lake, Massachusetts, just to the south of our modern homeland. It was of burlwood carved hollow when green, then stored in fat to prevent cracking. Many types of stone and metal gouges were used for large objects such as canoes or wooden mortars, while bone-hafted beaver-incisor knives did finer woodwork.[1]

Neighbors exchanged gossip, stories, and information inside the village, often visiting each other by night by the light of birch-bark torches. At other times they banded together to hunt, fish or gather wild foods. Neighboring villages met for ceremonies marking the annual cycle of Aki, the Earth, or the birth, death, or puberty of a young Alnôba. Each village had its own hunting and fishing territory, but quarries were for the use of all villages. During the spring fish-run harvest or the fall hunting, the village would be deserted, everyone moving to temporary camps close to the fish or game. There, the bounty of the land would be processed and brought back to the main village to be hung or cached in bark-lined storage pits. My grandfather said that a pit on an island in the stream was the best cache, since most land-dwelling pests couldn't get to it, though dogs and raccoons have been known to swim for a cache. By and large, village life went smoothly; those who had more gave to those who were less fortunate, both within and among villages; strife and war were almost unknown, although famine was a constant companion.

The spiritual world and the world of the common became tightly bound during the Years of the Log Ships. We knew that the Earth and its components were connected and cyclical. Birth, puberty, death, woman's menstrual cycle, the migration of waterfowl, and the cycle of the Moon and Sun were the heartbeat of creation. This cycle was reflected in the birth and childhood of an Alnôba youth. At birth, *dzizdiz*, the child was shown to his relatives and the world, then strapped to a joyously carved wooden cradleboard.

BABY STORY

We have an old story, where Koluscap is unable to quiet a baby, that teaches us of the strength inherent in youth. But there are other signs of that strength.

When your baby is born, don't let the doctors put that chemical in their eyes. Take your new baby and look deep into its eyes and you will see, for only a second, a purple flicker that is the fading fire of otherside, from where the baby's spirit came. That lets you know that the new baby is strongest spirit. But it will try to go back to the fire, so you should be good to it so it will stay with us humans.

Ruby Deal, 1961

I saw it. My son, Fred W. Wiseman was born 8 May 1980.

F. M. Wiseman, 1995

Children studied skills required of them as adults, making them into play. Aunts and uncles were instrumental in a child's upbringing. A boy of ten winters was expected to be able to kill a bird with a dartshot. In addition to skill, qualities of sharing, generosity, and respect for elders and the world were learned at an early age. Self-control was vital to a young person who had to learn to hunt wary and fleet-footed game. Children were treated with respect, and they could speak in councils. With the onset of puberty, our young were expected to take their place in Alnôba society, to marry, and to fulfill their family and village commitments. With adulthood came responsibilities not only to family and the ordinary world, but the unseen realms as well.

We understood the worlds of dream, spirit, and death, interpreted by *medlawinoak*, special men and women called shamans by modern scholars. *Wassobamit*, the "clear seers," or clairvoyants, also penetrated the veils separating the world of spirit from us. Our dead were buried with respect. (As part of this respect I must decline to share with you details of our burial customs. Euro-American anthropologists and archaeologists, who are fascinated with our dead, have much to say about them.) We talked to our neighbors about these things, teaching and learning. Crystals from the earth; wood, leather, fur, claws from the land; and plumage of birds from the air were adapted to objects of spiritual power that we could wear or place in shrines in our homes or on the land. We knew well our rooted, hoofed, taloned, clawed, and finned brothers, and we used their collective spirits as symbols of our lineage, band or village. *Megezo*, the eagle, valued for his sight; *alaskana*, the wolverine, for his tenacity; *kaskoi*, the heron, for his skill as a fisher; *awassos*, the bear, for his knowledge; *nolka*, the deer, for her kinship with women; *waukweses*, the fox, for his family instinct and skill in stealth; and *opweskak*, the golden seal, for its healing power, became personal and family symbols, to be asked for help in the hunt, healing, or trade. The spirit of long-departed *Tetraornis* and mammoth remained in our hearts and stories as thunderbird and *adebaskedon*. Water, from Nebizonnebik (Medicine Water, or Highgate Springs) or Nebizonnebizek (Little Medicine Water, or Alburg Springs) or Brunswick and Saratoga Springs (fig. 11) became powerful allies in our quest for balance and harmony with the world.

But during the Years of the Log Ships, the heavens became supremely important.[2] We had known the circuit of the great luminaries—the Sun, Moon, and Great Star (Venus)—for millennia. It was significant information for our spiritual lives and ceremonies with which we kept the balance

The High Rock Spring, Saratoga Springs, N.Y.

Fig. 11. Saratoga Springs, New York. *Wiseman collection.*

of creation. We knew the seasons were most significant: the cycles of spawning, birth, flowering, and death were tied to the great flame in our father the Sky. The Moon was tied to the rise and fall of the sea and the periodic purification that was the grace of women. We knew the constellations and wandering stars that moved with great slow cycles in the night. The connection of all things, an understanding given us by Koluscap long ago, caused us to wonder about the interrelatedness of the large and small luminaries that gyred about over our heads.

Centuries earlier, we had probably discovered that the thirteen-moon lunar timetable fell behind the solar year. There were problems with the solar year as well, for as the centuries lengthened, this foundation of our other calculations began to creep backward. We then learned, as have all

First Nations, that there was a complex and little understood interrelation between the luminaries that turn slowly overhead. Until the Years of the Log Ships we had little time and inclination to explore them. But the needs of our ship helmsmen and the shamans overseeing the harvest of fish and migratory beasts may have required calendrical precision and understanding. To fathom the interrelated cycles of sun, moon, and daylight with new precision, I believe that we began building observatories. Although this reconstruction is not held by mainstream archaeologists, it is geographically more plausible than having ancient European mariners come here to build observatories.

LUMP STORY

Yep, we have lots of hollow stone "lumps" around South Woodstock. I'd be glad to show you. My girlfriend has a lump in her front yard, and there are lots of them near the roads. Everybody says they're Celtic ruins. Nobody around here has much interest in them, but sometimes there are lots of out-of-state cars parked on the side of the road.

Jodie Loring, 1995

The most common observatories were semisubterranean stone chambers with stone slab roofs, perhaps mistaken by modern Euro-Americans for colonial root cellars or Celtic tombs. This type of observatory probably evolved from virtually identical small chambers such as those discovered by archaeologists in Labrador. Archaeologists accept them as native in subarctic Labrador, but not here. They were probably also influenced by skin-and-bark village sweat lodges and indeed could be used for this purpose. From a chamber observation point, the rising and setting of the sun at given times could be aligned with the center or walls of the chamber entrance. A more accurate observatory used long lines of sight from an observation point to a series of distant standing stones or natural landmarks set along the horizon. Movements of the sun along the horizon, the awaited positioning of the evening star against the side of a chamber wall—these all assured us that the world was connected, and we understood our place in the circle of the universe.

With the observatories, we could determine the winter solstice to properly set the Greetings Day, which hailed the return of the sun to its northward journey. The tiny, incremental movement north was enough to show that spring, with the assurance of life that it held, was on the way, even though winter's icy blast would still increase. With observatories on line, small problems in calendrical correlation that had long plagued us became apparent. With accurate measurement of the solar year, the other luminaries, from the moon to the planets (such as the synodical revolution of Venus) could be measured and calibrated. We discovered the eighteen-year "wobble" of the path of moon above and below the trail of the sun and marked it by sight lines on our observatories. We thus began the long research into the nuances of the relations between sun and moon that yielded eclipses. Our shaman-astronomers probably recorded these calculations on birch-bark scrolls and occasionally inscribed them on ivory tablets.[3]

Gathering the Bounty of the Land

We perfected our plant gathering and processing during the Years of the Log Ships. Indeed, by this time we became more vegetarian. We manipulated forests to encourage useful plants and discourage those of little use. Each season brought its wild plants to ripeness. Spring was still named for maple and birch sugar. We collected birch bark for increasingly specialized articles, from moose calls to houses. Summer saw collection of *sgueskimenal* (raspberries, *Rubus* sp.) and mountain and marsh-borne *satal* (blueberries, *Vaccinium* sp.). Minor berry foods and fruits were fire cherry (*Prunus* sp.), hawthorn (*Crataegus* sp.), rose hips (*Rosa* sp.), *mololdagwal* (grape, *Vitis* sp.), *saskibal* (elderberry, *Sambucus canadensis*), and *salonal* (sumac, *Rhus* sp.). The tiny but nutritious and abundant seeds of pigweed (*Chenopodium*) and buckwheat (*Eriogonum* sp.) were used as grains. The seeds were powdered on milling stones called *admikoganal*, which become common at this time. We collected many materials for cordage in addition to the basswood and spruce root. We made fine one- to four-ply cord from milkweed, *mazon* (Indian hemp), and nettle for twined bags, lashing, or lines.

Fall saw the nut harvest. *Pagon*, the cold-tolerant butternut (*Juglans cinerea*), still our favorite, was supplemented in warmer collecting areas by *pakimizial* (black walnuts, *Juglans nigra*), *bagimenakwamal* (hickory, *Carya* sp.), *pagonizal* (hazelnuts, *Corylus americana*), *anaskamenal* (acorns, *Quercus* sp.), *wajomozial* (beechnuts, *Fagus grandifolia*), and *wobimenal* (chestnuts, *Castanea dentata*). These were also processed in milling stones. Nut oil could be extracted by boiling the crushed nuts and skimming the oil from the top of the water. Medicines and dyestuffs were collected in late summer, although we have evidence of only the red or yellow dye-plant bedstraw (*Galium* sp.) and of an unknown blue vegetal dye. Pipes show the use of *odamo* (tobacco) or substitutes made from bearberry, red cornel, squawbush, or lobelia. Certain of our Old Ones became adept in plant-lore and taught this growing knowledge to the young who wished to walk the path of earth-healing. The internal medicines were supplemented by plants that could be used in other healing ways. For example, later healers treated broken bones thus: The bone was set, then a poultice of sphagnum moss, rendered sterile by acidic anaerobic bog environments and saturated with antiseptic balsam fir sap, was placed over the break and to cushion the injured limb. The limb and poultice were then wrapped in a naturally alcohol (betulinol)-laden antiseptic birch bark and tied with wood splints. The balsam sap was also a good "first aid" remedy in that it could stop the bleeding and antiseptically seal the cut. The spirit of leaf, bark, and stem became a source of our living and health.

Hunting the Uplands

During the Climatic Optimum, the uplands and marshlands and estuaries were abundant with game. *Nolka* (deer), *moz* (moose), *naama* (turkey), *bakkesso* (partridge), *kokw* (porcupine), and *awassos* (bear) roamed the uplands and dry thickets, while *moz* (moose), *tamakwa* (beaver), *moskwas* (muskrat), and *onegikw* (otter) ruled the watery worlds of marsh and thicket. Hordes of *pelzak* (passenger pigeons) and waterfowl cluttered the sky along the marshy lake margins and the seacoast. The salt coasts were abundant with *askigwak* (seals) and walrus, and the ocean was filled with marine fish and smaller whales to hunt.

To hunt forest creatures, we studied their behavior, made better prayer to their spirits, and developed wooden traps and snares with basswood, nettle, and milkweed fiber cordage. Grouse could be caught with a noose attached to a long pole wielded by quiet young hunters. Deadfall traps, called *klahigan*, were set for beaver, muskrat, and otter along their pathways to and from the marsh. Deer, bear, and even moose were caught by drag snares—loops of cord attached to logs that tightened and strangled the animal as it dragged the log down its trail. Deer and woods caribou were driven into corrals where they were dispatched at our leisure. We improved woodcraft so as to be silent in the forests or marsh—to be one with the land. We especially needed this skill in pursuit of *nahama*, the wild turkeys that were becoming common at this time. We developed improved *atlatls* of hickory and ash, weighted with soft stone ornaments, of a winged or "whale-tail" form. Our quivers bristled with darts adapted to specific prey of water, land, or air. A dart point with a flat or concave base, shallow side notches, and triangular point became so much the tool of choice for land animals, that it was almost a symbol for these times. (See fig. 8: the compass rose is an Otter Creek–style *atlatl* dart point.) They were made in various sizes for each preferred prey. Waterfowl such as Canada geese were hunted with blunt wooden-tipped darts; and fish, with detachable bone harpoon-tipped shafts. Geese were lured to the hunter with decoys made of grass-filled bird skins such as those reported by early Euro-American visitors thousands of years later. As our people ranged far to the west, south, and north, we could secure the best materials for stone points: quartzites and cherts from what is now Ohio, Kentucky, New York, northern Maine, northern Quebec, and Labrador. Of course we didn't neglect local quarries, such as the one on Hog Island (near West Swanton, Vermont) or on Mount Jasper (near Berlin, New Hampshire), but they often provided less than 10 percent of our projectile points.

The maple and hickory mainshafts became refined and flatted with the plumage of forest and water birds. An *atlatl* dart foreshaft was found in a bog just to the southeast of our homeland. This discovery is a lesson in our old hunting technologies. It was wooden, seven inches long, and split into two pieces. The stone point was sandwiched between the pieces in a hollow carved to accept it, and the whole glued together and wrapped with vegetal fiber.

Such hunting technologies brought the bounty of the land to our villages. We have zooarchaeological evidence that *gohkohkhas* (barred owl), *awassos* (bear), *pezo* (bobcat), *nolka* (deer), *olanigw* (fisher cat), *wokweses* (red fox), *kokw* (porcupine), *mihkoa* (red squirrel), and *agaskw* (woodchuck) were hunted in the uplands, while *tamakwa* (beaver), *woptegua* (Canada goose), *moz* (moose), *moskwas* (muskrat), thick-billed guillemot, *doleba* (box turtle), and *onegikw* (otter) attest to our use of the watery domain.

Freshwater Fishing

The Wazowategok (Missisquoi River), Wintegok (Lamoille River), and Winoskitegw (Winooski River) ran with *kwenoza* (northern pike), *maskwenoza* (muskellunge), and *monazigan* (black bass) Each spring *mamsalagikwsak* (walleye pike) congregated in shallows to remind us of cycles of life and earth. Bitawbagok was full of eighty species of sweet, edible fish, from the small lively perch to the massive sturgeon. *Woleskaolakw*, canoes hewn from tall white pines or other softwoods with polished-stone gouges and careful application of fire, allowed us to become people of the lakes, rivers, and sea. These shallow craft, late versions of which are sometimes fished from ponds throughout Wôbanakik, were twelve to eighteen feet long, one to two feet deep, and two to three feet wide, with half-inch thick walls. One needed to kneel on the bottom at first; but once we learned canoe safety, they were highly effective means of water travel and fishing.

FISH STORY

In the old days we didn't have fishing poles and fancy reels to kill a fish by wearing him out; the really big ones took patience. If you catch a fish too big to haul in with your hand-line, yet well caught, tie the line to the canoe and let the fish pull you around the lake until it gets tired. If you can move the fish a little after a while by pulling on the line, you need to "beach" him. Paddle over to a sandy beach if available, or any shallows that aren't clogged by marsh grasses and rushes. Slowly pull the fish in, guiding it carefully by hand or with a stick, to the shallows. Once the fish is caught by the bottom, get out of the canoe and wade over to the fish where you can kill it by hitting it on the head with a club—do not use your paddle. I've caught many a musky [muskellunge] that way. But one time I was in Missisquoi Bay and hooked something big that wasn't a sturgeon. It never tired, pulled me around all day and never gave in. As night fell, I cut the line and said good-bye. I wonder what it was?

Fred W. Wiseman, 1956

Hooks of willow wood or bone (often from wishbone) and copper gorges (thin bipointed rods with a fishline attachment in the middle) could be baited with fish scrap or meat. Fish lines were made from basswood bark or even rawhide and carried to the bottom with polished stone plummets. The rawhide fishline was a firethickened deerhide cut into a spiral one-eighth inch wide. This was worked into a round line with the fingers or between flat pieces of wood. When the fish swallowed the bait, the hook or gorge became lodged in the throat, allowing it to be pulled in. A related fishing technique was a "jig" of willow crotch with a fire-hardened point tied above a plummet weight. The jig was jerked up and down in a school of fish to snag and pull them to the waiting fisherman.

Seven- to nine-foot-long hardwood *astahiganal* (harpoons) armed with wicked-looking eight- to ten-inch barbed wood, antler, and bone points caught the great *kabassa* (sturgeon) during its spring spawning run. This fish could grow to four hundred pounds, requiring specialized hunting techniques. To catch sturgeon, two people would venture out in a canoe in the evening. The one in the bow was the harpooner; the other, in the stern, paddled and wielded the *maskwaiwagsanigan*, the birchbark torch-lure. If a sturgeon came to the light, the harpooner waited until the fish turned, exposing its soft underbelly, which was not protected by the thick, harpoon-resistant scales of the back. The harpooner would attempt to place the harpoon below the scales. If successful, the sturgeon immediately sounded, pulling tight the harpoon lanyard that was tied to the bow of the canoe. As the fish, in its fright and pain, darted this way and that, the stern paddler had to align the bow with the moving lanyard, or the fish could quickly pull over the bow, capsizing the canoe. The sturgeon quickly tired and could be dispatched with a lance and towed to shore to be processed. Sturgeon bone has been found at several of our old camps that date to this time.

We could attract other night fish to our canoes and harpoons with birchbark torches. Lures of deer hair and duck down caught the smaller fish, such as the brown bullhead or perch, and perhaps northern pike, bass, and *aligedaid*, the snapping turtle found at our old sites. Lines and dip nets of rawhide or braided vegetal fiber weighted with polished stone plummets brought the water's bounty to our canoes and drying rack. Dip-nets hauled *meskwamakw* (salmon) and *namoakw* (trout) from rapids and waterfalls. We made fish corrals, called *seniganial*, out of stone or sticks driven into the mud. Fish would swim into the corrals, become confused and be unable to swim out. Dipnets could then take the captive fish. One of our old corrals has been found in Wiwinebesaki, near Ahquedauke-nash (the Eastern Abenaki name for the outlet to Lake Winnepesaukee,

New Hampshire). The flat, perforated netting needles, found in many old habitation sites, attest to the ubiquitous fishnets used throughout Wôbanakik.

Saltwater Fishing and Sea-Mammal Hunting

Approximately 6,500 winters ago, our ancestors achieved a command of working the multicentury pine, cedar, and basswood trees that had so completely overtaken our lands. Groundstone adzes and axes, honed to a feathered edge by whetstone and burnisher and aided by fire, felled the great trees. But nowhere was the application of tool to wood so spectacular as with the building of the log ships, immense ocean- and lake-dwelling craft that could, for the first time, penetrate the heart of the Great Sea. Time has erased all evidence of these ships except for clearly incised pictographs in the westernmost sector of ancient Wôbanakik at Peterborough, Ontario (see fig. 13). These great vessels, with slender cedar or hardwood paddles, stroking the skin of the ocean, explored the lakes, rivers, and coasts in all directions. The log ships extended Wôbanakik far to the north, finally to the north-facing rim of the world. There we felt close again to the old land of the Frost Monsters as the pole star glittered almost at zenith. Once more we found almost forgotten Ponkiawassos and musk oxen. But it was the bounty of the ice-free Arctic summer that outweighed the effort of the 1,500-mile trek and kept us there. Every eighteen-hour day all along the rim land, whale seal, porpoise, and walrus fell to the skill of the harpooner. And just inland, the beautiful sugary chert (or quartzite?) of Ramah Bay fell to the ax of the miner. In that far rim of Wôbanakik, we built longhouses of bone, sinew, and rawhide held fast to the earth by lines of cobbles and boulders. They buffered the breath of the Ice Giants that, even in the high Arctic summer, still blew fiercely across the land. The bones of these remarkable ninety-meter long buildings still lie exposed. These old ruins are a testament and a challenge to the archaeologists who still stumble about trying to make sense of it all. They say, "But these people were but primitive hunters; it was certainly the Iroquois who brought the longhouse to the Northeast." These were mere outposts, fortuitously laid bare by land level rise and the low Arctic tundra.

Marine fishing and hunting were incomparable. Shell middens, scores of cubic yards in size, attest to collection and drying of *alsak* (shellfish) along the margins of the Great Sea. Moreover, *askigw* (gray and harbor seals) and walrus were hunted along the seacoast in a variety of ways. The cold months of early winter was a prime time to harvest the fat-laden animals. One common technique was to approach, in several canoes, a herd sunning on the beach. The animals would be confused by this advance; some would take to the water to be speared with slate-pointed lances. Animals fleeing on land were speared or clubbed. Seal oil, boiled and skimmed in hollow log kettles, was particularly esteemed for fuel and food flavoring.

Improving in concert with the canoes was the elegance of the tools we used to harvest the bounty of the deep. Deep-water fish and mammals such as cod, swordfish, porpoise, and the smaller whales were hunted offshore with ocean-going canoes guided by experienced mariners who knew the patterns of wind, wave, and seabird. Barbed and toggling harpoon heads were specifically designed for each kind of prey, from the swiftly darting *askigw* (seals) to the great *podabak* (baleen whales). These bone and ivory harpoons, carved and polished with care, were connected to a myriad of different whalebone foreshafts, then socketed to great wooden mainshafts, probably up to eighteen feet long. Vegetal and animal fiber lanyards and rope were held on polished-ivory line holders. The combination of expert harpooner and crew, skillfully wrought softwood canoe, and the proper reverence and ritual could not fail to convince the fish and mammals of the Great Sea to allow us to harvest them. Thus, we learned how our brothers of the water worlds lived, ate, and bred; and in learning we knew how to hunt them better. Killer whale and seabird amulets, which come to us from Aki the Earth, are a reminder of this covenant between people and our sea-dwelling prey.

Early every fall many log ships turned south laden with dried fish, Rahma quartzite, sea mammal skins, and meat for the heartland. Stone monuments, used for land-oriented religious ceremonies, also became coastal beacons, sitting on high promontories overlooking the coast, pointing the way home or to a safe harbor against the late summer storms that frequent the far north. And within and below these monuments lie some of our honored dead, who showed the way home for millennia until some were taken to museums by archaeologists. The ships that came down the Ktsitegok and Sobagwa coast were eagerly awaited by the villagers who came to see the year's animal and mineral bounty of the far north. Welcoming dances, feasts, and celebrations greeted the mariners on their arrival, their bounty insuring the villages against the cold of winter.[4]

Changes

As time went on, life began to be influenced by new people, ideas, and technologies. Our material world began to expand beyond Wôbanakik early in the Years of the Log Ships. We received quahog shell from our coastal southern neighbors. Marginella and columella shell came from the sandy margin of the Great Sea in southern Nibenakik (the Carolinas). Copper, the malleable bead- and blade-making stone, found us from far to the west, until we discovered a mine in the Cape d'Or region of what is today Nova Scotia. It was made into hunting and fishing tools such as gorges or lance-points, woodworking tools such as adze and gouge blades, domestic tools such as awls and knives, and ornaments such as thick rolled-copper beads strung on hemp rope. Its popularity declined at the end of the Years of the Log Ships, and the last evidence of it in western Wôbanakik (that I know of) was 1,800 years ago at Nonnigonikon Winooskik (the Winooski Site, near Burlington, Vermont), although it continued to be used by our eastern relatives.

Ancient bone, which has mostly faded into Aki, the Earth, in southern Wôbanakik, remains in cold northern soil, where the forces of decay are slower. From these northern sea-camps come expertly designed, made- and polished bone and ivory tools, with geometric patterns finely incised with precision stone tools. Images of waterfowl and sea mammals graced our tools and became effigies to help us in our quest for balance with the earth and its life. This is only the weakest remainder of a rich artistic tradition executed in perishable materials such as wood, shell, and birch bark. It is known that as recently as the eighteenth century we used finely incised birch-bark pictographic records, adapted to keeping records in a European manner.

Easily carved soapstone was occasionally found in our mountains or perhaps laboriously hauled by canoe up the Kwinitegw from the land of the Nipmucs (south-central New England). It was made into waterproof cups, plates, and bowls for processing or serving food, pipes for smoking, or ornaments to wear. Along the coast it was used for fishing weights called plummets.

The Kwinitegw and Bitawbagok Valleys were foci of stone bowl use; the remains of an extraordinary thin-walled cup were found at Skitchewaug, and numerous small fragments were found near the modern Euro-American settlement of Hartland, Vermont. However, a beautiful little hourglass-shaped *odamoganapskw* (stone pipe bowl) was recovered by a farmer from the Wintegok Valley, and other pipe fragments are common.

Chipped stone, used since we came to Wôbanakik for *ozigwaonak* (projectile points; see fig. 12) and meat and plant processing tools, was supplemented by stone shaped by laborious pecking to approximate shape, grinding with abraders to its final form, then polishing to give its final sharp edge and smooth surface. Much was locally quarried stone, but some beautiful banded slate made its way to us from the far West. Long, six-sided polished-slate "bayonet" points, attached to a sturdy ash or maple shaft with rawhide, became deadly moose lances. Polished stone hatchets, adzes, gouges, and celts, although hard to make, were more efficient woodworking tools and showed a new level of pride in manufacture—they became beautiful as well as useful.

This was a time of declining subsistence labor. We had time to spend on things other than wresting life from the land. Metal and polished stone made life more visually complex. They reminded us of those natural forces and spirits that were so close to us. Amethyst, clear quartz, galena, and calcite crystals, stones that had lived with us for thousands of years, had become symbols of personal identity, kinship, and place. Red ochre and graphite, ground by rotary motion into powder on red-slate tablets, became our paint. Soapstone from the Green Mountains, slate from the margins of Bitawbagok, and other kinds of soft stone were worked into beads or gorgets, plates of stone that were worn about the neck. Shell from our lakes or traded from the east or even mammal bone became large gorgets with up to three holes. Shell was made into small (6 mm by 4 mm) disc beads by drilling a fine hole in the center with a bow or hand drill. Then the chips were strung on a sinew cord held taut by a bow of a springy wood, such as ash or maple, and were ground more or less round by rubbing at an angle on a sandstone or granite abrading stone. Many graves of our honored dead have been opened by Euro-American archaeologists, revealing beautiful tiny worked-shell beads, but as a courtesy to the Dead, I decline to discuss these in any detail. Bone and antler were made into beautiful hairpins and combs, sometimes with a waterbird design cut into the top. Bone became whistles, beads, and pendants. A rectangular conch shell gorget was found weathering out of a gravel pit on Azeskoimanahan (Muddy Island or Isle LaMotte, Vermont) by Euro-American archaeologists, attesting to a long trade route that stretched to the tropical south. The porcupine, which had heretofore been such a nuisance that we hunted porcupines only when all other meat failed, became

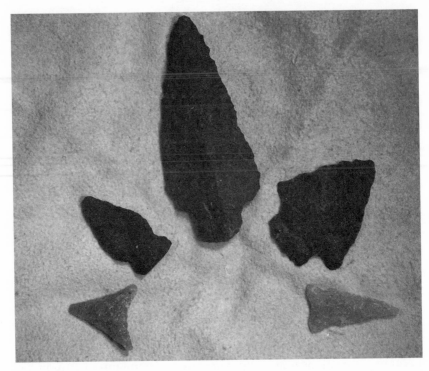

Fig. 12. *Atlatl* dart and arrow point types that define the Archaic and Woodland periods. *Wôbanakik Heritage Center Collection, photograph by Andrew Lee.*

the source for our embroidery "thread," complementing our painted leather clothing and bags.

To harvest the 30,000 or so porcupine quills, we would kill *kokw*, the porcupine, and pluck its quills if it had chewed our canoe paddles or food caches. Usually, we would ask a local porcupine to share its quills with us. To thank it in advance, we would give it a bit to eat, maybe a ground nut or two. While it was munching, we could throw an old, thin buckskin robe over it. The porcupine would "shiver," and we had a robe with enough quills for whatever project we needed to do. The quills would then be sorted by size and washed. The quills had to be kept away from children and especially the dogs, who would try to smell the quills, only to impale their lips and noses. We could then dye the quills yellow with ash bark or goldthread root, red with alder bark or hemlock root, green with moosewood or princess pine, blue with beech bark or rotted gray birch, purple from berries or silver maple bark, brown from tree bark moss, or black from fir or black spruce bark. The dyed quills could then be embroidered onto leather or birch bark. If embroidered onto wet birchbark, the quills would be gripped and held when the bark dried out and shrank. Various types of lock hitches were required when embellishing leather or wood.

The Great Sea

As our shaman-helmsmen became supremely adept at reading the ocean spirit and its signposts, we finally became deep-water mariners, venturing across large expanses of sea, fearlessly striking out for new territory beyond the horizon to see and to fish. We know this to be true, for the remains of deep-water dwellers such as swordfish found in our old living areas are testimony to ancient marine knowledge. This knowledge has not entirely departed.

SHIP STORY

There is a huge automobile ferry that travels from southern Maine to Nova Scotia. Many years ago the ferry was far out into the deep of the Gulf of Maine, miles from land . . .

Chunga, chunga, chunga. (the sound of the ferry's diesel engines)
The watchman noticed a tiny dot far to the northeast.
Chunga, chunga, chunga.
Upon closing in on the dot they were horrified to see that it was apparently a single person in a tiny canoe, bobbing up and down on the huge swells of the gulf.
Chunga, chunga, chunga.
The watchman went to the captain and said, "Looks like we've got a man in a lifeboat out ahead, we'd better steer over to offer aid." The captain gave the order.
Chunga, chunga, chunga.
As they approached they saw that it was an Indian in a canoe (the story does not tell whether it was a birch-bark canoe). "Must have been someone swept out into the deep sea! He doesn't look too excited however!"
Chunga, chunga, chunga.
The ship slowly pulled alongside the canoe where a single man was slowly paddling, apparently parallel to the invisible shore far to the west. He put

down the paddle to watch out for the swell made by the ferry and looked up
at the crew scurrying to help.
    "Ahoy, do you need help?"
    "Nope."
    "Is there anything you need?"
    "Well, I'd appreciate it if you could throw down a match for my pipe."
Chunga, chunga, chunga.
(See fig. 13.)

Flight of birds, currents of water, movements of fish, and the smell of current and land made the featureless sea a vast water trail by day. The stars circling quietly overhead became our guide at night. Every seafaring people has to know the heavens, for beyond the sight and smell of land only the tiny fires above show us our place in space and time. As with other maritime cultures, we knew that food on the great ocean was rarely a problem, fish were abundant and tame; they fell easily to the harpoon and leister. Drinking water was sometimes a dilemma. But as was the custom of traditional mariners, every rain squall was probably captured and concentrated in the bottoms of the hulls, where it was eagerly bailed into water bottles. These conservation measures prolonged the fading water store on long voyages beyond land. But death by thirst stalked a crew who forgot to follow the wind and stars or were unlucky. How far we went into the Great Sea remains a mystery. Recently, archaeologists have hypothesized that North America was populated by a European maritime society during the Ice Age, based on the similarity of stone tools. During the Years of the Log Ships, stone tools such as gouges and hooks were once again similar on both sides of the Atlantic.

"This new evidence suggests that cultural development may have been parallel on both sides of the Atlantic over seven thousand years ago. The evidence also compels diffusionists to ask whether these ancient ceremonial traditions were once carried from North America to the shores of Europe along the prevailing northern route of the Gulf Stream." (Will Lyman, narrator. "Secrets of the Lost Red Paint People" in *Nova*, WGBH, Boston. Telecast 1978.)

Far from being a frightful place, when respected, the Great Sea showed us its great calm and care. The great warm water trail just off the shore of Wôbanakik beckoned with its lush Caribbean fragrance to the greatest of mysteries, the land beyond the dawn. We could feel the great water trail of the Gulf Stream seize our ships from the toil of the paddlers and bear us inexorably dawnward. In Agomenikik (Europe), the ashen-skinned native

Fig. 13. Petroglyph of log ship, Peterborough, Ontario. *Drawn by Frederick Wiseman.*

peoples were astonished at the polished hulls of our great ships coming out of the warm mists of Wôbanakik. They welcomed our knowledge and tools of shipbuilding and looked with wonder on our crudely drawn illustrations of standing stones, stone rings, and markers. Soon we saw that they made gouges, celts, plummets, harpoons, and bone effigy combs in a style of Wôbanakik but always with a twist of their own. Later standing stones, stone rings, and circles designed at first with our guidance, made their land look more like home. But few Alnôbak made the trip to the island of fire (Iceland), the gateway to Europe; fewer made it to Europe, and fewest of all returned by the great northern gyre of current that was the road home. But enough returned to let us know that we were not alone in the world.

This reconstruction is as plausible and has as much circumstantial technological evidence as Eurocentric "ancient mariner" scenarios gaining popularity today. However, unlike mainstream scholarly thought, it makes the fundamental assumption that the Alnôbak were not passive recipients of sophistication but possibly even donors of worldwide cultural development. Whether you agree with it or not, it reveals the potential of "paradigm bias" in conventional cultural diffusion thought.[5]

During the closing Years of the Log Ships, new technologies crept into Wôbanakik from the southland. The first of these was the clay vessel. Every child playing on the riverbank knew that clay could be shaped and molded with the hands. We knew that clay hardened into a soft, crumbly rock when exposed to the hearth fire. Later came the knowledge of adding finely ground stone or clamshell to take up the crack-producing stresses as the clay dried and was fired. With this knowledge came techniques of making thin-walled clay containers—pots that did the same work as soap-stone vessels but could be made in less time. We learned to make a thin string of wet clay tempered with feldspar grit; then we coiled the strings on a "base form" (often a piece of an old bowl), and then coiled them vertically to make the form of a vessel. The coils could be "smushed" together with a deft motion of the fingers or cord-wrapped paddle to make a wall of the correct form. After drying, the next course of coils could be added to the wall. A water-polished stone smoothed the interior of the vessel. Decoration could be added to the neck to give the wet, greasy hands of the cook a gripping place. After drying, the pot could be eased from the base mold and fired in a hole six inches deep and three feet in diameter. The pots were placed in the middle, covered with hardwood fuel, then covered with sod to make a kiln. The fire was lit, perhaps with the help of a chert/pyrite fire-making kit, then allowed to burn out, the slowly declining heat producing finished pots. The advantage of the clay vessel was that it could be heated directly over the coals, suspended by thongs, or wedged in the coals with its pointed base. No longer did we have the laborious task of heating rocks in the fire, then transferring them, soot and all, to a bark, skin, or wooden pot with a pair of tongs. This was a considerable saving in labor and an improvement in taste. The first clay vessels, from two thousand years ago, were small cooking pots of uniform shape and size that held from one to three gallons. They had a conical base to allow them to be set upright in a bed of coals and a shell-edge type of decoration around the top. This type has been called by archaeologists "Vinette 1."[6]

The introduction of pottery marks the end of the Years of the Log Ships, for we now passed into a period when we looked inward. New political forces cut off our trade network to the south and west; Wôbanakik and the Great Sea became increasingly cold, as the Climatic Optimum gave way to cooler conditions. Formerly productive deep-sea fisheries declined or shifted into unknown areas, and the movements of seabirds such as the great auk became erratic, making navigation uncertain. The Gulf Stream declined and became moody and dangerous. The northern passage to the Arctic and Europe became increasingly hazardous as icebergs came farther south and lasted well into the spring. Hemmed in by climate and less than friendly neighbors, our life changed, for we became interested in the last great gift of the South: corn agriculture.

5

The Coming of the Others:
The Years of Corn

(1,000 to 400 Years Ago)

Asigwonit, the arrow, and *dobi*, the curved far-thrower that propelled it, came to us at this time. For millennia, the trap or *atlatl* provided all of our needs from our animal brothers. Then came the curved wood that could capture and hold our strength until we released the arrow toward the game. We used a simple bow made of one piece of wood, not bound with sinew or bone like those of our neighbors to the north. Our bow was made from a length split from rock maple, spruce, or ash, four or five feet long. *Bagiminakwam* (hickory) was the preferred wood in the south, where it grew straight and tall. It was made either flat or semicircular in cross section, often having a thickened hand-hold. It was tapered, then notched at each end to take the twisted sinew, gut, or hair bowstring. After the bow was made and polished, it was painted with designs and symbols to enhance its effectiveness against wild game and to make it easier to identify by the owner. Finally, the bow was given a case made from leather or rawhide, the tail of *bihtolo* (mountain lion) being preferred. Arrows, about two feet long, were made of serviceberry, dogwood, or ash. Fletching, of two or three split waterfowl- or raptor-wing pointer feathers, was lashed to *bakwa*, the shaft, with sinew and hemp thread. Arrows to be used on waterfowl were blunt, made by expanding the shaft to almost a thumb's width and rounding it. These were designed to stun the bird and, most important on canoe-borne water hunts, not to sink if we missed our mark. *Ozigwaonak* (stone points) graced the arrows used for rabbits or larger land animals. Fish were hunted with barbed-point arrows. When finished, the arrow was given the *bakwaikinawitgan*, the owner's mark that distinguished it from all others in the hunt or in war. The bow changed the nature of warfare, which had until now been relatively unimportant. We now needed *ajowanoganak* (woven wood shields) in the form of a large rectangle with a rounded top.

The years of the Log Ships lasted until about one thousand passages of the sun ago, when three things came to us; the first was golden-haired maize and her sisters; the second was the loss of our hunting lands to the west of Bitawbagok to a new group of people, and the third was the bow and arrow. Other than these changes, things in our villages were much the same as during the end of the Years of the Log Ships. We hunted and fished with the same technologies the same game throughout the year. There are remains of the following upland game animals found by archaeologists in our old village sites dating to the Years of Corn: *woboz* (elk), *moz* (moose), and *nolka* (deer), which we usually hunted in the fall; *mategwas* (rabbit), *segokw* (skunk), *agaskw* (woodchuck), *mihkoa* (squirrel), chipmunk, mouse, and shrew; *awassos* (bear), *alemos* (dog), *wokweses* (red fox), and *pezo* (bobcat). Animals from river, lake and marsh included *tamakwa* (beaver), *moskwas* (muskrat), *aligdaid* (snapping turtle), shad, *meskwamakw* (salmon), alewife, sucker, bullhead, *kwenoza* (northern pike), carp, *lapalsod* (yellow perch), *abonamagwas* (sunfish), catfish, *monazigan* (black bass), *makwhowikhozik* (dace), and *alsak* (freshwater mussel).

The Coming of Agriculture

But the arrival of *skamon*, the corn, signaled the beginning of a new life. We had known of Corn, the woman with the golden hair, for hundreds of years. Our neighbors to the south grew several varieties, from sweet to pop corn, and from time to time, a bit came up the ancient trade routes to be used as a curiosity, a rare food, or for beads. However, most of Wôbanakik was now too cold to grow it effectively, no matter how we tried. As time went on, new, more cold-hardy varieties of flint corn, beans, and squash developed and moved up the Hudson and Long River Valleys. The climate became slightly warmer about this time, helping spread these tender crops into our lands. Even these new cold-tolerant varieties were not foolproof in Wôbanakik's lowlands. Every few years a frost would wipe out the crop. We found that slight variations in the hill slope shape could determine a successful crop or failure. Low-lying cold pockets had to be avoided; windbreaks and other strategies probably were developed to assure protection. Fertilizers such as fish wastes speeded growth and maturation, giving us a better chance for a good harvest. Improved processing tools such as the *dawkwahogan*, or corn pounding mortar, made of elm, yellow birch, oak, or black gum, and improved storage in grass-lined pits made agriculture more attractive. We still relied on hunting, fishing and gathering wild foods—only a fool would be solely dependent on farming. (Fig. 14.)

Our *skamonikikonal* (cornfields) were not designed only for corn; we had many other crops. Red, kidney, or perhaps pinto and navy varieties of *adbakwa* (beans) were planted in groups of three or four seeds along with the corn and used the corn stalk as a trellis upon which to climb. The corn didn't seem to mind hosting the beans, and the beans certainly enjoyed the support the corn gave them. The smaller *wassawas* (squashes), such as summer squash, were eaten fresh, while the butternut and acorn squash could be stored for winter use. The flowers could be eaten as well. Pumpkins, our largest squashes, were very important food producers, but they had a long growing season and couldn't be harvested until frost was a threat. Thus, pumpkins could not always be relied upon. The related gourds also took a long time to mature but were important for containers and perhaps rattles. The six-foot-tall, yellow-flowered Jerusalem artichokes became an easy crop to grow. They didn't need fertilizer, didn't have any problem with our winters, and spread quickly by their fleshy, three- to four-inch underground tubers. As long as the ground wasn't frozen, they were available in a few minutes of digging. When the ground was frozen, they stored easily in baskets but were a prize target for rodents. The closely related *gizoskana* (sunflower) was prized as a finger food or to provide cooking or hair oil. *Odamo* (tobacco), raised in special beds by men, was important in ceremonies and medicinal offerings, and was smoked in pipes. By 1200 A.D. the stone bowls of these pipes were of steatite, the only common material objects made of this once important stone. The last crop of any importance was the husk tomato, or tomatillo, which could be eaten fresh or dried when harvested from the vine in the fall.

It became important to have our villages near the good agricultural sandy loams of the lower riverine flood plains. These could not be far from the areas used for fishing; for in the Planting Moon of spring we needed to harvest the walleye and suckers of Wazowategok, Wintegok, Winoskitegw, and Onegigwizibo and the alewives, salmon, and shad of Kwinitekw. Immediately after processing these fish we had to prepare our cornfields for

Fig. 14. Depiction of Abenaki hunter. *Wôbanakik Heritage Center Collections photograph by Andrew Lee.*

pakikan, clearing and fertilizing. In early to mid-May in the Kwinitegw and southern Bitawbagok, villages prepared and planted their fields. Northern villages planted in late May and early June. If there was no frost and the animals of the soil had spared the corn, the young plants emerged and grew in June. During the summer the families had to reside near the fields to tend the corn, beans, squash, Jerusalem artichokes, and tobacco. *Mkazas* (crows) and *segaukw* (skunks) were always a threat to the crop, digging or pulling up the young corn and often letting it lie on the ground to die. Women and children had to continually guard the fields from their incursions. Late summer and early fall was a time for gathering the still important blueberries, butternuts, chokecherries, hickory nuts, hazelnuts, raspberries, elderberries, grapes, and staghorn sumac. Sweetgrass, boneset, and other therapeutic and medicinal herbs were collected, dried, and prepared. By late August and September the produce of the fields was ready for harvest. After harvest in the early fall, the family could leave the village to go hunting. Thus, agriculture tied us to one spot for more of the year than before. It was probably just as well that we gave up our wanderlust![1]

The Coming of the Ganienkeh and Nadoueks

About four thousand winters ago, a people speaking an unintelligible language moved to the west of us in the Lake Ontario region from their homeland in Nibenakik (the south central Appalachian area). They visited and traded with us, and we knew them. They seemed interested in war as well as agriculture. War seemed to spread to them from their neighbors far to the south (modern Mexico): the great stone cities of 1,500 winters ago that fought one another, and little empires flourished and crumbled. By the end of the last millennium, the great earthworked city known as Cahokia (near St. Louis, Missouri) had erected its defensive palisade, showing that the need for defense had crept to North America.

Their villages, which may have originally looked like ours, by nine hundred passages of the sun ago became large settlements of longhouses shaped somewhat like our old buildings at Nonnegonnikon Nuliak. These villages were soon surrounded by high fences of upright stakes set well into the ground. The Wendat (Draper site) village in Ontario shows the first evidence of defensive palisades about six hundred winters ago. These villages were well planned—they were invariably set in defensible locations. The newcomers had some strange (to us) political and religious concepts and interesting ceremonies using carved wooden masks, and they endlessly analyzed their dreams. Although many of their ideas we understood and shared, it was perhaps good to have them at a distance. Soon that distance decreased. They spread to the east, first cutting us off from our trading partners and supplies of gray and mottled "New York chert" and "Ohio chalcedony." Then they approached our lands, which were then throughout the Wawobadenik (the Adirondack Mountains) and up into the Ottawa River. In numerous clashes, verbal and otherwise, the longhouse dwellers took over our hunting lands to the west. This warlike history is still remembered and celebrated by our Ganienkeh neighbors, who are now our friends:

A joke heard at Rebaska's Restaurant, Kahnawake Mohawk Reserve, Quebec, in 1998:
Q. What do you call an Abenaki in Mohawk? A. Lunch.

Our two peoples then agreed that the lake should become a boundary, and it received its final name "The Lake Between." Another group of these people moved up the Ktsitegw (St. Lawrence River), settling, according to interpretations of a single early European observer (Cartier), near Quebec City and near Montreal. There was plenty of land, and we didn't want to kill for it, for it belonged to the Great Spirit, not us. For all their aggressiveness and strange ways, it was not unpleasant to have them as neighbors, especially the people of the Great River, who quickly became our staunch allies and friends.[2]

They were very organized. If we set up a boundary with them, such as the east shore of Bitawbagwtegu (Richelieu River), we had to go into great detail about the nature of the boundary, where it began and ended, how it could be changed or crossed. But once all the seemingly endless verbal haggling was done, they honored the boundary. Thus, we learned to look at the land as something that can be cut up, like the carcass of a deer. These were foreign thoughts, but once mastered, they prepared us (slightly) for what lay ahead. Together we learned how to make more beautiful clay pots in a styles shared by the Nadouek and Alnôbak. By 1,400 winters ago, vessel styles became varied, ranging from pointed to rounded base types, but the neck decoration seemed not to be as important. The latest type from the Years of Corn was more globular and had a cord-wrapped paddle decoration and a punctate decoration made with the end of a tube, perhaps a reed. This vessel has been called by archaeologists "St. Lawrence Iroquoian." But as an advocate for the Abenaki people's ancestors, I propose that the pottery was developed by all of us, Iroquoian and Abenaki, as we shared our learning.

The St. Lawrence Iroquoian Problem:
An Issue of Political and Ceramic Sovereignty

In Massena, New York, is the St. Lawrence–Franklin D. Roosevelt Power Project. As part of the U.S. government's public art program, the project had Thomas Hart Benton paint a mural entitled *Jacques Cartier Discovers the St. Lawrence.* An Akwesasne Mohawk colleague pointed out that one section of Benton's mural depicts a group of Indian villagers preparing to meet Cartier at his first landfall in Gaspé, Quebec. That section is interpreted there (and in print) as "Iroquois warriors set forth to confront the arriving explorers." That publicly funded mural on federal property negated the Micmac people as our "first Contact" agents at Cartier's intrusion into our continent. The French explorer never saw an Iroquois warrior, unless one was visiting Hochelaga (a village probably lying under modern Montreal), during his sixteenth-century visit to that town. How can the American government portray an Iroquois village in ethnic Micmac country? This partially educated interpretation leads to a most vexing archaeological issue for those of us who believe that our homeland has always been ours: the so-called St. Lawrence Iroquoians.

The Two Iroquoian Villages of Cartier and a Regional Pottery

This concept was developed by archaeologists to explain certain cultural remains of the St. Lawrence River Valley. Unusual pottery vessels (fig. 15, left), pipes, and other remains have been found there since the nineteenth century. The pottery is technically excellent and decoratively distinct, with designs applied by incising, punctating, and molding. The problem scholars faced was that the St. Lawrence Valley was abandoned before sustained cultural "contact" with European observers was initiated in the early seventeenth century. This frustrating hiatus prevented a direct historical link with known modern ethnic groups of the northeast. A hint about who these people were came from the records of Jacques Cartier's sixteenth-century voyages to the St. Lawrence, published in English in the 1920s. Cartier encountered many travelers, hamlets, and two villages; one he called Stadacone, believed to be in the vicinity of Quebec City, and the other, Hochelaga, mentioned above. From these villages he collected, along with human specimens, some words in the dialect of the villages. (Note: vocabularies collected by Cartier from transient camps and traders are not "georeferenced" and cannot be used for such analysis.) Although the vocabulary was short and garbled by transcription bias, it seemed to relate to words known from a group of languages called "Iroquoian" after the League of the Iroquois, the best-known speakers of this large language family.

The inference was made that the people Cartier encountered at Hochelaga and Stadacone spoke an Iroquoian language, an assumption based on the meager data from two collection locales. However, the vocabularies are

Fig. 15. Wabanaki pottery, ca. 500 winters ago. *Drawn by Frederick Wiseman.*

believed by linguists to be more similar to Wendat than Six Nations Iro-
quois. The Wendat, for their own sovereignty issues, resent being called
Iroquoian, and the Iroquois themselves are divided; many of my friends at
Kahnawake and Akwesasne prefer Haudenosaunee rather than Iroquois.
But archaeologists are stuck with this "politically incorrect" term, and we
must deal with it. Native-proposed alternative names such as "Laurentian
Nadoueks" have gone unnoticed. Archaeologists tried with little success to
locate these villages to see what the pottery looked like. Nevertheless, the
secondary assumption was made that the (probably) Iroquoian speakers of
Stadacone and Hochelaga, or their direct ancestors, must have made the
beautiful pots then being found all over the St. Lawrence Valley but not
tied directly to the historically known Stadacone or Hochelaga. The result
of a series of inductive leaps was that the two "georeferenced" sixteenth-
century word lists taken by Cartier became connected to a modern ethnic
group, as did a pottery being found at increasing numbers of sites throughout the upper St. Lawrence. This created of the concept of a St. Lawrence

Iroquois ceramic style. This model is not without its detractors, for other historians have proposed that the inhabitants were actually Wendats or Mohawks, but that is a more distant debate.[3]

To this long-winded statement, you say, "What does it have to do with the Abenaki?" If the St. Lawrence Iroquoian pots had "stayed where they belonged," that would be fine for us (a headache for our Wendat friends, but that is their story). The trouble is that as archaeologists began digging in Abenaki country in the post–World War II era, they began finding these pots here, along with our standard "Algonquin" types. As time went on, it seemed that everywhere archaeologists dug, they found them until, by the last decade of the twentieth century, there seemed to be more St. Lawrence Iroquois pots in Abenaki (and our Wabanaki neighbors') country than in the St. Lawrence Valley. In November 1999, Dr. James Petersen of the University of Vermont showed an audience a dot-density map showing the known extent of St. Lawrence Iroquoian pottery in the Northeast. The St. Lawrence Valley seemed to be the northwestern quadrant of distribution of that pottery type. The rest of the area was what anthropologists would call Wabanaki country.

Now these semantic and geographic "games" are merely that. The problem is that the Abenaki people are still experiencing ethnic cleansing by governments that have power in our homeland. One of the forms of genocide is to disconnect us from our history, to show that we are transient with no rights here. The presence of pottery in our homeland that potential expert witnesses call St. Lawrence Iroquoian is a threat to Abenaki sovereignty, just as it is to the Lorette Wendat's land claims case in Canada.

Iroquois "R" Us? : An Abenaki-centric Perspective

Technically, I have no quibbles with the "St. Lawrence" appellation; archaeologists often name pottery after its "type site," the place where it was first discovered (or published). The pottery can subsequently be found far afield without any spatial judgments being made. However, as used by archaeologists in the Abenaki (and Wabanaki) homeland, this appellation is more than a type site identifier. It is used, in its more extreme incarnations, to imply colonization from the St. Lawrence Valley. Is this a reasonable conclusion?

I don't think that anyone working in the Colorado Plateau would say that the "Fourmile polychrome" that I excavated in the 1970s at the Homolovi site (Winslow, Arizona) implied a direct historical population movement from the Fourmile Site to the much larger Homolovi. Only through a well-dated and fine-grained stylistic progression through space and time could we begin to speculate on the movements of pottery-producing individuals, families, and groups. We are just beginning to reach this point in the Southwest, after seven decades of the most intense technical, systematic, tree-ring dating of materials and stylistic study of ceramics in the world. I read that Claude Chapedelaine and his Canadian colleagues may be beginning, in selected portions of the St. Lawrence Valley, to reach this level of geographic interpretation, with the help of neutron-activation testing for clay sources and microstylistic analysis of stylistic attributes. Without the precise dating control of dendrochronology (tree-ring dating) on numerous varieties of ceramics and/or their attributes, it would seem difficult to determine dated points of origins and directions of movement of *finished pots*. I suspect that their logic may rest on the still untested assumption of a "St. Lawrence hearth" or consistent point of origin of the ceramics. Sourcing raw materials shows that someone (the Innu, the Wabanakis?) went to clay banks in the St. Lawrence Valley to collect clay. It says little about ceramic manufacture and subsequent movement as trade goods or colonists' baggage. It says even less about ethnicity. I believe that a colonization model to explain this ceramic distribution may be premature, especially given its potential political impact. It is one of several reasonable hypotheses in need of testing within a tight chronological sequence in multiple regions of the Northeast.

The correlation of "Iroquoian ethnicity" with this widespread pottery is also in need of investigation. Close proximity of two friendly ethnic groups encourages stylistic borrowing and reciprocal trade of artifacts. Ritual exchange, trade, and political intermarriage are well known social "boundary maintenance" processes that cause styles, artifacts, and even craftspeople to cross permeable ethnic borders while maintaining those borders. The best-documented Native American process of this type is the potlatch, a ceremonial cycle of gift giving that held Indians of northwestern North America together in the face of high population densities and potential warfare. The result was that distinct ethnic peoples speaking languages about as closely related as English and Chinese eventually shared a remarkably homogeneous material and spiritual world without giving up their language or ethnic identity.

An example of this permeability as applied to ceramics is First Mesa

(Hopi) pottery, the finest native ceramic produced in Arizona. Loretta Houma, a potter from Hano village, First Mesa, told me years ago that two peoples make her pottery style: the ethnic Hopi, who have dwelt there for centuries, and her people, originally from the East (the Rio Grande area of New Mexico), who settled on First Mesa years ago. Two indigenous languages in two adjacent villages, one pottery. From my Hopi acquaintances and my mentors at the University of Arizona, I came to believe that artifact attributes and styles are independent variables that can, only with careful research, be correlated with other signals of ethnicity, such as language. The ethnic identifier is inferred after long, painstaking statistical, geographic and stylistic analysis, not as an a priori assumption. Upon beginning to study northeastern ceramic geographies, I learned of the sharing of Late Woodland Period pottery styles among ethnically Mohawk, Munsee, and Mohican populations to the southwest of our homeland. I note that the concept of "sharing," not "colonization," is used in that region, even in the secondary literature based on the original research, such as Robert Grumet's *Historic Contact* volume.

Dr. James Petersen's dot-density map of St. Lawrence Iroquoian pottery becomes necessary to our argument. The St. Lawrence Valley is clearly the northwestern quadrant of its area of "distribution." When I saw it, I thought, "It looks to me that it is 'New English Wabanakian' pottery that somehow made it up to the St. Lawrence valley and stopped." As much or more of the total area is what linguist/geographers would label as Wabanaki rather than Iroquoian. The Abenaki activist in me would draw other conclusions (St. L. Iroquois R us!), but I believe that a stylistic sharing model may be a competing reasonable hypothesis, given what we believe for other areas such as the Mohican Homeland (or the Southwest or Mesoamerica).

Now, the government bureaucracy and its attorneys care nothing for the geographic/historical semantic contests that engage mainstream scholars of the Northeast. Their goal is the denial of Indian sovereignty, which is an economic threat to its multiethnic constituency. To them, as with the mural interpreters at the power plant at Massena, New York, the St. Lawrence Iroquoian pots found in our homeland mean that the Iroquois, not we, are the heirs of our homeland. Other Native American factions in Vermont may also be happy to know this theory. As the director of a Vermont Native social services organization derisively said, "They [the Swanton Abenakis] are all Mohawks anyway."

New Connections with the Nadoueks

The Nadoueks learned from us how to make our traditional baskets. We probably learned from them how to build a village that could be defended in times of war. We traded them corn varieties and shell beads. For some reason, they were soon obsessed with these beads, called wôbôbi, or wampum, that were made by our relatives and a new people we will talk about along the margin of the Great Sea. Soon they learned to make them into necklaces, sashes, and belts that became markers of their prowess. Their villages were often very near ours. Dawskodasek, my family's home ground to the east of Masipskwibi (Missiquoi Bay, in Vermont and Quebec), was close to a Nadouek village. Thus, communication and exchange of ideas between our peoples was easy and quick. We intermarried with them and they with us. We began to learn their language. Those Ganienkakiiak (New York Iroquoians) who lived near us learned to be less uptight, and we learned to become more organized. They continuously fought among themselves until five hundred passages of the sun ago, some of the Ganienkakiiak to the west and south of Bitawbagok, near the land of the Mahiganiak (Mahicans), banded together in an alliance somewhat like our Wabanaki Confederacy. This allowed them to field large armies against their Nadouek brethren along the Ktsitegw. In the Christian year of 1570, they may have destroyed the Nadouek city of Hochelaga (at Montreal), ending the dominance of these people in the Ktsitegw and sending refugees to our homeland, a pattern that would be repeated many times in the near future. Their confederation's representative politics were strange, for we believed that at council every person has the right to say what he wishes and then the elders must hold peace for a day and a night to be sure that the decision was right for seven generations unborn.

PART II
The War for the Dawnland

6

Darkness Falls:
The Years of the Beaver

(Christian Years 1600 to 1820)

The fall of Hochelaga and Stadacone in the 1500s was the end of the serenity that had reigned for hundreds of generations. Our neighbors, the Nadoueks, were reduced to refugees seeking shelter among our villages and leaving their homelands vacant. The loss of the Nadoueks left their cherished farmlands and hunting territories along the Kitsitegw available for colonization. These deserted lands soon became refuges for a people from Wôbanakik during the Years of the Beaver. Filling in these long-abandoned lands, we were no longer separated from our northern relatives. Having destroyed their kin, the Haudenosaunee from the West began serious incursions into our lands—sometimes with our permission, sometimes not. Relations remained mostly peaceful for a while, although mutual raiding did occur. However, we decided that it would be prudent if we moved our villages to the bluffs overlooking our farmlands and surround them with a palisade of logs set firmly into the soil. (See fig. 16.)

First Contact

I name this turbulent period the Years of the Beaver because *tamakwa*, the beaver, is the animal upon which this time pivots. Disease from the East is the other singularity of the period. Beginning in the 1530s a series of afflictions washed over Wôbanakik, carrying away the knowledge of our elders, the potential of our young, and the srength of our adults. Whole regions

Fig. 16. Cultural map of Wôbanakik in A.D. 1500. *Drawn by Frederick Wiseman.*

had to be abandoned. This biological assault is still remembered with a prohibition to discuss it in detail, an interdiction that I will follow.

The Agomenokiak, whom I will discuss shortly, were entranced by the fur of the beaver and began to give us marvelous things in exchange for its pelts. The beaver, which was heretofore a relatively minor part of our annual hunting cycle, necessarily assumed a major role during this time. Access to beaver became critical, and friendly (or neutral) neighbors began to fight over beaver-hunting territories. The beaver trade affected the rhythm of the seasons—we now found it important to get as many beaver as possible so that the foreigners' technology could be ours. Our respect for conservation and game animals was challenged for the first time in scores of generations. To survive in a changing world, we could not refuse the new technology, no matter what the environmental consequences. For our neighbors, who looked upon our hunting territories with newly greedy eyes, were themselves acquiring new weapons' technologies against which we would be helpless. We became caught in an escalation of warfare and environmental degradation from which we could not free ourselves. It is said among some of my people that Koluscap became weary of this spiral, which hurt not only the land but the soul of the Alnôbak. Many say that his departure was due to the newcomers, but I believe otherwise. Departing in sorrow, he is not easily available to us anymore. Somewhere away from Wôbanakik, he awaits the time when Ktsi nwaskw will make things the way they should be.

THE DEPARTURE OF KOLUSCAP

Koluscap returned from a long journey and was walking through the forests of Wôbanakik when a group of animals came before him. "Koluscap, things are not well in the Dawnland," said Awassos, the bear. "The Alnôbak, who heretofore have been our respectful brothers are not treating us, especially my little cousin tamakwa, the beaver, with their accustomed courtesy and care." Since their lessons from the departure of the Ktsiawaasak, human beings have asked permission of Askawobid, the Watcher and the soul of their prey, to take any life. They have always taken only what they can use and no more; we have known that, for we listen to their stories and lessons on the air during long winter nights. Koluscap said, "What has changed in my short absence, that has all of you so disturbed ?" Moz the moose answered, "The humans have new tools, a horrible black metal that cuts our rooted kin with unmannerly swiftness and slays us even at a distance. With this metal, I have seen them kill many more beaver than they can use, wiping out whole families. Even worse, I know that they do not use all of the beaver, but covet only its skin and fur, which they do not keep, but give to a new hairy people in exchange for more of the horrid metal or little pieces of colored crystal. In the air is not their prayers, but concern that they must kill before someone else does it first. This is even a more troublesome thing than mere death of our kin, which is part of their life. I sense madahondo, *a bad spirit at work among them. And with this spirit in their heart is something else; it may indeed be good, but it is utterly foreign to the land, it does not belong." Koluscap said, "This spirit is called greed. I will go to the human beings and settle this."*

Koluscap went to a village of the Alnôbak. He looked about and saw that things had changed since he last came there. The village was surrounded by palisades, exuding a sense of fear and defiance. He smelled the scent of uneaten, unprocessed rotting flesh, something new to his nostrils, coming from a midden of meat beclotted with flies. Mingled with this stench was the smell of human sickness. The skins of beavers were stretched on racks all over the town, and women had left their traditional earth-lore occupations to become hide workers under the direction of men.

"Hey, you people, what are you doing? It is I, Koluscap." In response, a group of young men armed with iron tools and bright ornaments of silver,

came forward from the palisade gate. They looked troubled. "Stay, Koluscap, you must be hungry and we will give you some food, but you cannot come into our village," said a young Abenaki warrior. "The Black Robes say that you and your kindred spirits cause a sickness that causes us to rot and die. In remembrance of the old days, we give you this corn meal but you cannot come in." Koluscap saw something that he had never seen before in the eyes of his people, real fear and the green glint of greed. The tiny pieces of metal, especially the ones in the shape of a cross exuded a power of otherside that he had not felt since his birth; but it was different, cold and alien, as if it responded to currents not intrinsic to Wôbanakik. In the past, Koluscap had fought monsters and tricked his way into making the Dawnland right, but this force was from beyond his Earth to which the Great Spirit had bound him. The power in the metal and in the heart of the Alnôbak warrior was outside his authority, and he knew it. Only Ktsi nwaskw, the Great Spirit, could deal with that which was creeping over his beloved land.

"My people," said Koluscap, "I have been with you since the beginning of time. But now I see that my mission is complete." "The heart of the Alnôbak is no longer entirely the heart of The Land of the Dawn; you share it with spirits and forces which you do not even begin to understand." " New gods and desires are within you to change the land and its life for good or ill, and they cannot work with me. I tell you that some of the powers which you knew remain; Askawobid, the Watcher, and the small spirits of water, air, and wood; they continue, but some must depart. I am one who must go. But remember me, for I am not but the fabric of a good story. I await a changing of days." And with an air of maturity and sadness the people had not seen in their old hero ("How old?" asked some), he departed. Some Alnôbak started to move forward to say good-bye but were stopped by sidelong glances from others. "Let him begone, for we are sick enough," said one. "He is a ghost anyway."

It is said by some in the West that Koluscap did not depart but turned into a stone in the water. Others in the East say he waits on an misty island where he makes arrowheads to slay those who abuse the soul of the land that was once and will be his. The Saziboit, the River People, say that he paddles his magic canoe in the heavens between the sun and moon. As Ktsi alakws, the Evening Star, he gives hope to the Alnôbak who remember. Some whisper that if the heart is true, anyone who seeks Koluscap can find him, and he is not gone but merely quiet.

Medawas, 1995

How did this happen? As befell many times before, in the Years of the Log Ships and the Years of Corn, new things came to us from beyond Wôbanakik. For years we had heard of a dark malleable stone far stronger than copper. This metal was associated with a hairy race of people who had visited our Mikmoz (Micmac) and Beothuk kinsmen during the Years of Corn. These people had left, but there were stories circulating about the campfires that they would return. Around the council fire, elders speculated that they were the descendants of the "ashen-faced people," primitive humans we taught six thousand winters ago. Being bright and imitative, maybe they had advanced since we last saw them. The fabled hairy ones became a principal topic of news and gossip throughout Wôbanakik, and in our gossiping they became more real. Only our marine communities had sustained commerce with the these early ephemeral visitors. I like to see our coastal villagers as acting as "First Contact Ambassadors" to these strangers. This was an opportunity to unravel the mysteries of where they came from, what their motives were, could they be an advantage to us, and most important, did they represent a threat? These people, called Blacmonak, came from a far country called France, in large canoes with big pieces of cloth they developed from our ancient skin sails. They came to inquire of our neighbors about our land and life ways. Their European-made goods spread far inland from these tentative encounters on the perimeter of our homeland.

Some visitors were friendly, such as Champlain; others, such as the non-Blacmon kidnapper Weymouth, were treacherous. They wanted information on the geography of our homeland and old worn skins of beaver, marten, and other fur-bearing animals. For these furs, the visitors would exchange translucent beads of glass, woven cloth, and metals much stronger than our ancient copper. These wonderful materials fell into the web of exchange connecting our far-flung villages, spreading inland along with stories of the newcomers. These things were so valuable that they were often remade into new items that fit more appropriately into our culture. Now everyone began to receive the black metal from our eastern relatives in the flesh rather than as legend. Iron arrow points, spearheads, fishhooks, knives, axes, and needles revolutionized the way we interacted with nature (see figs. 17 and 26). They slew, cut, and sewed in a fraction of the time it took with chipped- or ground-stone tools. These magnificent early iron tools remain in the ground, lessons from our ancestors. A ten-inch iron spearpoint found in the Kwinitekw valley near the Euro-American settlement of Hanover, New Hampshire, attests to a hunter pursuing fall

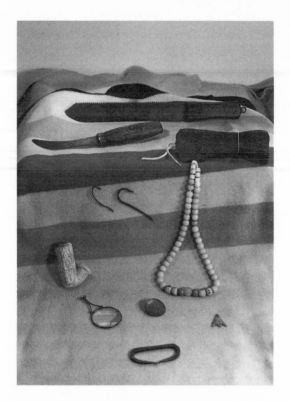

Fig. 17. Domestic fur trade and related articles found in
Wôbanakik. *Wôbanakik Heritage Center Collection, photograph
by Andrew Lee.*

game or winter moose in the mountains, while brass arrow points in the
valley attest to the hunt in the lowlands. Whoever possessed the black
metal became a powerful hunter, seamstress, or woodworker, for with
these tools, bark literally sprang from trees, saplings could be cut with a
single blow, and a new fineness of sewing prevented the winter's blast from
finding us inside snug parkas and leggings.

What trade tomahawks, tools, and guns did for the men, trade cloth and
beads did for the women. Our women had always strung shell, copper, and
seeds on twine and sinew and used porcupine quills and small shell beads
for embroidery, but this also changed. The earliest beads brought by Blacmonak traders were of an artificial rock that came in many colors. Today
we know these as trade beads, mostly from Europe, although some came
from the Orient.

Early Abenaki Trade Beads, Silver, and Brass

Most of the evidence we have of trade beads from the Years of the Beaver comes from archaeological sites. Many of these beads came from the graves of our honored dead who were disrespectfully disinterred and studied like a mineral specimen, yet another genocidal practice of the Bastaniak. However, some were taken from habitation areas such as Norridgewock and can be used in good conscience in this story. A few *nopkowanal* (necklaces) have amazingly stayed aboveground. There were three kinds of trade beads brought to us long ago. Necklace beads, called *mozobial*, were the largest type (see fig. 17). They usually had a large bore or hole for stringing on a leather thong. These were usually about one-quarter inch in diameter but ranged up to one-half inch and came in solid colors of amber, black, a dark purplish blue, dark blue, greenish blue, ice green, and opaque white. Multicolored neck beads came as the still popular "chevron" in a 1/4-by-3/8-inch size; a 1/4-inch cased variety with a colorless or green core with coral red cover (in fig. 26, the necklace with "cross of Loraine" has these beads), or as various sizes of black or dark brown beads with applied white or light longitudinal stripes. The second major type were bugle beads, long tubes of colored glass that could be strung as neck beads or sewn to clothing with sinew. Sometimes they were in white and dark blue, although more rust-red bugle beads have been found here. These were so quickly replaced by other types that the Alnôbak do not retain a word for them.

Small beads called *mozobizal*, between the size we call seed beads and pony beads (about an 8/o seed bead), were the third type. These were generally meant to be sewn to clothing rather than strung. They came in dark purple, dark blue, medium blue, ivory, black, white, and clear.

Along with beads came allied types of jewelry. Silver ornaments (fig. 26) began to be offered to us in quantity—from *aneskamonal*, the large, center-holed brooches such as one that lies at Chimney Point Museum, to smaller pins and buttons. We needed these tiny reflective amulets, for they repelled the influence of harmful spirits at the exact points on our bodies where we were most vulnerable. Beautiful little bells of yellow *wizowah-lakw* (brass) added their melodious tone to our bags and clothing. Silver and/or copper head and arm bands made their appearance. The new trade cloth quickly supplanted buckskin for all ceremonial and most village clothing. However enticing the trade goods, much of the year was too busy for making much jewelry and clothing. This could best be done in the quiet of Pebun, the winter, but it couldn't stop us from planning.[1]

Fur Trade and Conflict: A Small Case Study

As I said in the beginning of this chapter, the access to weapons brought a new reason for conflict to our land. I suppose this stage of the fur trade began when the Micmac Grand Council (Nova Scotia) or its antecedent gained an early monopoly on rights to these European visitors in the 1500s. With access to guns, navigation, and tools, they sought to turn their advantage in trade into a position as arbiter of the trade between the Europeans and Indians. This precipitated the Tarrantine Wars, perhaps the first of the so-called beaver wars to affect us. In the early 1600s, warfare had inundated the Gulf of Maine as far south as Massachusetts Bay. The Micmac Council apparently fought to prevent a southern fur trade from undermining the Micmacs' Gulf of St. Lawrence monopoly. During this bloody time our warriors from the village at Saco, Maine, rebuffed a Micmac seaborne assault; other times we were not so lucky. By the fourth decade of the seventeenth century, the Micmac lost their monopoly, as the French traders established new trading partnerships far up the St. Lawrence River, and the Dutch and English established trading centers to the south and west of our land. Our Passamaquoddy/Malecite allies in the Great Council Fire and the Gaspé Micmacs went to war for the last time in 1646. This was apparently the final bout of aggression between members of the Great Council Fire and the Micmac Grand Council. These new trading centers ushered in the next stage of the fur trade in the mid-1600s. Springfield, Massachusetts; Fort Orange (Albany, New York); and Montreal were soon built up along our borders, and we now found easy access to European manufactured goods, without the necessity of middlemen. This ease of contact had many implications. During the mid-1600s, European technology melded with our own to produce some of the most beautiful and distinctive artifacts known. This blended art has persisted in one form or another until today, yielding beadwork, sculpture, fashion, and naval architecture.

However, the Wendat and the Odawa, to our west, began an immense multidecade contest with the Haudenosaunee over organizing trade in the Laurentian economic corridor to the Great Lakes fur sources. We joined with the Wendat and Odawa in their struggles. For economic and other reasons, the Haudenosaunee often attacked us, until the Wendat competition was removed, at about the time that the Micmac quit their wars. The Years of the Beaver are a significant time; for this is the period that Euro-American scholars and lay people take great interest in. At this time we were "real Indians," worthy of Euro-American interest. Their scholars even to this day (see Calloway, 1990, for a meaningful update) use a totally inappropriate concept called the "frontier" to explain this time. The period when natives are at war with Euro-Americans seems always the most interesting to them. The popularity of movies such as *The Last of the Mohicans* and the "ravenous or pathetic warrior" prints of Lee Teter and Robert Griffing cater to this interest. It is also an extremely important time for Alnôbak lore keepers; for this is the time when we integrated alien ideas and materials into our millennia-old patterns, coming up with a new social and material synthesis that in some ways has been unsurpassed.

The Coming of the Alliance

By the 1500s we were caught in an endless cycle of war that moved up from the south, then shifted its focus with the coming of the fur trade. As we saw in the preceding section, the great city of Cahokia, near St. Louis, erected its defensive wall late in the first millennium. Six hundred winters ago, our Wendat allies to the west had perfected the twin defensive strategies of site (stockade building) and situation (easily defensible hilltop or bluff location). The reasons for the coming of this early regional conflict are unclear, but speculation includes ecological or agricultural misfortune, a "cult of war" (warfare for social advancement), and growing interrelated feuding between families and villages. This cycle of warfare was only exacerbated by the first tentative trade goods coming into our land from the northeast and southwest. This painful time is remembered in the oldest record of our Passamaquoddy relatives.

"Long ago the Indians were fighting one another. They struck one another bloodily. There were many men, women, and children, who alike were tormented by these constant battles"—*Wapapi Akonutomakonol*, Lewis Mitchell, 1990.

During this time of strife, messengers came to us with a message of peace and hope. Although some Haudenosaunee people advocate for the message coming to them a millennium ago, others prefer a 1400s or 1500s date. I will assume the later date, for it better fits the Wabanaki wampum records. I am also unsure of where these messengers came from, but the wampum records of the Passamaquoddy and the Haudenosaunee record evidence we can use.

Fig. 18. Chief Hassaki of the Odawa opens the Great Council of
1701. *Wôbanakik Heritage Center Collection, photograph by Andrew Lee.*

"At that time the wise ones thought that something had to happen.
What ever was to happen had to happen—and soon. They sent out messengers to different directions, to everywhere the Indians were located.
Some went toward the south, some to the east, others to the southwest
others to the west. They even came to the land of the Wabanaki. Very
long they journeyed, several months, before they completed their round.
. . . Every Indian to the farthest boundaries was informed that a great
confederacy was to be made"—*Wapapi Akonutomakonol,* Lewis
Mitchell, 1990.

"A council fire for all nations shall be kindled. It shall be lighted for
the Cherokee and for the Wendat. We will kindle it also for the seven nations living toward the sunrise."—Deganawidah of the Wendat ("The
Peacemaker").

From these records, it would seem that the alliance was originally con-
ceived to the west of our homeland. The Haudenosaunee tradition of their

The First Nations of the Great Council Fire, 1600–1880

Regional Subconfederacy (if applicable)	Nation	Villages (if applicable)
Independent Eastern nations	Innu (Montagnais)	
	Attikamek (Tete de boules)	
	Mahican/River Indian Confederacy (Early)	
	Penacook Confederacy (N.H. Abenakis) (Early)	
Micmac Grand Council	Seven Micmac districts	
Wabanaki Confederacy	Penobscot	
	Passamaquoddy	
	Malecite	
	Micmac	Bear River
	Abenaki	Odanak
		Wôlinak
		Missisquoi
Seven Nations of Canada	Mohawk	Akwesasne
		Kahnesetake
		Kahnawake (capital)
	Nippissing	Kahnesetake
	Abenaki	Odanak
		Wôlinak
		Missisquoi
	Wendat	Lorette
	Algonquin	Pointe du lac
		Kahnesetake
	Micmac	Restigouche
Three Fires	Odawa (ceremonial head of Great Council Fire)	
	Ojibwe	
	Potawatomi	

Note: The following nations were probably not formal members of the alliance, but these Midwestern nations had a formal military alliance with the Great Council Fire after 1701 (Some of these nations, such as the Fox, were at times at war with the Fire; it is unclear from Wabanaki records whether these nations were more than military allies): Delaware, Erie, Fox, Illini, Kaskaskia, Kickapoo, Menominee. Miami, Missisagua, Petun, Salteaux, Sauk, Seneca/Cayuga, Shawnee, Wenro, Winnebago.

messenger as Wendat (or a closely related nation) may be evidence of a southern Ontario place of origin. This was the beginning of a new era of international relations for our ancestors, a resumption of peaceful interaction that had reached back to the Years of the Log Ships. Today this alliance has many names: The Great Council Fire, The Seven Nations of Canada, and or the Wabanaki Confederacy. This alliance structured the way the Abenaki dealt with the Europeans when the latter began arriving in great numbers. In the late 1600s, Haudenosaunee people moved just to the north of our homeland and built a town we call Caanawagi (the modern Kahnawake Reserve, near Montreal). They soon became our close friends and entered into the wars to defend our homeland (fig. 18).

The success of the alliance was assured when the Haudenosaunee sued for peace at the council of the Great Peace of Montreal. After this 1701 juncture, Caanawagi became the capital of the Great Council Fire, and the Lake Champlain Abenakis became part of its division known as the Seven Nations of Canada; those to the east were in the Wabanaki Confederacy component.

These modern First Nations were allied politically and militarily. Until the 1750s they were nominally allied to the government of New France and the Catholic Church. These nations (see table) may be the modern "anthropological/linguistic/historical" equivalents of the fourteen nations recorded by the wampum records of the Sipayik Passamaquoddies.

The Political Nature of the Alliance

Village-nations, the basic unit of Great Council Fire, remained sovereign in all areas, including war. They were required to send delegates to the capital at Kahnawake every three years. These meetings were a mixture of politics, social events, and recreation. Immediate response actions (such as an attack on a village) required fast-moving ambassadors, accompanied by trained warriors and translators, to visit allied villages. The alliance had two basic systems of holding itself together, which I call condolence and consolation.

Consolation is the same idea as a chain of motels or fast-food establishments: standardization. When you arrive, you know how to order that hamburger (even in a foreign country). Many of the Council Fire Allies still use a variation of "Kwe" (Kwai in Abenaki, Kwe-kwe in Mohawk, Kue in Innu) as a greeting. This was a standardized greeting called the "common signal" that let people know the visitor was an ally. Village welcoming songs were virtually identical; "Kwanute" among the Wabanakis and "Inoria kwenoteni" among the Wendat are descendants. We find the same friendship, chief making, and other songs over huge distances. Condolence is based on the theory that the emotions must be addressed before politics. Before dealing with another village's delegate, the host needs to know his family and friends, joys and sorrows. This actually increases empathy as well as making each delegate seem more caring. Games, common hunts, and other activities were structural parts of councils, allowing the delegates to build emotional bonds in addition to political ones. This process decreased discord, which is usually due to an absence of understanding. Warfare will be addressed toward the end of this chapter.

External Political Actions of the Great Council Fire

Of course, the Council Fire functioned to reduce discord among member nations and to mediate warfare and peace with native and Anglo opponents, but as time went on it also became an agent to let the European powers know that we had not lost any war and were continually knowledgeable of our rights. As time went on, the Council Fire emerged as an important buffer between independent villages and the invaders. By the late 1700s various Anglo governments began decades-long programs of undermining the Fire. By the mid-ninteenth century it had gone into decline.[2]

The Yearly Cycle: Spring

I depict the Years of the Beaver as a yearly cycle, for at last we have ample historical, archaeological and remembered lore to reconstruct the life of the Alnôbak village during their last years of total sovereignty. Every season brought its sights and sounds to the new palisaded towns as well as to the older open villages. A village's year began in Zogalikas, the sugar-making moon of early spring, when it became warm enough for the sap to flow in the maple and birch trees. Trees were tapped with a V-shaped cut recalling the V-shaped patterns of geese flying north at this time. Into the cleft of the V we inserted a split sumac-wood trough and placed an elm bark bucket below the tap to catch the sap. With new tools from the foreigners, we changed from making a slash in the bark to drilling a hole in the tree. New types of sap spiles were made to be driven into the hole. As the days warmed, the sap flowed, and laden *maskwaijoak* (bark buckets) were taken back to the villages. The sap was boiled in large earthenware vessels. When it hung in "strings" from the stirring paddle, it could be poured through a basswood fiber filter into carved wooden molds to make sugar cakes. The loaves could be stored to enliven our food throughout the year. The syrup could also be poured into a granulating trough, where it could be stirred or "worked' as it cooled. This produced granular sugar. It felt good to be outside again, and the sweet warmth of the boiling kettles enlivened everyone. Syrup "accidentally" dribbled on the old snow by smiling elders was quickly devoured by children, if the dogs didn't get to it first (see fig. 6).

As the snow left, everyone waited for the breakup of the ice on the Wazowategok (Missisquoi), Molodemack (Merrimack), or other rivers. Wagers were made and excitement heightened until the inevitable happened: the ice let go, and the rivers, filled with great white teeth, flooded our fields, bringing new fertility. As the sun warmed the bosom of Our Mother, new life emerged. The first greens and groundnuts were avidly collected, replenishing vitamins and minerals sadly lacking in the boring late-winter diet of meat and dried corn. The tempo of life quickened, and there was much to do in this exciting first of the year. For this was Bapkwah, the bark collecting time, and we dispersed to *maskwahikonak* (the bark collecting camps), taking the *gadkanigan*, a wooden wedge for removing tough bark and the smaller *wigwashigan*, the barking knife. We knew which trees were for wigwams, which were *igua*, for canoes, and which were for smaller crafts (fig. 19).

While sap engorged the cambium, *wigmask*, the bark, could be made to spring from the tree, although later it yielded not at all. Before cutting, we asked permission of the tree, perhaps leaving some tobacco or another thing of value as a sign of respect. A quick I-shaped cut, reaching as high as possible could tear a plate of birch bark (also elm or cedar) from the tree. We made a horizontal cut with the *wigwashigan*, as high as we could reach, and another just above the root crown. We then connected these horizontal cuts by a vertical slit made so as to pass through blemishes so they would be at the edge of the sheet. Then, with the fingers or *gadkanigan*, the bark was removed by peeling away from the vertical slit. Blemishes and old knots held the bark to the tree like glue. In these places, the bark was pounded with the poll of a stone or iron ax to loosen its grip. Then the *gadkanigan* could pry the bark free. Sometimes even this failed, leaving a tear or hole in the panel. If the bark was for a canoe, wigwam, or other large project, the plates were supported by a cord wrapped around the

Fig. 19. Birch-bark container. *Wôbanakik Heritage Center Collection, photograph by Andrew Lee.*

tree so they would not tear, rendering them useless. The free bark panels were flexed against the natural curl, taken back to bark camp, and stacked on the moist spring soil, held flat with rocks to keep them flexible and soft until they could be worked. We collected not only the bark but the materials necessary to lash and build with it. Basswood bark could be taken and submerged in the swift spring streams until the shreddy lining could be removed to make tough but supple *wigibial* (lacings). Twenty-foot lengths of root were taken from the black spruce. The long, thin roots lay near the surface of thawing conifer forest and acid bogs. They were pulled up and coiled in long twists for taking back to the village to soak. Later the root bark could be easily removed and the root split lengthwise with a sharp knife to make *wadabal*, tough root lacings. Pine and spruce pitch, necessary for watertight *makuks* and canoes, was also collected, prepared, and stored. When each family had sufficient material, they returned from *maskwahikonal* to the village bearing the flexed bark rolls on their backs. Maple wood toboggans or sledges were quickly made from branches lashed together with roots. The bark was then spread on the moist spring earth, weighted with logs or stones, ready for use. Once the materials were ready, they could be used to make a canoe, house, or one of over one hundred different Alnôbaiwi domestic articles. The dwelling and the canoe were the greatest expression of bark craft of the Alnoba in those long-gone spring days; and the longhouse will be discussed in some detail.

Building the Longhouse

I am unsure when the longhouse came to the Alnôbak, although we have abundant evidence at Nonnigonikon Nuliak that our so called "red-paint" ancestors made ninety-meter-long multiple-family dwellings thousands of years before the Haudenosaunee developed them to the west of us. European observers recorded gable-roof as well as arched-roof longhouses among our Micmac and Eastern Abenaki kinsmen. These had six to eight fires, supporting thirty to sixty people. Archaeologists have found the remains of a quite recent one, twenty-five meters long by five meters wide, at Norridgewock and probably another in the Kwinitekw Valley near the Euro-American settlement of Claremont, New Hampshire.

To make the bark longhouse, a section of the village that was large enough was selected and the plan scored on the earth. However, the size of longhouses sometimes dictated that the palisade must be moved. We then made a shell framework of three-inch flexible wooden posts set two feet into the soil, with central six-inch supports set ten to twelve feet apart. Horizontal members were lashed to the uprights with basswood or willow withes. Rawhide, even though it made a tighter and stronger bond, was avoided, since it was the favorite food of the awobikwsosak, the mouse people, who would nibble on the lashings until they came apart, not a good idea in the dead of winter! The supports and framework were then covered by shingled plates of cedar, elm, or winter-harvested birch bark (or a combination), leaving doors in the ends and a series of smokeholes in the roof. Lightweight children worked on the upper sections, which usually consisted of birchbark. The panels were then sewn together and to the frame with root and bark lacings. An outside framework of flexible saplings was sewn through the bark to the frame. This strengthened the construction and held the bark panels against the frame. Bench supports that we slept on and stored food and equipment on were then made and attached to the frame. Of course there is no evidence of the numerous baskets and bags that hung from the frame, except for a few that are now held by Euro-American collectors or museums. Hearths, called laskeniganal, were built beneath each smoke hole. Flexible hide coverings sealed the doors and

Fig. 20. "English style" Wabanaki vertical log building interior. *Oil on canvas, Stephanie Stecklare, 1996; Wôbanakik Heritage Center Collection, photograph by Andrew Lee.*

smoke holes from ice and rain, and the longhouse was ready for its "moving-in" ceremony. Perhaps at this time the figures of animals reported to decorate wigwams and longhouses were added. Several related families moved into the longhouse, each of which had its own distinctive living area and hearth but shared warmth and sociability through the winter. To increase weathertightness, evergreen branches were laid against the bottom of the longhouse in winter.

The bark longhouse was quickly replaced by upright-log, then wood-frame construction in the European manner (fig. 20). By the mid-1700s, European writers report an almost universal use of European-derived architecture for village homes. Only seasonal camps continued to use the bark dwelling in a wigwam format.

Baskets

Another craft that was begun at this time of year was *abazenoda*, basketry. A light ax (such as the "heart-hole" example held by the Euro-American museum at Chimney Point Museum), was used to fell Mahlawks, the brown ash tree, with reverence and ceremony. Men pounded the wood with a special tool called a *wigebidemahigan*, to separate it along the spongy spring wood of each tree ring. The *wigebiak*, or ash wood strips, could be pulled off the log, bundled, and stored for making into burden and storage baskets. Both men and women wove the splints into a variety of utility baskets for our use and that of our neighbors.

During this time the fish ran in our rivers to spawn, as they always had, and the traps, weirs, and spears we used in the past continued to be important. Indeed, Seniganitegw (Lewis Creek, Vermont) was called "stone-works river" to commemorate the stone weirs that funneled the fish into our *adelahiganak* (basket traps), nets, and spears. The smell of spawning walleye wafting from Dawkwahoganizek (Swanton Falls) let us know that middle spring, the fishing moon, was upon us. We left our villages for *namaskon* (fishing camp) at Winooskik (known today as the Salmon Hole, near Burlington, Vermont), Dawkwahoganizek, Ahquedaukenash (the outlet of Lake Winnepesaukee, New Hampshire), Namaskik (the falls of the Merrimac, near Manchester, New Hampshire), and other places where the fish congregated. We remember families camping to repair and fill the fish drying racks with walleye, sucker, or salmon. Fish were abundant, and many were prepared, cooked, and eaten on the spot until we could eat no more. When the fish were dry, late spring's Kikas, the planting moon, was upon us. The fish were then placed in baskets, hide covers, or canoes to be taken back to the main village for permanent storage.

Late in the Years of the Beaver, Euro-American observers reported *skamonikikon* (cornfields) throughout the Bitawbagok valley. Others reported fields "four miles in length," along the Wazowategok floodplains. The "Burlington Intervale" had several hundred acres cleared; one individual field along the Winoskitegw was over twenty-five acres. The La Platte River had a twenty-five-acre field on its east side. These fields were cleared by men using a "slash and burn" technique still used by our relatives in the southern reaches of Turtle Island. The women then inherited the fields, where the crops we discussed under the Years of Corn—corn, beans, squash, and others—were planted when the threat of frost was past. European observers along the Saco River near the Soubagwa coast (southern Maine) in May of the Christian year 1605 reported that we put three to four corn grains and three to four beans into each hole. Around them were planted squash, pumpkins, and some tobacco. Now things really got busy, and the prohibition against storytelling came into effect—the world had too much to do in the present to dwell in the past, although the messages in the stories lived in our hearts as our backs toiled on the soil during Nokkihigas, the hoeing moon. The completion of the back-breaking hoeing activity signaled the end of spring. The crops now could overtop the weeds and were on their own.

Late spring began the season for trading, diplomacy, and war, since the rivers had receded from flood stage and the weather was warm enough to forgo heavy winter gear. The Blacmonak were then back in our villages for another season. They usually came in canoes made after our pattern. Their warriors and diplomats came at this time with gifts of metal and beads. They had an interest in making treaties with us to secure our furs and our help against another European people who were rapidly building an empire to the south of us. These new Agemenokak (European) people, of whom we began hearing dreaded rumors, we named the Bastaniak after their capital Bastan (Boston). Unlike the Blacmonak, who wanted our furs and help, the Bastaniak wanted our land. They treated our neighbors to the south like beasts, casually lied to them and killed them until they could not stand it anymore. Thus began the first of the exiles from New England, fleeing genocide and asking us, the Alnôbak, for asylum. But war and rumor of war were then far off, so we said to the Blacmonak that we would stand by them.

Following the Blacmonak warriors to our villages in the spring and summer were rugged woodsmen, blending their technology with ours, so that they almost looked and smelled like us except for their preposterous beards. They often married our women, lived with us through the winter, learned our language, and traded us goods for our furs. They regaled us with stories of our far relatives and the cities of Europe from whence they came.[3]

Another kind of Blacmon came in canoes those long-ago springs. He wore a black robe, often adorned for special occasions with a mantle of floral embroidery in a style that our women quickly adapted to our needs. He had no interest in furs, land, or women but wanted us to give up Ktsi Nwaskw, Koluscap, and all of our spirits and substitute his gods. He sought to discredit our shamans and religious leaders and said that we would all die if we stuck to our beliefs. If we did what he said, he gave us beads, brass rings, and beautiful tiny crosses of silver showing the Blacmonak's Dead God[4] (fig. 21).

These travelers were very sincere and peaceful and became accepted members of the community, sometimes living with us year around. They always liked to build a house for their god, so after securing our permission

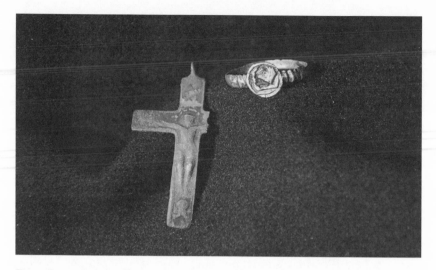

Fig. 21. Roman Catholic offerings. *Wôbanakik Heritage Center Collection, photograph by Andrew Lee.*

and labor, the mission chapel often became a fixture in our towns. As time went on, we had to make a personal choice whether to reject the Black Robes' religion, graft it onto our own, or accept it completely. But as time went on, we learned, as have native people in Latin America, to hold onto both belief systems, for each gives us strength in a different way. Spring was the time not only of planting but of becoming connected to a larger world, not all of which we could control.

Summer's Bounty

Early summer was a busy time. The women and children had to protect the tender young corn, bean, and squash plants from the crows, as well as clear the weeds. If the fields were far from the village, some family members would camp in or near the field, to deter nocturnal pests such as deer. Men hunted turkeys and smaller game birds and fished the lakes and streams with spear and line. The first wild fruits became available during Satalikas, the Blueberry Moon of early summer. Women and children dispersed to the berry patches to collect the sweet fruits that enlivened our summer diet or could be dried and stored for later use. In the summer, children played games of skill like *adowiz*, the ring and pin game, while their elders played games of chance such as *gagwenigan*, the dice game.

Adowiz, the Bundle and Pin game

This game is almost universal throughout Native America. We use a bundle of cedar or moose hair as the target, rather than a ring or perforated bone. Unlike other games, the name for the bundle and pin is almost identical throughout Wôbanakik. *Adowiz* is the Western Abenaki name as written by an anthropologist at Odanak, Quebec; the name recorded for the Abenaki at Kennebunk, Maine, was *artoois*; the Penobscot name is written *adu'is*; and the Passamaquoddy name is written *t'wis*. (Fig. 22, top, shows a modern "cedar bundle" *adowiz* game.)

   The bundle is an 8 1/2-inch-long cone made from needles of *koksk* (white cedar) or *mozipiaso* (moose hair) bound with cord (eelskin is traditional). It is attached to the midpoint of the *oskwaakwam*, an 8- to 9 1/2-inch, sharp, pointed, bone or wood implement by a 14-inch leather thong. The Passamaquoddy *t'wis* has an interesting addition. The thong passes through the cedar bundle and is fastened to a 4-inch-long, oblong moosehide piece that is perforated with numerous holes. The goal is to

Fig. 22. Wabanaki gaming equipment. *Wôbanakik Heritage Center Collection, photograph by Andrew Lee.*

impale the moosehide, and the cedar bundle merely functions as a swing weight.

Two people seat themselves on a robe or skin. The *oskwaakwam* is held in the hand (among the Passamaquoddy, it is said that the pointed stick is held like a pen) with the bundle hanging down. With a deft move of the hand, the bundle is swung up and impaled on the point. It is said that among our Penobscot neighbors the game is played by a young man and woman. If a man is interested in a woman, he will ask her to play the game. He begins and continues until he misses; then he passes it to the woman. If she is not interested in the man, she returns the *adu'is* to him after the first successful stab. If she is interested, she continues the play.

Each impaling of the bundle counts as one point, and the player continues until he or she misses the bundle. It then passes to the next person. The play continues until one person concedes; among the Passamaquoddy, one hundred successful stabs wins.

Babaskwahamawôgan: the Game of Lacrosse

Lacrosse was another almost universal game in Native America; only the people in the far west did not play it. Whole villages competed in games of lacrosse, often seen as "the little brother of war." The game was named and played slightly differently (for example, the name is *ebesquamogan* among our Passamaquoddy neighbors) wherever one went, except that the game always use a netted stick, a ball, and a delimited field, and few escaped unhurt after a game.

We use a variation of the lacrosse stick used by Euro-Americans until recent developments in plastic and aluminum: a crooked piece of ash (or hickory) in the shape of a bishop's crosier; hence the name given to the game by our French allies, "La crosse" (fig. 22). The stick is about thirty inches long and has a finely netted rawhide basket technologically related to the fish net. Lacrosse sticks are important individual possessions and were often adorned with carved or burned-in designs and attached ribbons and feathers. The *babaskwahamawôgan* (lacrosse) ball is of moose-hair filled-leather. A Penobscot example is made from a nine-inch disk of brain-tanned deerskin drawn up as a bag and filled with moose hair. A five-inch disk is put over the opening to seal it and the drawstring pulled tight so as to make a four-inch-diameter ball. Today, I use dog hair combed from my Samoyed as a filler and commercial leather as the cover, which is then laced with braided nylon fishline.

The game is played in a meadow near the village. The field is cleared. Two goals are made at either end of the field: both marked rings or shallow holes are traditionally used, although commercial lacrosse goals are now common. The players—men, women, or coed—determine the number of points to win the game, then form a ring at the center of the field. A referee goes into the center of the field and takes a *piakahiga*, or chip of wood. He spits on it and throws it into the air, the fall determining which side will get the ball. From that point on the scuffle begins, each side attempting to get their ball into the opponents' goal to score a point. Unlike the modern professional game, there are no rules of engagement and no fouls. Arms, knees, feet, and the lacrosse stick are wielded by all players in the fray to get the ball. Friendly games are played with a minimum of injury; but apparently, in the past, some games were played to settle grievances or to redefine boundaries or land rights—and these were as serious as Olympic competition. Among other First Nations, lacrosse is known as "the little brother of war," and it was. Winning a game was achieved by making a predetermined number of goals, as in the Euro-American form, but sometimes the game went on until one side became exhausted and conceded. There is no record of how long these indeterminate games lasted.[5] (Fig. 22.)

After the sun set, evenings often brought outside *bemowibem* (dances) and ceremonies. *Bagholiganal*, drums of cedar hoops or hollow logs, with woodchuck, deer, or moose rawhide, drumheads, sounded with gourd, rawhide, or the new *askanal* (cowhorn rattles) to complement voices in song and the shuffle and thump of feet in dance. Some dances such as the Gizosibmegawogan (Sun Dance), which uses large sunlike disks of feathers, were meant to influence the ripening crops; the Nolkaibmegawogan (Deer Dance) and Mesezoibmegawogan (Eagle Dance) related us to our four-footed and winged brothers. The war and friendship dances are self-explanatory. Of course, war was best practiced in the summer, when the serious work of fishing and planting was done, but as warfare spread through the Dawnland, it had to be done year-round.

Late Summer

Temezowas, the harvest moon of late summer, brought the first products of our fields, succulent green corn and the bean harvest. The medicine people were busy gathering the economic, medicinal (Appendix 2), and ceremonial plants, which had reached their maximum potency. Walmogwkil, the ceremonial sweetgrass, was collected in moist, sunny soils. It could be found on warm days by following the distinctive scent of cumarin ($C_3H_6O_3$) to the plants. This volatile wax remained sweet-smelling for years, making the grass a fine incense. Other incenses included red cedar, birch bark, and tobacco; later we obtained sage from the far west and began to use it as an incense. These were often fanned with a tail of bakkesso, the partridge.

Astiganak (dyestuffs) were also tracked down and harvested with care. No more than a few plants could be harvested from a colony, and we spread seed to replace that taken. Roots of red bedstraw (*Galium tinctorium*), and *babagakinihlog* (bloodroot, *Sanguinaria canadensis*) produced a flame and deep red respectively; *wdopi* (alder, *Alnus* sp.) bark yielded a distinctive reddish dye for birch-bark containers. Hellbore leaves and stalks (*Helborus trifolius*), goldenrod (*Solidago* sp.), or the branches of *pagoniz* (hazel, *Corylus americana*) made a yellow dye. Princess pine root made a green one. Bark of *wajomozi* (beech, *Fagus grandifolia*) gave a blue color. Violet was made from the dog whelk (a shellfish, *Nucella lapilluss*, along the coast), or from *mskwebagwes* (white maple, *Acer saccharinum*) bark inland; while wood could be dyed purple with *alnizedi* (hemlock, *Tsuga canadensis*) bark. Bound in clusters, these hung in drying racks, their perfume permeating our villages. The organic dyes were complemented by inorganic pigments such as *olamanjagw* (red and yellow ochre), charcoal or graphite for black, and clamshell for white. They were ground in a stone mortar in preparation for use. If for painting leather or bark, they could be mixed with egg or other binder; if for body paint, they could be mixed with bear fat or seal/porpoise oils.

Fall

In the early fall (Skamokas, or Corn Making Moon), the large *dakwahogan*, or corn pounding mortar, was moved into position beside every wigwam or longhouse or into the fields. Made from a hollowed tree trunk and a stone or long wooden pestle, it was used to process field corn into a coarse but sweet meal that could be stored or made into ash cakes or hunter's trail bread known to the Bastaniak as journeycake (johnnycake). It is said that at this time of year you could find a village in the fog by the sound of the *dakwahogan*. The mortar became a dangerous tool in the Years of the Beaver, for there is an old story among my people that men from Baliten (the Burlington, Vermont, area) would listen for the thumping of the *dakwahogan*

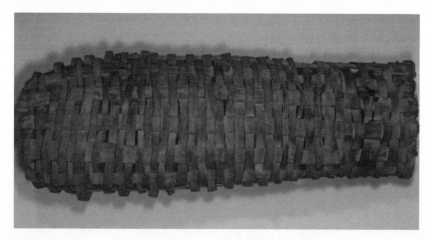

Fig. 23. Connecticut River ash-splint eel trap. *Wôbanakik Heritage Center Collection, photograph by Andrew Lee.*

to find Abenaki women. They would then chase them through the fields on horseback until they could be caught and raped. It quickly became prudent to carry the unprocessed corn to the villages and grind it there. Our grass-, mat-, and bark-lined storage pits were then loaded with the fall harvest of corn, beans, and wild nuts such as butternut, as well as smoked fish and dried meat. Remains of these pits, called "features" by archaeologists, are found all over our old villages, but mostly inside the remains of buildings, where they could be opened on a frigid winter's day. Another type of silo was used by the Alnôbak at the mouth of Sako (the Saco River), according to Champlain. Corn was placed in woven grass bags or sacks, which were then lowered into trenches five to six feet deep and the trenches filled. Obviously, this could be practiced only in places where the ground did not freeze; and I know that, except for the zone just in from the beach, the ground freezes at Wells, Maine, just south of this area. I doubt that anyone would want to dig through six feet of frozen ground in the colder regions of Wôbanakik.

Early fall was also eel fishing season; eels could be caught in special *adelahiganak*, splint traps (fig. 23) or simply speared as they made their fall migration. The oily flesh of these long snakelike fish was good in stew and dried easily for winter use.

Penobagos, the Moon of Falling Leaves, saw the dispersal of our people to hunting camp, a tradition that remains to this day. As the leaves turned red with the blood of the celestial Great Bear, the main hunt of the year began. From small *walligash* (spruce/hemlock bark) camps, such as the one reported by Euro-Americans at Franklin Pond (northern Vermont), or even rock shelters; the hunter, laden with bow and arrow (or rifle), knife, and killing lance and accompanied by hunting dogs set forth after deer, bear, or moose. This is a Sutton, Quebec version of an old story told from the Penobscot River to Lake Between about the dispersal of the Alnôbak in the fall. I am told that a related story has been collected by folklorists in Maine and that it may have even been published.

PLADLIQUE'S JOURNEY

Pladlique was a young man of eighteen summers who lived in the village of Dawkskodacek, a pleasant lowland to the east of Masipskiwibi. He lived in the longhouse of the Lineage of the Fox with his mother, father, sister, brother, grandparents, aunts, uncles, cousins, and his favorite dog, Vixen. One fall, during Penobagos, his mother came to him and said, "Pladlique, you need to go to Gwenaaden [Jay Peak] to get us nolka, the deer, for we have not enough food for our travel. Be back soon for we must go to deer camp within fifteen days." Pladlique said good-bye to his relatives and left the palisade, swiftly heading up the River of Rocks, through the valley of the Wazowategok until he came to the Mountain. At the base of Gwenaaden, he prayed, "Please Long Mountain, let me see a deer so that I may gather its flesh, for my family is hungry." To the Deer Mother, he said, "Here is odamo, the tobacco, which is so hard to grow yet so powerful; allow me to bring back that which will make my family live well on its coming journey." With his ceremony complete, he strode up the mountain. Soon he saw a fat doe but let it pass, to let Deer Mother know that he was not greedy. He saw a small buck that he knew he could have, and with a true shot from his ash-wood bow, he brought down the deer. He was happy and gave thanks to the Mountain that nurtured the deer; then to the spirit of the deer as he saw its life depart in his arms.

He was on his way down the Mountain, striding perhaps too fast, for time was short and he was young. He lost his footing in an unusual early mountain snow, and fell, dropping the deer. As he fell, he knew he had broken his ankle. Pladlique realized that he was too far from the materials to bandage and splint his leg. He was over a mile from the bog where he had to get the healing sphagnum moss and the antiseptic balsam fir sap, and the woods lacked the birch bark for the cast and splint. Pladlique also knew that unless he found shelter he would die of exposure or be the meal of the first molsem *(wolf) or* bihtolo *(mountain lion) that came his way. Painfully dragging the buck ("Thank goodness, it is a small one," he said), he soon found the small medicine cave that he knew of, a shelter that had a small spring in it. Painfully crawling to the cave, he set the carcass of the deer beside him, then extended his swollen leg on the soft soil . Piling newly fallen leaves under himself he made a rude bed, then arranged cool, moist earth over his bruised leg, as he had been told that his totem animal (*wokweses, the fox*) will do when it is injured. Then taking his knife, he butchered the deer and made a crude drying rack from its bones and sinew. He offered a quick orison to the mountain, then sat to wait for the power of his Mother, Aki, the Earth, to heal his leg. He waited. And waited. For fifteen days, he sat immobile until the deer meat, which was getting a bit high by now, was almost exhausted, and he knew that it was time to go. He bound his tender, half-healed ankle with splint and rawhide from the deer's carcass.*

Pladlique had a decision, to try to find his family, which he knew had left to follow swiftly moving game in the mountains or return home. He thought better (or worse) of it and headed painfully on rude crutches for his longhouse. He knew that there would be lots of food in the storage pits and he would await his family's return in Pebonkas, the Wintermaker Moon. Pladlique hobbled slowly out of the mountain, across the Wazowategok and across the River of Rocks to his home. He was expecting to see a lifeless village except, of course, for the village animals such as the nahamak *(turkeys) and* alemosak *(dogs), for all of his people, even the elderly, go to deer camp. But what he saw was amazing, for smoke came from the smoke holes of the longhouses, and people were walking back and forth before the palisade of his village. He knew that his people must have delayed their departure for some reason, but as he got closer he became troubled, for he did not recognize anyone. But when they saw him, they knew who he was. "Pladlique, Pladlique, where have you been?" they cried in loud, strangely accented voices that echoed about the palisade almost like the baying of dogs. "We have missed you and we thought you died on the hunt." Pladlique was more confused than ever. "Who are you people; and where is my family, my father, mother, grandparents, brothers, sisters, aunts, uncles, cousins, and my dog Vixen?" "Ah Pladlique, we know you and you know us, but we will talk of this later, for your foot is hurt." "You need to go to your longhouse where your friend will care for you." "My friend? Who do you mean?" said Pladlique.*

As Pladlique neared his home, a young woman of his own age, with long flowing brown hair and big beautiful brown eyes, emerged from the doorway, saw him and with a howl of joy and concern ran to him and hugged him. "Pladlique, I feared you were dead, but your foot, it is hurt. You must come inside and I will care for you." His head aching from confusion, he went inside his home and lay on his bed while the strange young woman sat before him on the floor. He said, "I know I have died, and you are the spirits that keep my village safe while we are at deer camp. Am I now a guardian spirit too?" "You have not died, "said the young woman. "You are very much alive." Pladlique replied, "Your eyes—I have seen them before; did I know you in another time?" The enigmatic young woman smiled and turned to get her medicine bag. The young woman of long brown hair tended Pladlique with herbs and soils that he had never seen before in the hands of his family, and she fed him strange vegetables and nuts but no meat. She would not sit with him but always sat on the floor, where she seemed most comfortable. In due time he recovered enough to easily walk to the River of Rocks with his nurse. He grew fond of his beautiful young kapinawos (caregiver) with the long brown hair and big dark brown eyes.

One star-shot night under the streamside willows he said to her, "You know, I love you." She said, "Ah Pladlique, I have always loved you, though perhaps you knew it not." He said, "Well, let's make love." The girl with the dark brown eyes looked horrified. "No! No, it can never be, you and I in that way, no matter what I may want!" She arose and fled to the village. The next night, under the willows that line the River of Rocks, he asked again. She looked worried but said, "OK just this once." They were both young, had no inhibitions and made glorious love together under their streamside blankets in the cool of the end of the Moon of Falling Leaves. Pladlique recovered now even quicker, and the elders of the village were amazed at his recovery. They said, "She is an amazing nurse, that one." Soon Pladlique said, "Will you marry me, my love, for I know my mother, father, grandparents, sister, brother, aunts, uncles, cousins, and my dog, Vixen, would just love you too?" The horrified look came back to her big brown eyes. "Oh Pladlique, that can never be, you and I in that way." But nevertheless, they made glorious love in the Moon of Ice Making, moving inside the longhouse as their spot under the willows became more and more snowbound.

One day, she seemed saddened and finally said as they walked by the ice-rimed River of Rocks, "Pladlique, the elders have said you must go back to Long Mountain to kill another deer." "But my love," said he, "the Moon of Winter is upon us and my family will return in fifteen days. I want you to meet them. You and your people don't even eat meat, so why must I go?" "Alas, Pladlique, you must kill another deer." Confused by her urgency, he *left after a final sweet, but somehow sorrowful lovemaking, and taking his snowshoes and winter clothing, went up to the Mountain without even a limp. Passing by the first deer he met, a small buck, he soon saw his prayer was answered and he shot a large doe. He gave thanks and said, "Now I can go back to my family and my love." Carefully, this time, for the snow was getting deep, he returned across the Wazowategok, across the River of Rocks to his village, where he saw the smoke of hearth fires and people walking before the palisade. To his relief they recognized him and he them. "Pladlique, Pladlique where have you been, we thought you had perished on the mountain two moons ago." Pladlique said, "No, I broke my leg, but was nursed back to health by wonderful people who live in this village while we are gone to deer camp." "Pladliqe, you must have hurt your head as well, for all that we leave at the village are the dogs and turkeys to guard our stores from the insects, raccoons, and squirrels."*

Pladlique was hurt by their disbelief but hurt more by the absence of the kind people he had grown to respect and love. "Well," he thought, "I'll tell my story to my kinsmen; they will believe me." That night he told his story around the hearth fire to his rapt familial audience: his mother, father, sister, brother, aunts, uncles, cousins, and his favorite dog, Vixen. He did not pay attention to the rolling eyes and disbelief of all but the elders, who smiled knowingly. He ended by saying, "There was a beautiful young woman who took care of me and I love her. When I find her, I want to have her for my wife." He said, "She has healing hand and heart and the most beautiful long hair and big dark brown eyes. The eyes I have seen before, and beginning tomorrow, I will search the Land of the Dawn until I find them again." And with that he stopped petting his favorite dog, Vixen, who sat in her usual spot his feet, for he now saw in the firelight that she had long brown hair and looked into his with beautiful, big, dark brown eyes.

For many years after that his family never could understand why Pladlique, always a successful hunter, left for deer camp a few days late and came back a few days early. And they could never understand why he didn't have any interest in women of the village until long after he finally laid his favorite dog, Vixen, to rest under the willows beside the River of Rocks. I know this is true because my family is from Dawkskodacek. My family is of the Lineage of the Fox.

Medawas, 1994

During Mezatanos, the Freezing Moon, the fat-laden game could be eaten or have its meat dried. Prime fall fur pelts could be stored for hair-on tanning into warm bedding and clothes or de-haired for rawhide or buck-skin. Bones, hooves, claws, and antlers were not neglected but saved for use as tools or ornaments, although this decreased slowly as the Awanokak's trade goods became increasingly available and attractive.

Winter Comes

Snow-fly and Pebonkas, the Winter-making moon, saw us returning to our villages dragging the animal harvest by ashwood, birch, or maple *odaboga-nal* (toboggans) or on our backs. Some people hauled fifty to ninety pounds of meat supported only with an *odebobi* (tumpline), a traditional finger-woven burden sash placed over the forehead and over the shoul-ders. Others used toboggans quickly made in the woods from the curved slats chopped from where the first branch enters the maple tree. Others brought the game back in sleds with runners of yellow birch or rock maple. Everyone retired to the warmth of the wigwam or longhouse to tell stories of "the one that got away" and renew interrupted friendships, fam-ily ties and romances. After a long day's labor in the cramped interiors, ten-sions could be relieved a bit by games, the most important of which was *gagwenigan*.

We name the moon after the winter solstice, Alamikos, the Greeting Moon, because of this social renewal as well as to greet Gizos, the Sun, on its return to the north. Early winter was an intense time. Everyone was crowded together and the people still living in the wigwam must have looked to their longhouse-dwelling kinsmen with envy and a resolve to build one next year. There was plenty to do. It still wasn't too cold, so adults and children could play outside with snow snakes and sleds.

Snow Snake

The snow snake game is played throughout North America wherever there is enough snow to warrant it. Most Native American snow snakes are quite long, from four to as long as ten feet, often thrown down a special lane made in the snow. The Abenaki game and snow snakes are somewhat differ-ent from the general pattern. Snow snakes are recorded by Euro-American observers from the Passamaquoddy and Penobscot people and the Abenaki at Norridgewock, Maine. Most of the snow snakes of Wôbanakik are shorter than those of the Haudenosaunee (Iroquois) or more western Native

people. Except for an exceptional 5- to 7-foot example from the Passamaquoddy people and a short Penobscot 14 1/2-inch-long example, most snow
snakes are 18 to 24 inches long. Among the numerous shapes are two
named varieties, the spoon mouth (called *mquon* in Passamaquoddy) and
snake head (called *atosis* in Passamaquoddy). A short variety is still known
as a "mudcat" (fig. 22).

If someone is interested in playing snow snakes, he goes through the village crying the name of the snow snake game in the local dialect. People
who are interested join him, bringing their snow snakes. The group pro-
ceeds to a place with a hard flat crust of snow. The snow snakes glide best
on such a surface. Each player advances to the throwing point, one at a
time. Calling the name of the snow snake and giving a quick throwing motion as if skipping a stone over the water, he skips it as far as it will go. The
next person moves to the station and throws. At the end of the first round,
the snow snakes are upended in the snow to serve as their own markers,
and the second round commences. Among the Penobscot, the farthest
stick wins all the rest. The winner gathers up the bundle of snow snakes
and with a yell throws them up in the air. The other players scramble to re-
cover their (or what they perceive as the best) snow snake.

Inside, there was the just-completed hide harvest to process. There was
ample time to sew *lalan* (trade cloth) and ribbon purchased the previous
summer. Buckskin was now supplemented by new clothing forms evolved
from the trade with the Blacmonak traders. The hood, which has emerged
almost as a symbol of Abenaki women, may have been developed for both
sexes from a European hood at this time. It was made from two rectangles
of black or navy wool trade cloth and adorned with contrasting bands of
red cloth or bright trade ribbon or appliquéd white seed beads. It was then
lined with another material. The hood was used by our people until the
early part of this century and is being revived as a ceremonial cap. Another
type of headgear, the conical or funnel-shaped hat was illustrated and recorded by early European observers. We adapted European tailoring to
our designs and needs, making beautiful new clothing, some based on
Alnôbak prototypes, such as leggings, and some based on Awanokak designs such as the "big shirt." Hunting and agricultural equipment, worn
and damaged during the year, needed to be mended or replaced. Steel,
brass, and copper were almost endlessly recycled to make new tools, weapons, and ornaments. By the Christian year 1670, iron and brass had superseded stone for arrow points. Sheet copper, salvaged or purchased, could be
made into conical shapes, such as the arrow point found at Norridgewock,

or tinkling cones such as those on an eighteenth-century Abenaki pouch from Pennacook. Rolled-copper cylinders became tube beads, identical to those used during the Years of the Log Ships. Copper pendants, such as a graceful one-by five-eighths-inch oval found at Norridgewock, and head-bands were quickly made with the new shears. Assuming the harvest was good and the storage pits full, there was leisure to pursue the more esoteric arts such as shell bead making, which remained important to the coastal communities.

Some shell *nopkowanal* (necklaces) from this time, such as the one found south of Norridgewock at the Euro-American settlement of Water-ville, Maine, had five hundred disk beads, while another from the land of our Penobscot neighbors near Bucksport, Maine, had five thousand quarter-inch-diameter shell beads. *Wôbôbial*, the longer tubular shell beads, called wampum by historians, did not become common until this time. In the early Years of the Beaver, wampum was scarce and expensive throughout Abenaki lands. Before the development of the steel drill, we could not drill a small longitudinal hole in the shell. Wampum was not made by any but the most southeastern Alnôbak. It is said among our neighbors the Passamaquoddy that it took a day to make and finish a single bead. European technology could produce it more quickly, more effi-ciently, and with less wastage. For us it was obtained in trade or given to us as gifts. By the Christian year 1680 it had become relatively common, due to the importing of iron tools. European steel files, drills, and wire sped up shell bead manufacture. It was reported that a shell bead maker could now make between one hundred and two hundred beads per day. These shell beads could be sewn directly to leather or trade cloth alone or in combina-tion with trade beads. Wampum was strung on sinew to make girls' and boys' necklaces and hair thongs or men's chokers, necklaces, armbands, and wristlets. It also appeared on the fringes of woven porcupine quillwork.

Winter evenings afforded the time to make the large ceremonial wam-pum belts required by ceremonies and treaties. (Figs. 29 and 30 show rep-lica wampum belts.) We had adapted our former pictographic birch-bark scrolls to the new woven wampum strings. These were strung on vegetal fiber or leather thongs with sinew to make complex mnemonic or sym-bolic messages. None remain to the Alnôbak. Euro-American collectors and museums have taken most, and the fact that they can be infinitely re-cycled made any but the most recent very rare. The Black Robes encour-aged us to make wampum articles for the glory of their Dead God, which Christian members of our community did. An early (Christian year 1684)

European report records collars of wampum and bugle beads adorning the altar of our chapel at St. Francis de Sales near Quebec City. Two of the largest wampum belts were not made by the Ganienkeh, as historians would have you believe, but by the Alnôba. These were made by our kinsmen in exile with religious sayings to be sent to Chartres Cathedral in Europe. The first was a large white belt, with black lettering " VIRGINIPA-RITVRAE" sent in 1678. In 1699 the Black Robe Vincent Bigot sent across the Great Sea our massive six-by-seven-foot belt, mostly of the rare black (purple) beads with the lettering "MATRIVIRGINIABNAQUAEIDD" executed in white. Today, these red and black porcupine quill–edged belts can be seen in the crypt at Chartres Cathedral in France. Wampum was used by our neighbors to recount stories as late as the 1870s.[6]

The long evenings of Biadagos, the Bough Shedding Moon (so named for the huge piles of snow that weighed down and broke limbs from trees) became theater. The magician, practical joker, and storyteller became the center of attention for both young and old. This was the time when our young learned the important stories of their heroes and ancestors and through them learned the subtle messages of honesty and manners. Games of chance and skill also livened up the long evenings.

The Dice Game

The dice are a series of six *mozasken* (moose bone) disks, commonly 3/4 to 7/8 inch in diameter among the Western Abenaki and Penobscot. *Magoliboasken* (caribou bone) is used by our Micmac neighbors to the east. They are domed slightly on one side and flat on the other. The flat side is incised with a series of arcs to form a Maltese cross or Pennsylvania German "hex sign"–like design. The incised lines are filled with carbon-black pigment to make them easily visible. The people of Norridgewock, Maine, reportedly used eight disks, made identically to the above but blackened on the flat side rather than incised. The bowl, called *wlôgan* by us or *waltahamogan* in Passamaquoddy, is quite shallow among the Micmac, Malicite, and Passamaquoddy and deeper, like a salad bowl, among the Penobscot. The bowl is traditionally made of *senomozi*, or sugar maple, sometimes with a beautiful burled or bird's-eye grain (fig. 22). The size is about 11 1/2 inches in diameter. An old shallow wood bowl from the attic or a garage sale usually suffices as the *wlôgan*. The bowl is struck sharply against a soft pad. In former times a brain-or-oil tanned *mozagen* (moosehide) sufficed; now a commercial blanket is often used to cushion the blow. The style of the *koksk* (white cedar) markers differ slightly, depending on the area. The length of the markers also varies from about 5.5 inches among the Passamaquoddy and some Penobscot, to almost 8 inches among the Micmac. The larger counting sticks are still usually thin splints of wood, carved in the appropriate traditional way. The Micmac and some Penobscot Abenaki use 51 cylindrical (or square in cross section) counting sticks 7.75 inches long (equaling 1/3 point each), three 7.5-inch counting sticks notched on one side (equaling 5 points each), and one 7.5-inch counting stick notched on both sides (equaling a 52nd 1/3-point counting stick until all the other sticks are exhausted; then it counts as 5 points). According to a published report by a Euro-American observer, the Passamaquoddy people apparently used a different counter system: a series of 48 thin wooden counters (equaling 1/3 point each); one snake-carved stick (equaling 1 point); and 3 carved flat sticks (equaling 4 points each). I wonder if this was a mistake on the part of the observer, since everyone else uses 55 markers.

Two people play at a time. They lay down the pad, put the bowl on the pad and place the six dice in the bowl with the marked faces down. They then place the markers to one side of the playing area. Sometimes a third person oversees the markers and keeps score. The contestants then seat themselves (or sometimes kneel) across from each other with the bowl between them. With a deft motion called *ômkawôgan*, the first player raises the bowl one to two inches above the pad, then quickly brings it down with considerable force to upset the dice. The lay of the dice is then counted. If a die falls from the bowl, it does not count.

The score:

6 identical dice	= 5 points (15 counting sticks or 1 notched stick)
2 successive throws of 6 identical	= 10 points (30 counting sticks or 2 notched sticks)
5 of one side	= 1 point (3 counting sticks)
2 successive throws of 5 of one side	= 2 points (6 counting sticks)
3 plain side	= 1 point (3 counting sticks)
Any other combination	= lose the turn

The game is played until the pile of counting sticks is exhausted. Among our Penobscot relations, this may signal the end of the game. Among other Abenaki peoples, the game may end or may continue. If the game is to continue, among some Abenaki groups, the players use the sticks in their respective piles to keep score. For each point, a single counting stick is removed from the personal pile and placed with the side toward the player; for each five points, a stick is placed with the end toward the player. In this way the game can go on for a very long time, until one concedes defeat.

The Norridgewock dice game was scored differently, since eight dice were used:

4:4 or 5:3 = no score
6:2   = 4 points
7:1   = 10 points
8:0   = 20 points.

By late winter's Mozokas, the Moose Hunting Moon, everyone was getting bored and cranky. The weather began to moderate; with some days above twenty degrees on a Fahrenheit thermometer. The men began to bestir themselves to go hunting. In some villages everyone went to hunting camp except the sick and aged. Winter clothing was the first necessity. Beaver robes and hats wrapped tightly prevented freezing of our heads and arms and torso, but the exertion quickly warmed us even in the cold evenings. Wool blankets worn shawl-like or made into tailored capotes quickly superseded peltry as a source of warm outerwear. Our thick brain-tanned moosehide *plejes* (leggings) were bound tightly with leather thong over the high *azazen* (collar) of our *mkezenal* (moccasins) (fig. 24). These moccasins were important winter survival tools. We had two types, the beavertail, with the sole drawn up all around and sewn to the vamp, and the *ojolkezen* (rabbit nose moccasin), a slightly easier moccasin to make that had a seam up the front. Winter moccasins had large "flaps" to cover the ankle and lower legs. They also had long laces to bind the leggings to the flaps. The moccasins were made large so that insulating fur, cloth, or moss insulation could be added.

Elk (reported from Norridgewock) or moose leather, sometimes with hair left on for traction and insulation, were the preferred materials. Leather bags and quivers, sometimes painted or ornamented with quillwork, carried the equipment of the hunt. Winter hunting, even with these well-adapted clothes and gear, was hard, dangerous work but productive. The *ogenak* (snowshoes), brought to perfection at this time by the Alnôba and their neighbors, were the key. On snowshoes we could pursue deer, elk, and moose, our feet gliding lightly over the snow while our prey struggled vainly through three- to five-foot drifts. Winter hunting required open-weave snowshoes so that the snow would not build up on top of the shoe,

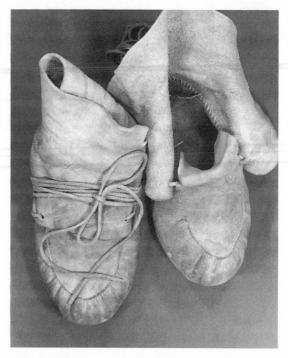

Fig. 24. Beaver-tail winter moccasins. *Wôbanakik Heritage Center Collection, photograph by Andrew Lee.*

slowing the hunter down. Once the animal was killed, the carcass could be processed, a quick *wdohogan* (sledge) made from wood, and the whole brought back to the hungry people in the village. Interestingly, the winter burden snowshoe had to have a close weave so that if game was carried with the tumpline the shoe would not sink in the light upper snow layer. For we knew that the new year was beginning. Our mother the Earth was waking again, her blood coursing from the ground up into trunks and branches of her mantle. As the days became warm enough to melt the snow, sap began to run, and the cycle began again.

The War for the Dawnland

As war spread throughout our land in the Years of the Beaver, we had to fight throughout the year. We did not practice war for total annihilation in the European sense of total war.

Fig. 25. Robert Rogers and the burning of Odanak. *Watercolor,*
Jon Young; Wôbanakik Heritage Center Collection, photograph by
Andrew Lee.

Europeans such as Robert Rogers attempted total ethnic cleansing by
destruction of whole village populations, such as Norridgewock, Missisquoi, and Odanak (fig. 25). Strategically, we saw war as a defense of our
homeland, yet it was other things too. We saw it as a complement to trade,
an agent of boundary maintenance, a way of achieving personal stature in
the community, a method of obtaining new tools and weapons, and a way
of obtaining new members for the village. We respected and honored our
enemies in battle. We even left messages from their captured kinsmen on
a tree at the village we attacked! In order to assure the minimalist impact
of war, all participants incorporated a series of strict ceremonies and protocols. There were many preparatory ceremonies for the war parties, which
even included warning the enemy and giving reasons for the impending
attack. There were returning ceremonies for both the warriors and their
captives, if any. The dreaded "running the gauntlet" that Euro-American
historians extol as a horrific initiation rite of our captives was actually more
symbolic than torturous. It would be the height of folly to maim a potential

productive member of Alnôba society. We neither attempted to degrade nor destroy our opponents, for in another part of the year we might become trading partners.

This time-honored system began to change during the Years of the Beaver, for the Haudenosaunee, on their own and stirred up by the Bastaniak, began to wage total war, even laying siege to one of our towns on the Kwinitekw. Then we Alnôbak, who were always the slowest to fight, became the fiercest warriors in what they called the Turtle Island. Even today, traditional people at Akwesasne (St. Regis Reservation, New York) and Caanawagi (Kanawake Reservation, near Montreal) remember us as being "nasty customers" as we fought together against the Bastanaik. After the Christian year of 1640, our armies were lightly armed, fast-moving guerrilla warriors armed with musket, pipe tomahawk, and knife. As technology evolved, so did the pace of war. However, the Alnôbak do not glory in old wars won or lost, so rather than a military history, which has been well crafted by Anglo historians, I will focus on an Abenaki perspective on the hows and whys of war.

Tools of War

For years we had obtained belt and ships' axes in trade with our neighbors, but they were burdensome when carried on the path of wood or war. The tomahawk was light, beautiful, and efficient in cleaving wood or a Bastaniak warrior's skull. Several styles of tomahawk remain in our land. The earliest type of which we have proof of is a triangular piece of plate steel embedded in a hickory handle, in the manner of prehistoric celts (wedge- axes). Later is a spike tomahawk, found near the first falls of Onigigiwizibo (Vergennes, Vermont). This tool was clumsy and easily broken. The lighter, more graceful pipe tomahawk was developed by the early part of the Christian eighteenth century. The earlier of the two pipe tomahawk styles found in our land is cylindrical-bowl form such as that found in Thornton, New Hampshire, and Elmore, Vermont. A later, more common style has a bulbous pipe bowl fitting. These have been found in archaeological sites in Wôbanakik, and one is on display at the state of Vermont's Chimney Point Museum. Two of this style have descended in Abenaki families. The best tomahawks had a steel bit forged into the blade. These cut cleanly and would not blunt or break in the heat of battle. An extension of the tomahawk was the battle lance. This was an eight- to ten-foot spear with an ashwood or hickory shaft. Affixed to the front was a long,

Fig. 26. The ancient tools of war found in Wôbanakik. *Wôbanakik Heritage Center Collection, photograph by Andrew Lee.*

thin steel blade, tapered or rounded at the back so that it could be easily withdrawn after use. They were hafted with a long tang going almost a foot into the shaft or fit over the shaft like a glove. Our French allies provided us with military pikes and spontoons, but we also recycled our old moose lances, and I even saw one eighteenth-century lance head in (from southern Maine) that was made from a military saber (fig. 26).

What we really needed were the "far throwers" used by Europeans to kill each other. By the 1640s in the Christians' calendar, we had obtained firearms and were reported by the Bastaniak as being proficient with them. These early muskets were matchlocks, which used a clumsy burning string to ignite the gunpowder. These were unreliable in the rain and revealed our position by its smoke or spark-light. During the eighteenth century our Blackmon allies provided us with military muskets made in France and elsewhere on the Continent (figs. 26 and 27). Of course we also took the Bastaniak "Brown Bess" musket from our foes (fig. 28). These were a vast improvement over the matchlock. Their flintlock firing mechanism could be used in the rain and was always ready to use. At the end of our wars, a special trade musket, identified by *shishigua*, the serpent, on its side, made its way to us in large quantities. Only one of these last muskets remain in our

Fig. 27. Abenaki warrior and spouse. ca. 1750. *Wôbanakik Heritage Center Collection, photograph by Andrew Lee.*

Fig. 28. "Kwai." *Wôbanakik Heritage Center Collection, photograph by Andrew Lee.*

land, captured in a museum at Cowass (near the Euro-American settlement of Newbury, Vermont). As time went on, we became proficient in maintaining and repairing the guns with parts cannibalized from other guns, or parts given to us by armorers at the French outposts. Lead was melted and cast to make musket balls, and we revived an almost dead craft as we chipped Vermont's stone for gunflints. The musket revolutionized hunting and warfare. It made obsolete the woven wooden shields and wood-slat body armor that we had used before the coming of the foreigners. Our men, now fast-moving lightly armed hunters of animals and men, carried the musket and the equipment to service it, a powder horn and soft gray lead.

How We Went to War

A seventeenth- or eighteenth-century Abenaki village was quiet but always alert. Often a messenger arrived at the wood's edge and gave the "common signal" of Kwai to let us know that he was an ally. With an honor guard escort he came through the village's palisade gate. He may have carried aloft a wampum belt with the design of a tomahawk executed in white beads on a purple background; the purple signifying war. A warrior ran to summon the Bonsawinno (fire keeper), who then kindled the sacred fire at the Council House.

As the fire was growing, a warrior summoned the Zôgômo (chief) and his Gaptinak (councilors). The messenger went to the Council House and delivered the belt to one who would receive it. This belt commanded respect and a quick response, for it bore the declaration of war against peoples outside the Great Council Fire. Rumors of war now circulated in the village. The chief and councilors took their places around the council fire chamber. The Bonsawinno brought forth the chief's or nation's pipe. It was then filled with tobacco and lit from the central fire. Beginning with the chief, the pipe was then passed from member to member to assure that nothing but the truth was to be spoken and that there would be no harsh words. At the conclusion of passing the pipe, the messenger stood and recited the message of war that came with the belt. All at the council listened to the ambassador, then each was permitted to speak, one at a time (some used the speaking-stick that must be held to permit speaking). A war council was then held where all—men, women, and even young people—were eligible to talk, for war involves all.

After the discussion, a somber but respectful meal was prepared to honor the belt carrier. At this time the people of the village knew the purpose of the messenger and considered their own responses. The elders kept peace for a day and a night, then met again to determine a response: to go to war or to remain neutral. The ambassador was summoned and given the response. If the response was war, the war chief rose, bearing the ceremonial red-painted war club. This symbolized the taking up of arms. He addressed the general assembly, asking if others would follow him to war. Other men rose and asked for volunteers for war parties that they would lead. (If the village nation remained neutral, there was nothing preventing warriors individually assisting the cause of a neighboring village or council fire.) (See fig. 27.) The warriors then painted their faces with their own design of war paint, which was different than that of their ceremonial or mourning paint pattern. After the discussion, a second somber meal was prepared, this time to honor the war parties. It was reported in 1703 that a dog was killed for the feast. The warriors then prepared for the first of many war dances. The Great Council Fire war dance is only dimly remembered. The Abenaki of Wôlinak call it the *nawadewe,'* which is merely the word for "dance," and remember that warriors danced with tomahawks or war clubs. After the feast and war dance, another round of pipe smoking occurred and the messenger departed to the next village.

What We Took to War

The first requirement of the warrior was seasonal clothing for the trail. Since the road was long and arduous, nothing more than the bare minimum was worn. A personal headdress, consisting of various feathers or a roach (a single surviving eighteenth-century Abenaki roach was of moose hair) and perhaps a silver headband, often called a crown by silver collectors (fig. 27). From the warrior's neck was suspended any or all of the following: a knife and sheath, a silver, or brass gorget (often the sign of a war leader), or perhaps necklaces made of wampum shell, silver, or trade beads, sometimes with a pendant silver cross or peace medal. Worn over a shoulder was the equipment pouch, which held fire-making tools, bullets, extra gun flints, a pipe and tobacco, concentrated corn and meat rations, and the few personal items required on the trail. Also slung from the shoulder was a powderhorn. Around his waist was a wide belt or sash, made of cloth or leather, which held up his breechcloth and leggings. His tomahawk and small pouches—and perhaps his pipe, separated into bowl and stem—were affixed to the sash. Moccasins completed the trail clothing. The warrior also carried a musket or, lacking that, a spear and bow/quiver.

How We Fought

We had two levels of strategy in warfare. The high-level strategy was to reduce the Bastaniaks' capability to invade our lands and perhaps bring them to peace council on our terms. A related high-level strategy was to aid our allies in their time of need, as much as could be done considering our own needs. A lower level strategy was to gather captives and war materiel. Captives were extremely valuable for selling to the Blackmonak, who would pay large sums for them, or to adopt into our society. It was interesting to us that many women and children captives said that we treated them better than they had been treated in New England. Our battle tactics varied, depending on the overall strategy.

Warriors were required to run long distances and then stalk quietly through the forest. Line battle (two equally equipped forces facing each other) was graded by weaponry. In long-distance encounters the musket or bow was used. When the opponent(s) closed in, the next weapon was the spear or lance. (I do not know whether our ancestors used the bayonet.) These would be used, if possible, with a thrusting motion rather than throwing. Only a novice would deliberately toss his spear. Next in was the tomahawk, the tool of choice for hand-to-hand combat. But I remember that Monkey Drew, a River Rat (whom we'll discuss soon) told me that it was always a good idea when fighting someone with a tomahawk to close in and use the knife. Let luck and plain meanness get you through. The best tactics were to always engage the opponent at a distance (shoot a person with a lance, lance a person with a tomahawk, tomahawk a person with a knife, and knife a person using only fists). It was, however, considered bad form to shoot a person who had only a tomahawk or knife. A second consideration was that killing an opponent was less desirable than capturing, so if we could inflict a disabling but sublethal wound to the arms or head or knock out our opponent, all the better—a captive with ruined legs was useless.

If we raided a settlement that was not aroused and ready, we attempted to capture rather than kill but did not hesitate to kill if necessary. Women and children were the most desirable, for they would be more docile on the retreat, which required all our speed and cunning. Being more lightweight than the men, they could be carried if necessary. Another important consideration was the capture of war materiel such as muskets or valuables such as clothing or jewelry. (Fig. 28.)

Returning from War

When we returned, we paused at the "wood's edge" and sent a runner ahead to prepare the village. Families needed to know who had been lost, who had been wounded, and who had come through unscathed. The welcome was a mixture of pain for those who had given their lives in defense of our homeland and rejoicing for the heroes who returned. The war chief gave the common signal (fig. 28), and the war party was brought into the village to await the council. A warrior summoned the Bonsawinno, who kindled the Council House sacred fire, as welcome for the war party. The war party then went to the Council House. The Zôgômo and Gaptinak took their accustomed places in the council fire chamber to hear the war party's report. The Bonsawinno again brought forth the nation's pipe, and beginning with the chief, the pipe was passed to the war party, then to the council. At the conclusion of the pipe passing, the war leader stood to describe the nature and situation of the combat, describing captives and booty taken and the distribution of these spoils of war. All at the council listened to the war chief, then each was permitted to speak, one at a time, words of praise, sorrow, or thanksgiving. If the village had suffered a defeat or setback that demanded quick retribution, the war chief rose bearing the red war club. He asked if others would follow him back to the war trail. The returning warriors now removed the war paint from their faces.

After the debriefing council, a respectful meal was prepared to honor the warriors who had given their lives. The village then prepared for the captive adoption ceremony. This may have taken the form of "running the gauntlet" but not in the spiteful way often reported by Anglo military records. The captives were given to families who had lost loved ones or perhaps to people to whom the war party owed favors. The captives might also have been kept for trading or selling to our French allies. After the captives were distributed, materiel was given to other families as thanks or payment for a past favor. Captured cannon, cannonballs, and gunpowder probably would have been considered village property. Following the distribution ceremonies came the first of many commemorative or celebratory war dances. The village then became quiet, each person's thoughts about the engagement now their own.[7]

The End of the World—I

But calamity fell. Our great allies, the Blacmonak, concluded a separate peace with the dreadful Bastaniak, leaving us and our allies at their mercy, of which they had little. To the west, our Odawa "elder brothers" fought on, and we sent warriors to help in their futile but glorious war. We soon learned that the Bastaniak were fighting one another, and our own councils were confused. We tried to let them kill each other, but that didn't work, and their feuds put boundaries between us and our allies to the north. We now had to deal with the blended people from the South, the Anglo-Americans.

7

Against the Darkness:
The Years of the Fox

(Christian Years 1820 to 1970)

The position of the state is that in the late 1700s the Abenaki ceased functioning as a tribe, and although they have regrouped, it still doesn't meet the legal test.
  —JANET ANCEL, Governor's Counsel, *St. Albans Messenger*, May 15, 1995

For academic historians, the turn of the nineteenth century were fading years of the Alnôba. Researchers find only the sparsest references to "a few Indians from St. Francis" or "old Joe, the last Indian left destitute" in the standard Euro-American sources. This dearth of information left ethnohistorians Gordon Day and Colin Calloway with the premise that the Western Abenaki were, by this time, essentially no longer in Wôbanakik except perhaps as visitors. Gordon Day, in an oft-cited 1981 article in the *International Journal of American Linguistics*, said that the "original inhabitants of this territory largely found their way to the St. Francis band." This set the tone for most future work. According to this logic, they had been largely exiled, during the Years of the Beaver, to the Kitsitegw valley, the former lands of the Nadoueks . With this dismissal, serious historical inquiry for the period almost vanishes. *The Original Vermonters*, by Haviland and Power (1994 ed.) stands as an excellent example of this phenomenon. Of its 272 pages of text, only 1.4 percent (pp. 247–250) deal with data on the critical period between 1800 and the Abenaki Renaissance. Prof. Colin Calloway's book *The Western Abenakis of Vermont, 1600–1800* (1990) explicitly avoids this apparently barren era by ending his research period at the critical turn of the nineteenth century. Actually, Calloway gives it a go in an epilogue, chapter 13, even providing a bit more data than *The Original Vermonters*. Other works on the Western Abenaki contain but a few vaguely written pages concerning this time, leading some to believe that the Alnôba truly faded but later than they had heretofore thought. It is true that the British government offered continuing refuge along the Ktsitegw, and some decided to head north into exile. In moving, they left a visible "paper trail" for ethnohistorians to make inferences from that are only partly true. This lack of scholarly research and writing has inadvertently provided the state of Vermont with a tactical tool in its campaign of disconnecting us from our ancestors, a strategic cornerstone in its ethnic cleansing program.

But exile is not the whole story, nor even a major story for those who remain. My ancestors chose to stay and merge, in the eyes of the Anglo-Americans, with our French neighbors. Yet we kept our beliefs and customs. Other families took the Path of the Fox, to fade into the mountains and rivers, seeing much and yet being unseen. A few families chose to be the intermediaries between the Alnôba and the Anglos, a visible reminder, to those who would see, that the Abenaki were not gone.

AGAINST THE DARKNESS

Let the visitors believe they have conquered,
that they have the land and its bounty.
Let them believe that we are gone, Indian Joe is dead.
The forests keep our secret.
The unseen fox has kits in its den.
The drums and rattles are not stilled.
They are heard in the far places,
they are heard on the air of night.
The visitors think they have won.
Yet the scent of sweetgrass troubles their dreams.

Medawas, 1994

As the Anglo-Americans flooded into Wôbanakik, each family band came to a new consensus about how to endure, since to remain unchanged in our old villages quickly invited genocide. There were five options: (1) exile, (2) fade into the forests and marshes, (3) live the "Gypsy"/"Pirate"/"River Rat" life between Native and European culture, (4) merge with the French community, (5) "pass" into English-American society.

Fig. 29. Representation of Abenaki delegate from the Seven Nations to Vermont legislature and wampum custodian in 1799. *Wôbanakik Heritage Center Collection, photograph by Andrew Lee.*

Fig. 30. Representation of wampum custodian and Abenaki delegate to the Great Council Fire at Kahnawake in 1840. *Wôbanakik Heritage Center Collection, photograph by Andrew Lee.*

The Years of the Fox are a joy and a frustration to write about. Anglo historians seem to lack research interest or tools to discover much about the Alnôbak of this time, so their lore is lacking. We left few records in censuses and village documents. They were unconcerned about us, for we retained neither wealth nor land that they could tax nor literary skills that they could exploit, and our children weren't considered fit for schooling. Even our names were unimportant and almost indistinguishable from our neighbors. But the trace was there to see, not in the written word, but in the Alnôbaiwi material world. No group that maintains a distinctive culture can do so only in the world of ideas and words, and the Alnôbak were no exception. As the modern historian laments the demise of the Abenaki, the art collector scours our land for "Indian art," which for some unaccountable reason is so common here. Abenaki baskets, tourist trinkets, and snowshoes crowd antique shops. Our pipes, beadwork, and buckskin clothing (figs. 27, 29, and 30) found at estate sales are quietly spirited away to New York, Scottsdale, or Santa Fe, to speak of our continuing presence and cultural continuity.[1]

Exile, Canada, and Their Political Implications

The British government continued to offer refuge for Alnôbak families in the reserves of Odanak and Wôlinak in the old Nadouek lands north of the original boundaries of Wôbanakik. Some continued the slow exodus to the north, where they joined their long severed kin. However, even these families often returned to Wôbanakik during the summer to sell their wares or during other times of the year to hunt or visit relatives in New England. The St. Lawrence mission villages were important for us in Wôbanakik, since the French Canadian people and the Catholic Church were much more accepting of Native people. The Alnôbak there remained "out of the closet" during the nineteenth and twentieth centuries. This had the important effect of allowing them to maintain highly visible traditions of language, music, dance, art, and public ceremony. Such traditions became unthinkable in western Wôbanakik as it became thickly settled by the highly genocidal English colonists. We would travel north to our sundered kin to renew our heritage and proudly sing and dance in the open. There we could also pursue political goals of protecting our homeland. During this time, the Seven Nations of Canada, one political arm of the ancient Great Council Fire, was empowered to treat

with the Europeans in western Vermont and northern New York. It continually let the Vermont government know that our land was "Indian
Country" (fig. 29).

HIS EXCELLENCY ISAAC TICHENOR ESQR. GOVERNOR OF THE STATE
OF VERMONT—VERGENNES

GREAT BROTHER
   We the Chiefs and Councilors of the Seven Nations of Canada Indians send our
love and respects to you and family by Five of our Agents which we the Chiefs have
sent to you to treat about our hunting lands—that lies in your State—beginning on
the East side of Ticonderoga from thence to the great Falls on Otter Creek and continue the same course to the height of land that divides the streams between lake
Champlain and the river Connecticut from thence along the height of land opposite
Mesisqua and then down to the bay—that is the land belonging to the seven Nations
which we have sent to settle for with you as we have settled with York State—so we
hope you will be pleased to receive our agents and that it will be settled to that both
sides will be contented.

Cochnawaga 29th September 1798

SIGNED BY TWENTY CHIEFS OF THE DIFFERENT NATIONS

	Gangage-Anasategen	Tahanageritsen
	Tareha	Shanagatee
	Garonistsioga	Thentaraganra
	Sotogen	Galentaterhou
	Anatahonne	Shagosanegatee
	Feyenetsshen	Shagenneganne
	Ganela tagee-rarontaksa	Aggeson
Tharki	Aggasne	Tionatogenhe
Enita	Otisggaioha	Teharoningethen

(MSS State Papers of Vermont, vol. 30, p. 348; see fig. 30)

   However, as time went on, the chiefs of Kahnawake began asserting that
Vermont was their land, not that of the Seven Nations or Abenaki. Such
actions, combined with other presumptuous activity, led to the decline
and failure of the Great Council Fire in the nineteenth century. This
chapter will focus not on the people in exile and their diplomacy, for they
have been dealt with elsewhere by Euro-American historians and their
own scholars, and I am preparing a manuscript to deal with it.[2] I will focus
on the largely unknown people who chose to maintain many of their traditional political, craft, and land use patterns intact in the face of increasing
hostility by their Anglo neighbors. These people, generally invisible to the

historian, have been given derogatory names, since they were visible to their neighbors yet seemed different enough to be seen as vaguely menacing. Called "Gypsies," "Pirates," or "River Rats" by their neighbors, they had to settle in areas not coveted by English Americans. These were marshes, pine woods, and mountains.

People of the Forests and Woods

Some families maintained a traditional "extended family band" lifestyle, relying little on Anglo society. However, they did maintain strong relations with their relatives who chose a more intermediate lifestyle. Hunting, fishing, and gathering continued to be the mainstay of the Alnôbak during this period. This traditional cultural/political system lasted into the twentieth century without much comment by Europeans, who often saw their seemingly isolated campsites in the mountains and on the margins of lake or marsh. It was among these people that the wigwam, the traditional dwelling of the Alnôbak finally gave way to the frame "New English" house in the 1800s. Very traditional music and dances continued among these people and are still remembered today by some elders. The last outward vestige of this lifestyle in the Lake Champlain area came to an abrupt end in 1941 when the U.S. government made a wildlife refuge from the delta of the Missisquoi River, expelling the last traditional families and forcing them into more mainstream American life.[3] These people never gave up their traditional forms of leadership but blended them into a more farm and village lifestyle.

River Rats and Pirates

Somewhat more acculturated than the traditional-lifestyle Alnôbak were people who kept mainly to themselves and did not participate in New England society to a great extent but nonetheless adapted European language, religion, and technology to their needs. Well before the turn of the nineteenth century they had adopted the frame house and much technology from their Anglo neighbors. The river- and lake-oriented Abenaki family bands were known to their neighbors as "River Rats" (as they were called in Swanton, Vermont) or "Pirates" (as they were called in Grand Isle County). The River Rats lived in shantytowns by rivers, while Pirates often lived out of their boats on the shores of Lake Champlain. In order to protect their traditional sovereignty, they sought out lands that were not coveted by the "English." The ultimate form of landlessness was achieved by some "Pirate" families who lived most of their lives out of houseboats. It is interesting that the River Rat settlements I know (at or near Swanton Falls, Milton, Vergennes) are invariably located close to Contact Period Abenaki towns, whereas Pirate families often congregated at important fishing, portaging, and gathering places. Older Euro-American observers remember "Indians" lingering long in such places, overseen by old burial mounds and village sites. These family bands were in fact the caretakers of long-established Abenaki subsistence, dwelling, and sacred grounds. While nowhere as nomadic as the "Gypsies" discussed below, these families were still mobile. They always had canoes or rowboats available to leave, with some pork and flour and a bedroll for a fishing, hunting, or gathering trip of one day to several weeks. Spring was the major fishing time, as the walleye and other fish ran in the rivers.

Perhaps the crowning glory of the nineteenth century River Rats was their bark canoe. The Wintegok, or Marrow River, commemorates Alnôbak canoe building at *mskitgw*, the lower, quiet stretch of the river. It was said that this area became ice free before the lake did and was therefore a good place to work on boat building. The marrow (*Win*) in the name Wintegok denoted the necessary moose bone marrow that was a critical component in good canoe building.

Building the Alnôbaiwi Canoe

The nineteenth century Alnôbaiwi canoe was a more advanced lake and river craft than the European rowboat. It was strong yet lightweight enough to be portaged around rapids. The paddler faced forward, seeing where he was going, unlike the rower who had to face the rear. It could be poled more easily as well. We made three basic types of canoe: the *mozolol* (moosehide skin-covered canoe), the *woleskaolakw* (dugout), and the bark canoe. We made two types of bark canoe, a quickly made and quickly abandoned canoe of spruce bark, called the *pkwahaol*, and the more permanent *wigwaol*, or birch-bark canoe, discussed here (see fig. 31). Of all New World naval architects, we were considered the best *nodtolidak* (birch-bark canoe makers). As with the makers of sailing ships, a whole terminology evolved around birch-bark canoe building, which I would like to share with you as part of the description of boat building.[4]

Fig. 31. Odanak, Quebec, birch-bark canoe. *Wôbanakik Heritage Center Collection, photograph by Andrew Lee.*

To make a *wigwaol*, we first had to determine which type of canoe we needed. Stream travel required a smaller, lighter weight canoe that could be portaged around rapids, while lake travel allowed larger *odoalagwal* (cargo canoes) or *madobaolagwal* (war canoes). Wind and water conditions to be faced by the canoe also needed to be considered. White water or waves could best be dealt with by a canoe having a high, water-shedding prow and stern. However, these high ends would be caught in the wind like a sail, making the canoe very hard to steer and keep on course, especially in a wide lake. A fairly standard *wigwaol* was sixteen feet long, three feet wide, and one and a half feet deep, carrying up to six adults or equivalent cargo. Thus, the canoe made at Mskitegwa (Milton, Vermont) would be very different if it was meant to go up the Wintegok or down to Lake Between. Much has been made of the differences between canoes made in various parts of our land; for example, western canoes were supposed to be lower than eastern varieties, although I have seen old photographs that show more variation in height within an area than between areas. Even the distinctive bowed-center Micmac-style canoe was used in the Ktsitegw valley at least as far west as the French settlement of Sorel, Quebec. Practical environmental considerations probably had as much to do with the style as supposed cultural differences.

As pointed out above, we had to have collected the materials, which consisted of igua, a strip of canoe-weight birch-bark, cedar strips for *wogino* (the ribs and the lining), spruce root for sewing the bark, and a spruce-gum mixture for a sealant. There is some confusion as to the best time to collect canoe bark; some say during a thaw in winter when the bark is toughest. An eyewitness in the Champlain Valley noted April 1881 as the date, while the Mikmoz (Micmac people who live in a *warmer* area than the Western Abenaki) are reported to do it as late as June. The bark could be harvested from an upright tree by cutting as high as one could reach, then making an I-shaped incision to peel the bark back. The wide bark needed to be supported by cords to prevent splitting. However, to get really large pieces of bark, the tree was often felled, then peeled. *Agwanus*, bark peeled out of season, stuck to the tree like glue and was not used except for repairs.

The sealant, constructed by women while the men made the gunwale frame, was made as follows: *Pego* (spruce gum) was collected in little *maanikwoganal* (bark pails) fastened below slashes in the bark. The resulting sap was boiled until it thickened, then mixed with finely powdered wood charcoal to give it body. Marrow or animal tallow was added to the mixture to give the sealant a degree of flexibility. This addition was necessary or the gum/charcoal mixture would quickly harden to a glasslike consistency. It would then crack in use over the flexible-bark canoe covering, causing leaks.

Our men split and carved the gunwales (the wooden upper sides of the canoe) with the *belaghagenigan* (crooked knife) from clear white cedar, made mortises for the thwarts, then bound them together at the front and rear ends with *wadabal* (spruce-root lashings). Maple, larch, or white cedar *bakagaokwtagil* (thwarts) were carved and inserted into the gunwales to spring them apart to the shape of the canoe. The completed frame was then laid on a flat, loamy-soiled building site, often on a layer of sand specially modified to help shape the bottom of the canoe. A series of stakes about one meter long were then pounded into the soil around the periphery of the frame.

The stakes were pulled carefully from the soil and laid beside their holes, facing outward. The frame was removed, and a roll of moist igua bark was laid, white side up, on the ground in the space left by the stakes. The craftsman then had to judge the bark and its blemishes. Repairs to the bark and any "piecing-out" of bark, such as adding the *kohigan* (the extra piece of bark below the gunwale on most canoes) was done at this time. Any "shingled" overlaps had to face to the rear of the planned canoe. The frame was then placed on the bark roll exactly in its former position within the rim of stake holes and weighted down with large cobbles. The bark was carefully pulled up around the frame until a hole was revealed; then the stake reinserted in the hole and pounded fast to the soil. This was repeated for the rest of the stakes, carefully working and cutting slashes in the bark so as to not tear the moist bark in the wrong place. Opposite side stakes were lashed together so that the frame mold wouldn't spread, making a deformed canoe. The bark was pulled up and lashed to the vertical stakes. The stones were removed and the frame was raised to its height. It was independently lashed to the mold, and the ends of the frame sprang upward in a graceful curve that is characteristic of our canoe.

When the moist bark was on the frame, it was sewn together by the women. They first folded the moist bark over the gunwales. A *spogan* (deer-bone awl) was used to pierce the bark, and then it was securely lashed to the frame with spruce root, which was sometimes dyed with vegetal dyes. Cedar-strip outwales were then lashed to the gunwales with root. The canoe had to be continually kept wet while this was being done. The *cidohiganal*, the curved front piece of the canoe frame, was placed into the ends of the canoe, then sewn in with a distinctive spiral sewing called *adebigwonsahigan*. After the canoe was taken off the mold and turned upside down, the women added lashings to the ends of the canoe to bind it together and did any fine repair work or additional lashing as required. They could complete this process in about a day. The hot gum mixture was applied to each joint, seam, or hole to make the canoe waterproof. The canoe was then given back to the men to complete.

While the women did the lashing, the men split thin, light strips of *molodakw*, clear white cedar. Some of these strips were used to line the inside of the canoe longitudinally, to protect the bark from the occupants and to give strength to the whole. These were kept tight against the bark by the *koskiwogin* (canoe rib), slightly thicker strips whittled so as to carefully fit under the gunwale and to spring outward to give the canoe its final shape. The fitting of these, a process called *abonskan*, was the most delicate step in the manufacture, for an ill-fitting rib could deform or tear the rest of the canoe. They had to be pounded (*kwakthigan*) carefully into place. The ribs were then sewn to the gunwale with spruce root, and a final gunwale cap-strip was pegged to the gunwale to protect the lashing. Cedar headboards, snapped into the bow and stern, completed the construction. The canoe was then allowed to dry for several days. If if it had a tendency to warp, it could be straightened during its drying by tying it to stakes. Designs, if wanted, could be scratched or painted onto the bark during the drying process. The canoe then underwent final inspection and repair after being checked for leaks.

In general it took about a week to build a sixteen-foot canoe. The canoe lasted for about a year of heavy use or decades of light use. It was easy to repair with materials available from the forest. Although old canoes may be good in the spring, some would probably fail sometime during the summer when bark was hard to remove. Repair would be very inconvenient, or in the case of the war canoe, very dangerous. Therefore, the prudent Alnôba village had canoe making as an important activity every spring.

The birch-bark canoe became harder to make during the mid- and late nineteenth century, as large trees from which the *igua* (the single large piece of birch-bark) came, became almost nonexistent, at least near rivers. The Alnôbak soon developed the *kokskolagw*, a canoe made of cedar strips supported by the ribs. The strips had to be more finely made than those that just fit between the bark and ribs of the *wigwaol*. The strips were nailed or stapled to the ribs, and the whole was covered with canvas to render it waterproof. These were made by *nodtolidak* into this century. This technology was the basis for the wood-and-canvas canoe that was the mainstay of the northwoods during the late nineteenth and early twentieth century and formed the basis of the famous Adirondack Guide Boat and other highly collectable "woodies" so esteemed today.

Odaoganak (canoe paddles) were split from cedar, ash, or maple and laboriously carved to shape by hand. (Fig. 39 shows a paddle made by my family in the late 1800s.) It took one person longer to make a paddle than it took the group to make the canoe, but it lasted longer. I still use the paddle my father made in the Christian year of 1944. Remains or descriptions of early paddles are rare, but they appear in old Euro-American paintings, showing that they were often carved and painted with ownership or spiritual markings.[5]

Summer saw many River Rats hired on as camp cooks and guides at the resorts and camps that lined Lake Champlain (fig. 32). During the fall they subsistence-hunted and guided *odowinoak* (Euro-American sportsmen) for waterfowl and upland hunting. They also made ends meet by continuing the craft traditions of their forebears. Except for one family in Swanton, the River Rats and Pirates apparently did not make tourist wares such as baskets and miniature snowshoes, but they did perpetuate crafts associated with fishing and hunting. Small carved-burlwood *amkwonak* (canoe cups) were remembered as the specialty of one River Rat who lived just above Swanton Falls, while canoe paddles (fig. 39), decoys, fish decoys,

Fig. 32. Missisquoi Abenaki guides and camp cooks with their clients. *Wiseman collection.*

snowshoes (fig. 40), rowboats (fig. 1), wooden duck calls, and even cedar furniture have been traced to these makers. There is some evidence that one family in the Swanton, Vermont, area made canvas and cedar canoes and Adirondack Guide Boats. These were made for themselves as well as other fishermen and hunters. One of the guide boats remained parked on the river until around 1970, when it was sold to a collector in New York. The Rats were part of their communities and contributed to community life. For example, during the 1927 flood, my father remembered them as instrumental in saving lives, cattle, and property; often braving dangerous eddies and currents in their seemingly fragile handmade boats. They were seen by many of their neighbors as wardens of the rivers and lakes, but others saw them in a different light. Unlike the Gypsies, most River Rats and many Pirates had some formal education, often attended the Catholic Church, and had an interest in town politics. I remember the *saziboit*, or the River Rats in the 1950s, at the end of their reign, and they taught me much. My mother was afraid to let me go down there by the river until "Monkey" Drew, a childhood friend of my father who lived on the river, told her that she needn't worry: if any River Rat did anything to me or let anything happen to me, he would die, and rather slowly. (See fig. 33.)

I remember these weathered, sunbaked men, smelling of tobacco, motor oil, and some kind of alcohol, as the kindest and gentlest people.

They talked of wives and family, yet always seemed to be alone, continually doing something—whittling a new paddle, tinkering with an almost dead outboard motor, or filleting the day's catch. At night someone would take out a fiddle, which by now had replaced the drum and rattle as the instrument of choice among some Alnôba (but not all) families, and play old songs in French and English. They taught me how to whittle fish decoys and lots of other things that I now know were Abenaki traditions of respect for the land and other people. They were always proud of me every time I caught a big fish. (Alas, Monkey Drew died before I caught my twenty-five-pound muskie.) More than that, they introduced me to the lore of the river: The first stories that I heard of the fortified village of Missisquoi came from them; they told me of "Indian mounds" that had slowly been leveled by plowing and of the tiny magical island that lay off of Highgate Springs. I knew that the *molsemak* (wolves) and *bihtolak* (cougars) were still around and that the serpent of Lake Champlain would only reveal

Fig. 33. Monkey Drew with my father's trophy muskellunge, 1957. *Wiseman collection.*

Fig. 34. Crooked knife with "Fred W. Wiseman, June 1913" inscribed on blade. *Wiseman collection.*

himself to those who were true (my father saw it six years before his death).
The Black Pool, below the second falls of Wazowategok (at Highgate Falls,
Vermont), was known to be the home of a *tatoskog* (giant lizard or serpent)
that would stir up the mud on the bottom. Only when I learned from my
father that it was methane made by rotting bark from an upstream lumber
mill did I stop being afraid. I still get goose bumps there, especially when
evening sets in and the gas really starts boiling. I heard how Bastaniak men
from Charlotte and Colchester would ride up to Missisquoi to chase Abenaki women like game animals. I heard of two battles on the Missisquoi
that are still entirely unmentioned in Euro-American scholarly work. I
shared their sorrow at the loss of their traditional hunting and fishing
grounds to Anglo regulators when in 1941 the Missisquoi delta was made a
wildlife refuge. I heard stories of continued use of their traditional lands
even as the "feds" tried to clamp down.

DUCK HUNTING STORY

*I was up beyond the slough hunting ducks one dawn in '44. It was during the
war, and we couldn't get any meat. I knew that I could get away with one or
two well-placed shots and the feds wouldn't come after me. Well, I saw two*

lone early ducks whistling over the bulrushes and let fly. Bang! Well, it seemed the whole world exploded, ducks came up in rafts all around me, must of been a million of 'em sleeping. More damn ducks than I'd ever seen. I knew I'd better high-tail it out of there 'cause the feds'd be coming. I did get the duck though.

Frederick Kermit Wiseman, 1961

I saw crooked knives (fig. 34) and pipe bags, moccasins and carved walking sticks. I learned that if you were fighting a person with a tomahawk and you only had a knife, you needed to close in quickly and "let plain meanness and a little luck carry you through." I learned of the creatures on Camel's Hump that only ran clockwise around the mountain until they came up behind you to bite your rear. I learned of what lay under the root of the mountain we call the Pinnacle (and why that ski development still hasn't been built there). I heard echoes of Koluscap and of the lore of wind and cloud. The quickness with which the wind could change on Missisquoi Bay was enshrined in this saying:

> *"The wind she blow a hurricane*
> *the wind she blow some more*
> *When the wind she blow on Lake Champlain*
> *'tis better to stay on the shore"*

I sometimes think the River Rats may have trained me in a traditional First Nations way. They would let me try out my own ideas or fears, only coming to my rescue when I had made such a fool of myself that I understood the implications of my actions:

MONKEY DREW AND THE MOSQUITOES

I was out fishing one time in the late 1950s or the early 1960s with Monkey Drew on Missisquoi Bay, when a thunderstorm came up from over Alburg Spit (to the west). The lightning started coming down, and the wind came up. I began to get scared that we were going to be capsized or struck by lightning. Monkey, who always had a cigarette stub attached to his lower lip, ignored me as I quit fishing, even though the smallmouth bass were really biting now. I couldn't concentrate. Finally, I started crying. Monkey finally acknowledged me and said, "You scared and want to go in?" I told him about lightning hitting the tallest thing around and we were the tallest thing on the flat lake. Muttering something like "lightning don't hit me," he cranked up his old beat-up outboard. We headed up the mouth of Dead Creek, an outlet of the Missisquoi River as the rain started lashing at us. He found an old raised camp (they are all gone now) on Metcalf Island. He said, "We can get out of the rain under there." Well, when we got under there, it was dry, but was home to every mosquito between Swanton and Montreal. As we sat there in the swarm, I noticed that they didn't seem to trouble him. Maybe his cigarette stub repelled them. But they loved me! I tried to be cool, but they got in my nose, in my ears, and bit me mercilessly. We were too cramped to swat properly. I tried to be cool. Finally, I couldn't take it any more. I jumped up and hit my head on the rafters and began crying again. I was completely soaked and mosquito bitten and now had a concussion. Finally, Monkey Drew acknowledged my wailing. "Well," he said, "you want to go back out?" We went back to Missisquoi Bay. We caught some great smallmouth bass in the wind and lightning. I'm still scared of thunderstorms on the lake though.

Every bit of geography had a story associated with it. The lore of the dangerous currents that could catch a boat just above Dawkwahoganizek (Swanton Falls) and pull it over the falls was repeated in one of the many stories about the two foolish brothers. When the boat was inevitably caught, it was said:

FIRST BROTHER: Throw out the hank (anchor)!
SECOND BROTHER: We ain't got no hank!
FIRST BROTHER: Throw it out anyway, we go bomp (bump)!

Another, "the two brothers and the wildcat," is associated with the caves in Highgate Springs. The two brothers are walking by a small cave in Highgate, Vermont, when they see a wildcat (bobcat or fisher cat) run into the cave.

FIRST BROTHER: Hey, why don't you go in there and get that kitty?
SECOND BROTHER: Guess I will. (He begins crawling into the tiny cave.)
FIRST BROTHER: (Hearing an awful shrieking and growling commotion coming from the cave orifice, he calls over the din): Hey, ya got him?
SECOND BROTHER: Y'er g*d d*mn right I got him, now come in here and help me let go of him!

There is a whole cycle of "city slicker" stories encapsulated in the "rich Texan" or "rich guy from Boston" stories. These functioned as important "boundary maintenance signifiers," (as the anthropologists say) between the Rats and "outsiders." In addition to a measure of sovereignty, these stories let us know that the outsiders were not quite so smart as they seemed to think. This story commemorated yet another place, the building of a golf course years ago on the road between Swanton and St. Albans, a larger town seven miles to the south. The River Rats considered golf a silly sport, but that's another story.

GOLF CLUB STORY

A River Rat was a very successful guide and had a rich Texan as his client for bass fishing in the summer and waterfowl hunting in the fall. The Texan loved both of these pastimes and was good at them, with his Montegue fish rod and Model 21 Trap shotgun. Finally after years of successful guiding, the rich Texan asked the Rat if he could possibly repay him for the best years of his life. The Rat thought a bit about retiring. He knew that all the "big-wigs" in Swanton who retired went to Florida to play golf. He hated Florida but thought golf might be interesting. "I'd like a set of golf clubs," said the Rat. The Texan replied, "How many clubs in a set?" The Rat replied, "I think there are nine." The Texan looked worried, but the guide knew he could afford them. The next year the Texan never came. Nor the next year. Finally, in the third year the Texan came back, this time on a commercial flight to Burlington rather than his own plane to Highgate Airport. Greeting the Texan, the Rat asked expectantly: "Did you get the clubs?" The Texan said, "Yer damn right I got them, but only seven have swimming pools."

When the historians say that tradition faded long ago into the margins of villages and cultivated lands, I laugh a bit inside. I could cast a fish lure from my grandmother's prim Victorian porch down to where the River Rats kept the fire of cultural and political sovereignty burning. The drums and rattles sang their song (as violin music and story) even as Anglo life went on. The River Rat and Pirate family lifestyle declined during the 1930s. Men continued to linger on the rivers and lakes through the 1950s, when local and state government severely restricted their subsistence hunting and fishing by increased enforcement. Their traditional family lifestyle was severely curtailed by offering welfare and the threat of removing their children from their culture and placing them in foster or state homes. This forced the Rats underground. I inherited from one Rat a "pike spear" for the tribal museum, that was used illegally at night by fire or lamplight to spear walleye pike during their spring run. This spear was, in his eyes, a true symbol of resistance and sovereignty. It was used until 1994. (It is ironic that this spear and its fishing style, outlawed by Vermont, is crucial evidence for federal recognition.) Today, there are a few men who practice this as a part-time lifestyle, but their families live a life little different from their neighbors.[6] However, they never gave up any form of political sovereignty—it became one of the stimuli for the "fish-in" protests discussed in the next chapter.

Indian Craftspeople

Some families adapted specific traditional craft technologies, which had earlier been a mainstay of trade between the Alnôbak and New Englanders, to tourist wares. During the nineteenth century, Anglos began coming to northern New England as visitors to grand hotels, spas, rustic "camps," and other tourist enclaves. These visitors had it in their mind that "Indians" went along with scenery (fig. 35) and began to demand "Indian Goods" as items to take back with them as trinkets or curios to their faraway homes. The most important curio was the "Indian basket." Men made most of the heavy, utilitarian baskets traded to the Anglo storekeeper or farmer, but these were too "clumsy" to be acceptable as curios. Women, who traditionally made smaller, lighter weight utility baskets, began making them for the tourist trade. The first lightweight baskets were made for European collectors in the 1860s and 1870s. They were often painted or stamped with designs or had the splints dyed with vegetal dyes on the outside. As production increased, so did demand, until everyone, tourist and local, had to have an Indian basket to sit on a shelf (figs. 36 and 37). The baskets quickly evolved into the fancy basket seen everywhere for sale in Wôbanakik antique shops. In time the production of the women eclipsed that of the men, who, toward the end of the basket maker era, were reduced to cutting trees and pounding the ash to make splints for the women.

Making the Victorian Fancy Basket

Two materials were necessary for making the fancy basket. *Mahlawks*, the ash tree, was felled and the bark removed. The bare log was placed on

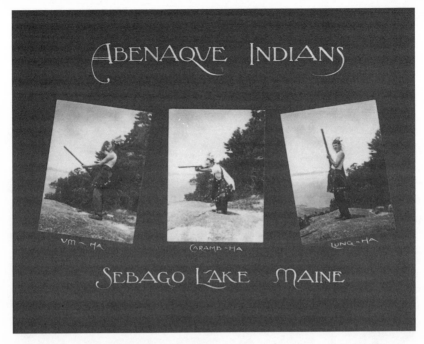

Fig. 35. "Abenaque Indians, Sebago Lake." *Wiseman collection.*

transverse logs to give it some height, then pounded with a tool called a *wi-gebdemahigan*. The pounding separated the wood into thin plates along the annual growth rings, which could be pulled from the log as *wigebiak* (ash splints). The rough splints could be used for coarse utility baskets or fish traps. However, fancy baskets required more processing. They first were run through a "gauge" to cut them into uniform widths, then shaved down with a steel blade to make a smooth surface. The finished splints could then be coiled and stored (fig. 36).

Another material necessary for some baskets was *walmogwkil* (sweet-grass), often found growing in moist sunny locations. Permission was asked of the patch of sweetgrass and a percentage taken home to dry. We soon learned that it would be good to start cultivating it in larger quantities, which we did. Unlike the widely available sweetgrass used as incense, basketry grass was left unbraided. In the 1930s a grass from the Orient began to supplant some sweetgrass.

By 1875, the Alnôbak made three varieties of fancy ash splint basket: the sweetgrass basket, the *cowwiss* basket, and the varying-splint basket. The sweetgrass basket was usually circular with a radial splint pattern on the lid

Fig. 36. Abenaki basket maker and baskets. *Wiseman collection.*

and base. The ash splints were tapered toward the middle, then soaked in water, often mixed with a commercial dye. The splints were laid in a radial pattern; then wet sweetgrass was woven in a spiral pattern around the radial splints. Thin ash splint "weavers" may alternate with the sweetgrass. When the desired diameter is reached, the splints are carefully bent upward to make the sides. Here the sweetgrass was often braided to make the weavers. Thin splints could sometimes be added for decorative affect. The

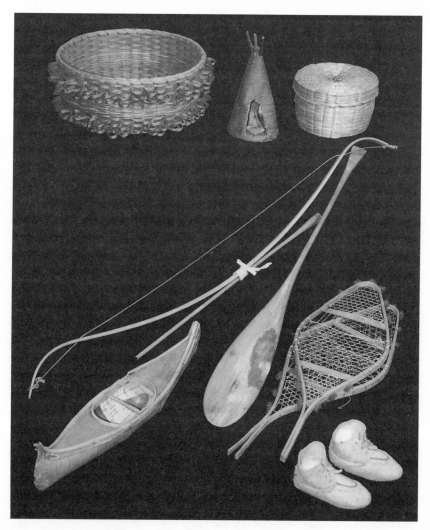

Fig. 37. Tourist trade articles. *Wôbanakik Heritage Center Collection, photograph by Andrew Lee.*

sides are ended out by attaching a circular splint rim and bending the uprights over it. Another rim ring of splint or grass was added and lashed to
the basket with a thin ash splint. The *cowwiss* basket was made in a similar
way, but sweetgrass was usually not present. Decoration was achieved by
adding an "over weave," or second layer of decoratively curled splints.
These weaves have special names, such as "standard diamond weave,"
"periwinkle," or "porcupine." *Cowwiss* baskets are often left undyed. The

last major variant of Victorian basket lacks sweetgrass or over weave. A direct descendant of earlier baskets, it uses the variation in width of the weavers to achieve a decorative effect. These underornamented baskets are the most eagerly collected by modern Euro-Americans since their simplicity goes well with their stereotypic notions of "Indian art."

These decorative baskets were made in large numbers by families in the Lake Champlain and Connecticut River Valleys. We have evidence of some basket makers in the Lake Memphremagog and White Mountains areas. Although Alnôbaiwi baskets were sold at Lake Winnepesaukkee, New Hampshire, and Poland Springs, Maine, we do not yet know whether they were made by us or by citizens of the Penobscot or more easterly nations.

In addition to baskets, the tourists wanted canoes, bow and arrow sets, and snowshoes but in miniature, as trinkets. Men began making these specifically for the tourist trade. At first, about six generations ago, the objects were full-sized, such as a four-foot bow, but by four generations ago they had become small, two-foot models of their former glory (fig. 37).

Men made six- to twelve-inch canoes and two- to six-inch snowshoes in addition to their full-size counterparts. The 1909 Champlain three-hundred-year celebration saw us selling miniature canoes and wigwams, even as the festival denounced us and extolled our old Haudenosaunee opponents. But it seemed that, in general, times were changing; it might be a good time to be recognized as an "Indian." In selling their baskets, miniatures, and other crafts, our craftspeople were probably the first Abenaki to learn that our Anglo clients had a desirable exotic image of Indians. Heretofore, Anglos had simply ignored or cleansed the Abenakis in their midst. We began to experiment with catering to this newly discovered image, which was of princesses and war-bonneted men, to lure customers to our sales booths, as well as affirm our First Nations identity. New clothing in line with the Plains prototype was developed, combining traditional beadwork with Plains-style headdresses. One family, on the shores of Bitawbagok, did exhibitions of basket making and sold their wares in full "Indian" costume (fig. 38). This process of discovery and adaptation cannot be stressed enough, for it laid the material and symbolic groundwork for the late twentieth century Abenaki renaissance. The tourists wanted to see us in costume, and we gave that to them, but our traditional clothes remained locked in our trunks.

Thus, when we sold to the Indian-loving tourists we presented an Indian face. We had, of course, always been somewhat mobile, and we now

Fig. 38. Pan-Indian "cut-cloth fringe" clothing, ca. 1900. *Wôbanakik Heritage Center Collection, photograph by Andrew Lee.*

gravitated toward tourist enclaves in our mountains, such as Mozeodebe wadso (where we sold porcupine-quill trinket boxes in what collectors now call a Huron style). We also frequented lakes such as Bitawbagok and Win- nipesauki. Here we could set up camp and present ourselves in costume to sell our wares during the tourist season. We could sell right out of our camp or travel by foot or canoe from camp to camp and sell that way. When the tourists left, so did we. The "tourist enclave" became merely an- other stop on our millennia-old seasonal round. At other times of the year, we sold to our neighbors. But we knew from long experience what the peo- ple of Vermont and New Hampshire thought of Indians. So when we hitched up our teams to peddle our wares to the Anglo-Americans of the Lamoille or Winooski valleys, we were merely "Gypsies," never Indians. Basket making went into eclipse in the late 1920s because of increasing ra- cial hatred of our neighbors and deteriorating economic conditions.[7]

Gypsies

Our extended "Gypsy" families and groups of families lived in upland en- vironments, often in tarpaper shack shantytowns. In addition to each family's semipermanent home was a wagon and horses to draw it. With this, Gypsies maintained a partly mobile lifestyle, each year following a geographic circuit where they peddled their wares. Families congregated in their villages during the winter, where they made crafts for sale during the traveling part of the year. Men also cut ice and went ice fishing on lakes and ponds. In the spring the men would go fishing, collect ash or birchbark for crafts, work in the lumber industry, or help their relatives with the maple syrup harvest. Summer saw Gypsy families disperse to their peddling routes. Then they would gather their families, wares, camping gear, and provisions and take to the road for periods ranging from one to many weeks. They traded baskets and other crafts for money, food, or hay for their horses. People still vaguely remember one of our Gypsy families from South Burlington that plied what is now Vermont Route 15 from Essex Junction to at least Hardwick, Vermont, selling baskets and other tourist items. I have recovered many things sold by them, including a set of four baskets purchased in the 1930s by an Anglo family in Johnson, Ver- mont, a "French Canadian"–style chair sold in the early 1900s to an inn in Jeffersonville, miniature snowshoes and more baskets sold in Underhill, and a final basket in Jericho, Vermont. The family was also supposed to have made gloves, moccasins, and jackets from hand-tanned moose, wolf, and deer hides, although none of these materials have come to light with a provable Gypsy association. Fall saw them return to their shantytowns, where the men could go hunting. Winter began the cycle again.[8]

Five generations ago everyone knew of the Gypsies; as they stopped at the edges of their villages and sold baskets, needlework, ax handles, and tools. They knew that the villagers thought that we came from "somewhere else." The Gypsies are the source of stories, common in almost every town during the nineteenth and early twentieth century, of Indians who come from somewhere, often thought to be Canada, set up camp on the town's outskirts to sell crafts, dispense herbal remedies, and tell stories to the courageous few who would listen, then suddenly "disappear" back to Canada. Other New Englanders did not perceive them as Indians but as a mysterious, vaguely dangerous people who made good crafts but were best left alone or encouraged to leave. The Gypsies knew that the villagers told their children to be wary of them, for they could see it in their eyes and hear it in their taunts. But however much New Englanders detested what they saw as the Gypsy lifestyle, they appreciated their workmanship. The requirements of a peripatetic lifestyle and providing tools and crafts to the Anglo Vermonters made Gypsies almost invisible historically. By four generations ago we had the amusing situation of being "Indians" to tourists, "Gypsies" to our Vermont customers, "French" to the people we lived with, and "Alnôba" among ourselves. No wonder historians had a hard time tracking us down.

Farm and Village Life with the English

During the Years of the Fox, other Alnôbak adapted to village and farm life, taking what we wanted from it and keeping what we needed from our past. We may have looked little different from our neighbors, but the heart was still of the forests and rivers (fig. 39).

Many families, including my own, blended in with the working "French" class in northern New England. We converted our knowledge of the Earth and its gifts to masonry; of wood, to carpentry and cabinetmaking; of canoe building, to boat building. We village-dwelling Alnôbak soon discovered that we could make things needed by our new neighbors as they adapted to Wôbanakik. They could be sold directly to the general store for credit or to neighbors from our porches. Basketry, a long-held tradition, was

Fig. 39. Abenaki hunter with .303-caliber Savage Model 1903 rifle. *Wiseman collection.*

in demand by farmers and townspeople, as were canoe paddles (fig. 39), tool handles, and snowshoes.

"I remember we had an Indian family here, and the woman made baskets and used to come around door to door to sell them. We didn't make a big thing out of it and neither did they" (Lucille Bell, Swanton, Vermont, ninety-eight years old, quoted in the *Burlington Free Press*, January 7, 1996).

Snowshoes

Ogenal, or snowshoes, were used by Native Americans wherever deep winter snow-drifts hindered effective winter travel. Skis, an alternative form of winter travel, were developed in the Old World. Each region of northern North America had its own distinctive snowshoes. For example, people in the far West made a thin, canoe-shaped snowshoe, while more southern people made oval snowshoes. We Alnôbak and our neighbors made a teardrop-haped snowshoe that is the prototype of the modern snowshoe used by winter backpackers and campers (fig. 40).

No one is sure how many years ago or where in North America this wonderful invention was developed, but early colonial records contain numerous references to Abenaki snowshoes. The snowshoe was often credited by Europeans for the ability of Abenaki warriors to strike English settlements at will during the winters of the long wars for the defense of the Abenaki homeland. Paintings from the eighteenth and early nineteenth centuries and photographs from the late nineteenth century illustrate woven snowshoes being used for hunting and travel by the Abenaki and their neighbors. In the Western Abenaki area, we have oral and artifact evidence of snowshoes being made on the eastern side of Lake Champlain, and in the White Mountains. Remember that the Eastern Abenaki, Passamaquoddy, and Micmac also made snowshoes. One Abenaki maker lived near the modern Euro-American village of Swanton, Vermont. A pair of adult snowshoes, miniature snowshoes, and a snowshoe mold (fig. 40) from Swanton date quite late, from the early to mid-twentieth century. The Obomsawin family of Thompson's Point, Vermont, is remembered to this day to have made many snowshoes for sale. We have recovered one pair of children's snowshoes from this area that the former owner identified as being Abenaki-made; perhaps it hails from this family. Lastly, a very old, decrepit pair of snowshoes, beautifully made in the Abenaki style, was stated by the seller to have been made "by Indians near Conway, New Hampshire, who made lots of snowshoes before the First World War." There are no records of current production of snowshoes by Western Abenaki here or in Canada. During the late nineteenth and early twentieth centuries the Abenaki made thousands of miniature snowshoes of split cedar and heavy yellow or tan thread for sale to tourists. These ranged from tiny three-inch models (fig. 37) to very detailed one-foot examples. General manufacturer of these ceased only recently, and there may still be a few being made.

The Abenaki snowshoe maker had to procure clear (knot-free) ash wood. The wood could be easily bent to make the snowshoe frame while green, but if the wood dried, it had to be steamed in a special steam box. The wood was split to the approximate dimensions, often leaving distinctive marks on the frame, then planed or shaved down with a drawknife to

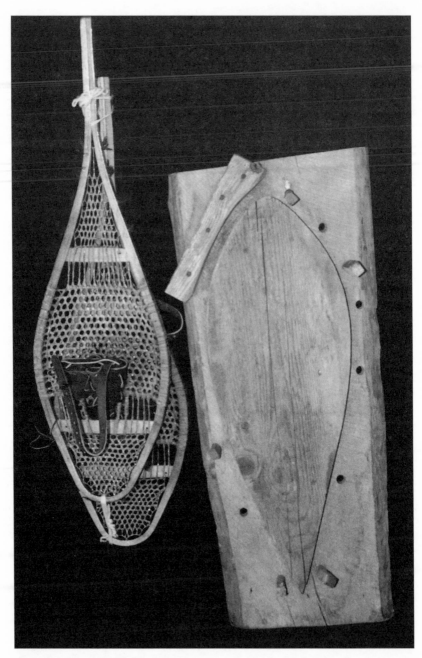

Fig. 40. Recent Abenaki snowshoes and snowshoe mold. *Wôbanakik Heritage Center Collection, photograph by Andrew Lee.*

the desired thickness. The wood was thinned a bit in the center to facilitate bending. Holes for the lacing were marked and drilled, and mortises for the two crossbars were then marked and cut. The flexible wood was then placed on the frame mold. Every snowshoe maker had a series of these molds to make the various sizes required by his customers. The mold was fitted with the splint across the upper left side, with the central thin section just above the "keeper." The splint was carefully bent with the hands, and retaining pins were placed to hold the splint in shape. By working carefully down the mold, the splint was forced into shape. The tails of the splint were aligned and clamped together. The frame was then allowed to dry into shape for two weeks. The crossbars were whittled out of wood three-sixteenths of an inch thick. After the frame dried into shape, it was removed from the mold and spread apart to allow the crossbars to be inserted into the mortises. Two or three holes were drilled through the tail; nails were inserted in the holes and clenched. After a light sanding and trimming, the frame was ready for the hexagonal-weave filling.

Next, a section of rawhide was wet, and a spiral cut made with shears produced a long continuous thong. Thongs were cut in two thicknesses for the finest snowshoes; the thicker for the central weight-bearing section between the crossbars and a finer thong for the toe and tail sections. For children's or less expensive snowshoes, the thong was the same size throughout. First, the wet thong was run around the outside of the frame, threaded through the frame holes with tufts of red hair or yarn attached to the outside, then tied and clipped. Then, with a special bipointed wood or ivory needle, the snowshoe lattice was woven in moist rawhide. This was a time-consuming process and one that is difficult to replicate. When the rawhide was dry, it tightened up and became taut. Then the snowshoe was varnished. The boot harness, sold separately, varied from simple leather tie-ons to elaborate stirrups more appropriate for horse tack. Families in the Missisquoi continued to make snowshoes until three generations ago, and there are people alive who remember their parents making them.[9]

Making these necessary goods provided a substantial income for many families, who continued to use time-honored traditions of materials procurement and fabrication. Materials could be collected in the spring or other appropriate times and dried and stored until the item could be manufactured. Winter continued to be a good time to make many articles. Many of these were made by men, such as the utility baskets and canoe paddles. I remember stories of canoes and canoe-like boats being made by several Alnôbak craftsmen at Dawkwahoganizek (Swanton, Vermont) four generations ago. They remained on the waters even when I was a teenager. My family continued to make a distinctive lightweight cedar canoe paddle until 1978.

Although we became a part of the new Anglo economic and social world, our reliance on the land was undiminished. We obtained more modern and efficient tools from the general store, but hunting and fishing remained key to our existence. As the bow and arrow gave way to the muzzle loader in the Years of the Beaver, the muzzleloader gave way to the breech-loading single-shot and repeating rifle (fig. 39). The hand line and net was superseded five generations ago by the fishing rod and hand-cranked reel. Our hunting and fishing expertise also began being sought by our New English neighbors. Our men became guides and camp cooks for the first sportsmen who ventured into Wôbanakik seven generations ago, a role they maintained throughout the Years of the Fox.

My relatives from Dawkskodacek often worked the hunting camps in northern Vermont four generations ago (fig. 32). Stories from the Indian past and lessons about how to navigate on the river and lake were repeated over flickering campfires. Old photographs taken of sporting expeditions in Wôbanakik's waters and mountains often show Abenaki men looking on as the *odowino* ("white hunter") shows his trophy fish or bear. As time went on, sportsmen were supplemented by visitors who came merely to rest or pursue recreational activities such as boating. The old seasonal cycles were unbroken; fall was the time for deer camp whether as guide or hunter. If the tarpaper shack and Winchester rifle replaced the wigwam and bow, the time and place of deer camp and the respect for the game was unchanged. Indeed, the insanity attending the fur trade had abated during the Years of the Fox, and we once again had the political and economic freedom to express our respect for the land and conservation of its bounty. But Koluscap did not return. Spring was the time for fishing, and Wazowategok and her river-sisters continued to feel the presence of the village-dwelling Abenaki. Midsummer got a new name, Temashikos, the hay making moon (which was inserted into the lunar calendar every three years), as my great grand-parents helped their Anglo and French neighbors with the harvest.

Although our family band sovereignty persisted undiminished, the increasing respect we garnered for our craft arts and guiding abilities encouraged us to reveal more complex political systems.

"I remember when I was a kid; we had a (Indian) Chief in town" (Ben Gravel, Swanton, June, 1968).

According to the St. Francis family, this was probably Nazaire St. Francis, who was, at the time of Gravel's youth, respected by the Swanton Abenakis as an able leader and chief. His home was a center of meetings and discussions within the Abenaki community, maintaining an important continuity. This political/cultural leadership had always existed at Missisquoi, but it seemed OK in the first decades of the twentieth century to let others see it. But things were afoot that would drive our arts and culture underground once again.

The End of the World — II: The Genocide Years

Background

Times were changing; in the 1920s the Anglo Vermonters had come to believe that their northern New England was the quintessential America, with people as white as their houses and picket fences. I believe that four Euro-American social processes merged during this time to bring yet another round of genocide to the Abenaki. The first was the "domestic hygiene movement" which began in post–Civil War America; it stressed cleanliness and organization in the household. By now interior plumbing was rapidly expanding, the kitchen was evolving into our modern form, and farm animals were no longer allowed inside. Medical advances also pointed the way to the necessity for personal hygiene as a way of thwarting disease.

A second late-nineteenth-century social process was put into motion by shifting patterns of immigration into the United States. More settlers from abroad were arriving each year from the eastern and southern Mediterranean. To the older Anglo/Dutch/German immigrants, this seemed somehow menacing to their way of life. A strategy pursued by the "New English" was to psychologically distance themselves by elitist genealogical organizations such as the Daughters of the American Revolution or social associations such as the Society for the Preservation of New England Antiquities. People romanticized the good old days and began collecting American antiques, something these immigrants would (hopefully) never have. Another response was to put actual space between them and the new people. This ranged from a few miles—a flight from Boston to Cambridge—to more remote genteel towns, such as Concord. Yet this was not enough; the New English had to rub shoulders with America's new adoptive citizens in the workplace and market. A third social peculiarity combined the vague unease of the nineteenth century with the horrors of international conflict, as in World War I. Xenophobia, a fear of foreigners, rose to its zenith in the post–World War I era and was expressed in many ways, from isolationism to immigration controls to the spread of the Ku Klux Klan. The rail lines and the new "touring" automobile offered the prospect of evading the increasingly disliked racial and ethnic diversity of southern New England. Perhaps correlated to this "new racism" was the popularity of the eugenics movement, the fourth process. Developed in Europe in the mid-nineteenth century, eugenics applied the concepts of scientific plant and animal breeding to humans. Combined with Victorian ideas of racial and ethnic superiority and inferiority, eugenics became another prospect for protecting the northwestern Europeans in New England from the infusion of undesirable ethnic traits into their midst.[10]

Vermont Hope

People had long known about Vermont (and portions of adjacent New Hampshire and northwestern Maine) as sportsmen's paradises (guided by Abenakis) or as a place for a "cure" in an Abenaki medicine spring. Now increasingly, they looked to Vermont as the last "great white hope" of New England. This area seemed to be a New England without the increasing tide of ethnic "others" that seemed to be plaguing the coastal urban zones. Perhaps in response to this southern New England phenomenon, the state of Vermont created the Commission on Country Life in the 1920s to study, fine-tune, and perpetuate this image. Although Vermonters on a community level knew of the persistence of the Abenaki people in their different manifestations, they had to be denied on an official or academic level. As Vermont (and to a lesser extent, New Hampshire) explicitly codified its lily-white image, people who did not fit the image were at first written out of their geography. The image sold to tourists became beloved by residents. Academics and writers such as Dorothy Canfield Fisher, who defined the lily-white penultimate image of Vermont, portrayed it as a "no-man's land without permanent Indian residents." Even if there were any Indians in the past, there certainly weren't any left. But as scholars studied the social geography of the state to reinforce their emerging stereotype, they unfortunately began to reveal the hidden ethnic diversity that was under the surface of the lily-white small towns.

The French Canadians (all of whom were supposed to have "moved down" in the nineteenth century—another historical essay in racism),

River Rats, Gypsies, and Pirates didn't always look or act like "real" Vermonters. First, they were often Roman Catholic, contradicting the religious cleansing of the seventeenth and eighteenth centuries, which was one goal of New England's wars against France and the Indians. Although rarely seen on village greens, the Catholic Church was in each town. The Black Robes of generations past had laid a solid religious foundation in northern New England. The church's parishioners often came from the Back Bay or French Hill, areas elite Vermonters rarely frequented.[11]

In addition to religious propensities, many of the Abenaki people's darker eyes, skin, and hair and nuances of behavior descending from their Amerindian ancestry set them apart from their more stylish neighbors. Persistent Abenaki political and cultural sovereignty, which was manifested in communalism, social and genetic isolation, subsistence hunting and fishing, disregard for increasingly restrictive new laws and social programs, and the persistence of a seasonally mobile lifestyle, reinforced this ethnic distinction in the scholars' research. Fashionable social beliefs, such as "settled life is superior; nomadism is primitive" and everyone must have indoor plumbing and separate bedrooms combined with more insidious biological ideals concerning racial purity to make these revealed people seem an anomaly. "Overall, what could be a purer place than Vermont?" said the academic/social elite. All they have to do is get rid of these few "rough" families that cloud the picture.

The Vermont Eugenics Survey

Led by Henry Perkins of the University of Vermont, the Eugenics Survey in the mid-1920s attempted to find and isolate (with the help of town clerks, police departments, and the new social service departments and agencies) those village- and farm-dwelling families that had bad (i.e., non-White Vermonter) genetic traits.[12] Soon the lens of genocide was trained on the Gypsies, Pirates, and River Rats, as well as other ethnic groups. Employing the latest genealogical research and statistical record keeping techniques, the survey added new technologies to the list of ancient genocidal procedures used by New English authorities against the Abenakis. In addition, they provided social and police organizations with lists of families to "watch." Unfortunately, the social gulf between elite Anglo culture and the village-dwelling River Rats and Pirates was not so wide that they could entirely escape notice. Major Abenaki families at Missisquoi were especially at risk. The more "hidden" families and the Gypsies

Fig. 41. Copy of a photograph of Henry Perkins. *Oil on board, Laura Pinter; Wôbanakik Heritage Center Collection, photograph by Andrew Lee.*

partially escaped unheeded—for a while. But then began ethnic conflict incidents as Gypsies and Pirates had their children taken from them. The theft of children and the hatred emanating from the burning cross and Ku Klux Klan rallies are still recalled by Abenaki and French Canadian elders in Barre, Vermont. Any family who still had thoughts about standing forth as Abenaki, due to the tourists' continued interest in our arts and culture, quickly retired to obscurity as the tide of intolerance rose. We continually needed to be on our guard with the police, the tax man, and the school board, the eyes and ears of the survey.

With the passage of An Act for Human Betterment by Voluntary Sterilization (Senate bill 31) in 1931, racism, harassment, and even sterilization came to the Abenaki as it was coming to the Jews of Europe. I know families today, from Swanton to Barre, whose elders were singled out and harassed by the Eugenics Survey because they were perceived as "different." It was reported that over two hundred people were sterilized during this campaign. It is my opinion that the "new racism" of Vermont's elite eventually permeated Abenaki society, leading to shame at being different or fear that we or our children would be "discovered" by the state of Vermont and have evil things done to them. This mixture of shame and anxiety that visited the Alnôbak caused families to repudiate their Native American ancestry and "pass" into other, less despised segments of society. The safest ethnic refuge during the 1930s was the French Canadian community, the descendants of our ancient allies, since they shared our religion, economic status, and other social and geographic traits.

Genocide Recedes

Eventually, the genocidal fever died down somewhat as we prepared for war with an empire that was taking these ideas, tentatively tested in Wôbanakik by its university faculty and its legislature, a few steps farther. But the University of Vermont taught eugenics into the 1950s. As the tactical "eugenic" weapon declined, state and federal social services agencies remained aghast at our "nonmarrying, illiterate, nomadic," "environmentally destructive" lifestyle. The Abenakis' political and cultural sovereignty was proving remarkably resistant. Once again agenda of ethnic cleansing shifted, as it continued to erode Abenaki cultural and political sovereignty through the mid-twentieth century. The new tools were not the surgical scalpel and the fear it engendered but improved record keeping, compulsory schooling, and increasing harassment by environmental, land tenure, and zoning regulations. The legacy of the 1920s Country Life Commission, scientists at The University of Vermont and lawmakers at Montpelier, lives on.

I remember certain families, even in Swanton, that were perceived as "different"; they were tolerated but always marginal. Each town in Wôbanakik had its poor "French" section, where the old hunting, gardening, and social and food-sharing networks persisted more or less invisibly until the coming of the Years of the Bear. But the years after the war were very quiet years. We Alnôbak had by now cunningly hidden our lore and culture so successfully that our neighbors didn't know who we were, and we thought it best that they remain ignorant. As pointed out above, the River Rats and some isolated rural families overtly retained the old ways more than we village dwellers did. But in the villages, Abenakis also kept the old fires burning. Homer St. Francis recalled that meetings of Abenaki people occurred regularly at his childhood home in the 1950s. Issues of sovereignty had not disappeared but were safely underground. April Rushlow recalled that her grandfather, Nazaire St. Francis, was extremely interested in trans-border crossing rights for Native Americans at the time, years before it became an issue with other First Nations.

8

The Darkness Ends:
The Years of the Bear

(Christian Years 1970 to 1994)

Introduction

Although it was always unsafe, we constantly developed new strategies and tactics to be recognized as a distinct group of indigenous people. This was a long and arduous trail, fraught with danger. The trailhead to the modern Abenaki Renaissance needed to be traversed two ways. The first was the road of education, based upon a carefully reasoned and detailed explanation of our history and culture. At the time, Vermont was believed to be "empty" of Native people, and the Abenakis, living in Canada, were evil. The following is an excerpt from *Vermont Our Own State*, a 1960s textbook read by Vermont's young: "The Indians who gave the most trouble to the English. . . . were the St. Francis Indians. They had been very cold blooded and cruel. . . . The English decided to do something about the St. Francis Indians . . . Rogers and his men attacked the village and killed most of the tribe. The danger from the St. Francis Indians was gone forever" (Hope Kellerup, quoted in Moody, 1987).

The problem was that due to our need to hide during the Years of the Fox, this information was then (in the Christian years of the 1960s) too dispersed to be useful. This was compounded by the low economic status of the Alnôbak which precluded, at that time, any literate, Abenaki-generated rebuttal to the image of the cold-blooded St. Francis Indians and drunken Frenchmen asking for a government handout. This is a theme that manifested itself time and again: accommodation for the present and hoped-for sovereignty through long-term educational goals. The second path was the road of the warrior, a more forthright approach. This path made the assumption of sovereignty primal, and all else followed from that premise. Civil disobedience, confrontational rhetoric, and an unwavering commitment to not letting the state of Vermont "get away with" anything were cornerstones of our second approach. These two themes came to be encapsulated in the leadership of two major Missisquoi family bands. The latter part of the Years of the Bear are the fruits of these twin trajectories: the results of a bewildering explosion of knowledge of the Abenaki and the concomitant political factionalism.[1]

The Road to Recognition: 1965–1976

First Beginnings

The civil rights movement of the 1960s offered glimmerings of hope to the Alnôbak family bands meeting around their kitchen tables, hope that the most recent bout of attempted ethnic cleansing had ended. The emerging "Red Power" movement and its successes and failures convinced some of us that perhaps we could openly reconvene our political leadership. Nineteen seventy-two saw the beginnings of the modern Abenaki struggle for recognition and respect. (Fig. 42.)

For years, Abenaki leaders such as Wayne Hoag, Kent Ouimette, Richard Phillips, Harold and Homer St. Francis, and Robert Wells had been meeting around kitchen tables in Swanton and Highgate, Vermont, discussing the memories of their elders and the Red Power Movement. Old connections with Akwesasne and Odanak, languishing since the eugenics years, were revitalized, and their news seemed good, that the time might be right for the Abenaki people to come out of the closet *as a group*, not just as individuals or family bands. However, not all leaders agreed to this course of action. Chief April Rushlow remembered that Leonard Lampman, who later became an important chief of the nation, was not interested in participating at the beginning. Homer St. Francis remembered the animated discussions around his and other kitchen tables in the Back Bay of Swanton. There was argument about how to proceed, because our community was traditionally a system of semiautonomous family bands, an ancient and enduring form of government. However, some community members, as well as First Nations visitors more knowledgeable about

Fig. 42. Artifacts of the early Missisquoi Abenaki Renaissance. *Wôbanakik Heritage Center Collection, photograph by Andrew Lee.*

White bureaucracies, suggested setting up a government that would be recognizable by White people. During the eugenics years the U.S. government had passed the Indian Reorganization Act, a public law that forced diverse tribal governments into a format that the United States could properly deal with and control. Although this tribal pattern was alien to our ancestral family band sovereignty, it was decided to adopt that format as the legitimate political organ of the Abenaki community. This decision has proved to be a great strength and great weakness of the political manifestation of the Abenaki Renaissance.

The St. Francis–Sokoki Band

The St. Francis–Sokoki Band of the Abenaki Nation was the tribal name chosen for the Swanton Abenakis. St. Francis denoted Odanak, the northernmost village of the Western Abenakis, represented in Swanton, Vermont, and Sokoki (central Connecticut River area) the southernmost. Choosing a name was the easiest of the issues facing the political reawakening. The Indian Reorganization Act required an executive branch or chief. How was the chief to administer? How was he to take and hold office? What would the legislative and judicial branches look like? These and many other issues needed to be hammered out. It was decided that there would be a chief, elected by popular vote of the citizens of the St. Francis–Sokoki Band, advised by a tribal council also elected by popular vote. The judicial branch would eventually be vested in a single person, the tribal judge. Slowly the tribe organized, appointing Wayne Hoag as its first chief. So the Abenaki Nation once again became visible on the land-scape of northeastern North America.

The Anglo community was astonished, indignant, and perhaps even a little frightened by the apparently "new" ethnic community forming in its midst. My favorite quote of the early seventies was from a fishing friend of my father's (and a member of the Vermont Federation of Sportsman's Clubs): "I thought we fought the French and Indian War to get rid of this mess." On April 19, 1974, the band held its first "Fish-In," a form of civil disobedience (fishing without a state-issued license) to call attention to past injustice and force Vermont to legally confront the Abenakis. The government and news media lashed back, ridiculing the Abenaki commu-nity and its leadership. In the forefront of the media attack were the *St. Al-bans Messenger* and the *Burlington Free Press*. A perusal of old issues from the 1972–1976 period reveals articles, opinion statements, editorials, and letters to the editor with a consistent anti-Indian slant: "Why of course the Vermont Abenaki Tribe deserves unlimited hunting and fishing rights. But why not give it to them the way they had it, i.e. only with handmade birch and gut bows and flint arrows" (John Outwater, letter to *Burlington Free Press*, December 23, 1976).

One estimate reported to me by Jeff Benay, the chair of the Governor's Commission on Native American Affairs, was that 90 percent of the news coverage was negative. The consensus of the Anglo community was that we were a "bunch of crazies." Officially, the state of Vermont ignored the Abenaki community, but there was an undercurrent of suspicion that was most obvious in its law enforcement branches.

Academia Discovers the Abenaki

Euro-American historians and archaeologists, who had largely ignored us until this time, saw the stirring of the Bear and came to us. Once one of our bands was "visible" politically; perhaps there was new academic turf to study. The "new Abenaki" were seen as an endangered ethnic community—something that academics found hard to ignore. In 1973, archaeologists from the University of Vermont and other institutions were called in when excavation revealed an Abenaki graveyard. Eventu-ally, archaeologists removed large numbers of artifacts from eighty-five of our dead from the great cemetery along the Wazowategok, known to them as the "Boucher site." For the first time that anyone in the Abenaki community remembers, scholars sought us out for our opinion and remembrances. Gordon Day, in his researches on the Odanak Abenakis, pursued library research on Missisquoi and other ancient Vermont communities to help explain his Canadian research subjects. Lawyers came to us too, scenting court settlements. All of a sudden, Alnôba families faced not only hostile reporters but sympathetic scholars with microphone or pen in hand. We did not know what to do, and we began giving up our story and our material history, so that it could be used for the scholars' professional advancement. Hopefully, some of this knowledge would "trickle down" to the media and the Vermont government and be a benefit to our struggles.

KOLUSCAP AND THE RED-FACED ANTHROPOLOGIST

Koluscap was sitting on a rock by the water smoking his big pipe and making arrowheads when he heard stumbling and heavy breathing. Soon a red-faced Bastaniak anthropologist came into view, burdened by papers, cameras, and tape recorders. "Koluscap," panted the anthropologist, "I have read so many things about you in the published stories of the Abenaki." "I have been searching for the road to find you for months," he said, sitting down heavily on a rock before Koluscap. Koluscap smiled and asked what the red-faced man wanted. "I know that if a person finds you, you will grant him wishes, and I want to know all about you, how—you were made, all the wonderful things you did, and why you left the Abenaki and await here" came the breathless reply. Koluscap said "This is true, Red-Face. You may hear my story, but what do you want to do with this knowledge?" The anthropologist said, "I want everyone to know about the Abenaki and their gods so that the government will take them seriously and not harass them." Koluscap said, "Proceed, Red-Face, and I will tell you all." As he interviewed Koluscap, he absently noticed that every time he took a picture there was always molsem, the wolf, in the background; every time he wrote notes in his book, there was mesezo (eagle) flying overhead; and when he recorded Koluscap's voice, there was awan, the breeze on the water. The anthropologist shared Koluscap's hospitality for quite a while, until his notebooks were bulging and his audiotapes and film were spent. Then he said good-bye and left Koluscap by his pile of arrowheads smoking his pipe.

Months later, the anthropologist was on television promoting his new book, Koluscap: The Secret Life of a God. *He had carefully edited, organized, and rewritten his notes, tapes, and photographs and sent them to a publisher who had accepted them almost without question, for "Indian books" were hot items among the Europeans who were disenchanted with their own spiritual path. The publisher had already sent him a hefty advance, which he used to buy a new luxury sedan. The publisher wrapped the project in secrecy and determined that it was best to release the book on the day the anthropologist would be on national television. The anthropologist came on stage, his mind filled with the prospect of the endowed chair of anthropology promised by his university chancellor, the worship in the eyes of his female graduate students, and the hefty royalties of his best-selling book. Things did not go well though, for every time he opened his new book, all that could be seen was the white and yellow markings of bird feces; every time he showed a picture of Koluscap, it was so smeared with wolf dung he couldn't make out what was being photographed; and every time he played his recordings to all you could hear was the sound of the wind and waves. The red-faced anthropologist was once again true to his name.*[2]

Medawas, 1995

By 1974 the fine-tuning of the political process allowed the Abenaki to vote in their first constitution, another requirement of the Indian Reorganization Act. The community was well on its way to much needed political stability in the face of continued media and governmental hostility. In that year there was a slight shift in government policy toward the St. Francis–Sokoki Band. The older "empty Vermont" heralded by the historians was being refuted by archaeological work in Vermont and the studies of anthropologists in Canada. The ancient and historical Abenakis could no longer be portrayed as nonexistent. The word began "getting out" to the public. A measure of this "Abenaki presence" was that the the band was able to collect 1,400 signatures on a 1975 hunting and fishing petition to the Vermont Fish and Game Commission. The new "fall-back" position of the state was to subtly challenge the St. Francis–Sokoki Band on all levels, to demand that they prove that they were the direct descendants of archaeologically and historically known Abenakis. The media followed suit, also shifting to exploring any possible disconnection of the band from their forebears. The situation deteriorated. In an attempt to get at the truth, then-governor Thomas Salmon commissioned Jane Baker to independently investigate the claims of the St. Francis–Sokokis. Her research, although containing a few inaccuracies and implicit raciological value judgments, supported the St. Francis–Sokoki claim that they were the descendants of the historic Abenakis. On the other hand, anthropologist Gordon Day disagreed with the report, saying that from his Canadian perspective only ten families at Missisquoi were of proven descent. On Thanksgiving Day 1976 (this always seems to be the "Indian Day"!), Salmon issued an executive order giving state recognition to the St. Francis–Sokoki Band.

But developments presaging later controversy occurred. Rivalry and the pressures of rebuilding a nation fractionated the original "around the coffee table" leadership. Kent Ouimette split off to form a Missisquoi Band, Wayne Hoag formed the Green Mountain Band, and Richard Phillips formed the Eastern Woodland Band, short-lived political groups that mostly rejoined the St. Francis–Sokoki Band. In 1977 a tribal vote was symptomatic of these times: there had to be two votes for chief. These developments had unintended positive effects, including the creation of a larger potential membership base and forcing the Vermont state government to face several political entities, not just one.

The Rise of Missisquoi 1976–1992

The Loss of Recognition

The executive order extending recognition to the St. Francis–Sokoki Band created a firestorm of protest by Vermont constituencies who believed that they had something to lose to the newly recognized Abenakis. Once again, the *Free Press* archive is a mine of information on resentment and stereotyping by Vermont's Anglo population. Doomsayers from powerful sportsmen's organizations implied that the St. Francis–Sokoki Band would take over hunting and fishing, causing widespread game animal and fish extinction. Others said that land claims would kick everyone out of Vermont. State recognition, for all its evil backlash, had positive benefits. In 1976, Abenaki Self Help Association, Inc. (ASHAI) opened, as a way of channeling federal and state moneys to the needy in the now-recognized Abenaki community (as well as their French and Anglo neighbors). ASHAI began setting up social, economic, educational, and cultural programs for Vermont's most disadvantaged ethnic community.

Unfortunately, the political recognition given by Governor Salmon was an executive order, an instrument that could be revoked by any successor. The next Vermont governor, Richard Snelling, had a more conservative political bent and constituency. The ideological gulf that separated the new governor from the St Francis–Sokoki Band was summed up in this sarcastic statement disseminated to New Englanders in *Yankee Magazine*: "When they told me the land was given to them by God, I told them what I couldn't find was where God registered the deed—" (Gov. Richard Snelling, 1977, quoted in *Yankee Magazine*, 1991).

In January, after taking office, Governor Snelling promptly revoked state recognition and instituted a series of little understood executive and judicial actions to protect the state from future legal action by the St. Francis–Sokoki Band. While Snelling's actions mollified hunters and fishermen who had feared that their fishing rights would be hurt by recognition, it militarized the Abenakis. The band decided to pursue legal action in the courts. Under Chief Homer St. Francis, we chose nonviolent civil disobedience as a forensic tool to force the state to recognize us. In 1979 the band held its next Missisquoi River Fish-In. This civil protest had been used successfully by tribes in Washington state to prove their aboriginal rights to hunting and fishing. In the Missisquoi River Fish-In, Abenaki citizens fished without valid licenses below Swanton Falls, their ancient fish-harvesting place. One interesting implication of this well-publicized activity was that the 1980 census showed almost one thousand people self-identifying as Native in Vermont. The Abenaki were coming out of hiding!

A Change in Leadership

Homer St. Francis, the contentious chief of the nation, left in 1980 due to an arrest conviction unconnected to tribal activities. "I can do more on the sidelines. . . . There's more than one way to skin a cat" (Homer St. Francis, April 16, 1980; quoted in the *Burlington Free Press*).

The interim chief appointed by the tribal council was not from the original "kitchen table leadership" but from the Lampmans, a major family band in the Swanton area that had adopted a "wait and see" attitude. This expanded the Abenakis' presence in Swanton. Leonard "Blackie" Lampman, who was elected chief in the next election, is remembered as being more conciliatory to the Vermont and federal governments, attempting to work within their parameters rather than strongly asserting sovereign rights. His approach yielded different but much needed social and educational initiatives. Under his administration the band persuaded schools in north-western Vermont to set up Abenaki awareness programs. At that time, young Abenakis had suffered high schoolyard abuse and high school drop-out rates. At the time (1980) the dropout rate for Abenaki youth was 70 per-cent, and less than 5 percent went on to college. These programs began the long painful process of getting the Vermont educational system to real-ize that they had a racial/ethnic problem in their midst. The Abenaki Youth Group provided extracurricular instruction and encouragement in Abenaki arts and culture for our young.

As part of this, the Lampman administration obtained the first federal as-sistance grants for children and the elderly. In 1981 ASHAI became Vermont's first nonprofit organization to build a Section 8 Low Income Housing project. Called Abenaki Acres, it provides homes for low-income people of all ethnic groups. ASHAI was so active and well respected that in 1982 the federal commissioner of the Agency for Native Americans (ANA) commended ASHAI as one of the twelve best Indian social services agencies in the United States. But probably the most important long-term initiative during his administration was the decision by the Abenaki leadership to pur-sue state and federal recognition. In an apparent change of heart, Governor Snelling did issue a limited "Proclamation of June 22, 1983" recognizing the St. Francis–Sokoki Band as the legitimate representatives of Vermont Aben-akis. I suspect that this may have been in response to the new Abenaki bands "spun off" in the late 1970s. The governor pointed out that the proclamation was for the purpose of gaining federal aid for the Abenakis and did not com-promise the state's sovereignty. Snelling also promised aid to the band in seeking federal recognition. This is a lengthy, detailed petitioning process by which the applicant tribe basically has to prove the following things:

1. That the modern applicants are the descendants of a tribe known to have inhabited the area from what anthropologists have called the Con-tact Period.
2. The applicants can show a persistence of culture from that time period.
3. The applicants can show unbroken political authority.
4. The applicants have been seen as a distinct population by their Euro-American neighbors.[3]

Sympathetic Anglo researchers had shown, in the 1970s, that the Abe-naki culture had existed in Vermont during the crucial Contact Period and indeed had persisted much later. The genealogical evidence was, at least for a few Swanton families, complete enough for the petition. However, the other links were unknown or unprovable in the early 1980s. Researchers began combing old state and federal records, newspaper archives, and other new sources for data on the critical nineteenth and twentieth centuries. After years of feverish research, the Abenaki were ready to begin the petition for recognition.

In 1982, the recently created Indian Education Office published *Finding One's Way* (see Appendix 3) and began to promote Abenaki awareness by having community members combat stereotypes and advance the cause of diversity. From this point on, the organization slowly grew and became more effective.

The Turning Point of 1987

After six years of leadership, Blackie Lampman passed away in 1986. The tribal council, effectively keeping the power in the Lampman family, appointed Blackie's son Lester interim chief. This perhaps had the effect of creating a certain amount of dissension between the two major family bands. According to people who remember these times, as well as numerous (mostly negative) newspaper articles, it seemed that the Lampman family and its supporters wished to keep Lester Lampman in power. It also seemed that former chief Homer St. Francis, who had been defeated in previous elections by Blackie Lampman, wished to be chief so as to pursue his more militant goals. The tribal elections of November 1986 were contentious, with emotions high in both the Lampman and St. Francis factions. It was also one of the biggest elections, with both sides doing lots of politicking and bringing voters to the polls. In order to assure the fairness of the election, a tribal election committee was formed, with three from each "side" and Ted Greenia, an "outsider" as head. The vote was confusing. April Rushlow, a member of that committee, remembers the hours of counting and recounting and the problem with ballots that were incorrectly filled out. After the votes were tallied, St. Francis won by the slim margin of three votes. Former interim chief Lester Lampman and community member Joan St. Pierre attempted to have the results of the election voided, citing fraud, in that the incorrectly filled out ballots were not counted. St. Francis denied the recount, and the ballot box was sealed by the committee and stored in the tribal safe.

When that attempt failed, Lampman and his supporters apparently made a strategic decision to appeal to the state of Vermont, which had been relatively friendly to Lampman's father's administration. According to Abenaki citizens, newspaper articles, and *Yankee Magazine*, he persuaded the state to have the funds for ASHAI frozen, potentially undoing all of the community service aid that the Abenaki community was receiving. One faction took their grievances to the hostile Anglo press, a foreboding of future tactics. At this point, the built-in conflict between the ancient family-band form of government and the new tribal form required by White government structures became painfully obvious and set the stage for anguish in the Abenaki community. Tribal politics had become a power struggle between two family bands that spilled over into the courts, and social programs suffered. The old processes of condolence, consolation, and consensus in chief-making were forgotten in the heat of the moment. Also, the new, government-required form of electoral succession was probably inappropriate for the political fabric of mid-1980s Missisquoi.

The St. Francis family perceived that this was a direct attack on their right to the chieftainship, using their oppressor, the Vermont state government. In response, St. Francis and his backers used their power from within rather than seeking outside aid, making a strategic decision that would have lasting effects on the development of the Abenaki Nation. They nurtured a rewrite of the tribal constitution to increase the chief's executive power. It also made St. Francis chief for life, blocking the capacity of the electoral process for resolving interfamily political conflict. He also quickly moved to have Lester Lampman and his supporters voted out from positions of power in tribal government.[4]

The response of the state and media to these political actions was to ridicule the openly hostile Homer St. Francis; and the relations between the St. Francis–Sokoki Band and the Anglo community deteriorated again. The attorney general's office and the state and local police stepped up their surveillance, beginning a low-level harassment of Abenaki citizens. In response, the always fiery Homer St. Francis launched a counteroffensive of civil disobedience. Spring 1988 saw another Missisquoi River Fish-In followed by arrests that would have far-reaching implications. However, the St. Francis administration was not all fire and guns. I remember that plans were made for a community center to provide a neutral location where Abenaki citizens of all ages could meet. Longer-range dreams for a tribal museum and health center began to be discussed. December 12, 1989, saw the first meeting of a committee to discuss a cultural center in Swanton. It was attended by Abenakis, museum professionals, and politicians. An old village site on the Monument Road in Highgate was purchased by the State Division of Historic Preservation. In June 1989, Johnson State College, in conjunction with the Abenaki community, began a summer archaeological survey field school on the Monument Road. These dreams and endeavors laid a solid foundation for what has come to pass.

Sovereignty Moves to the Fore

A major focus of the St. Francis–Sokoki Band during the late 1980s was to prepare for the Fish-In trial. They argued that they were free to fish under the concept of aboriginal right, that any indigenous group has claims to the land and its resources unless they have been explicitly "extinguished" by legal means such as treaties or obvious techniques such as extermination. Anglo researchers for the Abenaki side knew there were no documents that explicitly transferred legal title to Vermont or anyone else from the Swanton Abenakis, except for a late-eighteenth-century lease that had expired years ago. They were confident of the outcome. The trial went on in the summer of 1989. The state of Vermont claimed that it had the rights to the land under the doctrine of transfer of sovereignty between European colonial powers. This argument has been long overturned in constitutional and international law. In August 1989, noting that the state of Vermont could not show any evidence that it had extinguished title, Judge Wolchick dismissed the charges of illegal fishing against those who could prove that they were Abenaki citizens. This judgment had the opposite effect of calming down the situation. Led by the news media on the surface, with low-level police harassment as an undertone, the Anglo Vermont community stepped up its semicovert campaign against the Abenaki people. A personal experience from this period illustrates a thrust and parry between the state and the St. Francis–Sokoki Band.

One of the programs to promote sovereignty was to purchase and display Abenaki tribal license plates. Abenakis were being harassed for displaying them in Franklin County, Vermont. Michael Delaney (the tribal judge) and others told me personal stories of car impoundments and physical abuse attending what was technically a charge of driving without a valid license plate. It seemed to me that the police targeted the relatively powerless Abenaki citizens of Franklin County. At the time, I lived in Johnson (Lamoille County), Vermont, and was active in college and community affairs, cub scouts, Johnson and Lamoille County Planning Commissions, and the board of the Vermont Council on the Humanities.

I attempted to use my stature and community involvement to dramatize the increasing police pressure put on the Abenakis. I registered with the tribal council and obtained one of the plates for my car. Would I be arrested? Well, I tried. The Lamoille County deputy sheriff's son was in Cub Scouts with my boy, and I parked next to his car. I even talked to the deputy with my foot on the rear bumper—nothing. At the time, the Vermont Council on the Humanities office was across the street from the sheriff's office, so I parked next to the sheriff's car—nothing. Well, if I couldn't get nailed in Lamoille County, maybe I can get arrested in Franklin County on my trips to the tribal headquarters—nothing. I drove with those plates for six months and attracted no attention from the state or local police. In an act of personal irony, I had to remove my plate to lend it to Middlebury College for their upcoming publication to celebrate the Vermont Bicentennial. (Fig. 43.)

However, a family of modest means living near me also displayed the Abenaki plates. Within seventy-two hours their car was impounded. It was assessed exorbitant storage fees, that would have forfeited their only transportation, had not the Abenaki Defense Fund paid the authorities the fee. Months later, I asked the deputy sheriff why I had not been detained. He said, "We know you're just trying to be a do-gooder and we don't need the aggravation." When questioned about the other family, he replied, "Oh them—well, that's a bad family anyway, and they don't do anything without us knowing about it." I later learned that this family was targeted by the Vermont Eugenics Survey for extinction. Long shadows of eugenic ethnic cleansing remain.[5]

Nineteen ninety-one saw the establishment of the Governor's Advisory Commission on Native American Affairs, composed of Miles Jensen, its head, and equal representation appointed by the governor and the St. Francis–Sokoki Band. It was chartered to deal with native issues related to educational, cultural, and economic development. It also laid out the bipolar attitude the state was to follow by recognizing "the historic and cultural contributions of native Americans to the state," but "nothing in this executive order shall be construed as according official recognition to any Native American tribe or tribal entity" (draft of executive order of June 30, 1990; on file at the Abenaki Tribal Museum).

In 1992, a Barre law firm prepared a land claims case on behalf of Abenakis, a third thrust against the state. This was in part based on the favorable action of Judge Wolchick three years earlier. This juridical thrust was intolerable to the security of the state's wealthy constituencies. Several title

Fig. 43. Swanton Abenaki license plate. *Wiseman collection.*

insurance companies immediately attempted to amend their policies' language to exclude coverage for Abenaki land claims. State banking officials said a protracted legal battle could make it hard to buy or sell a home in Vermont. The enforcement arms of the state quickly took up this "threat" to the financial elite, and justice receded a bit more. The disrespectful position of the state was well summarized: "The average white Vermonter cannot conceive that Chief Homer and his crazy little group of followers will win this thing. . . . Vermonters are going to fight like hell before they give up their land and or give Chief Homer anything" (Howard Van Benthuysen, Franklin County state's attorney; quoted in *Yankee Magazine*, 1991).

By the spring of 1992, police harassment had gotten worse, and the Abenaki community had become more alienated and confrontational. Homer St. Francis reported to aghast Vermonters that the Abenakis were willing to "spill anybody's blood if it comes down to it." This was probably the high point of the anti-Abenaki sentiment in the media. The chief was portrayed as alternately a joke and a threat: "His indiscreet language and intemperate acts have been livening up slow news days since the early 1970s when he declared war on Vermont and the United States" (*Yankee Magazine*, 1991). The Governor's Advisory Commission on Native American Affairs attempted to mediate the problem. In October, Abenaki and police attended a historic meeting with federal (Border Patrol), state, and local police and the Vermont Department of Fish and Wildlife to work out proper protocols to use in arrest and arbitration and to create lines of communication between the antagonists.

The late eighties and early nineties were probably the most cohesive era for the Abenaki, as political, social, and economic initiatives abounded, even with active antagonism on the part of the state. In 1990, 1,696 Native Americans self-identified for the U.S. census, a significant increase over the last census. However, during this time the fabric of Abenaki community showed the first signs of unraveling. The power struggles between the St. Francis and Lampman families in the 1987 election and its aftermath had given the St. Francis family unprecedented power; they had also curtailed the representative process by which differing views could be heard and integrated into Abenaki tribal policy. Certain influential citizens and families began to distance themselves from the confrontational strategies of the St. Francis leadership. While much of this dissension was internal, some individuals began to undermine the St. Francis–Sokoki Band, establishing independent relationships with the state and other native nations. Naturally, the Anglo community, believing that these people were more pliable, cultivated such relationships, perhaps as a way of undermining the administration of Homer St. Francis.

In 1991 the state of Vermont celebrated its bicentennial but left out the Native 95.5 percent of Vermont's human history. The only Abenaki participation was limited to a single mobile exhibition describing the many uses Natives made of birch bark, and the Abenaki Cultural Center's (the predecessor of the Tribal Museum) lending of a few artifacts to museums for their displays.

I will not dwell in detail about the legal thrust and parry between the state of Vermont and the Abenaki Nation at Missisquoi during this period This is fodder for Euro-American historians, who dwell on such things because they leave such extensive records. The story of the Alnôbak is necessarily greater than the state of Vermont or the Abenaki Nation at Missisquoi. However, both are political entities and as such represent much larger processes of social justice and repression. The first stirrings of the Bear may have been political, but the awakening is much more.

Academia Publishes the Abenakis, and Abenakis Become Academics

For many years our neighbors and relatives, the Native people of Maine and Canada, have long joined with the New English in downplaying or denying our existence. Also damaging was the *Wabanakis of Maine and the Maritimes*, produced by the Quakers and Eastern Abenaki peoples for use in schools. Only two paragraphs of this book were devoted to the peoples who occupy the vast Wabanaki lands west of the Penobscot River:

"Of all the groups of Wabanaki people probably the least is known about the *so-called* [emphasis added] Western Abenaki who were living inland when Europeans were exploring the coast" (p. D 10).

"As defined in this book the term Wabanaki refers to all groups on this list except the Swanton Abenaki group" (p. D 8).

Thus, we were defined out of existence by our own relatives in the minds of any New England teachers who used this otherwise excellent book.[6]

The first stage of a change in this attitude was discussed above, marked by Euro-American anthropologists, folklorists, and historians delving into their own forebears' records concerning the Alnôbak or by archaeologists excavating old habitation sites and the graves of our honored dead. Thus, the late 1970s and early 1980s were the era of the *Manakazoit*, the people hungry for our lore. The Christian year 1981 saw the publication of two important books: Gordon Day's academic *Identity of the St. Francis Indians*, which went into great detail concerning our people, and the more popular *The Original Vermonters* by William Haviland and Marjory Power. In the mid 1980s, two very influential figures entered the scene. Folklorist and storyteller Joseph Bruchac in 1985, with his small but groundbreaking *Wind Eagle* volume, was quickly followed by others focusing on Native stories. From that time, Bruchac, who is of Abenaki descent, and his family became important contributors to the Abenaki Renaissance, in the arts (the whole family), material culture/reenactment (Marge Bruchac), environmental education (Jim Bruchac), and language (Jesse Bruchac). Their continuing contributions, especially within a larger United States and world context, cannot be understated. Historian Colin Calloway entered the ongoing "information rush" with his "Green Mt. Diaspora" article in the 1986 *Vermont History*, followed by the mass-market *Abenaki* (1989) and the academic *Western Abenakis of Vermont, 1600–1800* (1990) and the 1991 *Dawnland Encounters* volume. The effect of these books was substantial. Few could deny, after reading these volumes, that the Abenaki were here from 12,000 B.C. to A.D. 1800; and the "empty Vermont" model espoused by earlier historians continued to crumble. This hard-won data forms much of the pre-1800 information base that I attempted to reorient to a "sovereign Abenaki" viewpoint for this book.

In response to this tide of new historical and archaeological information, the state of Vermont grew more bipolar concerning the Swanton Abenakis. The enforcement and judicial branches of the state government chose not to listen to this new data and persecuted the Alnôba with renewed vigor in scenes reminiscent of the 1920s and 1930s. The social arm of the state, represented by the Division of Historic Preservation, the Vermont Historical Society, the Vermont State Colleges, and an increasingly repentant University of Vermont became great supporters in our struggles. Other divisions, such as the Vermont Agency of Natural Resources, were divided and usually followed the whims of the current administration. These movements originated with work done by the Euro-American scholarly, political, and social services community, but this was to change in the late 1980s. The Abenaki Research Project (ARP), founded and steered by the pioneering ethnohistorian John Moody, began to involve Abenaki citizens as researchers rather than as mere subjects. A cadre of Native women scholars coalesced in the ARP and grew during this time; it included Dee Brightstar, Cheryl Bluto, and Jeanne Brink. Each developed unique skills and began taking them to the Euro-American community directly, without the Anglo middleman. Dee Brightstar, who had training in prehistoric archaeology, became an advocate for the Abenaki dead and the sacred aspect of the lands and waters. Cheryl Bluto espoused a similar message. Jeanne Brink, a descendent of Alnôba basket makers, pursued academic goals in Native American studies, then became an advocate for the Alnôbaiwi arts, emerging as the force behind a series of museum exhibitions in the early 1990s.

The Bruchacs, discussed above, became active *within* the Abenaki community. My role began in 1988, when I began a study at Johnson State College to track down and record every piece of Abenaki material culture that I could find in southern Quebec, Vermont, New Hampshire, and western Maine. This project expanded, and a grant written by a student at Johnson was accepted by the Vermont Council on the Humanities. I asked Jeanne Brink if she would administer the grant, and it went splendidly, recovering data on over 1,100 objects and culminating in the 1992 groundbreaking exhibit "Spirit of the Abenaki." The exhibition at the Chimney Point historic site in Addison, Vermont, was quickly followed by another featuring modern artists, including the world-renowned Gerard Rancourt Tsonakwa. A more important legacy of the research was the documentation of cultural survival through the nineteenth century, the time that the state of Vermont asserted that we were not here. Another was a template for artistic revival, as will be seen below.

The Restoration of Ceremony

A second issue of great importance in the late 1980s was the reestablishment of cultural gatherings. For years we had a "harvest supper" in October, but that was generally closed to the public. In 1989 a racial incident in a "Vermont History and Government" class at Johnson State College sparked a commitment by the Sadler administration to create an Abenaki Awareness Day. I was placed in charge of the college's participation for the event, and convening the Missisquoi Abenaki leadership and college administration, we decided to format it somewhat along the lines of a pow-wow but including a lecture series. In April 1990 we prepared a ceremonial area, an area for vendors, a lecture hall for indoor talks by Abenaki leaders, and a dance arena for people to dance to Abenaki musicians. We made sure that publicity reached the Abenaki as well as the Euro-American community.

The day went well; its central location also drew people from New Hampshire. I remember discussing the day with Chief St. Francis, Tom Obomsawin, Tribal Judge Michael Delaney, and others, who believed that it should continue but under Abenaki leadership. The next two summers the Abenaki celebration was held at Sandy Point Field Station, a small lake-shore facility then run by Johnson State College to the west of Swanton, Vermont. These gatherings were relatively small and mainly for Abenaki citizens, although the general public came as well. Due to limited space, a pow-wow format had to be abandoned. We had pipe ceremonies and other social and religious ceremonies for adults and children, as well as food sharing, but we also continued with the education theme, with lectures and displays of artifacts and herbal medicines. Friends from Odanak and Akwesasne attended. But other processes were afoot that would change the location and scale of our now established yearly celebration.

The Restoration of Art

The arts also underwent a renaissance in the late 1980s and early 1990s. Abenaki artists such as Jeanne Brink and Dee Brightstar began working in basketry and jewelry media. Jeanne Brink preferred to place herself within her family's well-known tradition of nineteenth-century ash fancy baskets. Dee Brightstar pursued traditional bead and bark work but also extended into more contemporary media such as paint and silversmithing. Except for the still green basketry, snowshoe, and wood-carving traditions, artisans were one to several generations away from their stylistic, technological, and symbolic Abenaki artistic heritage. Beginning in 1989, I endeavored to isolate significant, well-documented traditional Abenaki artifacts from other Native art styles discovered by earlier research projects mentioned in the section above. I hoped that these well-documented pieces could

provide a strong stylistic background for modern artists. To rediscover Abenaki technological and manufacturing nuances of these objects, I began
experimenting with wood and metalwork replication, media that I had
previous experience with. This led to the founding of the Laboratory for
Traditional Technology at Johnson State College in late 1989. Experiments in beadwork, clothing, woodwork, and feathercraft began in that
year. In 1991 we obtained a budget for materials and expanded our experimental work to the more expensive wampumwork and silversmithing. In
concert with the Audubon Nature Center in Huntington, Vermont, we
began planning architectural replication. The products of this experimental work were donated to Native and civic organizations throughout Vermont and southern Quebec. More important, information on sources,
materials, and construction that we had discovered was first made available in late 1991 to any who needed help in making their own regalia and
ceremonial materials. Some Native people were hesitant about multiethnic Johnson State College students' creations and information. As time
went on, most came to understand that this was yet another form of restitu-
tion by the Vermont community and were accepting.

In 1994, the short-lived College of the Missisquoi debuted, through the
assistance of the Governor's Commission on Native American Affairs and
Burlington (Vermont) College. It offered Abenaki language and Abenaki
and Native American history courses. It lasted through 1995, when Burlington College withdrew financial and administrative support. Attempts
at forming links with Johnson State College and the Community College
of Vermont did not materialize. The college is now on a "back burner."

The Coming of Factionalism: 1992–1995

The first new separate Abenaki band appeared in early summer 1992,
marking a shift in the direction of the Abenaki Renaissance. The Northeast Woodlands–Coos Band was organized by Howard Knight, a disabled
veteran. Like many Abenakis, Knight discovered his ancestry in the 1970s.
He spread the word of a new Abenaki group up and down the Connecticut
Valley, attracting, according to Knight, over seven hundred members.
Some joined because they were Abenakis from the old Coos region; others joined because they were dissatisfied with the St. Francis–Sokoki
Band. Immediately, Knight and St. Francis began a conflict for hege-
mony in the Abenaki homeland. As far as I know, this was the first time

that Abenaki people began accusing other Abenaki people of not being "Indian." This tactic spread in the coming years, greatly destabilizing the Alnôbak. This new emerging leadership confused the state's decade-old program of marginializing the Abenaki. On one hand, this was classic "divide and conquer,": the Abenakis had fractionated and were fighting with one another in the media. This certainly delighted the judicial and enforcement branches of the Vermont state government, since Abenakis were calling each other "wannabes" (fake Indians). This lent credence to the state's position that the St. Francis–Sokoki Band and other Abenakis were not Indians. On the other hand, Knight seemed as volatile and antagonistic as St. Francis, sharing the same intolerable goals of sovereignty and recognition.

The Investiture of Grand Chief St. Francis

In 1994, Homer St. Francis was diagnosed with a life-threatening cancer. In response to this diagnosis, Chief St. Francis's supporters took three unilateral steps that would have lasting effects on the Abenaki community. First, St. Francis appointed his daughter April (now Rushlow) as acting chief, with the power to run the affairs of the band on a day-to-day basis. (Fig. 44.) This political action was perhaps similar to the appointment of Lester Lampman as interim chief at the time of Blackie Lampman's passing. It effectively kept power in one family band. In a second controversial move, the band tribal constitution was changed again, to create chiefly succession within the St. Francis family, independent of future will of the larger Abenaki community. Although there are conflicting stories about this time, which are different from what I remember, I will try to reconstruct events. I remember that Carol Neptun of the Abenaki Research Project, as well as the tribal lawyer, Mark Nestor, had confidential advice for the Abenaki tribal council that may have led to this unique action. These suggestions resulted in a rewrite of the constitution, which we discussed in a November 5, 1995, general meeting, and ratified on February 25, 1996. Lest there be any confusion concerning the ratification, Chief Rushlow has graciously given me permission to quote a clause from the Tribal Constitution in this one instance: the chieftainship will "rest exclusively within the traditional hereditary families of chieftains."

Chief Rushlow has also given me permission to list the official signers of the constitutional change. They indicate that the "core" families were represented at the time and signed the ratification: Lance Lampman, Dorcus Pellesier, Lisa Lampman Rollo, April St. Francis, Harold St. Francis, and

Fig. 44. Copy of a photograph of Homer St. Francis
in 1995. *Watercolor, Laura Pinter; Wôbanakik Heritage
Center Collection, photograph by Andrew Lee.*

Homer St. Francis II. While Homer St. Francis was directly quoted by the
media as saying that "native American practice made it appropriate to
keep the chieftainship in the St. Francis Family," this form of constitutional succession of power was, I believe, unprecedented in the modern
Wabanaki world. Even though it is clear from his statements published in
several Vermont newspapers that St. Francis's intent was to keep the chieftainship within his lineal descendants, the wording of the constitution is
broad, with the plural "families" and an absence of geographic specificity.
There were other families that had successions of able leaders, who could
conceivably run for chief . It is even in line with documented aboriginal
Wabanaki practice before the adoption of constitutions. Unfortunately
those political stratagems among nineteenth-century Maine Wabanakis
became so contentious that the Great Council Fire was, by some accounts, called in to mediate.

The investiture of St. Francis as grand chief was another decisive historical experience, with as many remembrances as there were participants. Also, continuing political, cultural, and even spiritual implications

are unclear. Since the creation of a new Abenaki political status is critical to the continuing history of the Abenaki, I will attempt a reconstruction, knowing full well that virtually all of the participants will disagree with it. As we have seen in the historical sections, the Abenaki had never, by themselves, had a grand chief. This title was traditionally reserved to the chief of the Odawas at the Great Council Fire at Kahnawake. Our Micmac neighbors had a grand chief tradition, but that was a unique case with political roots in the sixteenth century Micmac Grand Council and its singular relation to the Catholic Church. The title of grand chief in intertribal confederacies was given to a highly respected leader who could hold several politically distinct communities together and speak on behalf of all of them.

At the Abenaki Heritage Celebration in May 1996 (there is even debate about the date, although it was not so long ago!), a group of Abenaki political leaders met and determined that Homer St. Francis should be inducted as grand chief. There are conflicting accounts of the relations between this leadership and St. Francis. In an unprecedented move, the chief of the St. Francis–Sokoki Band, which never acknowledged the authority of any group but itself, accepted the title of rank from these "external" leaders. In a sense this was literally the crowning glory of St. Francis's rise to power, from achieving chief-for-life in 1987 through extending his chieftainship into an incipient dynasty just months before.

The implications of accepting the grand chief investiture from Abenakis outside Missisquoi were complex and subtle. The inauguration also created a vulnerability inherent to the rank: First, after St. Francis accepted the title, he seemed to abandon his previous title of chief-for-life. He began using Grand Chief on correspondence and in interviews. This acceptance of universal authority may have left his daughter, Acting Chief April St. Francis (now Rushlow) the titular political authority specifically at Missisquoi. This unilateral change in authority has unexplored constitutional potentials. Second, in accepting the title from other Abenakis he explicitly acknowledged their political authority to confer title of rank. These people now retained authority independent of the Abenaki Nation at Missisquoi. This political status was morally irrevocable as long as St. Francis held the grand chieftainship. Third, these leaders had achieved the political authority to revoke the title of grand chief. This authority was also external to St. Francis's well-consolidated authority base at Missisquoi. There is anecdotal evidence that some of these leaders soon reconsidered their offer at the following Littleton, New Hampshire, pow-wow.

At this point the record becomes a mass of disharmonious accounts. The result of these enigmatic stratagems was that Homer St. Francis continued to hold the title of grand chief while denying the authority of the coalition that appointed him. A second result, according to some accounts, was that Walter Watso of Odanak, Quebec, seemed to now have the grand chief rank that was previously offered to St. Francis. The remarkable outcome was that the Western New England Abenakis, who had never had grand chiefs, may have had two! A derivative problem quickly emerged on the Canadian Abenaki reserves. The Canadian Odanak and Wôlinak communities, always recognized by Missisquoi, were already alienated by the clandestine maneuvering of St. Francis's foes and were in no rush to claim an American as their grand chief, nor did they recognize Watso's title. It is said in Odanak that actions such as this by American Abenakis disrupted social and political ties with Canadian Abenakis, ties that had been building since the 1970s. It increased discontent with other New England family bands, who saw their participation reduced to passive approval of chiefly plans. Third, some Abenakis slowly abandoned their activities with the Abenaki Nation of Missisquoi's social and economic programs.[7]

These events are critical for understanding the political course of the Abenaki renaissance. Although Chief St. Francis's actions are at odds with what some may believe is a "correct" tribal structure, it began the conversion of an inappropriate U.S. government–sponsored form of government into something more approximating the millennia-old family band structure. Family bands did have patriarchs, such as Homer St. Francis, and they held that position for life, unless they were removed for actions not consistent with the chiefly vows. Succession was in the family, since it was a family band. Loyalty and kinship were also elements that held the family band together. Therefore, the St. Francis–Sokoki Band, as it became the Abenaki Nation at Missisquoi, began a slow movement toward a more authentic system of administration.[8]

Nonpolitical Alternatives to Missisquoi and Coos

During this time, the Title V Indian Education Office, which had been created in 1981, assumed more of a quasi-organizational role in the Swanton Abenaki community. Its director, Jeff Benay, was appointed chair of the Governor's Advisory Commission on Native American Affairs by Governor Dean. The Parent Advisory Committee and the Title V's year-round activities attracted Franklin County Abenaki parents to this increasingly active and powerful organization. Precisely because it was avowedly not political and seemed to lack personal agendas, it was an attractive alternative venue for Abenaki revival. The Dawnland Center, another "nonpolitical" organization arose in central Vermont during this time. Developed in early 1994 by Lorraine Landers and Dana Pictou, the Dawnland Center was envisioned as a social services agency for the region's Native community. Drug and alcohol abuse counseling, conferring with prison inmates, and other social services were soon provided. However, right from the beginning, the Dawnland Center had a strong, semiautonomous spiritual component. This organization, called the Shooting Star Lodge, was explicitly based on the beliefs of its founders. This gave the center a focus unique in the Abenaki country that became increasingly inviting as time went on. It attracted a talented board of directors from the Abenaki and other Native communities in Vermont. The center soon expanded from social services to cultural programming, sponsoring elders' gatherings and pow-wows. By late 1994 it had assumed all the traditional organizational powers of an Indian community except an overtly political stance. Its members, however, were not adverse to entering into the political fray.

Also in central Vermont, the nonpolitical Abenaki Dance Troupe, organized and spearheaded by Jeanne Brink in 1992, began learning Western Abenaki dances from our exiled kinsmen from Odanak. The group began small but slowly grew. As the troupe learned dances, they learned the lore of what the dances mean. In 1992 the Laboratory for Traditional Technology began a project, supported by student labor and funds from Johnson State College, to manufacture their dance equipment and regalia, including clothing, rattles, drums, and props. Dance Troupe membership and performance etiquette developed over time and formed a social nucleus of activists, artisans, and spokespeople. Today the organization, called the Wa'banaki Dancers, is a politically and socially active force in Vermont. As Abenaki society began to be divided along unclear political lines, these organizations assumed a crucial neutral role in offering support and a sense of community for many Abenaki citizens.

The Heritage Celebration and Other Abenaki Nation Initiatives

As we saw in the previous section, the Abenaki community had developed a unique summer observance to rejoice in our reemerging heritage. It was relatively small and not widely publicized. The Governor's Advisory

Commission on Native American Affairs discussed this ongoing celebration and how to make it a more effective communicator of Abenaki culture. In 1992, Governor Howard Dean transmitted to the commission his interest in a state of Vermont–sanctioned Abenaki heritage celebration. The previous summer celebrations were held when schools were not in session and families dispersed for vacations. We wanted schools and colleges to be in session for our continued educational purposes, but the weather had to be warm enough for outdoor vendors, drums, and dancing. I conducted a survey of educational institutions as to what would be a good time for the event. We determined that early May would probably be the best time and turned over the organizing to commission member Mark Mitchell and others to oversee. (Fig. 45.)

The weekend of May 4, 1993, was the first Abenaki Heritage Celebration, and it was attended by over two thousand people, including Governor Howard Dean. It consisted of vendors, dancers, storytellers, and refreshments. Most important, it retained the distinctive educational component from the previous years. Lectures, storytelling, and educational demonstrations were planned for the mornings, before the noon "Pow-wow Grand Entry." Evenings, after the tourists went home, saw a ceremonial meal, where we shared our food with honored guests from other nations. This also was a tradition persisting from the previous summer celebrations. But Governor Dean had proclaimed the whole first week of May as "Abenaki Cultural Heritage Celebration Week." Following the weekend celebration, a group of performers went throughout the state spreading the news. In 1994 a better-organized Heritage Celebration expanded on the previous concept but added a theme; that year being the return of the Drum to the Abenaki.

Two other Abenaki Nation initiatives premiered in 1994. The River Keepers Project was begun with grass-roots volunteer labor, small grant funding, and cooperation with the local high school. The Swanton Abenaki community has always been a river people, and this was merely a continuance of its age-old "River Rat" commitment to the waters. Instead of ceremony and tradition alone, the River Keepers now added chemical monitoring of the Missisquoi River for pollution, litter, and garbage collections, alerting environmental authorities concerning possible violations and presenting educational programs for the public. The project obtained watercraft and began patrolling the ancient river home. A second initiative was the Abenaki Trading Post. For years, the Abenaki community had made crafts for sale as well as personal use. The tribal headquarters had a

Fig. 45. First Abenaki Heritage Celebration poster. *Dee Brightstar; Wiseman collection.*

small area available for display of a few of these items. The Abenaki Nation decided to create a showcase for these wares, called the Abenaki Trading Post. The nation received a significant grant in 1993 to create a place to sell Abenaki arts and create a register of Abenaki artists. A coordinator was appointed to do this survey of artists to discover their artistic media and find out if they would be interested in being part of the planned cooperative venture. The planned trading post was designed to give all Abenaki artists a venue for selling their wares and a place to purchase craft materials at cost. A building behind tribal headquarters had been refurbished for the trading post and the Abenaki Research Project. The portion to be the trading post then had heating and store fixtures installed. The trading post was launched in 1994 and today, in our new headquarters, still sells Abenaki arts but has expanded to include posters and books by Abenaki writers.

Another critical issue of the early 1990s was the Western Abenaki language, almost entirely forgotten in Wôbanakik. I remember place-names in Abenaki and a few Abenaki words (pronounced very differently from the way they are spoken at Odanak) mentioned by the River Rats. For example, the remembered (in Canada, over one hundred miles away) name for the first falls of the Wazowategok is written by a Euro-American scholar as Dawkwahoganizek while its name, still spoken by people who lived within two hundred yards of it into the 1950s, was Tawnkwahunka. Only a few words remained in the most traditional branches of my family. As the dances are returning slowly to Wôbanakik, so is the language. In 1992, Gordon Day and Jeanne Brink published a small Abenaki language primer and tape for use in school systems. Cecile Wawanolet, an elder from Odanak, and her son, Elie Joubert, have taught Abenaki grammar to people near Missisquoi. Jesse Bruchac, son of prolific writer Joseph Bruchac, also began teaching conversational Abenaki, first at the local high school, then through the Abenaki Tribal Museum and Cultural Center, before leaving the region in 1999. Day's English-Abenaki dictionary was published in the 1990s by the National Museum of Canada, making much of the language, as spoken by our exiled kinsmen at Odanak, Quebec, much more accessible.[9]

The Advisory Commission Endures Hardship

The Governor's Advisory Commission on Native American Affairs was hit by controversy in 1994. The commission had asked Governor Howard Dean to give the Abenaki Nation limited state recognition. Governor Dean rejected the proposal because he believed that it would open the door to gambling and hurt the state's position on land claims. This was the first time that the Indian gaming issue had surfaced as a potential stumbling block. Other outstanding issues were the inaction on the state's promise to purchase and set aside an ancient burial ground in Highgate Town and a 439-acre Maquam (Swanton) parcel that the Abenakis consider sacred. This parcel was important to the Lampman family, and the agreement was concluded in September 1994. Finally, the actions of the State's Attorney Howard Van Benthuysen (such as the quote above) caused the Abenaki community to believe that they were being treated disrespectfully in court proceedings, in violation of the understanding of October 1992. Two of the commissioners quit in the controversy.

All of the forces of creation and destruction that mold the modern Abenaki world developed in these years. The forces of creation included acceptance of the Abenaki people that they were Indian, acceptance by the Abenaki people by academia, building organizational and political structures to deal with Anglo Vermont, and rediscovery of our material and symbolic heritage. The forces of destruction unleashed included a constantly shifting, overtly hostile state of Vermont and a built-in political instability caused by friction between traditional family-band politics and Anglo-imposed tribal and social organizations run by authoritarian leaders.

9

The Modern Abenaki

(Christian Years 1995–)

*1995: The Explosive Beginnings of the
Contemporary Abenaki World*

Nineteen ninety-five was the most momentous year of the Abenaki Renaissance. On March 30, the Vermont Supreme Court affirmed misdemeanor convictions for nine Abenaki Indians. After months of debate and waiting, the Vermont Supreme Court overturned Judge Wolchick's August 1989 pro-Abenaki ruling. Ignoring testimony from archaeologists, anthropologists, and historians, the experts in this field, the court listened to law officers and determined that the Abenaki's case was voided by the "weight of history." In an interesting twist, the court raised the "weight of history" issue. It was *not* used by the state in its pleadings. This determination was contrary to federal Indian law and condemned by experts throughout the United States. Native people familiar with what they call "the Eliott case" always ask me how any court in the United States could come to this conclusion.

The "increasing weight of history" rule enunciated by the Vermont Supreme Court should not be allowed to displace the traditional requirements of Aboriginal title doctrine. If followed by other courts, the rule would hamstring Indian tribes in asserting their interests. Other jurisdictions considering extinguishment of aboriginal title should take the opportunity to expressly reject Elliot as an unsound departure from long-established doctrine. By vigorously advocating for reliance on the Aboriginal Title doctrine's basic tenets, practitioners may prevent other courts from reproducing the Elliott Court's dangerous mistakes. (John Lowndes, *Buffalo Law Review* [1994])

There was one hopeful note. Obviously knowledgeable about the overwhelming proof that the St. Francis–Sokoki Band was the actual heir to the historically known Abenakis, the court accepted the fact that the modern Abenakis were a "bona fide Tribe of Indians," then proceeded to show that their land had long ago fallen into Anglo hands. Unfortunately, the attorney general and other judicial and enforcement arms of the state chose to ignore this and continued their genocidal strategy of disconnecting us from our ancestors.[1]

"Hopefully this [the Supreme Court ruling] will finally put to rest the litigation between people claiming to be Abenaki Indians and claiming defense because of that" (Howard Van Benthuysen, state's attorney, *Burlington Free Press*, March 30, 1995). This unenlightened assertion that we are "claiming to be Abenaki Indians" became the cornerstone of the state of Vermont's official position on the Abenakis, even after the Supreme Court accepted our tribal status as a basis of their pernicious 1995 ruling. This ruling caused a wave of anguish and anger in the Abenaki community, alienating some and making others feel hopeless. I remember Chief St. Francis saying that was the end of dealing with the state; now we would pursue federal recognition with extra vigor. The Abenaki Nation at Missisquoi had earlier decided (in 1993) to seek federal recognition through a Bureau of Indian Affairs (BIA) petition. They had withdrawn their previous (1981) petition after it became obvious that the federal government had released confidential data to the state for use in its case against the Abenakis in *Eliott*. Armed with much more cultural information, the St. Francis administration now pushed forward, especially after the disastrous Supreme Court ruling. However, a possible stumbling block lay embedded in the tribal rolls that must be included in the petition. Individuals and families, including many well known to be Abenaki by the Native and Anglo communities, did not have their genealogical paperwork in order. It was the opinion of the tribal lawyer and the head of the Abenaki Research Project that the Nation had to ask for confirmatory information from all its citizens to meet federal standards of genealogical proof. This painful decision, made to enhance the BIA petition, led to yet more controversy within the Nation. Many people refused the request, which prevented them from maintaining their former level of citizenship.

Mazipskwik

In the early fall of 1995, political, social, and genealogical rifts within the Abenaki community widened into a split similar to those of the late 1970s. In October the Traditional Abenakis of Mazipskwik and Related Bands was formed. This accelerated a loss of officials and employees at the Missisquoi Tribal Headquarters that began with the tighter genealogical requirements. The new Native organization named Connie Brow, Homer St. Francis's niece, as chairwoman. The new tribe's board members included Dave Gilman, a former coordinator of Missisquoi Riverkeepers; Ina Delaney and John Lawyer, formerly on the Abenaki Self Help board of directors; and Mike Delaney, the former tribal judge. The new Abenakis of Mizipskwik met in the Swanton Village Complex, perhaps a symbolic gesture of accommodation to Anglo political reality. Chairwoman Brow told reporters in 1995 that Mazipskwik wanted to work with the state, not seek federal recognition, and that they were opposed to gambling.[2]

This was the second time that an Abenaki faction had attempted to "fight their battles" in the Anglo press. There was also dissatisfaction within the Abenaki community concerning a concentration of power in Homer St. Francis and his family at Missisquoi and the Nation's new tougher application of its rules regarding citizenship. Grand Chief St. Francis quickly responded, saying that Native American tradition makes it fitting for the chieftainship to stay in the St. Francis family. He noted that those who left "could not make the grade" regarding the more rigorous genealogical requirements for membership. In late fall 1995, the division became wider as another group of Abenakis proposed a meeting in the Upper Connecticut River Valley. Organized by Tom Obomsawin, Newt Washburn, Wayne Hall, Karen Porter, and Charlie Richardson, this group became the nucleus of a third dissident group in eastern Vermont and western New Hampshire. Yet another Abenaki entity entered the fray when David Hill-Docteau informed the Vermont community that *he* was the hereditary grand chief and prince of the Abenaki Nation and tried to claim the New England Kurn Hattin Homes campus in Saxton's River, Vermont. By the end of the year there were four entities claiming to represent the Abenaki people.

The Cultural Context of That Memorable Year

The 1995 Abenaki Heritage Celebration was the peak in public attendance and artist participation. It was the last year Odanak and the Abenaki Dance Troupe attended in an official capacity and the first year that our Mohawk friends from Kahnawake attended. Basket makers, wood carvers, storytellers, professional dancers, and others made this a memorable experience. Several state officials attended to see the renaissance in action. The

Abenaki touring group that followed the two-day event was in high demand. Governor Dean supported the advisory commission's desire to publish a curricular framework on Abenaki studies for the middle schools of Vermont. On the cultural side, things looked positive. Other Native institutions began their own events, which amplified the Abenaki presence. The Dawnland Center Pow Wow in central Vermont attracted many people, and another group descended from Howard Knight's pioneering organizing had a successful pow-wow in Evansville, in north-central Vermont. The exhibition "Long Shadows: Henry Perkins and the Eugenics Survey of Vermont" opened on Sept. 29, 1995 at the Fleming Museum in Burlington (Perkins was Fleming Museum's first director). This was the first major public venue dealing with the eugenics movement in Vermont and the impact it had on its people. In addition, the university hosted an evening symposium on eugenics on October 24, attended by Abenaki representatives. The long suppressed relation of the Abenaki and the Eugenics Survey began to creep into Vermont's consciousness.

In November 1995, IBM donated $15,000 worth of computers and peripherals to the Abenaki Nation for use at the Title V Indian Education Office. The six "Eduquest" computers and two printers were to be shared by Title V and ASHAI for the training of adults and children in computer skills. This was accompanied by a refurbishing of the Tribal Learning Center and making it more responsive to the current needs of the Abenaki youth, such as the "After School Program." At the same time, the importance of Title V grew among Abenaki citizens as it was seen as an relatively calm, apolitical organization in the midst of political unrest and destabilization. In the summer of 1995 the Johnson State College administration closed down the six-year-old Laboratory for Traditional Technology. The collection was divided; materials purchased with JSC moneys were stored in my college office and the balance moved to Swanton. I also moved my Abenaki research library to Swanton. These collections became the nucleus of Wôbanakik Heritage Center in late fall 1995. I purchased book and artifact storage and display materials and outfitted a small classroom research facility for use by the Abenaki community and the public.

The Dead Come Home

As discussed earlier, the ancient Abenaki burial ground on Monument Road was excavated in 1973 by the University of Vermont. Remains of about eighty-five Abenaki were found. An ongoing passion of the St. Francis leadership was the recovery and reburial of the dead who had been removed by archaeologists. In a series of thrust-and-parry moves, various organizations in Vermont and as far afield as Texas and Maine agreed to return the burials to the Abenaki. The remains trickled back in the early 1990s and were stored in a state warehouse in Berlin, Vermont. The next phase was to purchase the land for the reburial. In the spring of 1995, Vermont lawmakers authorized $200,000, supplemented by an anonymous donation of $125,000, to purchase the two-acre parcel from which the burials were taken. The state was able to purchase the property in late summer. Anglo neighbors were fearful that the Abenaki would use the property and thereby lower their property values. In a similar vein, the owners, when originally approached by the state and the Abenaki community, responded with colorful but unprintable words. They eventually realized a huge markup on the value of their property, probably because they knew that it was going to the Abenaki community. The town of Highgate did what it could in December 1995 to stymie Abenaki aspirations. Although town officials knew that the property was to be an unmarked, undeveloped cemetery with no infrastructure; the Abenaki were required to put up a five-foot chain-link fence around the parcel, add ten off-road parking spaces, and pay a property tax assessment on the land. But that did not stop the return of the Dead. In a ceremony closed to the public but attended by dignitaries such as Chief Obomsawin of Odanak, the remains were reinterred in their original burial areas. Following the ceremony, other factions came to the site to give their blessing to the return of the dead. There are some things that transcend even band rivalry.

The Modern Abenaki World

The forces of destruction and recovery are well balanced in the Abenaki world of northern New England. Abenaki youth now have a low, 3 percent dropout rate, lower than the state average. Fifty percent of graduating Abenakis go on to college. This points the way to a brighter economic future for individual Abenakis within the Anglo American dream, but its implications for tribal sovereignty and cultural continuity are problematic. Due to Anglo scholarly activity, virtually everyone in northern New England sees the modern Abenaki Nation as the heir to an unbroken cultural history. (Fig. 46.) New connections to other First Nations are

Fig. 46. Women at the May 1999 Abenaki Heritage Day celebration. *Photograph by Andrew Lee.*

being explored, and a new tribal museum has opened. But there are unresolved problems that continue to haunt the Abenaki Renaissance.

Factionalism Rises

The decades of hard-won political successes of the St. Francis–Sokoki Band, combined with a widely disseminated academic revision of history, had finally paid off. But the toll was high. The camaraderie of the early years was long gone, the casualty of power struggle, BIA criteria for recognition, and damaged egos. But Vermont was a much safer place to be Abenaki than it had been. Organizations and independent individuals supporting or representing self-identified Abenakis have blossomed in the last few years. Some such as the Clan of the Hawk and the Coos Band have their roots in the tumultuous events of 1995. Others such as the Cowasuck Band–Penacook Abenaki People in Franklin, Massachusetts, have been around for years, independent of the struggles in northern Vermont, while Charles True of Epping, New Hampshire, is in the process of gathering southeastern New Hampshire Abenakis together. These southern and eastern groups have come to represent a viable alternative to the geometrically expanding number of Vermont bands. One of these groups, perhaps representing a future trend in the Abenaki Renaissance, will be discussed as a case study.

Nineteen ninety-six was a quiet year; everyone seemed dazed by the tumult of the year before. Mazipskwik had grown and was now hosting its own pow-wow, and the Dawnland Center and Title V Indian Education Office were expanding. Johnson State College produced *Abenaki Memories*, the first theatrical program reviewing Abenaki history and reopened the Laboratory for Traditional Technology. *Abenaki Memories* premiered at Highgate Falls, Vermont, in May. With all the new players, it became difficult to discern any direction for the Abenaki renaissance.

In 1997, the Lampman family, which had almost ceased its participation in the Abenaki Nation at Missisquoi, finally attempted to force a constitutional referendum at a tribal general meeting, to open up leadership opportunities to others. Since this was a general, not a constitutional meeting, the strategy was fended off by St. Francis's supporters. The Lampmans did not press for a constitutional meeting. As a result, the Lampman family seemed to dissolve all but the most tenuous ties with Missisquoi. Continuing the focus of her father, Ms. Lampman-Larivee emerged as a guiding force behind the Missisquoi Health Center in the early 1990s, through its creation in the middle of the decade, and continues today. The Lampmans are very involved educationally, working closely with the Title V Indian Education Office and its connections to the University of Vermont and numerous other programs. The deepening association of the Lampman family with the influential Title V altered the balance of power in Swanton yet again. Early 1998 saw the ending of the externally funded Abenaki Research Project at the Abenaki Nation at Missisquoi, which forced the termination of its researchers. Some past employees became informal yet powerful associates of the Lampman family band. The Lampmans have, at the time of this writing, not formed any official tribal organization, nor have they allied themselves with other dissident bands, even though offers have been made.

Today this increasingly influential group functions remarkably like the traditional Abenaki extended family band, with Larivee as its focus of authority. Recently, informal lines of communication have been established between the Lampmans and the Abenaki Nation at Missisquoi, which has necessarily evolved toward a family band political organization due to the many alternatives for people not aligned to its leadership. However, representatives of both the Lampmans and St. Francis have let it be known that they are there for each other if an external threat looms. At the time of this writing there are at least twelve entities representing or supporting Abenaki people in Vermont alone. Although many Abenakis and Anglos feel anguish due to the fractionating of Vermont's Abenakis, I believe that it is a good thing in the long run, in that it more truly represents the ancient and enduring political reality of the Abenaki world. What we now lack is an organizational device to unite these into one force. The old protocols of condolence (understanding the other family band's hopes and fears) and consolation (standardized ceremonies of welcome, entertainment, and conflict resolution) have not yet been revived, and I am sure that the Vermont government fears it highly. Perhaps if they can keep us fighting . . .

Selective Recognition: The State's Final Ploy

"The Governor's Office argues that the Abenaki claim to recognition is flawed because they lost their claim to cohesiveness 200 years ago, then regrouped recently" (Susan Allen, Governor Dean's spokeswoman, *Burlington Free Press*, April 9, 1999).

At the time of this writing, Vermont governor Howard Dean continues to make his dualistic pro- and anti-Abenaki case to the Vermont public. It is now accepted by the politically liberal establishment (to which Dean belongs) that the Abenaki people have always been here. The decades-old strategy of disconnecting the Abenakis from their ancestors, while still asserted by the governor's and attorney general's offices, has had to shift once again. Do you remember that in chapter 1 I talked about the desirable "exotic other" Abenakis and the vaguely menacing "interior" Abenakis? This dualism has become the crux of modern Abenaki-Vermont relations. The state recognizes our "bead and buckskinned exotic other" as we bring a whiff of politically correct "pow-wow diversity" to a Vermont almost ethnically cleansed. It even has to recognize our excellent community services branches such as Title V Indian Education or ASHAI, and the potential for "heritage tourism" represented by the new Abenaki Tribal Museum and Cultural Center (see fig. 49). But Governor Dean will not recognize our distinctive "interior" rights explicitly held by other Native peoples in the Americas. The attributes of this form of discrimination include (1) openly affirming those portions of cultural persistence that lead to Vermont tourism development, such as museums, cultural celebrations, and the

like, or a sense of "cultural pluralism" now so desperately needed by a politically liberal elite; (2) alleging that the people practicing this cultural
persistence are not the cultural/ political descendants of the ancient Native Americans, thereby (3) denying portions of cultural persistence that
are a threat to politically forceful institutions such as the banking and insurance industries, or sportsman's organizations. This institutionalized racism is based on an unprovable allegation (no. 2 above) and the belief (no.
3) that denying a group's constitutional rights will keep the economic
status quo. These long discredited implicit ideals are so politically incendi-
ary that neither the governor's nor the attorney general's office cares to
touch them in open discussion. But recent patterns of immigration into
Vermont, especially of people of Asian and African descent, provided an
opportunity for the state of Vermont and the media to refocus on those ethnic groups. This process caused a recent political shift to a more generalized "diversity" theme in the state of Vermont, which poses little economic
threat to the Anglo community yet has obvious benefits for the liberal elite.
The Abenaki communities now can be portrayed as but one of the many
newly emergent "minorities," with no special rights or priorities.

The Media Divides and Strikes

Not all in the Vermont state government ignored or were hostile to the
Abenakis. In late winter 1998, Vermont senator Julius Canns and other
lawmakers crafted a resolution proposing limited state recognition of the
Abenaki. Canns said that one of the purposes of the resolution was economic opportunity. He noted that recognition would free scholarship
money, which is given to self-identified Asians and African Americans in
Vermont. The spirit of the resolution was identical to Snelling's June 22,
1983, "limited recognition" proclamation. The Abenaki, among all self-
identifying minorities, had to be officially recognized by Anglo authorities.
The governor would not do this. The Senate resolution was carefully
worded so that it would not be a political tool for any action by the Abenaki community. This came to naught, for Senator Susan Bartlett, a Dean
administration supporter and chair of the Senate General Affairs and
Housing Committee, blocked the resolution, keeping it in committee.

Although the resolution went nowhere, it provided a convenient forum
for buffeting the Abenaki Nation in 1999. A diffuse, yet sophisticated
"spin" and misinformation program, only now being understood, focused
the media on widespread feelings against the ailing Homer St. Francis and

his supposed support for gambling. This invented pro-gambling position actually came from misquoting an article in the 1995 *St. Albans Messenger*. In the original quotation, his position was that, when federal recognition came, it would be the nation's decision on gambling, not the state of Vermont's, and this has always been his position. In addition, any proposal to set up a casino would have to be brought to a vote of the citizens of the Abenaki Nation; and from my sense of the community, the proposal would probably fail. Even I, who hate gambling, was quoted out of context and portrayed in three Vermont newspapers as a pro-gambling champion.

By the end of the twentieth century, the state and the media learned how to exploit dissident groups and individuals and could now afford to marginalize and discredit the Abenaki Nation at Missisquoi. This broad divisive approach provided an innovative, politically sanctioned environment within which estranged Abenakis and organizations could now safely come forward to criticize leadership of the Abenaki Nation at Missisquoi. The following quote went out on the Associated Press wires and was picked up by several Vermont newspapers: "'Where does he get the idea that the Abenaki want gambling?' Brink asked of Dean. 'Homer, well who says Homer speaks for all the Abenakis in the State of Vermont?'" (Jeanne Brink, *St. Albans Messenger*, April 17, 1999).

For anyone who may think there is no pattern to this campaign; below is a portion of what the *Burlington Free Press* said about the results of recognition only five days after the above quote (fig. 47):

NO TO RECOGNITION
[F]ormal state status will not alter Abenaki tribal pride for good or ill. It will not resolve schisms within the Abenaki people. State recognition would be a preamble to federal recognition, and that would be like whacking a policy hornets' nest with a stick. Around the country Federal Recognition has led to regions of dire violence. It has led to gambling, a parasitic industry, and development entirely out of scale with the casinos' host region. It might even lead to nuclear waste storage against state wishes, if one tribe has its way. (Editorial, *Burlington Free Press*, April 23, 1999)

Keeping its pressure on Missisquoi, the *Free Press* then sponsored a "Dialog on Diversity" two days later, on April 25, 1999. Its panel included but three Native people among the eleven listed (remember that the Abenaki are now but one of a group of minorities). Two had Abenaki ancestry, but neither was enrolled at the Abenaki Nation at Missisquoi or the Canadian reserves. Two, certainly, and perhaps all three of the Native panelists had spoken out publicly against Missisquoi. In late 1999 a state-sponsored health survey of Vermont's Native Americans was contracted to the Dawnland

Fig. 47. "The Future Abenaki Reservation according to the Burlington Free Press." *Pen and ink,*
Laura Pinter, 1991; Wôbanakik Heritage Center Collection, photograph by Andrew Lee.

Center. Missisquoi was not contacted. The Dawnland Center's priorities
and criteria were incorporated into the state survey. This led to a lively discussion between state officials and the Abenaki Tribal Council in early
November 1999. A personal example of this diffuse exclusionary practice
occurred about the same time, in the November 1999 University of Vermont symposium on Vermont's Native people. One of the organizers, although a former employee at Missisquoi, was now very connected to one
of the other Swanton political groups. Missiquoi was not contacted. Ethnohistorian John Moody pushed hard for my inclusion after I was not
named on the original list of participants. Chief Rushlow, who was invited
well after the organizers had set the agenda and speakers, refused to participate. It was an interesting thrust-and-parry exercise that illustrated the personal and professional hazards of organized factionalism. It even included
the release of my personal letter written to one of the university organizers
to the other faction. This person used the letter, as Chief Rushlow put it, "to
make more trouble for us." The result was that I was the only active citizen
of the Abenaki Nation at Missisquoi who attended the Abenaki conference,
out of scores of Native people. The two University of Vermont organizers

were initially unaware of the organizational pitfalls of dealing with internal Native politics. Organizer James Petersen was very supportive of my participation, and the conference was a great success on many fronts. But factionalism still remains beneath the surface, waiting to confound us all.

By 2000 the war had finally come full circle. The Abenaki community has internalized the ethnic cleansing of the last four hundred years, routinely threatening one another and calling each other "wannabe Indians," a common process in Indian country called "lateral oppression" by sociologists. We not only had to fight Vermont but our brethren as well, and the media spun their own tale. However, the renaissance moves on, for with each year, more truth about our history is revealed, exposing the falsehoods and racism (such as those illustrated above) of those who would stand in our way. The rebirth of a nation is a hard thing, and we are being tested, but we will emerge the stronger for it.[3] At the time of this writing, Missisquoi is awaiting active consideration for Federal Recognition.

New Abenaki Initiatives

On a positive note: In the summer of 1998, the Abenaki Nation moved from its decades-old offices in the Swanton Railroad Depot to a more modern and central facility (fig. 48). One side became the tribal offices, a much improved modern facility. One section, however, was reserved for a proposed tribal museum. Its message was chosen specifically to promote Abenaki cultural continuity and sovereignty. A selection of original and replicated artifacts was transferred from the Wôbanakik Heritage Center to the new museum. It opened on November 15, 1998, and has been an immense success. Visiting politicians seem enthusiastic, so much so that by May 29, 1999, the official opening of the Tribal Headquarters, the legislature appropriated $25,000 for an expansion. (Fig. 49.)

The museum has become an important component of the Abenaki Heritage Celebration, opening its doors to honored First Nations guests from the United States and Canada. It has greatly increased understanding of our culture by our Native brethren. As of this writing, the museum is moving into expanded quarters. Following the museum's mission, every program and every lecture has promoted continuity and sovereignty, as does this book. With the transferral of its Abenaki collection to the museum, Wôbanakik Heritage Center refocused its mission in 1998. It now promotes a revival of the Great Council Fire, the ancient alliance of the Abenaki and their neighbors.

Fig. 48. Abenaki Tribal Headquarters in 1998. *Photograph by Andrew Lee.*

The Last Best Hope for Peace

As I close this narrative, the Abenaki people are in an ambiguous position. So much of our history and culture is now known that there is no remaining doubt that state and federal recognition are warranted, a significant change from just ten years ago. New England's Anglo elite, as well as tourists, are consistently entranced by our "exotic other" pow-wow and cultural event presence. On one level, it is the best time since 1609 to be a Native person in Vermont. On another level it is a terrible time to be Native. Necessary but controversial decisions by the Abenaki Nation at Missisquoi, such as tightening membership requirements and consolidating chiefly power, triggered a certain loss of standing within the larger Abenaki community. This engendered an environment for the blossoming of dissident groups and gave the media an opening to further destabilize the Abenaki community. This "lateral oppression" within the Abenaki community is more apparent than real. Each of the current twelve Abenaki organizations consists of a single (or perhaps two) strong-willed (usually male) charismatic individual surrounded by a group of devoted followers. My hunch is that the oppression is the result of inflated sense of self, hurt feelings, and jealousy among these leaders rather than doctrinal differences between the groups—in other words, politics as usual.

Fig. 49. Inside the Abenaki Tribal Museum and Heritage Center in May 1999. *Photograph by Andrew Lee.*

Other First Nations have vast differences based on religion, centuries-old family band rivalries, externally imposed tribal governments, relations with organized crime, and real revenge. Perhaps the only real divisive issue is that of the definition of an Abenaki citizen. I have reports from most (not all) of the various factions that the community would stand together if push came to shove. This is evident in the reburial of our dead and preventing real estate development of sacred lands. The only real barrier to ending lateral oppression is an absence of any political means to heal wounded egos and engender a greater sense of unity. The greatest threat to the state's and media's agenda of keeping the Abenakis disorganized and weak is the internal development of procedures to allow these charismatic leaders to work together. A common theme discussed by my spiritual elders at Missisquoi, as well as Odanak and Passamaquoddy, is that the current leaders, who are of my generation, have absorbed so much hatred from the attempts at ethnic cleansing, foreign wars, and family tragedy that they cannot work with anyone. Yet they refuse to cede any real power. It is an Abenaki belief that this destructive life force is neutralized by correct burial ceremony, freeing following generations to act independently. But I refuse to believe that my generation must pass before healing can occur (I want a happy ending for the sixth edition of this book!).

There is a last best hope for peace. Years ago we were fighting each other over the new powers given to us in the fur trade. But an ancient genius came up with the inspiration of condolence, the commitment to address emotions before business; and consolation, providing a hospitable environment for visitors. These ceremonies, slowly, over a decades-long transition, ended bloodshed based on differences far greater than those we have today. I have recently began trying condolence on my opponents, and the results are still problematic. At least people are beginning to hear of the old ways of soothing egos and coming together. My hope is that as time goes by this also will dampen lateral oppression, well before burial does. But for this we need help. Unity cannot come only from within. Beginning in the summer of 1998, connections between the Wôbanakik Heritage Center and the Mohawk reserves in the United States and Canada, as well as our Penobscot, Passamaquoddy, Malecite, and Micmac kinsmen, have been made and are expanding. This has opened our horizons to areas of mutual concern with our Native neighbors, making our dissentions seem petty. These people have watched the ebb and flow of the Abenaki from afar and are sharing their wisdom and perspectives (some of which have been incorporated in this book). The Seven Nations of Canada, which pressed the Abenaki land claims against a 1799 Vermont, are reviving, and Missisquoi is an active participant. Perhaps down the line, we will build mere understanding and communication into something more enduring: an international solidarity, our last best hope for victory.

Thus, as the Bear awakens, families are talking, sharing old lore, learning that they are not alone. As the renaissance began at Missisquoi, it is spreading throughout our land, from southeastern New Hampshire to Lake Between. Families are coming forth from obscurity and getting to know each other. New bands are forming in western Vermont, in New Hampshire, and even in Maine and Massachusetts. No longer is the sound of drums and rattles muffled by hiding. Our squabbles are more appearance than substance and seem increasingly confined to a few aging agitators. The frenzied current government/media offensives show that the Anglo seats of power finally comprehend that the greater Abenaki Nation will realize its dreams of sovereignty. As always, the major weapon against the forces of darkness is the truth, and this book is my account of the truth. The Bear is awake, and Koluscap is returning! *Eyah*, it is done.

Appendix 1

The Place-Names of Wôbanakik

Introduction

Wôbanakik, "The Place of the Dawn," is a pleasant Native American land that includes what is now called northern New England and the Canadian Maritime Provinces. It is the land occupied by the Wôbanakikiiak, known to Euro-Americans as the Western Abenaki, Penobscot, Passamaquoddy, Malecite, and Micmac peoples. Each nation, from the Penobscot Nation eastward, has consistent scholarly and government recognition and the formalized political geography that goes with it. This glossary applies the general term Wôbanakik to the little studied, politically ambiguous "western" Wôbanakik area bounded by the sovereign Penobscot Nation to the northeast, the lands formerly occupied by the Wendat (Huron) people to the north, the lands of the Iroquois and Mahicans to the west, the Nipmuc Nation and their relatives to the south, and the Atlantic Ocean to the southeast. Place-names within Wôbanakik are descriptive of the locality, like "rocky river." They may refer to a river, a settlement at that river, or even to the people who live there, reinforcing in a geographic way, the

Sources for this appendix: Western Abenaki names are from: Gordon M. Day (1981a and 1994), Henry L. Masta (1932), Joseph Laurent (1884). Three Penobscot place-names are used in eastern-most Wôbanakik, since there are no recorded words for them in published Western Abenaki sources: Apikwehkik (Pigwacket or Fryeburg, Maine), Asepihtegw (Ossippee, New Hampshire), and Laesikɑntegw (Androscoggin River, New Hampshire and Maine). These are from *The Wabanakis of Maine and the Maritimes* (American Friends Service Committee).

idea that people are part of the natural landscape. This naming is unlike European place names which commemorate people or far away places. Place-names listed below do not include all that are known; names of purely local interest are omitted.

Since the names come from sources that wrote and pronounced the names differently, I leave them mostly as written, with minimal editing. "Correct" pronunciation of the place-names is complex and is not the goal of this listing. But if the vowels are pronounced as if they were in the Spanish language, the place-names will probably be understood by a speaker of Western Abenaki. The ô and α symbols are required for writing Abenaki languages; the former is a Western Abenaki nasal sound, "ohn," and the latter is a Penobscot "uh" sound. Place-names in parentheses are outside Wôbanakik but have Abenaki names and are important to Abenaki history and geography. Also note that the English meaning is only an approximation, since Western Abenaki words have different connotations and meanings from those in English. For example, the *k* suffix common in the list is the Abenaki locative ending and can mean "at the," place of," or "location."

Modern Name	Abenaki Name	Approximate English Meaning
Atlantic Ocean	Sobagwa	Great Ocean
Connecticut		
(Mashentucket Pequot)	Mazôntegok	Wild Hemp River
Connecticut R.	Kwinitegok	Long River
Maine		
Androscoggin R.	Laesikαntegw	Rock Shelter River
Fryeburg	Apikwehkik	At Land of Hollows
Kennebago L.	Kwenôbagok	Long Lake
Kennebec R.	Kenebec	Deep River
Kennebunk	Kinibôka	Rough Ground
(Malecite Nation)	Moskwas	Muskrat
(Micmac Nation)	Micmôz	Micmac Person
Moosehead L.	Mozôdebinebesek	Moose Head Lake
Mousem R.	M'mosem	My Moose (River)
Norridgewock	Molôjoak	Deep-flow River
Ogunquit	Ogwaômkwik	At the Accumulated Sand
Pejepscot	Pejepskw	Bad Rock
(Penobscot Nation)	Panôbskaik	Place of Penobscot
Saco	Sokwakik	At the South Place

Modern Name	Abenaki Name	Approximate English Meaning
Saco R.	Zawakwtegok	South River
Sebago L.	Sobagwa	Ocean
Village of Wawenock	Wôlinak	At a Bay
Massachusetts		
Connecticut R.	Kwinitegok	Long River
(Pocumtuck R.)	Pokwômtegok	Very Narrow River
Squakeag	Sokwakik	At the South Place
Merrimac R.	Molôdemak	Deep River
New Hampshire		
Ammonoosuc R.	Ômanosek	Fishing Place
Androscoggin R.	Laesikɑntegw	Rock Shelter River
Concord	Penokok	Down Hill
Connecticut R.	Kwinitegok	Long River
Dover	Wiwinijoanek	Water Flows around It
Mt. Kearsarge	Gawasiwajo	Windfall Mountain
Mt. Washington	Gôdagwajo	Hidden Mountain
Manchester	Namaskik	Place of Fish
Massabesikick Pond	Massabesik	Large Lake
Merrimac R.	Molôdemak	Deep River
Mt. Monadnock	Menonadenak	Bare, Silver Mountain
Ossippee	Asepihtegw	River Alongside
Pemigewasset R.	Pemijoasek	Swift Current
Piscataqua R.	Pesgatakwa	Dark River
Salmon Fall R.	Nôwijoanek	Long Rapids
L. Sunapee	Seninebik	Rocky Lake
Suncook	Senikok	At the Rocks
L. Umbagog	Wôbagok	Clear Lake
White Mts.	Wawobadenik	White Mountains
L. Winnepisaukee	Wiwinebesaki	Land around Lake
Winnepisaukee Village	Wiwinebesakik	Land around Lake Place
New York		
(Adirondack Mts.)	Wawobadenik	White Mountains
(Ausable Chasm)	Nagwiajoak	Underground Stream
(Ausable R.)	Senapskaizibok	Rocky River
(Land of Iroquois)	Magwak	At the Iroquois
(Land of Mahicans)	Mahiganek	At the Mahigans
(Saranac R.)	Salôntegok	Sumac River
(Saratoga)	Nebizonbik	Medicine Water
(Schaghticoke)	Mskitegwa	Quiet Water
Split Rock	Zobapskwa	Split Rock
(Ticonderoga)	Tsitôtegwila	Waterway Continues

Modern Name	Abenaki Name	Approximate English Meaning

Quebec

Ash Island (Richl. R)	Odebesek	Head Place
(Land of Algonquins)	Osôganek	Algonquin Place
Chaudiere R.	Kikôntegok	River of Fields
Coaticook R.	Goategok	Pine River
Durham	Kwanahômoik	Long Point in River Bend
Megantic L.	Namaskonkik	Fish Field
L. Mephramagog	Mamhlawbagok	Wide Water
Missisquoi Bay	Masipskiwibi	Flint Water
Odanak	Odanak	Dwellings (Village)
Phillipsburg	Dawkskodasek	Open Meadow
Richilieu R.	Bitawbagwizibok	Lake Between River
St. Francis R.	Alsogôntegok	Empty Cabin River
St. Lawrence R.	Ktsitegok	Great River
(Land of Hurons)	Ktsitegwiiak	Great River People
Wolinak	Wôlinak	At a Bay

Vermont

Alburg Springs	Nebizônnibizik	Little Medicine Water
Mt. Ascutney	Pemapskadena	Rocky Mountain
Bellows Falls	Ktsipontegok	Great Falls
Black R.	Mikazawitegok	Black River
L. Bomoseen	Bonsawinno	Fire Keeper
Camel's Hump	Dowabodiwadjo	Saddle Mountain
L. Champlain	Bitawbagok	Lake Between
Connecticut R.	Kwinitegok	Long River
Dead Creek	Pibesgantegok	Roily River
Fair Haven	Skokagik	Snake Place
Grand Isle	Ktsimenahan	Great Island
Highgate Springs	Nebizônnibik	Medicine Water
Holland Pond	Massawippi	Clear Water
Island Pond	Menahanbagok	Island Lake
Isle la Motte	Azibijizikok	Sheep Dung Place
Lamoille R.	Wintegok	Marrow River
Lamoille R. Mouth	Kwenosakek	Pike Place
La Platte R.	Kwenaskategok	Long Point River
Lewis Creek	Seniganitegok	Stone Works River
(Land of Mahicans)	Mahiganek	At the Mahigans
Mt. Mansfield	Mozeodebe wadso	Moose Head Mt.
Maquam Bay	Tamakwa	Beaver
L. Mephramagog	Mamhlawbagok	Wide Water
Milton	Mskitegwa	Quiet Water

Modern Name	Abenaki Name	Approximate English Meaning
Missisquoi Bay	Masipskiwibi	Flint Water
Missisquoi R.	Wazowategok	Crooked River
Newbury	Goasek	Place of Pines
Nulhegan R.	Klahigantegok	Wooden Trap River
Otter Creek	Onegigwizibok	Otter River
Passumpsic R.	Pasômkasik	Clear Sandy River
Mt. Philo	Mateguasaden	Rabbit Mountain
Pike R.	Kwenozasek	At the Pike Place
Mt. Pisga	Pisgah	Dark
Sand Bar St. Park	Kiilesagwôgan	Land Bridge
Shelburne Point	Kwinaska	Long Point
Swanton	Mazipskoik	Flint Place
Swanton Falls	Dakwahoganizek	Little Mill Place
Thompson's Point	Kwazôwapskak	Extended Rock
Vergennes	Natami pontegok	First Falls
White R.	Wasabastegok	Clear Stream
Winooski	Winoskik	Onion Place
Winooski R.	Winoskitegok	Onion River

Appendix 2

The Herbal Medicine of Wôbanakik

Introduction

The Native people of Wôbanakik believe that the natural state of things is health and balance. Sickness or accident is intrusive, entering one's mind or body, a force that must be neutralized to reestablish the balance in one's life. Therapy is holistic, treating the whole person, mind and body—a technique recently rediscovered by the Euro-American medical profession. Every mother, then as now, has quick, effective remedies for childhood's illnesses, while the shaman uses specialized expertise to diagnose and treat more complex and troubling diseases. The parent or shaman has a group of trusted allies: plants that can be processed so as to protect or enter the body to fight disease with the aid of proper ritual or ceremony. Techniques were developed long ago for taking the spirit inherent in the plant and transforming it into a tool that could enter the ailing body and treat the illness. Infusions, poultices, even smoke carried the healing properties of the originating plant to the disease. There the plant and ritual could work together to draw out or alleviate the disease. Before the introduction of European and African diseases, there were few life-threatening viral or bacterial afflictions other than a form of bone tuberculosis, which left its imprint on the bones of our hallowed dead, as the invasive analyses of Euro-American scientists have revealed.

I have included some additional published material from our Innu

Sources for this appendix: Aroostock Indian Resource Center, n.d. Nicholas Denys (1908), Frank G. Speck (1915a), Frank Speck and R. W. Dexter (1951, 1952).

(Montagnais), Algonquin, and Haudenosaunee (Iroquois) neighbors, since their curing practices were often shared with us. Below are listed a few of the recorded herbal medicines of Wôbanakik. They need to be made in a specific way and given to the patient in a specific dosage. Therefore, I have not included exact recipes and do not recommend attempting to use any of these medicines without extensive training.

Remember: misuse of this information may lead to complications or even poisoning!

Herbal Preparation

The Alnôba herbalist knows the medicinal qualities of great numbers of plants, information discovered centuries or millennia earlier and carefully transmitted by an elaborate apprenticeship system. The herbalist knows what part of the plant is best for which disease and when that part would have its maximum potency. Leaves and twigs are most potent in the late summer; bark is most efficacious in the spring and early summer. Some plants should be used green, the essential spirit departing with freshness; others retain their power for some time if dried correctly. The herbalist knows to ask permission of a patch of medicinal plants, even leaving an offering of tobacco or cornmeal. Only a portion of the resource is harvested from any patch, yet another way of showing respect for the spirit of the healing plants. The customary practice to prepare plants is to handpick and clean or rinse the leaves, twigs, and bark to remove any extraneous plant parts, insects, dirt, etc. The plant material is usually added to a specific amount of water and boiled or steeped in hot water. The theory is that the power in the plant is liberated and transferred to the hot water. The herbal tea can be drunk or applied to the offending element. Another technique is to mash or shred the plant material, perhaps mix it with a little water or sap, and apply it as a poultice to the affected area, where the spirit will pass directly from the plant to the body. Occasionally, the plant is chewed, releasing more of the power directly. The Penobscot people use another technique: sweet flag (*Acorus calamus*) is steamed through the house to keep away disease.

Psychiatric and Neurological Medicine

The Alnôba traditionally engage the shaman to diagnose and cure mental and neurological illnesses. Diagnostic and curative technique involves discussion of dreams, visions, etc., a real form of psychoanalysis. The shaman also uses trance and ritual to further assist the patient to understand what troubles him or her. However, certain problems, such as weakness or nervousness, are amenable to treatment with plant medicine.

Weakness and Nervousness

Wild sarsaparilla (*Aralia nudicaulis*) root is steeped for weakness (Montagnais).

Ground hemlock (*Taxus canadensis*) is mixed with ground pine for weakness (Montagnais).

Yellow lady's slipper (*Cypropedium calceolus*) is good for nervousness (Penobscot).

Paralysis and Epilepsy

Bunchberry (*Cornus canadensis*) is steeped for paralysis (Montagnais) and for fits (Malecite).

External Medicine

External medicinal plant treatments usually consist of poultices of crushed leaves, or saps applied directly to the affected area. However, an infusion is sometimes used, as in the case of common juniper needles, which are steeped to make an antiseptic and stimulating (and sweet-smelling) hair wash.

Skin and Hair Problems, Boils

Balsam fir (*Abies balsamea*) resin for frostbite (Malecite).

Common juniper (*Juniperus communis*) is a hair wash (Micmac and Malecite).

Hemlock (*Tsuga canadensis*) is for chapped skin (Micmac and Malecite).

Jack-in-the-pulpit (*Arisaema triphyllum*) is steeped to make a liniment for general use; LIQUID IS POISON (Penobscot).

Pin cherry (*Prunus pennsylvanica*) wood is good for chafed skin (Malecite).

Pitch pine (*Pinus rigida*) as poultice is for boils and abscesses (Penobscot).

Spotted wintergreen (*Chimaphila maculata*) can be steeped and applied to blisters (Penobscot).

White pine (*Pinus strobus*) pitch is for boils and abscesses (Penobscot).

White spruce (*Picea glauca*) gum is a poultice for boils (Micmac).

Cuts and Wounds

Alder (*Alnus* spp.) leaves and bark for festering wounds (Micmac).

Balsam fir (*Abies balsamea*) resin for cuts (Micmac and Malecite).

Basswood (*Tilia americana*) inner bark sutures wounds (Algonquin).

Common juniper (*Juniperus communis*) gum is for healing cuts (Micmac and Malecite).

Spikenard (*Aralia racemosa*) root is for wounds (Montagnais).

White pine (*Pinus strobus*) bark poultice for wounds (Micmac and Malecite).

White spruce (*Picea glauca*) salve is for scabs and sores, cuts and wounds; gum is a poultice for boils and abcesses (Micmac and Malecite).

Bleeding

Bloodroot (*Sanguinaria canadensis*) roots are strung around the neck to prevent bleeding (Penobscot).

White pine (*Pinus strobus*) tea is for hemorrhage (Malecite).

Sores and Infected Wounds

Balsam fir (*Abies balsamea*) is for bruises, sores, wounds (Micmac and Malecite).

Bloodroot roots (*Sanguinaria canadensis*) are for infected wounds and cuts (Malecite).

Slippery elm (*Ulmus rubra*) bark is for draining infected wounds (Malecite).

Tamarack (*Larix laricina*) bark is for festering wounds (Micmac and Malecite).

White pine inner bark (*Pinus strobus*) is for sores and swellings (Micmac and Montagnais).

Burns

Balsam fir (*Abies balsamea*) is for burns (Micmac and Malecite).

White cedar leaves (*Thuja occidentalis*) is a poultice for burns (Micmac and Malecite).

Eye Problems

Red osier dogwood (*Cornus stolonifera*) is for sore eyes (Malecite).

Spikenard (*Aralia racemosa*) root is for sore eyes (Montagnais).

Swelling of Limbs

Blue flag (*Iris versicolor*) is crushed and mixed with flour to make a poultice for any pain (Penobscot).

Clustered snakeroot (*Sanicoula gregaria*) is for swelling and inflammation (Algonquin).

Moosewood (*Acer pennsylvanicum*) bark is steeped for a poultice for swelling of limbs (Penobscot).

Twinflower (*Linnea borealis*) mash is made of the plant for inflammation of the limbs (Montagnais).

Water lily (*Nymphaea tuberosa*) leaves are made into a mash for swelling of limbs (Penobscot).

Water lily (*Nymphaea tuberosa*) root is boiled and made into a poultice for swelling limbs (Micmac, Montagnais, Penobscot).

White cedar leaves (*Thuja occidentalis*) is a poultice for swollen hands and feet (Penobscot, Micmac, and Malecite).

Communicable Viral and Bacterial Diseases

After the European invasion, alien viral and bacterial diseases swept through Wôbanakik. Most of these debilitating diseases had associated fevers. It became obvious that several thousand years' experience with medicinal plants was ineffective against them. There was little time to experiment, as many thousands died. Nevertheless, some old prescriptions, such as willow bark, did reduce fevers and alleviate suffering, so that it became the basis for aspirin and its acetominophen and ibuprofen descendants.

Communicable Diseases

Alder (*Alnus* spp.) bark tea for diptheria (Montagnais).

Black spruce (*Picea mariana*) bark with white maple (*Acer saccharrinum*) bark make a tea for the flu (Montagnais).

Highbush cranberry (*Viburnum* sp.) berries make a tea for mumps (Micmac and Malecite).

Pitcher plant (*Sarracenia purpuria*) is for smallpox (Montagnais).

Spotted wintergreen (*Chimaphila maculata*) is for smallpox (Malecite).

Sweet flag (*Acorus calamus*) root is for cholera (Penobscot).

Water avens (*Geum rivale*) root tea for dysentery (Penobscot).

Colds, Fever, Headache

Alder (*Alnus* sp.) leaves and bark make a tea for fever (Malecite).

Angelica (*Angelica atropurpureum*) root is for cold in head.

Aspen (*Populus tremuloides*) bark is steeped and made into a tea for colds (Penobscot and Malecite).

Balsam fir (*Abies balsamea*) or tamarack (*Larix laricina*) is for colds (Micmac and Malecite).

Black spruce (*Picea mariana*) bark with white maple (*Acer saccharrinum*) bark make a tea for colds, cough, flu (Malecite).

Ground hemlock (*Taxus canadensis*) is made into a tea for fever (Micmac) or colds (Penobscot).

Hemlock (*Tsuga canadensis*) bark makes a tea for colds (Micmac and Malecite).

Juniper (*Juniperus communis*) berries for colds (Malecite).

Labrador tea (*Ledum groenlandicum*) leaves and twigs are for chills (Montagnais).

Red osier dogwood (*Cornus stolonifera*) is for headache (Malecite).

Seneca snakeroot (*Polygala senega*) root is used for colds (Malecite).

Shining willow (*Salix lucida*) bark is steeped and made into a mash and put in a bandage for headache (Montagnais).

Speckled alder (*Alnus rugosa*) bark boiled or partridge berry (*Mitchella repens*) berries are cooked into a jelly for fever (Montagnais).

Spikenard (*Aralia racemosa*) root is for colds (Montagnais).

Sweet flag (*Acorus calamus*) root is for colds. (Penobscot).

Tamarack (*Larix laricina*) bark tea for colds (Micmac and Malecite).

White cedar leaves (*Thuja occidentalis*) is for headache (Micmac and Malecite).

White pine (*Pinus strobus*) tea is for colds (Micmac and Malecite), and gum is for colds (Montagnais).

White pine (*Pinus strobus*) bark, needles, and twigs with hemlock (*Tsuga canadensis*) tea for colds (Micmac and Malecite).

Wild lily of the valley (*Maianthemum canadense*) tea is for headache (Montagnais).

Willow (*Salix nigra*) bark or common juniper (*Juniperus communis*) needles and twigs are steeped for colds (Penobscot).

Sore Throat

Angelica (*Angelica atropurpureum*) root or red osier dogwood (*Cornus stolonifera*) is for sore throat (Malecite).

Pitcher plant (*Sarracenia purpuria*) roots are for sore throat (Micmac).

Staghorn sumac (*Rhus typhina*) berries make a tea for sore throat (Montagnais).

White pine (*Pinus strobus*) gum alone or with white spruce (*Picea glauca*) twigs boiled with root of sour grass (*Oxalis* sp.) for throat trouble (Montagnais).

Chest Problems

White spruce (*Picea glauca*) twigs are boiled with root of sour grass (*Oxalis* sp.) for lung trouble (Montagnais).

Coughs and Grippe

Angelica (*Angelica atropurpureum*) root is for coughs (Malecite).

Black cherry (*Prunus serotina*) bark is steeped for coughs (Penobscot and Malecite).

Black spruce (*Picea mariana*) bark with white maple (*Acer saccharrinum*) bark make a tea for cough (Malecite).

Black spruce (*Picea mariana*) is a cough remedy (Micmac and Malecite).

Black spruce (*Picea mariana*) twigs are boiled for cough (Montagnais).

Hemlock (*Tsuga canadensis*) is for grippe (Micmac and Malecite).

Red osier dogwood (*Cornus stolonifera*) is for catarrh (Malecite).

Water avens (*Geum rivale*) root tea for coughs.

Water lily (*Nymphaea tuberosa*) juice of root is for coughs (Micmac, Montagnais).

White pine (*Pinus strobus*) tea is for cough and grippe (Micmac and Malecite).

White pine (*Pinus strobus*) bark, needles, and twigs with hemlock (*Tsuga canadensis*) tea for cough and grippe (Montagnais).

Wild sarsaparilla (*Aralia nudicaulis*) root is dried and crushed to powder and steeped for coughs (Montagnais).

Consumption and Spitting Up Blood

American elm (*Ulmus americana*) bark tea for spitting up blood (Penobscot).

Black cherry (*Prunus serotina*) bark tea is for consumption (Malecite).

Bloodroot roots (*Sanguinaria canadensis*) are for consumption (Malecite).

Cleavers (*Galium aparine*) is for spitting up blood (Penobscot).

Common juniper (*Juniperus communis*) gum is for tuberculosis and consumption (Micmac and Malecite).

Jack-in-the-pulpit (*Arisaema triphyllum*) root bulb treatment of tuburculosis; TOXIC (Malecite).

Liverberry (*Streptopus amplexifolius*) is steeped for spitting up blood (Penobscot).

Moosewood (*Acer pennsylvanicum*) bark is steeped for a spitting of blood (Penobscot).

Pitcher plant (*Sarracenia purpuria*) is for spitting up blood (Penobscot, Malecite).

Spotted wintergreen (*Chimaphila maculata*) is for consumption (Malecite).

Star flower (*Frientalis borealis*) is steeped for consumption (Montagnais).

Tamarack (*Larix laricina*) bark is for consumption (Micmac and Malecite).

White cedar (*Thuja occidentalis*) leaf poultice is for consumption and cough (Micmac and Malecite).

White pine gum (*Pinus strobus*) is for consumption (Montagnais, Penobscot).

Sexually Transmitted Diseases

Cleavers (*Galium aparine*) or spikenard (*Aralia racemosa*) is for gonorrhea (Penobscot).

Moosewood (*Acer pennsylvanicum*) bark or liverberry (*Streptopus amplexifolius*) is steeped for a gonorrhea remedy (Penobscot).

Internal Medicine

Internal medicine includes problems with the internal organs other than those associated with communicable diseases such as influenza. The mouth could be treated with poultices and chewing the medicinal plant part, but the more inaccessible organs needed an infusion to carry the healing principal to the disease.

Teeth and Mouth

Black alder (*Alnus incana*) bark is boiled for ulcerated mouth (Montagnais).

Gold thread (*Coptis trifolia*) stems are chewed for cankers or sores in mouth or sore gums (Penobscot).

White cedar leaves (*Thuja occidentalis*) is a poultice for toothache (Micmac and Malecite).

Asthma

Shining willow (*Salix lucida*) bark is smoked to relieve asthma (Penobscot).

Stomach Problems

Alder (*Alnus* spp.) bark tea for retching (Indians of Maine).

Common juniper (*Juniperus communis*) is for ulcers (Micmac and Malecite).

Jack-in-the-pulpit (*Arisaema triphyllum*) root bulb stomach medicine; TOXIC (Micmac).

Juniper (*Juniperus communis*) underbark and berries make a tea for ulcers (Micmac).

Mountain ash (*Sorbus americana*) bark is boiled and drunk to stimulate appetite (Montagnais).

Mountain ash (*Sorbus americana*) bark is boiled and drunk to cause vomiting or for stomach pain (Micmac and Malecite).

Raspberry (*Rubus* sp.) runners make a tea for stomach problems (Micmac).

Spotted wintergreen (*Chimaphila maculata*) is for stomach trouble (Malecite).

Sweet flag (*Acorus calamus*) root is for indigestion (Micmac).

White spruce (*Picea glauca*) or hemlock (*Tsuga canadensis*) is for stomach trouble (Micmac and Malecite).

Wild ginger (*Asarum canadense*) is for stomach ills (Indians of Maine).

Colic in Infants

Balsam fir (*Abies balsamea*) is for colic and is a laxative (Micmac and Malecite).

Mountain ash (*Sorbus americana*) root is boiled and made into a tea for colic (Micmac).

Sweet flag (*Acorus calamus*) root is for stomach pain in babies (Indians of Maine).

Expel Intestinal Worms

Aspen (*Populus tremuloides*) bark is dried and steeped for worms in children (Montagnais).

Intestinal Tract

Balsam fir (*Abies balsamea*) is for colic and is a laxative (Micmac and Malecite).

Hemlock (*Tsuga canadensis*) is for diarrhea and bowel troubles (Micmac and Malecite).

Choke berry (*Aronia arbustifolia*) bark is steeped for diarrhea (Micmac).

Chokecherry (*Prunus virginiana*) bark is steeped for diarrhea (Malecite).

Elder (*Sambucus canadensis*) is made into a purgative (Malecite and Micmac).

Ground hemlock (*Taxus canadensis*) is a tea for bowel and internal trouble (Micmac).

Mountain ash (*Sorbus americana*) bark is boiled and infused as a tea; acts as a diuretic (Malecite and Micmac).

Speckled alder (*Alnus rugosa*) bark is boiled for cramps (Montagnais).

Yellow birch (*Betula allegheniensis*) bark tea is for diarrhea (Malecite and Micmac).

Hemorrhoids

White oak (*Quercus alba*) bark is steeped to make a drink for bleeding piles (Penobscot).

Urinary Tract Problems

Labrador tea (*Ledum groenlandicum*) leaves are made into a diuretic (Micmac, Montagnais).

Spotted wintergreen (*Chimaphila maculata*) is for a cold in the bladder (Indians of Maine).

Trailing arbutus (*Epigaea repens*) tea is for gravel and urinary tract problems (Iroquois).

White pine (*Pinus strobus*) bark needles and twigs make tea for urinary trouble (Micmac and Malecite).

Kidney Problems

Cleavers (*Galium aparine*) is for kidney trouble (Penobscot).

Hemlock (*Tsuga canadensis*) is for cold in kidneys (Micmac and Malecite).

Liverberry (*Streptopus amplexifolius*) is steeped for kidney trouble (Penobscot).

Moosewood (*Acer pennsylvanicum*) bark is steeped for kidney trouble (Micmac).

Pitcher plant (*Sarracenia purpuria*) is for kidney trouble (Penobscot, Malecite).

Trailing arbutus (*Epigaea repens*) tea is for kidney problems (Iroquois).

White pine (*Pinus strobus*) tea is for kidney trouble (Micmac and Malecite).

Yellow clintonia (*Clintonia borealis*) expressed juice of root is for gravel (Montagnais).

Blood Problems

Labrador tea (*Ledum groenlandicum*) leaves and twigs purify the blood (Montagnais).

Mountain ash (*Sorbus americana*) bark is boiled and drunk to purify the blood (Micmac).

Speckled alder (*Alnus incana*) twigs are boiled for impure blood (Montagnais).

Spotted wintergreen (*Chimaphila maculata*) is for purification of the blood (Malecite).

Trailing arbutus (*Epigaea repens*) tea is for blood problems (Iroquois).

Bone Breaks and Sprains

Balsam fir (*Abies balsamea*) is for fractures (Micmac and Malecite).

Juniper (*Juniperus communis*) gum with eelskin bandage is for sprains (Indians of Maine).

Rheumatism

Beaked hazel (*Corylus conuta*) twigs are made into a tea for rheumatism (Micmac).

Blueberry (*Vaccinium* spp.) leaves are a tea for rheumatism (Malecite and Micmac).

Common juniper (*Juniperus communis*) is for rheumatism (Micmac and Malecite).

Yellow birch (*Betula allegheniensis*) bark makes a tea for rheumatism (Indians of Maine).

Midwifery and Childbirth

Childbirth is not generally considered a disease warranting hospitalization as is common among Euro-American people. Childbirth is usually at home with assistance from family members and a midwife, a professional who assists in the birthing process. Herbal medicines are prepared by the midwife for easing the pain and disorientation attending childbirth, as well as cleansing and healing agents for the mother after the birth has taken place.

Birth Control

Turtle head (*Chelone glabra*) is for prevention of pregnancy (Malecite).

Childbirth

Black ash (*Fraxinus nigra*) leaves are given to women after childbirth to cleanse them (Penobscot).

Ground hemlock (*Taxus canadensis*) tea brings out clots and alleviates afterbirth pain (Malecite).

Yellow lady's slipper (*Cypropedium calceolus*) is good for women in the throes of childbirth (Penobscot).

Appendix 3

Educational Resources: An Annotated Resources List for Students and Educators

Introduction

It is only within the last three decades that European scholars have shown interest in the Alnôbak, thereby changing our perceptions of history and diversity within Wôbanakik. This renaissance has been sparked in great part by activism on the part of Native people, especially in the northwestern part of what is now Vermont. As a response, many teachers, museum professionals, archaeologists, and state officials have shown an increasing need for books, audiovisual and other resources, conferences, and coursework pertaining to the Western Abenaki. This appendix is a first attempt to provide, in one place, a coherent listing by topic of the current resources available to professionals.

In addition to resources on the Alnôbak, I have included important materials concerning the closely related Eastern Wabanaki of Maine and the Canadian Maritimes. These people, especially the Micmac, have been extensively studied for many years and have by far the most written about them. The Alnôbak lived in an almost identical way and had a very similar material and spiritual world, so the more "polished" productions (such as the Mi'kmaq video listed below) are appropriate for our students until analogous materials are produced.

In this appendix, I will use the somewhat confusing Euro-American term "Abenaki" rather than Alnôbak, since that is what most people are familiar with. This should make these materials easier to use.

Abenaki Studies, General

This section includes books, periodicals, and other resources that are specific to the Western Abenaki. It also includes works that consider the Western Abenaki as part of a group of closely related peoples sharing similar language, beliefs, art, and culture.

Periodicals

First Light. Dawnland Center, P.O. Box 1358, Montpelier, VT 05601.

This monthly newsletter is from the Dawnland Center in Montpelier. The Dawnland Center, while not specifically an Abenaki institution, holds many seminars and activities that are focused on Abenaki-area issues and are attended by many Abenaki people. For people interested in Abenaki studies and current events this newsletter is critical. *Rating* ***

Articles and Booklets

"The Abenakis: Aborigines of Vermont." 1955. Stephen Laurent. *Vermont History*, pp. 286–95. Reprinted 1993 as "The Abenakis of Vermont," Vermont Historical Society.

This important article, published in the entirely Euro-American—biased *Vermont History*, was a milestone. Steven Laurent, a recognized Abenaki elder and scholar, put the cards on the table: the Abenaki were in Vermont, and they are still here. Two decades ahead of its time, the article fell on deaf ears, and it wasn't until Euro-American ethnohistorians such as Day and Calloway came forth that the Euro-American community began to listen. This article is good for people interested in the Abenaki renaissance. *Rating* ****

Books

The Abenaki. 1989. Colin Calloway. Chelsea House, New York. 110 pp.

This is the best short introduction to the people of Wôbanakik, which includes the Western Abenaki. Designed as a part of a Native American series for middle and high school students, it is even useful for younger or more mature audiences. It is well written and includes many archival photographs of Abenaki peoples surrounded by traditional clothing, lodging, and crafts. Color and halftone photographs of Abenaki artifacts complement the text and archival photography. While focusing on the better-known eastern groups, it makes a strong case for the persistence of the Western Abenaki and puts them into a regional context. This is a must for inclusion in any library on Abenaki materials. *Rating* ****

Les Abenaquis du Canada. 1986. Honorius Provost, Textes # 8. Quebec, H.ville. 32 pp.

An important introduction to the Abenakis north of the border, in French. It is a quick historical sketch of history and culture. Important for francophones, it could also be used in anglophone areas as a text for intermediate French-language coursework. *Rating* **

Abenaki Legends, Grammar and Place Names. 1932. H. L. Masta. La Voix des Bois Francs, Victoriaville, PQ.

This book is a necessary addition to the Abenaki library, in that it represents an attempt by a gifted Abenaki scholar to put in one place a wealth of linguistic, folkloric, and geographic detail. I have found this much more useful in my work than the books of Laurent or Day. I always prefer to hear what the Abenaki say about themselves first, then fill it in with Euro-American scholarly material. This book is a valuable resource for teachers or museum professionals. *Rating* ****

A History of the Abenaki People. 1977. Ken Pierce. Instructional Development Center, University of Vermont, Burlington, VT 05405.

This small book, somewhat dated, was the first attempt to give teachers and other interpreters information necessary for Vermont children to understand the Abenaki experience in Vermont. This is of historical interest only. *Rating* **

In Search of New England's Past. 1998. M. K. Foster and William Cowan. University of Massachusetts Press, Amherst.

This is a selected compendium of the late Gordon Day's published research. Primarily for scholars, it gives an insight into his motivations (in part, to save the Abenakis' dying culture for posterity), techniques (a mix of scientific, social scientific, and historical inquiry), and material he uncovered. If you need to have access to his research, this and *Identity of the St. Francis Indians* (see below) are good places to start. *Rating* ****

New Dawn: The Western Abenaki, a Curricular Framework for the Middle Level. 1987. Linda Pearo, Frederick Wiseman, Madeline Young, and Jeff Benay. Franklin Northwest Supervisory Union Title IX Indian Education Program, 14 First Street, Swanton, VT 05488.

This book is a first attempt at converting the wealth of data on the Abenaki into a format usable by teachers. It is wide-ranging and covers most of the information out there that is applicable. The archaeology sections are somewhat dated and simplistic, and the history also does not take into account much of Colin Calloway's excellent and detailed work. I do like its use of all sorts of different sources, from newspaper clippings to articles to sections of longer published works. A good start but needs a second edition. *Rating* ***

Northeast Indian Resource Secrets. 1997. Thomas Ford. Audenreed Press, Brunswick, ME. 129 pp.

This book is a very interesting compendium of Ford's thoughts and resources for teachers who are attempting to portray the Wabanaki peoples in their classrooms. Laced with his own spirituality and beliefs about what is appropriate to teach and what isn't, this small book gives another, much needed perspective to teachers. *Rating* **

A Semi Annotated Bibliography: The Wabanakis. 1982. Boston Indian Council, 105 S. Huntington Avenue, Boston, MA 02136.

This is an excellent resource for professionals or high school teachers; however, it shows the very distinct "Maine bias" that implies that Maine is the only place in the Abenaki area that contains Native people. Also somewhat dated. *Rating* *

The Wabanaki: An Annotated Bibliography of Selected Books, Articles, Documents about Maliseet, Micmac, Passamaquoddy, Penobscot Indians in Maine, Annotated by Native Americans. 1982. Eunice Nelson. American Friends Service Committee, Box 286, Orono, ME 04473.

This is a very valuable resource, although somewhat dated, showing the "Maine bias" that implies that Maine is the only place in the Abenaki area that contains Native people. Good as a reference for high school or college students. *Rating**

The Wabanakis of Maine and the Maritimes. 1989. American Friends Service Committee, Maine Indian Program. PO Box 1096, Bath, ME 04530.

This is the premier book treating the whole "Wabanaki cluster" of peoples. It is designed for elementary school teachers but contains a wealth of information on almost every aspect of life from 1600 until today. It includes both informational sections and lesson plans. Included in the back are various resources available for teachers. It suffers from one major flaw: it considers that the Western Abenaki of Vermont are not true Abenakis. This racist attitude is inexplicable given that the book was produced with the oversight of Native people by the American Friends Service Committee. If we disregard this flaw—*Rating* ***

"The Western Abenaki." 1978. Gordon Day. In *Northeast,* vol. 15 of *Handbook of North American Indians,* pp. 148–59.

This is one of the best short introductions to the Western Abenaki, written by their first great Euro-American exploiter and champion. Although relying heavily on material from the Canadian Mission Abenaki people, it nonetheless lays out the boundaries of the Western Abenaki homeland and discusses the culture in some depth. Its inclusion in the *Handbook of North American Indians* allows a quick comparison with neighboring people such as the Eastern Abenaki or the Mahicans. A must-read for teachers or students from middle school up. *Rating* ****

Videos

Our Dances. Penobscot Student Dance Troupe. Penobscot Nation, Indian Island, ME 04468.

This short but very nice video was done by the Indian Island Elementary School, using dances, interviews, and an animated sequence. This is an excellent resource for elementary schoolchildren to see what their neighbors in Maine can do with local and state support for their culture. *Rating* ***

Penobscot: the People and Their River. Penobscot Nation Museum, Indian Island, ME 04468.

Another well-done Penobscot production, this time focusing on their spiritual and ecological relationship to their river. It is analogous to Vermont Abenaki relations to their river. Good for fifth grade up. *Rating* ****

Wabanaki: A New Dawn. Maine Indian Tribal-State Commission, Box 87, Hallowell, ME 04347.

Probably the best introduction to the Wabanaki peoples, but like all Maine Indian productions, it leaves the Vermont Abenakis out of the culture. Good interviews and scenic shots, well integrated. *Rating* ****

Museums with Western Abenaki Materials

Abenaki Tribal Museum. 100 Grand Avenue, Swanton, VT 05488.

The Tribal Museum is the only Abenaki–run cultural center in the United States. It has an exhibition room with original and replica artifacts, as well as a large meeting and arts room. The museum is currently undergoing a major renovation and expansion. *Rating* ****

Bennington Museum. West Main Street, Bennington, VT 05201. (802) 443–1571.

The Bennington Museum, made famous by the theft of their Grandma Moses paintings, contains a small collection of Vermont artifacts and ethnographic material. Don't go there specifically for Native American materials. *Rating* *

Bixby Memorial Library. Main Street, Vergennes, VT 05491. (802) 877–2211.

The Bixby Library has collections of archaeological materials from the western portion of the Western Abenaki area. Important collections of Contact Period beads are displayed. A major problem is that many of these materials may be from desecrated graves and belong in the Earth rather than in a display case. I would not take Native people to see the materials. *Rating* *

Chimney Point State Historic Site. Rd 3 Box 3546, Vergennes, VT, 05491. (802) 759–2412.

Chimney Point is the state of Vermont's museum of Native American and French culture. It was designed with some input from the Abenaki Nation, unlike many other museum installations listed here. They sponsored the "Spirit of the Abenaki" exhibit, which was the first all-Abenaki art show in Vermont. Excellent destination for all levels of schoolchildren and young adults. *Rating* ***

Ethan Allen Homestead. Winooski Valley Park District, Burlington, VT 05401. (802) 865–4556.

The Ethan Allen Homestead has a nice, small interpretive program on the Abenaki. They have been quite responsive to the Abenaki renaissance, sponsoring symposia, handbooks, and a map of the Abenaki homeland. *Rating* ***

Robert Hull Fleming Museum. University of Vermont, Burlington, VT 05405. (802) 656–2090.

The Fleming is the premier anthropological museum in the state. It has extensive collections of materials, but the curation is in flux and it is almost impossible to find anything. This may be taken care of by the time you read this. Good as a general field trip destination *Rating* ***

Laboratory for Traditional Technology. Department of Humanities, Johnson State College, Johnson, VT 05489. (802) 635–2356, ext. 352.

The Traditional Technology Laboratory has a small but nice collection of documented historic Abenaki materials, as well as numerous replicated materials for loan to schools and other organizations. Not primarily designed as a field trip destination, it nonetheless has a good lending system of artifacts and audiovisuals. Has traveling lectures as well. *Rating* ***

(*Note*: The laboratory was closed in February 2000; we await a possible reopening.)

Lawson Middle School. Middle Street, Essex Junction, VT 05452. (802) 878–3361.

The David Marvin Collection has extensive artifact collections from throughout North America. One case contains materials from the Western Abenaki area. It would probably be OK for a general archaeology tour for a small group of middle or high school students, but it is not arranged or displayed properly for large numbers of students. *Rating* *

Mt. Kearsarge Indian Museum. PO Box 142, Kearsarge Mt. Rd., Warner, NH 03278. (603) 456–2600.

This is an excellent small museum, basically devoted to western Indian groups. There are some Abenaki and Micmac materials. It has an excellent museum shop, the Dreamcatcher. The museum sponsors seasonal celebrations attended by local Wabanaki people. Call ahead as the museum is not open all year. *Rating* *** (If we consider it as an *Abenaki* museum, *.)

Musee des Abenakis, 58 Wabanaki, Odanak, PQ JoG 1Ho. (514) 568–2600.

The Musee des Abenakis gives tours in English during the fall, spring, and summer seasons. An excellent long day trip for all ages and levels of expertise. It may be a tiring trip for young children unless coordinated with other attractions in southern Quebec. Remember that children must have appropriate permission from parents to cross the border. Check with the feds on this one. If you can get through the red tape, the trip is worth it. *Rating* ****

Vermont Historical Society. Pavilion Building, State Street, Montpelier, VT 05602. (802) 828–2291.

The Vermont Historical Society has many archaeological and ethnographic materials in the collections. However, due to the concerns of the Abenaki people, many of these are being held "in trust" for the Abenaki community and are not on display. Occasionally, the society will sponsor exhibitions in which Abenaki materials are featured. Good as a general field trip destination, not primarily for Abenaki materials. *Rating***

Wôbanakik Heritage Center, 17 Spring Street, Swanton, VT 05488.

The Heritage Center contains historic diplomatic and military artifacts used by the Abenaki people to preserve their land against British-American assault. Although not able to give tours, the center does lend materials and sponsors talks by its staff. *Rating* ****

Abenaki Archaeology General

This section includes works whose main focus is the period before A.D. 1600, although historical materials may be included.

Books

Manitou. 1989. James Mavour and Byron Dix. Inner Traditions International, Rochester, VT 05767.

This 390-page book discusses stone walls, chambers, and monoliths common throughout Wôbanakik. This stonework was long believed to be European, but this book raises the possibility that it is of Native American origin. It has had the unfortunate effect of making Western Abenaki sacred areas "attractions," such as has happened to the earthworks and calendrical sites of our western and southern neighbors. On the other hand, it settles once and for all the implicit belief that the interior Abenaki were somehow less "advanced" than the Maritime Archaic people of coastal Maine. Good background reading for someone who knows Abenaki archaeology; may confuse other people. *Rating* *

The Original Vermonters. 1994. William Haviland and Marjory Power. University Press of New England, Hanover NH 03755.

This is the standard work on the Western Abenaki area from the perspective of anthropology and archaeology. It is a must for anyone who has any interest in the prehistory of the Abenaki area. The current edition is up to date and includes modern anthropological thought. It is important historically in that its first printing made the strongest case at that time for the presence and persistence of the Western Abenaki, and therefore deserves our greatest respect. The current edition does suffer from several basic flaws when looked at from a Native perspective. For example, it reveals the location of sacred sties and burial grounds to the public. This information, while permitted under Vermont and U.S. law, is considered in bad form by traditional people, who believe that it encourages looting (unlawful excavation of graves and sacred goods) or defacement of sacred monuments. A second problem is that materials from graves are shown and discussed explicitly. This is also considered in very bad taste by traditional people. If one takes these faults into account, this remains a very important, if flawed work—the best that modern social science can do. Excellent resource guide for middle and high school teachers or museum people, OK for high school students. *Rating* ***

Vermont Division for Historic Preservation Plan. n.d. [1991?]. Division for Historic Preservation, Montpelier, VT.

This publication, not primarily for public use, gives a fine concise resume of Vermont prehistory with an excellent bibliography. *Rating* **

Multimedia

12,000 *Years of Vermont's Past.* Available from The Discovery Museum. 51 Park Street, Essex Junction, VT 05482. (802) 878–8687.

This multimedia package consists of a videotape, games, teacher's guide, and two booklets. Although dated, this is the best teaching module for the Western Abenaki area. Developed by the Division for Historic

Preservation, it goes into great detail about Abenaki archaeology. Good for teachers only. *Rating* ***

Events with an Abenaki Archaeology Theme

Vermont Archaeology Week. For information contact Division for Historic Preservation, Montpelier, VT 05602.

Generally in September, this statewide celebration has many events, lectures, short courses, and the like, scheduled each year. This is an event that is not to be missed, as it affords a clear look at the Abenaki Renaissance and is a chance to meet people who are active in it. *Rating* ****

Abenaki Studies: 10,500 Years Ago to 2,000 Years Ago

This section deals with resources dealing with the first 9,000 years of Abenaki occupation of their homeland.

Articles

"A Probable Paleo-Indian Site in Vermont." 1953. W. A. Ritchie. *American Antiquity*, 18: 249–58. *Rating* **

Books

Diversity and Complexity in Prehistoric Maritime Societies: A Gulf of Maine Perspective. 1995. Bruce Bourque. Plenum Press, New York. 413 pp.

Bourque's years of work with the Turner farm site is put into a regional context. While this deals mostly with coastal Maritime Archaic materials, including much burial data (which many Native people consider inappropriate), it is an important contribution to our understanding of the Abenaki's coastal and deep-sea adaptations. Excellent for researchers, OK for college students. *Rating* ***

Multimedia

"Secrets of the Red Paint People." *Nova.* WGBH Television, Boston, MA.

This excellently done video presentation is one of the few nationally broadcast presentations that focused on Wôbanakik. It shows the relations of coastal Wabanaki people to cultures of the south-central United States and aboriginal Europe. Turns the "European influence" idea around and suggests that prehistoric contact went from America to Europe. The only problem is that it implies that the coastal Wabanaki people were more "advanced" than the people of inland Wôbanakik. Excellent resource for high school up. *Rating* ****

Abenaki Studies: 2,000 Years Ago to 500 Years Ago

This section deals with resources discussing the period right before the Abenaki lands were invaded by European people.

Multimedia

Mi'kmaq. American Friends Service Committee, Audiovisual Resources, 2161 Massachusetts Avenue, Cambridge, MA 02140.

This film, consisting of six episodes for elementary or middle school students, explores in depth the life ways of the Micmac people during the Late Woodland Period. It is probably the best "stereotype breaker" available in that the people portrayed in the dramatic sections dress in clothing that is far removed from what children believe to be "Indian dress." The Western Abenaki probably lived in a virtually identical way. Highly recommended. *Rating* ****

Micmac: Their Daily Life. McIntyre Educational Media Ltd. 30 Kelfield Road, Rexville, Ont. M9W 5A2.

This filmstrip for elementary school students is accompanied by a sound tape and teacher's manual, focuses on much the same material as *Mi'kmaq* (see above) but puts it within a daily routine format. This also shows students that the Wabanaki people did not dress or behave like the stereotypical "Indian." *Rating* **

Micmac: Their Seasonal Life. McIntyre Educational Media Ltd. 30 Kelfield Road, Rexville, Ont. M9W 5A2.

This filmstrip, second in the McIntyre educational series, is also accompanied by a tape and manual. This multimedia resource focuses on the Micmac seasonal activities of fishing, hunting, gathering, and craft work. *Rating* **

Books

The Micmac: How Their Ancestors Lived 500 Years Ago. Ruth Whitehead and Harold McGee. Nimbus Publishing Ltd., PO Box 9361, Sta. A, Halifax, NS 3BK 5N5.

This small book, designed for elementary school students should be in every school in New England, for it shows in a well-illustrated and well-written way how Wabanaki peoples lived on the eve of contact. The illustrations of clothing are especially choice, since they destroy stereotypes about how "Indians" dressed. *Rating* ****

Abenaki Studies: 500 Years Ago to 100 Years Ago

This section deals with historical information concerning the Abenaki during the first two hundred years of contact between them and the European invaders. This period holds much interest for Euro-American historians in that it is a time of war and diplomacy. This section also deals with the Abenaki during the time that the European invaders attempted to adsorb and extinguish the Abenaki peoples. During this later period the Western Abenaki went "underground," hiding their distinctive culture and presenting a French, River Rat, or Gypsy face to the incoming tide of British Americans. This later period holds virtually no interest for historians, so very few materials exist.

Books

Identity of the St. Francis Indians. 1981. Gordon M. Day. Canadian Ethnographic Service Paper No. 71. National Museum of Man, Ottawa.

This book was the first major Western Abenaki work undertaken by Professor. Day. In it he discusses at some length the history of Coos and Missisquoi villages. Intended for other scholars, it is somewhat wordy and pedantic. It maintains the old idea that everyone left Vermont and headed to the Canadian mission villages. For those who are interested in the fine details about the Abenaki from an ethnohistoric point of view, it is an excellent resource. A good book for researchers and museum professionals; perhaps for high school teachers. *Rating* **

North Country Captives. 1992. Colin Calloway. University Press of New England, Hanover, NH. 160 pp.

It is said that the "captivity narrative" is the oldest form of American literature. Calloway has compiled a series of narratives that are extremely revealing about the Abenaki world during the wars with the British Americans. Great data on war, social customs, material culture, and other aspects of life from hostile observers. A must-read. Good from middle school up. *Rating* ****

Northeastern Indian Lives. 1996. Edited by Robert Grumet. University of Massachusetts Press, Amherst.

Although generalized to all of the Northeast, it is an excellent series of biographies of important Native people of the region. While only the biographies of Rawandigon (chapter 5) and Molly Ockett (chapter 15) deal with Abenakis, it is worth using as a text in college courses or placing in every high school library. *Rating* ****

Western Abenakis of Vermont. 1990. Colin Calloway. University of Oklahoma Press, Norman.

Colin Calloway has emerged as the foremost historian interested in the Western Abenaki. This well-researched and documented 346-page book goes into exhaustive detail concerning the stuff historians are interested in: "guys, guts, and guns". There is information for those interested in the social and material history of the Abenaki, but it must be combed and sifted from innumerable descriptions of the diplomacy and war that engaged the men of both worlds during the first two hundred years of Euro-American–Abenaki contact. It is probably the best work on the period available and is therefore a must-read. A good book for high school or college students and their teachers, researchers, and museum professionals. *Rating* ****

Dawnland Encounters. 1991. Colin Calloway. University Press of New England, Hanover, NH.

This book gives more detail on the military, social, and economic relations between the Abenaki and the European invaders. Still thick with guys and guns but more good social and economic data included. probably a good direction for historians to be moving. An excellent book for researchers and museum professionals; perhaps for high school teachers. *Rating* ****

Abenaki Studies: 100 Years Ago to 30 Years Ago

This section deals with historical information concerning the Abenaki during the recent past—how they almost became culturally dominated by the states of Vermont, New Hampshire, and Maine. During this time they were seen as Gypsies or other undesirable "White" people who should be marginalized and exterminated by sterilization.

Articles and Handouts

"Gypsies, Pirates and River Rats." 1994. Frederick M. Wiseman. Laboratory for Traditional Technology, Department of Humanities, Johnson State College, Johnson, VT 05656. (802) 635–2356.

This little handout for all teachers details the experiences of Abenakis during this time of extreme genocide, how they were seen as vaguely menacing people always at the edge of proper society always under pressure to move on or become sterilized. *Rating* ***

"Review of Eugenics in Vermont." 1926. H. F. Perkins. *Vermont Review*, September-October, 56–59.

This short article, written by Professor Perkins of the University of Vermont, is one of the most chilling documents ever published in Vermont. Well written and benignly worded, it lays out the groundwork for the surgical extermination of undesirable people who don't fit into the well-behaved, White Vermont stereotype. A nomadic, basket-selling, and horse-trading family of obvious Abenaki affiliation is targeted toward the end of the article. The German scholars interested in eugenics found Vermont's Eugenics Survey useful for crafting the Final Solution that was later pursued by the Nazis. A must-read for anyone who believes that genocide never happened here. *Rating* ****

Books

Breeding Better Vermonters. 1999. Nancy Gallagher. University Press of New England, Hanover, NH.

While Nancy Gallagher does not specifically confront the eugenics issue as a tool of ethnic cleasning of the Abenaki people, she does an excellent job of uncovering the history, philosophy, and methods of the Eugenics Survey.

Thus is a must-read for anyone attempting to understand recent Abenaki history in Vermont. *Rating* ****

Abenaki Studies: 30 Years Ago to Today

This section deals with historical information concerning the Abenaki during the most recent past, how they regathered their spirit and their culture and turned around the tide of genocide that attempted to destroy them.

Articles

"Return of the Natives." 1994. Yvonne Daley. *Vermont Life*, Autumn, pp. 38–45.

A very important article, in that it is one of the first serious attempts of *Vermont Life*, long a cultivator of the "lily white," British American Vermont stereotype, to seriously consider that Native people may actually live in the state. *Rating***

Books

The Western Abenakis: Maintenance, Reclamation and Reconfiguration of an American Indian Ethnic Identity. 1996. Mariella Squier. University Microfilms, Ann Arbor, MI.

Squier's dissertation caused a firestorm of controversy in Abenaki country when it was released. It contains good data, but according to other reviewers it has an agenda of promoting one group of Abenakis from the Clyde River, Vermont, area over other groups. It also contains questionable data concerning many of the people discussed in the work. I would be very careful using the data in the work; please compare it with other sources. *Not rated*

Finding One's Way: The Story of an Abenaki Child. 1988. Franklin Northwest Supervisory Union Title IV Indian Education Program.

This little book and its accompanying guide for elementary and perhaps middle school teachers was instrumental in bringing contemporary Abenaki issues to the Vermont classroom. This is a fictional story of a child who faces the day-to-day racism still found in northwestern Vermont and slowly, through the help of his family, becomes more comfortable with his ethnicity. No teacher who expects to interpret the Abenaki experience can afford to be without it. *Rating* ****

Odanak: Chez nous. 1998. Kim Chamberland. Musee des Abenakis, Odanak, Quebec.

This small but colorful book is an excellent French-language introduction to the modern Quebec community. This may be used in the United States in French-language coursework. Its writing is simple but elegant, and the pictures help with understanding. A must-have, even if you have to go to Odanak to get it. *Rating* ****

Western Abenaki Language

This section deals with the Abenaki language during the most recent past, told to us by both Native scholars and Euro-American ethnographers.

Multimedia

Alnobadowa: A Western Abenaki Language Guide. 1987. Gordon Day and Jeanne Brink. Jeanne Brink, 130 Tremont Street, Barre, VT 05641.

This inexpensive little introductory book and cassette tape is an excellent resource for anyone interested in a primer of the Abenaki language. It is especially useful for teachers in the elementary grades who wish to acquaint their pupils with Abenaki. *Rating* ****

Books

French Abenaki Dictionary. 1995. Stephen Laurent. Chisholm Brothers, Portland, ME. 528 pp.

I love this book. Although arranged in the format of the original eighteenth-century work by a priest to the Abenakis and keyed to French rather than English; it contains a wealth of data on the culture of the Abenakis during their long war with the British Americans. It also contains names for objects and actions that have passed out of use, undetected by Day. Useful for researchers only. *Rating* ****

Western Abenaki Dictionary. Vol. 1, *Abenaki-English.* 1994. Gordon M. Day. Canadian Ethnology Service Papers, no. 128. And *Western Abenaki Dictionary.* Vol. 2, *English-Abenaki.* 1995. Gordon M. Day. Canadian Ethnology Service Papers, no. 129. Mail orders: Mail Order Services, Canadian Museum of Civilization, 100 Laurier Street, PO. Box 3100, Station B, Hull, Quebec J8X 4H2.

This monumental work is a comprehensive listing of Abenaki words and their English translations. The Abenaki-English format of volume 1 makes back-translating English words a nightmare and is therefore not recommended except for researchers and other linguistic masochists. The English-Abenaki translations of volume 2 are highly useful. Get the second one! A must-read book for all interested in the Abenaki people. *Rating* ****

Abenaki Indian Legends, Grammar and Place Names. 1932. Henry L. Masta. La Voix des Bois Francs, Victoriaville, PQ.

This work was done by an Abenaki scholar fluent in both Native and non-Native voice and does not suffer as much from the biases and ignorance of a non-Abenaki scholar. I find that the information is delightful and well organized. The place-name data is crucial to understanding Western Abenaki geography. A good resource for researchers and museum professionals and perhaps for high school teachers. *Rating* ***

New Familiar Abenakis and English Dialogues. 1884. Joseph Laurent. Leser Brousseau, Quebec, PQ.

This delightful dictionary has a wealth of information on Abenaki names and gives the reader an insight into how the Abenaki language expresses the Abenaki worldview. Much pleasanter to use than the pedantic works of Gordon Day and much closer to the pre-Contact Abenaki culture in both time and the fact that it was written by a member of the Abenaki Nation. The place-name data is crucial to understanding Western Abenaki geography. A good book for researchers and museum professionals; perhaps for high school teachers. *Rating* ****

Traditional Material Culture

This section deals with information concerning Abenaki material culture from the recent past and modern materials made within older traditions.

Articles and Handouts

"Western Abenaki Snowshoes." 1994. Frederick M. Wiseman. Laboratory for Traditional Technology, Department of Humanities, Johnson State College, Johnson, VT 05656.

This short handout for teachers gives a concise description and history of what is known about Western Abenaki snowshoes, which, unfortunately, isn't a whole lot. *Rating* **

Books

Abenaki Basketry. 1982. Gaby Pelletier. Canadian Ethnology Service Papers, no. 85. National Museum of Canada, Ottawa K1A 0M8.

This book, which focuses on the basketry of the Mission Abenaki communities of Canada, is well researched and documented. Similar wares were made extensively by the Western Abenaki in their homeland. The halftone photographs are muddy and unclear, but until someone revises the work with better illustrations, this is the best that we have. A good book for researchers and museum professionals; perhaps for high school teachers and students. *Rating* **

Elitekey. 1980. Ruth Holmes Whitehead. Nova Scotia Museum and Education Resources Program, Department of Education, Province of Nova Scotia, Halifax.

I find that little book is the best single reference on material culture. Although it focuses on the Micmacs, whom some Euro-American scholars would separate from the Abenaki, it is a valuable resource in that the Micmac, due to their relative isolation from intense Anglicization, retained much more of their ancient lore into the twentieth century than did the more westerly groups. Therefore, this book explains analogous well-documented Western Abenaki artifacts—how they were made, what their makers thought of the objects, and how they were used. Splendid for students, middle school and up, or any teacher or researcher. *Rating* ****

Gift of the Forest. 1995. Frederick Wiseman. Abenaki Education Series, no. 1. Ethan Allen Homestead, Burlington, VT.

This short handbook for elementary and middle school teachers concerns small and large bark crafts of the Western Abenaki, ranging from small trinket boxes to canoes and bark architecture. It is ideal for children in the primary and middle school curricula and would be a useful addition to the bookshelf of adults in that it has some new information on Abenaki material culture. *Rating* ***

Western Abenaki Clothing. 1995. Frederick Wiseman. Abenaki Education Series, no. 3. Ethan Allen Homestead, Burlington, VT.

This short handbook for elementary and middle school teachers concerns later historic Abenaki clothing. It dispels the image that the Abenaki had to look like the "Last of the Mohicans" or like the Plains Native people. It is ideal for children in primary and middle schools and would be a useful addition to the bookshelf of adults in that it has some new information on Abenaki material culture. *Rating* ***

Indian Double Curve Secrets. 1996. Tom Ford. Audenreed Press, Brunswick, ME.

This is an unusual small book, mainly available in Maine bookstores. It presents Ford's compilation of the basic Abenaki design motif, the double scroll, and gives it a wealth of cultural meanings, some of which are well known, such as the symbol for the Wabanaki Confederacy. Other meanings are obscure. This is a good work for art and craft classes or anyone who us interested in an exhaustive treatment of the scroll. I wish the author had given us more data on the origin of the meanings. *Rating* **

Indian Handcrafts. 1990. Keith Wilbur. Globe Pequot Press, Old Saybrook, CT.

This book, while treating people mostly to the south of the Abenaki area, has the most extensive known series of drawings and graphic interpretations of Native American technology from prehistory through the supposed disappearance of native peoples about 1700. Much of this material culture was certainly analogous to that of the Abenaki. This book is especially useful for children from the fifth grade up and for adults interested in a quick view of prehistoric and contact period crafts. *Rating* ***

Micmac Quillwork. 1982. Ruth Holmes Whitehead. Nova Scotia Museum, Halifax.

A splendid book, well researched, written, edited, and illustrated, on a specific Abenaki people and craft. While the Western Abenaki did not make quillwork boxes in a style identical to the Micmac people, the sections on technology, materials, and dyes are very important to apply to quilled boxes from our area. Excellent resource for researchers and museum professionals. *Rating* ****

New England Indians. 1978. Keith Wilbur. Globe Pequot Press, Old Saybrook, CT.

This book, like Wilbur's *Indian Handicrafts*, describes people south of the Abenakis. It also has an extensive series of drawings and interpretations of New England Native American life. Useful for children from the fifth grade up and for adults interested in a quick view of prehistoric and contact period culture. It also perpetuates the stereotype that Native people disappeared from New England. If we bear that in mind, *Rating:* ***

Our Lives in Our Hands. 1990. Bunny McBride. Tillbury House Publishers, 132 Water Street, Gardiner, ME 04345.

This small book relies heavily on interviews and biographies of people who still make traditional baskets, adding an important dimension to the study of material culture. Excellent for elementary, middle, and high school students. Important for anyone interested in material culture of the Abenaki. *Rating* ***

Videos

Our Lives in Our Hands. Harald Prins and Karen Carter. Documentary Educational Resources, 101 Morse Street, Watertown, MA 02172.

This film discusses the survival of basket making among the Aroostook County, Maine, Micmac people as a means of continuing their culture and making a decent living in a very economically depressed area. Lots of detail on technique and materials. *Rating* ***

Modern Arts and Crafts

This section deals with information concerning the most modern Abenaki arts, those that are in the mainstream of Native American arts. This shows that the Abenaki are not necessarily constrained by the past but are looking to contemporary arts to craft a bright future as players on the international art stage.

Books

Legends in Stone, Bone, and Wood. 1986. Tsonakwa and Yolaikia. Arts and Learning Services Foundation, 4632 Vincent Avenue South, Minneapolis, MN 53410.

This little book is a jewel, for it deals with both the Abenaki spiritual world as well as showcasing the exemplary art of two of our most gifted artists. Good for middle school students up. *Rating* ****

Welcome the Caribou Man. 1992. Tsonakwa and Yolaikia. San Diego Museum of Man, 1350 El Prado, Balboa Park, San Diego, CA 92101.

This little book, second in the series, is also a jewel, for it again deals with the Abenaki spiritual world as well as showcasing the exemplary art of Tsonakwa and Yolaikia. Good for middle school students up. *Rating* ****

Light of the Dawn. 1994 Tsonakwa. LL Publishing, 2937 Avenida Destriao, Tucson, AZ 85746.

This book unfortunately lacks the polish of the first two in the series; the photographs are muddy and the typesetting is obviously done on a desktop machine. However, it is an important work in that new stories from Tsonakwa are included; and for the first time other Abenaki artists are at least mentioned, even if their artwork is not shown. For people interested in the Abenaki art renaissance, it is a must-read; for others, ho-hum. *Rating* **

Subsistence

This section deals with historical information concerning Abenaki hunting, agriculture, gathering and fishing during the most recent past.

Books and Articles

The Abenaki People and the Bounty of the Land. 1995. Frederick Wiseman. Abenaki Education Series. no. 2. Ethan Allen Homestead, Burlington, VT 05401.

This short handbook for elementary and middle school students is the first attempt at collating and organizing information on Abenaki plant foods and their use. The data, from primary historical sources, other Abenaki peoples, experimental work carried out at Johnson State College, and discussion with modern Abenaki people who collect and use these resources, is listed by geographic resource use zone and by plant species. Abenaki names, if known are included. *Rating* ***

"The Diet That Made the Red Man." 1955. Stephen Laurent. *New Hampshire Archaeologist*, no. 4. pp. 6–9.

This little article includes much material, published for the first time, concerning Western Abenaki subsistence. It is a must for anyone teaching Abenaki studies that include food and cooking. *Rating* ****

In the Three Sisters Garden. 1995. Joann Dennee, Jack Peduzzi, and Julia Hand. Food Works, Montpelier, VT 05602.

I love this large book on gardening in a northeastern Indian way. While somewhat Iroquois-centric and "New Agey," it is by far the best work for teachers attempting to use gardening as a way of connecting with their students and connecting them to the earth. A must-read! *Rating* ****

Collections of Stories

This section deals with information concerning Abenaki religion, spirituality, and child rearing during the recent past. These stories were often taken by folklorists and anthropologists from storytellers who were unaware that the stories were going to be retold for the professional advancement and financial gain of later anthropologists and storytellers.

Books

Algonquin Legends. 1992. Charles Leland. Dover Publications, New York.

This book is *the* source for all professional storytellers and researchers. Direct translation of Penobscot, Passamaquoddy, and Micmac stories abound, complete with the scatological humor and outrageous sexual and eating practices that we need to "clean up" before telling these to our young people. The author was convinced that the Wabanaki were heavily influenced by the Vikings and their religion, and maybe they were—or perhaps Viking religion was influenced by Wabanaki beliefs. The illustrations, done by a talented Passamaquoddy artist, are the only traditional depictions that we have of many of the characters featured heavily by storytellers. There is an enigmatic reference to collections of stories from the Canadian Abenaki Mission Villages, but none are included—what a shame! *Rating* ****

The Faithful Hunter. 1988. Joseph Bruchac. Greenfield Review Press, Greenfield Center, NY.

This booklet was the second book of Abenaki stories for children by the gifted storyteller Joe Bruchac (see *The Wind Eagle*, below). After this book he left the Abenaki to expand first to the northeastern Native people and then to the North American continent with the *Keepers* series, coauthored by environmental educator Michael Caduto. However, the book is slightly misleading for people interested in *Western* Abenaki materials.

The stories are mostly from our neighbors to the east. But the stories are splendid. *Rating* ***

Six Micmac Stories. 1985. Ruth Holmes Whitehead. Nimbus Publishing and the Nova Scotia Museum, Halifax.

This book, by the doyenne of Micmac studies, relates Micmac stories in a way that the author hopes is true to the original meaning and nature of the stories, even though they are derived from secondary anthropological and folkloric sources. They have a much grittier feeling than the more polished productions of Joe Bruchac but don't make as many allowances for telling to children and are therefore more of anthropological interest. If used in storytelling, they need to be edited somewhat. *Rating* ***

Stories from the Six Worlds. 1988. Ruth Whitehead. Nimbus, Halifax, NS. 242 pp.

I am only sorry that this book is specifically about the Micmac. Whitehead's book has given me the best Euro-American scholarly insight into the Wabanaki worldview. It makes clear many questions that I had about our own Abenaki belief systems. I cannot recommend this book highly enough! *Rating* ****

The Wind Eagle and Other Abenaki Stories. 1985. Joseph Bruchac. Bowman Books, Greenfield Center, NY.

This small booklet was the first book of Abenaki stories for children by the gifted storyteller Joe Bruchac. However, it is misleading for people interested in *Western* Abenaki materials. The introduction, by John Moody, focuses on the Western Abenaki of Vermont, while in actuality the stories are mostly from our heavily studied and anthropologically exploited neighbors to the east. Also, there is some controversy as to the character of Tabaldak in the stories, whom some would see as an importation of Yahweh, the Judeo-Christian God from the forced Christianization of the last several hundred years. However, if we suspend disbelief, the stories as told are splendid. *Rating* ***

Tapes, CDs

Gluskabe Stories. 1990. Joseph Bruchac. Yellow Moon Press, PO Box 1316, Cambridge, MA. (617) 776–2230.

This tape was the first audio presentation of children's Abenaki stories by the gifted storyteller Joe Bruchac. However, it is slightly misleading, for the stories are mostly from the Penobscot and more easterly Abenaki people. As pointed out in *The Wind Eagle* review, there is controversy as to the character of Tabaldak. The stories, told in Bruchac's enchanting voice, are splendid. *Rating* ***

Voice of the Night. 1987. Tsonakwa. Soundings of the Planet, PO Box 43512, Tucson, AZ.

This tape is a jewel for anyone, child or adult, for it deals with both the Abenaki spiritual world as well as showcasing the exemplary art of Tsonakwa, one of our most gifted artists and storytellers. It also features Carlos Nakai's magical stop-flute. Tsonakwa's stories, told to music, have a spirit that us unrivaled in the audio production world. *Rating* ****

Welcome the Caribou Man. 1993. Tsonakwa. Old Pueblo, 4420 E. Speedway, Tucson, AZ 85712.

Another excellent retelling of Wabanaki tales by this gifted storyteller. Not quite so polished as his first but seems closer to the spirit in his publications. *Rating* ***

Light of the Dawn. 1994. Tsonakwa. (No publication data on the cassette, but it may be available from the Dawnland Center. PO Box 1358, Montpelier, VT 05601).

The most recent collection of his excellent stories but once again not quite so polished. *Rating* **

Abenaki Fiction

I would personally like to see a novel that portrays modern Abenaki people and their struggles. *Finding One's Way* is good but not targeted to an adult reader population. The other books reviewed are nice but once again have the Abenaki in buckskins and beads. I have heard that Joe Bruchac has completed a book from a later period set in Maine. Keep your eye out for it when it comes out.

Abenaki Warrior. 1997. Alfred Kayworth. Branden Publishing Co., Boston. 261 pp.

This is probably the best fictionalized historical biography available for the Abenaki area. It reads like a historical novel, until you see exact historical-geographic references. Although it takes place in the "guys, guts, and guns" era of the British American wars, it would captivate students from middle school up and is OK for college survey courses. *Rating* ***

Cave of Falling Water. 1992. Janice Ovecka. New England Press, P.O. Box. 575, Shelburne, VT 05482.

This is a "costume drama" that involves both Euro-American and Abenaki female protagonists, but once again gives us the feeling that the Abenaki have faded from the scene and leave only their artifacts and stories for us to enjoy as "cultural resources." Good for middle school and up. Not for researchers, of course. *Rating* **

Dawnland. 1993. Joseph Bruchac. Fulcrum Publishing, Suite 350, 350 Indian Street, Golden, CO 80401.

This is the first full-length novel by the storyteller Joe Bruchac. It is good to see him try his hand at a long story crafted to intertwine the political, social, and mystical worlds. He does so with great success, making a book that can be read again and again and still have something new to find. Good for middle school and up. Not for researchers, of course. *Rating* ***

Finding One's Way: The Story of an Abenaki Child. 1988. Franklin Northwest Supervisory Union Title IV Indian Education Program.

This little book and its accompanying guide for elementary and perhaps middle school teachers were instrumental in bringing contemporary Abenaki issues to the Vermont classroom. This is a fictional story of a child who faces the day-to-day racism still found in northwestern Vermont and slowly, through the help of his family, becomes more comfortable with his ethnicity. No teacher who expects to interpret the Abenaki experience can afford to be without it. *Rating* ****

Western Abenaki Music

Tapes, CDs

Alnobak. The Dawnland Singers and Awassos Sigan Drummers. Good Mind Records. PO Box. 308, 2 Middle Grove Road, Greenfield Center, NY. 12833. (518) 583–1440.

This tape is for anyone, from children to adults. Contemporary musicians Joe, Marge, and Jesse Bruchac use Native Abenaki themes and apply them to modern songs of spiritual consciousness. Some have called it slightly "New-Agey" but good. *Rating* ***

Zahkiwi Lintow8ganal: Voices in the Woods 1999. Marge Bruchac and Justin Kennick. Good Mind Records, Northhampton, MA.

A very nice new production by a talented pair of musicians. You can hear the Abenaki language and its cadence here. Good for both children and adults. I look forward to more productions by this group. *Rating* ****

Abenakis. 1990. Thomas Obomsawin. Canyon Records Productions, 4143 N. 16th. Street, Phoenix, AZ 85016.

This tape, for high school students and adults by contemporary musician Tom Obomsawin, uses Native American themes and applies them to modern songs of social and political consciousness. If you want to see how the Abenaki fit into the modern Native American musical world, Tom's tape is a must. *Rating* ****

Bibliographic Notes

In this section I would like to expand on some philosophy, ideas, and materials, discuss in some detail the sources that most influenced me in writing this book, and discuss some experimental work that I have done over the years.

1. Introduction and Methods of Research (pp. 1–9)

1. Berkhofer's 1979 classic *The White Man's Indian* was followed by other works, such as *Playing Indian* by Philip Deloria (1998) and E. S. Bird's (1996) *Dressing in Feathers* (see especially her introduction). These works are very important for anthropologists, archaeologists, and ethnohistorians to read so as to understand how they are influenced by their own culture. A more academic work, *Natives and Academics*, edited by Devon A. Mihesuah, develops this "image" with regard to Native and non-Native perspectives on ethnohistory. See especially Mihesuah's introduction, pp. 1–18; Donald Fixico's "Ethics and Responsibility in Writing American Indian History," pp. 84–95; Elizabeth Cook Lynn's "American Indian Intellectualism and the New Indian Story," pp. 111–38; and Laurie Whitt's "Cultural Imperialism and the Marketing of Native America," pp. 135–71. Cook Lynn's work has greatly influenced my own philosophy concerning writing about the Abenaki. I am what she calls an "urban mixed blood" writer, few of whom are concerned with tribal sovereignty but instead express an accommodation to mainstream individualism over ethnic solidarity.

2. The calculation of ancestors assumes a twenty-five-year generation, two unrelated parents, and no lineal crossbreeding. The discussion of language can be found in Haviland and Power, *The Original Vermonters* (pp. 3–7). I like the genealogical-geographic model of ethnic descendance, since it is the intuitive one we all use in our ordinary life, rather than a fixed cultural geographic model. An attempt to disconnect us from our ancestors aired on *Discovery News*, December 3, 1999 (Discovery Channel), where Euro-American scientists, using DNA and facial reconstruction techniques, imply that ancient populations of North America are not the ancestors of modern First Nations, whom they see as a recent immigrations. Featured archaeologists quickly used this logic to block repatriation of our Old Ones, perhaps indicating that scientists *really* don't want us to have our ancestors but want to keep them for their own analysis. This is a major destabilization of relations between us and the scientists, if it moves from the sensationalist media to mainstream academic thought.

3. I developed the Iroquois supremacy paradigm in *The Great Council Fire* (Wiseman, 1997) and "The Last Alliance: The Abenaki and the Great Council Fire (Wiseman 1999). This is an interesting but little understood raciological tradition in ethnohistory

that has crept over to archaeology and even folklore studies. Vine Deloria, in his *Red Earth, White Lies*, takes on the Bering Land Bridge hypothesis. Unfortunately, my training was at the Laboratory for Paleoenvironmental Studies, University of Arizona, and I had Paul Martin and Vance Haynes on my Ph.D. committee, so I was trained as a Land Bridge believer. However, Wôbanakik was under ice at this time, so I can safely avoid the problem concerning the Abenaki people.

4. Pan-Indianism has been a continuing problem for my work in repatriating data to the Abenaki. An example of how ridiculous this had become was when an "elder" (who, by the way, uses the term "elder" on her private stationery) told Chief April St. Francis in early fall, 1999, that I was White, not Indian, because I "gave everyone a ten-minute break" during a presentation to First Nations People in Quebec in 1998 (St. Francis, personal communication, 1999). I understand that there is a scramble for the "high ground" of spiritual leadership, but it seems that it is based too much on denigrating those who are perceived as threats.

5. I am following the lead of Haviland and Power in *The Original Vermonters*, also published by University Press of New England.

2. The Coming of the Great Animals (pp. 14–25)

1. This is a widespread and important tale, also figuring in the title of N. Howard's 1989 book, and a well-done version is in Tsonakwa and Yolaikia, *Legends in Stone, Bone and Wood* (1986), p. 22.

2. The early history of the glacial and periglacial landscape comes from the excellent but dated summary in Chapman's 1937 "Late Glacial and Postglacial History of the Champlain Valley" and from more recent works by Carr and Davis (1977); Flint (1971), especially the excellent maps on pages 492 and 494; Shaefer and Hartshorn's "The Quaternary of New England" (1965), pp. 113–28; and Margaret Davis's "Phytogeography and Palynology of Northeastern United States" (1965), pp. 377–402. I also use Haviland and Power *Original Vermonters*. The pros and cons of the idea that not all mountains were overtopped by Wisconsinan glaciers is discussed in Flint (1971), p. 486. I am not sure of Mount Monadnock's status as a *nunatak*. The reconstructions are mine, combined with local detail.

3. An excellent description of deglaciation is by Larsen (1972), pp. 301–9.

4. This reconstruction is based on some of Borns's (1973) work on Paleo-Indian migration routes, Richie's (1953) "A probable Paleo-Indian Site in Vermont" in *American Antiquity*, and Gramly's work at Vail (1982, 1984) and Adkins (1988, esp. pp. 36–39), combined with some data on Arctic/subarctic subsistence summarized by Colin Taylor (1991), pp. 182–203, and Maxwell (1992), pp. 329–53, as well as with the paleobiogeographic data and Pleistocene geography discussed in note 3. It is rounded out by comparison with Haviland and Power. There is controversy about whether we got there while the whales were there (Loring [1980] is where I got the sea mammal hunting idea), because there is no archaeological data from that period. The data begin about one thouand years later (Petersen, personal communication, 1999).

I take a looser view: the land was open, the food was there, people have routinely lived in the wake of receding ice, so why not? Boats? Well, we know that boats were in use at this time elsewhere (the Australia connection); and recently James Dixon (2000) and Stanford and Bradley (2000) have stated that Solutrean fisherfolk from Europe came to North America across the Atlantic by boat, so our small boat in the illustration is nothing compared to these assertions! I know that I'm going out on a limb with the *mozolol*, but I'd hate to waste the excitement of the reconstruction and the painting. Chasing a beluga in a raft in an area where there is no wood just wouldn't cut it.

5. Hibbard, Ray, Savage, Taylor, and Guilday (1965), pp. 509–26, and Jennings (1989) provided information on the bestiary, extinction (pp. 59–60), sites, technology and hunting (pp. 91–98) used here. Haviland and Power (1981), whom I also use, go into a lot more detail than I do, and I recommend their work.

6. This comes from pollen data in Davis (1965).

3. The Forest Closes In (pp. 30–32)

1. This reconstruction comes from pollen data and paleobiogeography from Anderson and Race (1982), and Bradstreet and Davis (1975), along with the speculations of archaeologists (Haviland and Power (1994), pp. 40, 287) about the seeming diminution in archaeological evidence, which is more apparent than real.

2. The coastal reconstruction assumes an early perfection of dugout canoes, hinted at by the presence of the full-channel gouge and a well-developed maritime adaptation in coastal areas to the northeast of us. I'm using late examples, such as the one at the Abenaki Tribal Museum in Swanton, Vt., as analogs. The toggling harpoon and technological data are from L'anse Amour in Newfoundland, summarized in McGhee, 1976. Yes, I know that it is a burial, but our claim to precociousness requires at least a vague description of this material.

4. The Land Becomes Warm (pp. 36–54)

1. A good paleoclimatic résumé of the time is Bradstreet and Davis (1975). I may be reaching a bit on my reconstruction of the treeline and its interaction with the Labrador Maritime Archaic. I know that Gordon Day preferred a dome-type wigwam (J. Brink, personal communication, 1996). My wigwam description is from more easterly examples (Calloway 1989:21) as well as the lithograph of an Abenaki village north of Lake Mephramagog (Tremblay, 1999). As far as I know that is the only documented example of a traditional wigwam in Wôbanakik, so for now, I reject the dome wigwam. Experimental work that we have done over the years at the Laboratory for Traditional Technology at Johnson State College help me to envision the construction, the rotisserie, and the ability of a child, not an adult, to easily ascend the wigwam to work on the upper reaches. Furniture descriptions come from subarctic dwellings, which have also been replicated. Lots of the inland artifact detail comes from the various publications from Jim Petersen listed in the bibliography, as well as *The Original Vermonters* (Haviland and Power, 1981).

2. Spiritual issues are from comparisons of modern Wabanaki practice with that of their linguistically related neighbors such as the Innu and Algonquin peoples. There is a distinct possibility that widespread practice implies significant age (the other possibilities are diffusion and multiple origins). Ruth Holmes Whitehead's (1988) *Stories of the Six Worlds* has probably the best model of the basic Wabanaki world-view, and I use selected portions of that here.

3. OK, here we go with the decades-old observatory–root cellar controversy. There are three competing views that I know of (four, if aliens built them):

a. Archaeological canon: The ruins of these stone structures are federal or neoclassical period root cellars. Indeed, some of these, such as the "Calendar II" site in South Woodstock, are closely associated with the ruins of a historic brick building and probably functioned as such. While at MIT, I worked on one of these on Cape Anne, Massachusetts, with local historian, Mike Bowie, and that one had definite associated artifactual materials dating from the 1780s (lead-glazed creamwares) to the early nineteenth century (wishbone-handled phosphate porcelain teacups and pearlware dish fragments). However, we could find no materials beneath the structure or in definite association with initial construction.

What seems odd to me is the aberrant use of inappropriately large cut-stone lintel and roof construction members and anomalous placement of the structures, given what we know of built-environment proxemics of federal and neoclassical period Anglo-American dooryards. I have had some analytic experience with southern New England architecture through my antiques consulting practice (Wiseman, 1986), and these seem to me an anomaly in British-American construction. Also, their rather limited distribution, while Anglo-American federal architecture is widespread, also needs to be explained. And only a percentage are associated with documented historic Anglo buildings. The "lump" in Jodie Loring's friend's front lawn (from the quote) is on a hillside plateau over a mile from any early-nineteenth-century construction. Its only associated built environment are two anomalous stone cairns (on a well-sorted old clay-loam terrace; the nearest rock over one hundred yards away downslope!). Although I didn't give this stone chamber the time it deserved, it seems that it required a lot of labor to haul several tons of stone to a nonagricultural area and erect a system of buildings and alignments.

b. "The Early (Bronze Age?) European discovery" model describes the structures as the result of prehistoric visits by Europeans and perhaps Africans (see B. Fell, 1989, for an overview). Much of the logic of this school appears anguished, but there are lots of "spot finds" here that, if authentic, will haunt mainstream archaeologists. Warren Dexter and Donna Martin's (1995) book is probably a good place to start, in that it has the most detailed photographs applicable to our area, despite its tortured prose. See also Hanz Holzer's (1992) work on Mystery Hill, a large site on our southern border, which is now a tourist attraction ("America's Stonehenge") in southern New Hampshire. I have no problem with all kinds of people coming over here early on, but why did they not leave their diseases behind? I can believe the Vikings because of a thinning out of diseases to the north, but if a Mediterranean vessel hit Cape Anne, there would be hell to pay.

c. The Amerindian hypothesis. Of course, this is the simplest explanation, given the high "strangeness coefficient" of the sites. Hints come from the Maritime Archaic period of Labrador and Newfoundland. The L'anse Amour mound (McGhee, 1976) is also about as early as stone-constructed mound building gets in the Americas, and the small linteled mound shown to us in detail by Fitzhugh in the Nova video "The Secrets of the Lost Red Paint People" looks an awful lot like a miniature prototype of the Calendar II site in Vermont. The cairn and standing-stone coastal markers of the treeless north of ancient Wôbanakik point to at least a line-of-sight alignment system. These are accepted as First Nations construction by Fitzhugh 1975a, 1987.

The solar/lunar corrections discussed are the basis of current Wabanaki calendrical systems that we use for ceremony. (See Adney's undated manuscripts at the Peabody

Museum and Maine Historical Society, as well as Wiseman, 1995c). There is a growing respect for astronomic and geographic knowledge of the Wabanakis (also see Ray, 1983), and I am assuming that the alignments worked out by the "Early European Hypothesis" people with regard to the 18.6-year cycle of the moon at Calendar II have some merit. If we can have Woodhenge at Cahokia and Fajada Butte Sundagger at Chaco Canyon, why not Calendar II here? If we *really* believed that the Abenakis ancestors could be as "advanced" as the Anasazi or even the Mississippians, perhaps our view about these buildings would change. As an advocate for Abenaki sovereignty, I go with the hypothesis that they are First Nations buildings and that the alignments are related to the known sophistication of other ancient Wabanaki material talents.

4. The hunting, fishing and gathering reconstructions rely on archaeological data summarized by Haviland and Power (1981), for Vermont and Bourque's (1995), Fitzhugh's (1987), and Tuck (1975a, 1975b) extensive and detailed work for coastal Wôbanakik. I fleshed it out with generalized northern hunter models presented in works such as Maxwell (1992, pp. 111–53, 329–53), and Taylor (1991, pp. 182–203, 224–49). This gave me the size and description of spears, dead falls, harpoons, etc.

For the saltwater fishing and sea mammal hunting descriptions, I rely once again on the extensive work of Tuck, Bourque, and Fitzhugh. I believe that I am stretching the data to say that the Nuliak colonists returned to places such as Swanton, Vermont, each year, but the abundance of Rahma quartzite there shows that there were connections; perhaps they were as extensive as I suggest. Others believe the Nuliak colony was a year-round fishing station.

5. My section on the Great Sea is another place where I assert Abenaki equivalency with other world cultures of similar advancement. I love the story about the Ferry that introduces this section, because it puts to bed the stereotype of the Wabanaki people as being landlubbers.

I know diffusion is out now, but the new mitochondrial DNA haplogroup X has us coming by boat from Europe (D. Stanford and B. Bradley [2000], and haplogroup B may even have us coming across the Pacific. (Dixon, 2000; Schurr, 2000). Everyone wants us to be the receivers of artifacts, genes, and spirituality from the more advanced Old World. Diffusion is OK when it goes from Old World to New, especially if the physical anthropologists can convince the feds that the Old Ones are actually not Indians. Then they get the big prize—bodies to study! Let's turn it around; if I'm not mistaken our carbon 14 dates on Maritime Archaic sites at Brador and L'Anse Amour are as early or even a bit earlier than analogous examples from coastal Europe (McGhee, 1976), so why not have the gouges, fishhooks, and other circumboreal diffusion start here? The *Nova* documentary "Secrets of the Lost Red Paint People" interviewed European scholars, who don't seem to have as many problems with circumatlantic connections as archaeologists do here and even propose a west-to-east movement of ideas. Remember, that because of the Gulf Stream and the wind currents of the North Atlantic, Europe is much easier to reach from here than it is to reach here from Europe. The strange big boats that I christen "Log Ships," with their circular sails and steering oars are from the Peterborough petroglyphs; you may want to view the petroglyphs from the easily obtainable but disconcerting *America BC* (p. 304). Finally, there is a cute children's story built on the premise that we made it to Europe, it is called *The Voyage of Wood Duck* (Trottier, 1995).

6. The ceramic introduction story is based on Petersen, Heckenberger, and Basa, 1989, as well as Haviland and Power (1981) for Vermont, and Bourque (1995, pp. 255–56), and Petersen's (1980, 1985) résumés of ceramics in the area.

5. The Coming of the Others (pp. 59–60)

1. The first part, concerning subsistence, is based on Haviland and Power (1981) and Heckenberger and Petersen's 1988 data from Skitchewaug, with colorful additions from Wilbur (1978, pp. 28–34). I am extrapolating the presence of some cultigens, which are a bit marginal here, such as gourds (they grow fine most years at the Ethan Allen Homestead's garden at the Intervale in Burlington, Vermont, but I'll be darned if we can grow them at Swanton, Johnson, or other colder places in Vermont. Husk tomatoes are also dicey. On the other hand, Jerusalem artichokes would take over Wôbanakik if given a chance; even in the colder sections they spread mercilessly. I wish I liked the slimy things!

2. The Iroquoians are believed to have arrived from the west, perhaps from the Ontario Peninsula between Lakes Huron, Erie, and Ontario (F. Jennings, 1989, p. 249) and settled in New York about four thousand years ago (Lounsbury, 1978, p. 336). Furthermore, there is the belief of an ultimate southern origin before that (Lounsbury, 1978). (Snow [1992] argues that the northward movement is quite recent). This is a linguistic/cultural model that goes in and out of fashion. I hear rumors that some Iroquois ethnohistorians and linguists are beginning to have the Iroquoian languages and peoples develop locally up here. I will stick to an intrusive model. I realize that some may accuse me of being somewhat judgmental and stereotypic in portraying the Iroquois as warlike. Most Iroquois nationals whom I know personally are rather proud of their martial image and even attempt to perpetuate it, even when it is not strictly true. Others prefer that I focus on their diplomacy.

Actually, Kahnawake was our old ally, not our enemy, but they have deconstructed their history, buying into the flawed work of Anglo scholars (Wiseman, 1997a). I doubt that anyone would doubt that the Wendat were our friends and allies (Sioui, 1992), and indeed they remain so today.

3. I know that probably the most irritating thing in this book is my critique of the St. Lawrence Iroquoian model (Trigger and Pendergast, 1978). First, I am an outsider. Second, I am advocating an intellectual position based on a perceived political threat, naturally a poor basis from which to argue. As a defense; I guess a bit of intellectual history is in order. It is true that I am an outsider, but I learned ceramics during the rough-and-tumble days of the "New Archaeology" from Pat Culbert, Bill Longacre, and Gwynne Vivian, and a little from Paul Martin when he visited the University of Arizona. I worked off and on with Bill Robinson and Jeff Dean and their colleagues at the Tree Ring Lab in 1969–1972. I apprenticed myself with Hopi potters. I learned that you can't make any a priori assumptions of ethnicity (an old rule: pots don't have sex, nor do they speak). You work from a well-defined series of epistemological and methodological rules that allow you to test hypotheses of ceramic variation through space and time, which better be well documented by tight excavation and dendrochronological control. I am almost twenty years out of date (my last ceramic work was in the early 1980s) and I have not gotten too far into the local literature, but this kind of stratigraphic/temporal control seems lacking here (beginning, as far as I know, with Brumbach's (1975) résumé of the ceramics in Algonquin territory, through Chapedelaine's and Tremblay's works, unfortunately mostly in French and hard for me to read, except Chapedelaine (1992), which is bilingual. Tremblay (1999, 2–8, 41–52) has attempted to deal with the anthropologists', Wendats', and Mohawks' claims on the St. Lawrence in a dispassionate

manner but doesn't completely understand that a disconnection from the past gives Euro-American governments a political tool to use against First Nations people.

Petersen's excellent work in Maine and elsewhere in northern New England is distributional and comparative and stands or falls on an Iroquoian "hearth" model (now known as a "fast center" in the contemporary historical geographer's jargon), diffusing to a backward Algonquin/Wabanaki hinterland (the geographer's "slow margin" — here we are "slow" again!). Petersen's publications on the subject with which I'm familiar (1990, 1992, 1999) seem closer to allowing an independent Wabanaki production in many places but still sees the stylistic influence moving unidirectionally from the Iroquoians. I also believe that the geographic-linguistic basis of the assignation seems problematic. Biggar's (1924) translation of Cartier doesn't give me a whole lot to go on, perhaps there are other more precise sources originally used in the construction of the St. Lawrence Iroquoian model. I suspect that someone who is current in archaeological epistemology could take this one on and have a field day. I hope that my exposition here and in the text at least points the way to an alternative model.

6. Darkness Falls (pp. 75–113)

1. The structure of the discussion of the fur trade is loosely based on the model in the introduction to Gilman's *Where Two Worlds Meet*. This is the best widely available contemporary discussion of the trade that I know of, although focusing on an area to the west of us. Other sources include Innis's classic 1930 work on the fur trade in Canada, and Peter Thomas's specific work on the Connecticut River (1981). An interesting ecological view, though not specific to our area and maybe not all that applicable, is S. Krech (1981) The fur trade material culture section is based on artifacts found by archaeologists such as Thomas, cited above, as well as material found in the collections of the Wôbanakik Heritage Center. I used illustrations from Gilman's *Where Two Worlds Meet*, Woodward's *Denominators of the Fur Trade*, and Hanson's *Voyagers' Sketchbook* to look for similar items with a local provenance.

2. The discussion of the fur trade wars and the alliance is summarized from my work on the Great Council Fire (Wiseman, 1997a, 1997b, 1999). I used the wampum records, most commonly available as *Wapapi Akonutomakomal*, by Leavitt and Francis (1990) as the underlying basis for the alliance. Local early influence of the fur trade is from Snow (1976a), and description of the Tarrantine Wars is based partly on A. H. Morrison's (1975) description and discussion about Membertou's attack on southern Maine. Another good resume is Bourque and Whitehead (1985). The conjectural date of the beginning of the alliance is based on the assumption that the Peacemaker of the Haudenosaunee was actually one of the messengers described by Leavitt and Francis. I make the assumption that the various confederacies were subdivisions of a larger inclusive "Great Council Fire" based on the data collected at Old Town by Frank Speck (1915a, 1919). He noted that the four nations of the Wabanaki Confederacy were formally integrated into a larger alliance based at Kahnawake and that the Odawa (leaders of the Three Fires Confederacy) were the titular head of the alliance. Other hints are found in the independent relations of the Micmac Grand Council with Kahnawake described by Speck in Leavitt and Francis (1990). Others, such as Jean-Pierre Sawaya (1998), and Peter Macleod (1996), who focus on the Canadian Seven Nations, tend to believe that the alliance was independent and merely had diplomatic relations with

the other alliances. I will go with the Penobscot and Micmac data and use an inclusive "umbrella alliance" model.

3. The annual cycle is a fairly common literary device used by archaeologists and ethnohistorians to reconstruct life. Haviland and Power (1981) use this. Phenological and cyclic data, such as ice breakup, syrup-collecting time, and fish runs are from phenological notes taken at Johnson, Vermont, Wells, Maine, and Swanton, Vermont, over the 1991–1999 period. Correlation of these with Abenaki months are from Wiseman (1995). There is controversy as to whether sap collection and processing is pre-Contact, and even some First Nations scholars seem to agree (V. Deloria, 1998, p. 72), but since we have old stories about Koluscap and maple sugaring I'm going to assume we've done it for a long time. Bark data comes from many sources, including Whitehead (1982), and Bernard Mason's (1974) discussion of bark work. The longhouse discussion comes from Cowie's Tracy Farm site data (1999). I combined it with data from our own experimental longhouse being constructed at the Audubon Research Center at Huntington, Vermont. Data on cornfields and corn are discussed in Haviland and Power (1981), with additions from Champlain's (Biggar, 1922) data from Saco for the coastal Abenaki.

4. The issue of Christian conversion is complex and controversial (Axtell, 1981; Conkling, 1974). Our elders are mostly Roman Catholic, but many of our young are rejecting their beliefs as anti-Indian, leading to generational conflict. This is true in non-Abenaki communities as well; friends at Kahnawake report the same conflict. In order to resolve this dilemma, I went to the Southwest and Mexico in the fall of 1999 to observe how First Nations people there were dealing with this apparent conflict, only to discover that there was no conflict. Integration of both systems, such as seen in the well-known Yaqui Easter Celebrations, is commonplace. But more subtle appropriations of Christian spirituality abound, such as the miraculous organ pipe cactus at the Catholic Church at Aduana, Sonora. This cactus is believed by the Mayo First Nation people to be sanctified and as a means of holding their widespread communities together. I doubt that the Vatican would consider a living plant a direct link to the unseen realms. I get the same feeling at Potlotek (Chapel Island, Nova Scotia) on St. Anne's Day. The Micmac captain I conversed with explained that 90 percent of the Micmac People were Roman Catholic, and this religion was part of their pride and separation from the Anglo government that is still oppressing them. He further stated that the Micmac people had a special agreement with the Vatican, called the Concordat, that gave the Micmac Grand Council a combined political and religious power. He further stated that there was no conflict between the Micmac worldview and that of Catholicism, and he believed in both the "little people" and St. Anne. An interesting Euro-American scholarly view is K. M. Morrison (1981).

There are deep currents here, including a rising anti-Catholic, anti-Francophone movement, which seems to be engulfing the Quebec Mission Villages, as well as northern New England communities; and I cannot address them in a short note. I believe that to be Abenaki is to honor the old spirits, as well as the portions of Christianity that support our autonomy, such as St. Anne, representing the Moon and Women, and the Archangel Michael, whom we petition in our continuing fight against Anglo genocide.

5. The games are from Culin (1907) and other minor sources (Brown, 1889; Favour, 1974; Wiseman, 1995d), as well as original artifactual materials held by the Wôbanakik Heritage Center. Experiments and play conducted at Johnson State College also figure in the reconstructions.

6. Data on wampum is summarized from Wiseman (1997b) and Speck (1919). Other good sources for Wabanaki wampum are reviewed or summarized in Leavitt and Francis (1990).

7. The discussion of war comes from several sources. The artifacts of war data have come from the collection and analysis of trade weaponry with good Wôbanakik provenance (some featured in Wiseman, 1999). This material is important for the Abenakis' current petition for federal recognition. These materials are mostly shown in the figures. The reconstruction of the ceremonial cycle of war from notification by wampum-bearing messengers to distribution of captured materiel, is based on Leavitt and Francis (1990), Speck (1915a, 1928; for the war dance, 1940), and N. N. Smith (1955, 1977). An interesting analogous view, which I adapted for the war strategy and tactics discussion, comes from MacLeod's (1996) exhaustive work on the Seven Nations.

7. Against the Darkness (pp. 118–147)

1. I pretty much discuss the problem in the text, but I need to expand it a bit. The Vermont state government is serious when they "know" that the Abenakis disintegrated during the period 1791–1972. Their official position, to be developed in chapter 8, is that we are "wannabes." The lack of recognition given to this time period by ethnohistorians and anthropologists bolsters this attempt at ethnic cleansing by disconnecting us from our ancestors. I would make a plea to all scholars out there: *Ignore our prehistory and the guys, guts, and guns era; please work on the archaeology and ethnohistory of a people who had to go underground.* The camps of the River Rats still remain. I know of "Indian hideouts" of the late nineteenth century with easily dated bottles and graniteware. I know it is too late to dig the "Gypsy" camp under the tarmac at Burlington International Airport, but what about other ones on the banks of the Winooski near Williston? Cultural geographers can follow and reconstruct the itineraries of "Gypsy" basket makers, and track down demonstrable "Indian" products they sold. Antique pickers and collectors are a gold mine of data here. I am sure that I will catch hell from Abenaki friends who consider working in our old ruins (even sixty years old) or studying recent artifacts as sacrilege, but if scholars are going do it, at least give us some ammunition we can use to defend ourselves!

2. *The Identity of the St. Francis Indians* by Day (1981b) is the primary source, as well as his many other works cited in the Bibliography. Many of these have recently been combined in a volume edited by Foster and Cowan (1998). Also consult Speck (1928), where he takes a short look at Wôlinak before plunging into the stories.

3. Unfortunately, this information is currently anecdotal—from two sources. The first is an interview with a neighbor, a former farmer on Route 15 in Underhill, when I lived there in 1993. He told me that his grandparents told him of an Indian family who lived in the foothills and sides of Mount Mansfield until the 1920s. He showed me the remains of their camp, and I collected some materials for the Wôbanakik Heritage Center. He indicated that they rarely came out of the woods—only to get sugar, flour, and coffee. The owner of the general store in Underhill Center also remembered stories in his family of ruffian "hill people" who traded baskets, brooms (?), and snowshoes. The second source is my father's remembrances, shared by "Monkey" Drew and Ernest Larocque, of the family "kicked out" by the feds and of their troubles getting along in Swanton and Alburg (Vermont) villages. I remember seeing, as a child, the ruins of their camps, and I investigated one of them in 1991. Almost all of the wooden structures are gone or pillaged, but there are scatters of glass, metal (including fishhooks and a reel), and even ceramics, some of which were pearl wares quite a bit older than I expected. These collections are housed at the Wôbanakik Heritage Center.

4. The canoe data comes from Adney and Chapelle (1964) and Guidmark (1989) and from analysis of a well-documented Abenaki canoe in the Abenaki Tribal Museum in Swanton.

5. My family made canoe and Adirondack Guide Boat oars and paddles.

6. The section on the River Rats comes from personal remembrances of these people, who greatly influenced my early years. I could write a whole book on them. Monkey Drew never admitted to me that he was Indian, although a newspaper clipping (August 29, 1963) says that he had Indian ancestry. He used to start a story with "This is what the French and Indians used to do." I have some of his artifacts, as well as some given to me by Ed Hakey. These are now housed at the Wôbanakik Heritage Center. Others there, I have reconstructed from memory.

7. Fancy basket data is from Pelletier (1982) and interviews with basket makers such as Sophie Nolet of Odanak. The miniatures are not published for our area; these come from intensive collection in Wôbanakik from 1989 to 1999, combined with tracing their provenience. The clothing likewise comes from documented examples in the Wôbanakik Heritage Center collection. One item, a man's outfit (ca. 1900), is a an interesting story. At first glance it resembles the regalia made and used by the Improved Order of Red Men, an Anglo fraternal order (see P. Deloria, 1998, pp. 58–68, for a résumé and a photo on p. 67 of the regalia). Unlike published examples or museum pieces, which use seed beads, often with patriotic American flag designs, this outfit used the coarser "Niagara-style" beadwork common on tourist whimsies sold by Iroquois and Abenaki people at the time. In tracking down the provenance , I was able to show that the regalia was used by an Essex, Vermont, family that "sold baskets on the Lake Champlain islands." Indeed, the sweat staining and use-wear patterning hints at rough daily handling rather than occasional ceremonial use, supporting the native origin hypothesis. This points out that there is lots of data out there, but it needs to be looked for in unconventional ways.

8. The Wôbanakik Heritage Center has a documented collection of the artifacts made by this extended family.

9. Snowshoe measurements and specific characteristics are from examples of northwestern Vermont and White Mountain Abenaki snowshoe molds, incomplete snowshoe frames, and snowshoes in the Wôbanakik Heritage Center collections. Techniques of rawhide weaving and finishing are from interviews with workmen at the Tubbs Snowshoe Company, Stowe, Vermont, in 1992 and from experimental work with frames and lacings obtained from the company.

10. An interesting place to really explore these regional social processes is in the various books tracing the history of antique collecting. Stillinger's 1980 *Antiquers* is excellent, if you read between the lines of this elitist text, especially pp. 48–50, concerning the xenophobic aspect of New England's historic preservation and antiques craze. *The Documentary History of American Interiors* (E. N. Mayhew and M. Myers, 1980) goes into the architectural and furnishing proxemics of the domestic hygiene movement and leads to back to the important works of Catherine Beecher (especially 1868) and C. Beecher and H. B. Stowe's *American Woman's Home* (1869). These and their social implications are summarized in Wiseman, 1986.

11. Anti-Roman Catholicism is still an issue among some Abenakis and French Canadian Vermonters. For those of you who disagree, there is a demonstrable cultural geographic legacy of social exclusion. There are few Roman Catholic churches on village greens in Vermont. They may come within feet of it, as in St. Albans and Cambridge, but still not be on the green. For those of you with a touring bent, there are some. How many can you find?

12. The last word on the Eugenics Survey is Nancy Gallagher's new (1999) book *Breeding Better Vermonters: The Eugenics Project in the Green Mountain State*. The shame associated with the eugenics years is well remembered and relived today in Vermont Abenaki families, some of whom I interviewed for this work.

8. The Darkness Ends (pp. 152–177)

1. This chapter has been by far the most difficult to write. Due to the factionalism, hurt feelings, and egos involved, many sections have two divergent interpretations, plus a third recorded by the hostile *St. Albans Messenger* (early on, they are pro-Abenaki now) and the *Burlington Free Press*. I have been scrupulous in showing drafts of this chapter to representatives of the two factions and have received fairly insulting corrections, such as "you still don't get it" and "you've got it all wrong." I am sure to draw the wrath of some recent Vermont and New Hampshire factions by basically ignoring them, yet they have done little that I know of, as of this writing, to advance the general Abenaki cause. They are currently consolodating their power base. The backbone of this chapter is from sixty-seven newspaper clippings (too many to cite) from various newspapers in Abenaki country, arranged in a matrix of political and cultural "columns" with yearly "rows." The documented base data are then fleshed out with interviews with the players (or children of the players) over those years, as well as my own activities and remembrances after 1987, when I became a citizen of the Abenaki Nation at Missisquoi. Material From M. Davis's *Encyclopedia of Native Americans in the Twentieth Century* (1996) contributes to the discussions on federal recognition (pp. 78–80) and the Indian Reorganization Act (pp. 218–20 and 262–65). I then add other specific materials, such as an excellent, relatively unbiased *Yankee Magazine* article from 1991, various Vermont government officials' statements, Jeff Benay's chapter in *New Dawn* (Pearo et al., 1996), as they are needed to construct the expository points that I wish to make.

2. This is a conversion of a modern Dine (Navajo) trickster story that circulated among graduate students at the University of Arizona in the mid-1970s. I have grafted it into the Koluscap cycle by changing place and detail and adding Abenaki animal names. As subcreator of this story, I now have responsibility to it. As I am typing this note, I have, but have not deposited, my advance for this manuscript, for I need to be sure that it supports my work in defense of Abenaki sovereignty. I want you to be able to read this, not get your hands messy!

3. A concise discussion of the hurdles required for federal recognition is on pages 78–80 of the *Encyclopedia of Native Americans in the Twentieth Century* (Davis, 1996).

4. This is a best guess about what happened; my three informants all disagree with each other on specifics, and they disagree with newspaper accounts. I remember it differently again, but that was my first year as a citizen of the St. Francis–Sokoki band.

5. This story still disgusts me.

6. I believe that things are quite a bit different now. We have excellent relationships with the Sipayik and Indian Township Passamaquoddies, and the Penobscots at least know that we exist, even if not all are happy with recognizing us.

7. Same caveat as in note 4.

8. This is my own model, one that may have merit over the long haul. It is based on the tension that was created between actual sociopolitical structure (extended family bands) and Anglo-induced tribalism. I believe that eventually, the best form of

government for the Abenakis is the form that they have always had. The problem is that traditional political integration of family bands at the village and confederation levels was based on condolence and consolation, discussed in chapter 5. Today, ego, personal agendas, and differential media access reinforce divisiveness, and these mechanisms are almost forgotten. However, all is not lost. At the 1999 UVM conference discussed in the Introduction, I was confronted by a longtime opponent. We put our grievances on the table, and even though I'm sure she didn't believe me—and I certainly didn't believe her—we decided to try to use condolence and consolation at the end of the confrontation. I agreed to not pursue some actions I was taking if she would stop telling people untruths about me. I gave her a gift. We agreed (I think!), and I have kept my part of the bargain. She was, as far as I know, my most virulent antagonist; and if our accommodation holds, as I sincerely hope it will, it points the way to hope for the future.

9. I fear for the fate of the Abenaki language. Just when we get an able teacher, something happens and he or she has to stop teaching. Age forced Cecile Wawanolet to cease her classes at the tribal headquarters several years ago. Jesse Bruchac recently moved from the area, and Elie Joubert is unable to continue his teaching at this time. I believe that we need some help from funding sources to do this right, perhaps an immersion course at Odanak. I am trying to do my bit with the Abenaki language names in this work, but I can just barely understand a simple sentence.

9. *The Modern Abenaki (pp. 180–190)*

1. For a review of how dangerous the Vermont Supreme Court decision is considered in Indian law, refer to the *Buffalo Law Review* (Lowndes, 1994).

2. Mazipskwik has the best Abenaki web site by far. I know that web sites published in books make the book quickly dated, but you need to go to it if it is still up. Type in "Mazipskwik" or "Abenaki" on your search engine, and if it is still up it will appear. The logo is a turtle.

3. This is a most hurtful issue and the most inexplicable. Excluding a historically oppressed people from their rights, based on potential adverse economic effects, has not been in fashion since World War II. I cannot see how the media have not picked this one up and run with it. Perhaps I am oversensitive and biased (one I admit), but in light of the current administration's commitment to diversity in Vermont, this must be an issue!

Notes to the Illustrations

1. The author in Monkey Drew's boat, 1956. The boat was a handmade flat-bottom boat commonly used by River Rats in the mid-twentieth century. They were usually rowed, but this boat had a small two-horsepower Johnson outboard motor.

2. Wôbanakik and environs, 10,500 winters ago. Note the stagnant glaciers in what will later be known as Maine and Nova Scotia. Sites discussed in the text are labeled; other sites marked. Compass rose is a Clovis-style lance point.

3. Whale hunt on the Champlain Sea, 10,500 winters ago. This conjectural 1997 painting by Lewis Pusey portrays a group of Abenaki hunters pursuing narwhals in the Champlain Sea, with a mammoth looking on. Mozeodebe wadjo (Mount Mansfield) and Dowabodiawajo (Camel's Hump) are on the horizon.

4. Depiction of Paleo-Indian hunter. The hunter wears little but breechcloth, leggings, and moccasins to aid speedy travel. He carries the large repeating lance, made, in this case, of spruce with woolly mammoth ivory socket. Inserted into it is an ash-wood foreshaft with rawhide hafted stone point. In a long quiver he holds an *atlatl*, or spear thrower, and several shafts.

5. Wabanaki hunters pursue a woodland caribou by canoe. Postcard image before 1910. Early hunters would have used a *mozolol*, or skin boat; this is the distinctive Micmac-style canoe. The prey shown here is the once common woodland caribou. This species is extinct in the Canadian Maritimes and remains in Wabanaki country only in the Chic-Chocs Mountains of the Gaspé Peninsula of Quebec.

6. Traditional and transitional maple sugaring equipment found in Wôbanakik. *From top to bottom:* French-Abenaki metis syrup mold (north central Vermont, ca. 1900), sumac-wood sap spiles (northern Vermont, ca. 1880), "sugar cone" for molding hard maple sugar (western Maine, ca. 1880), birch-bark sap bucket (southern Quebec, ca. 1880). These are not ancient styles (except, perhaps, for the bark cone) but represent the culmination of ancient technologies discussed in the text. Before European influence the spiles would have not have been tubular at the back and driven into a hole drilled into a tree but open all the way and jammed into a notch cut in the bark below a V-shaped pair of notches in the bark. The sap bucket would have had a vegetal or leather bail, not metal. The sugar mold is a rather recent invention, probably not more than a couple centuries old, but the cross motif, indicating Catholicism, is an important detail.

7. Dugout canoe, white pine (replica, 1995). The canoe was made in 1994–1995 by Johnson State College students from white pine in dimensions reconstructed from an average of known ancient dugout canoes.

8. Wôbanakik and environs during the Years of the Moose and Log Ships. This map basically depicts the Maritime and Laurentian Archaic of the Archaeologists as one culture area, with different facies depending on the local ecological constraints and potentials. L'anse Amour is extremely important to my argument about the west-to-east movement of culture bearers, in that it is older than equivalent sites such as Teviac, on the

European coast. Note that Wôbanakik may have extended to the west, but this may be contested. The compass rose is an Otter Creek *atlatl* dart point.

9. Kennebec River Valley at Norridgewock, Maine. Postcard image before 1911. Broad alluvial valleys such as this were prime sites for early villages.

10. Wabanaki cone wigwam. Postcard image before 1904. Note the cloth door flap and external log weights to hold down bark sheets. Although this image is from the Canadian Maritimes, identical buildings have a nineteenth-century documented distribution as far west as Lake Memphramagog in Quebec. A photograph taken at the lake in northern Vermont in the 1910s may show one in the background, but the image is too vague to tell if this is a traditional building or a "rustic reconstruction" of some type.

11. Saratoga Springs, New York. Postcard image before 1914. Note the conical wigwam and turn-of-the-century cut-cloth fringe clothing. This speaks more to emerging stereotypes about eastern Native people than about reality.

12. *Atlatl* dart and arrow point types that define the Archaic and Woodland periods. *Clockwise:* Monkton quartzite deltoid woodland arrowhead; Mount Independence chert side-notched *atlatl* "bird point"; medium-game Mount Independence chert tanged or stemmed point; small-game Mount Independence chert deltoid *atlatl* point; small-game Monkton quartzite side-notched, concave-base atlatl dart point. Replicas made by Andy Lee, 1999.

13. Petroglyph of log ship. Date conjectural. The Peterborough, Ontario, petroglyph field is one of the most important rock art sites in eastern North America. Numerous humanoid and naturalistic figures and what are obviously some kind of canoes with passengers are depicted all over the rocks. Archaeologists have speculated for years that the large ground-stone gouges found all over Wôbanakik were used to hew large dugout canoes. But there has been no other evidence of what these canoes may have looked like. The Peterborough glyphs have been cited as evidence of European vessels penetrating North America, a hypothesis not widely held by academic archaeologists and First Nations people. If we combine this iconographic representation with the documented woodworking technology, we can hypothesize that this is an actual image of a log ship. It has intriguing detail, including a deep draft unlike other canoe petroglyphs at the site; what appears to be a steering oar, such as is known from the Pacific Northwest; and perhaps even a representation of an irregular moose-hide sail, such as was described by early European observers in the Western Atlantic.

14. Depiction of Abenaki hunter. He wears replica brain-tanned "sleeves" as a top, with ochre and carbon-black pigment decoration. The necklace is of steatite tubes alternating with red catlinite beads. Catlinite has been found as far east as the Penobscot Valley of Maine. The breechcloth is interesting in that it is a Vermont deerhide with the clawmarks of a mountain lion. The mark is enclosed in a circle of double-scroll designs. The leggings are also brain-tanned with pigment decorations. Moccasins are detailed with porcupine quill designs. He holds an original (early 1700s) bow with twisted-gut bowstring.

15. Wabanaki pottery, ca. 500 winters ago. Idealized types illustrating differences in overall form and position of incised, punctated, and molded decoration fields.

16. Cultural map of Wôbanakik, in A.D. 1500, with overlay of boundary of the Great Council Fire in A.D. 1750. Note that the Nadoueks were extinct during the reign of the alliance. Their homeland was colonized by Abenakis, Wendats, and Mohawks in the 1600s. The boundary outline is a conservative estimate of the distribution of the fully integrated allies of the Abenaki. It would be instructive to compare this map with the distribution of the Six Nations of upstate New York, which was supposedly the largest confederacy in the East.

17. Domestic fur trade and related articles found in Wôbanakik. Although many of these artifacts were widely available to both Euro-American and First Nations people, they were also specifically listed by various references as being important fur trade items. While the provenance is good, there is little hope of determining the ethnicity of the artifacts' first owners. *From top to bottom:* Multipurpose trade knife (LL Barbour, Skowhegan, Maine, nineteenth century); skinning knife, "Riggs" (probably Massachusetts, eighteenth century); fishhooks, eighteenth century; trade ax head (southern Maine, eighteenth century); white, blue, and clear wound glass "neck beads" (central New Hampshire, ca. 1740); kaolin pipe (central New Hampshire, date unknown); burning glass (southern Maine, ca. 1760); bronze medallion (north-central Vermont, ca. 1700); bronze arrowhead (southern Maine, seventeenth century); fire steel (southern Quebec, ca. 1740).

18. Chief Hassaki of the Odawa opens the Great Council of 1701. He holds an eagle-wing fan and T-shaped calumet. He is wearing a prairie grizzly bear-claw necklace and a buffalo-skin robe. Delegates are wearing body tattoos and clothing appropriate to the period. A French colonial honor guard is seen to the right. The chief holds a belt that exists today but is held in European hands. Watercolor, signature unclear, 1998.

19. Birch-bark container. Sewn with dyed and split spruce root. Handle, hinge, and tie-downs from leather (Sutton, Quebec, ca. 1900). This has an excellent provenance, although its design is similar to Attikamek and even some Passamaquoddy bark work.

20. "English style" Wabanaki vertical log building interior. We have numerous references to Abenaki and Wabanaki people living in English- or European-style buildings in the eighteenth century. This is an adaptation of an early-nineteenth-century painting of a Wabanaki house interior from New Brunswick, which may illustrate this type of architecture. It is an upright-log, earthfast (bases of logs set into the soil) building. There are also early references to bark shingles being used on the roof. This kind of building is not unknown in Native America. Variations were common on the eastern and southern margins of the so-called woodlands culture area and were used by French colonials as well. Note absence of interior furniture.

21. Roman Catholic offerings. Silver crucifix (southern Maine, ca. 1680), brass platform or Jesuit ring, "heart and hand of God" motif (southern Quebec, ca. 1710). The crucifix is a widely distributed seventeenth-century type found at French-influenced First Nations sites. It was probably made in France. According to conventional wisdom, the Jesuit (platform) rings were supposedly given to Christian converts. However, there are records of brass rings, probably identical to this one, listed as fur trade articles. Perhaps those created for ecclesiastic use had different motifs from the fur trade examples. More research may shed some light on this.

22. Wabanaki gaming equipment. *Top to bottom:* Cedar bundle *adowiz* game (new in 1995); ash-wood lacrosse stick with deer-hide webbing (southern Quebec, ca 1880); *gagwinigen* set (replica, 1994, except for bowl, which is western Maine, ca. 1800); maple "mudcat" snowsnake (provenance unsure, ca. 1880). It has a pewter-weighted head that does not show in this photograph.

23. Ash-splint eel trap. Splint traps were used all over eastern North America; this one is important for its Vermont provenance. One end contains a tapering funnel-like entrance that acts as a one-way gate for eels, who come in for bait but cannot exit. The other end is blocked by a stone or wood slab when in the water. The trap can be easily lifted from the stream and quickly emptied into a storage basket on shore (Connecticut River, Brattleboro, Vermont, ca. 1780–1810).

24. Beaver tail winter moccasins. These are a widespread northern type with high flaps and long lacings to bind up over the leggings to seal out snow and drafts. These

may not be of Abenaki make, but provenance data indicates that they were used by them (southern Quebec, ca. 1900).

25. Robert Rogers and the burning of Odanak. This is an adaptation of an often reproduced plate of Rogers in a benign pose with subservient Indians behind him. We have given him a more appropriate visage surrounded by flames.

26. The ancient tools of war found in Wôbanakik. Most of these materials were commonly available to civilians and military and to both First Nations and Euro-American users. Even the tomahawks and trade silver, usually thought of as "Indian," were often used and worn by Euro-Americans and Europeans. Therefore, while I can control the geography of the provenance, the ethnicity of the original owner must always remain in doubt. I am reasonably certain of the diplomatic silver gorget and the tomahawk, since they seem quite specifically designed for giving to First Nations allies. *Left to right:* Powderhorn with steel and brass fittings (central New Hampshire, ca. 1750); *fusil a' domino* (musket with barrel bands, originally from Holland, ca. 1730, depinned and banded after 1740; found in southern Maine; predates Revolutionary War period "Hessian" musket); French flints for flintlock, from a ca. 1740 shipwreck in the Gulf of St. Lawrence; "screw bowl" pipe tomahawk with brass deer inlay on blade, handle probably a replacement (central New Hampshire, ca. 1800); tanged steel lance head (Connecticut River, eighteenth century); trade-silver "Cross of Lorraine" (mark unclear, probably Montreal, ca. 1790), restrung with transparent blue wound glass beads (Europe or China, ca. 1800); trade-silver nosering with pendant heart (mark unclear, ca. 1750); early Continental-style measuring powderhorn; ramshorn, compass-incised decoration; iron and brass fittings (France or Quebec, ca. 1690, found in central New Hampshire); diplomatic silver gorget, Philadelphia-style engraving (north central Massachusetts, dated 1757.

27. Abenaki warrior and spouse, ca. 1750. This is a reconstruction of the costume of the period with appropriate accessories. *The Warrior:* He wears a silver crown copied from one believed to be from this region that was available for auction on the Internet. It is surmounted by a loose "turban" of blue silk and a round "roach" adorned with vulture, hawk, and owl feathers. His shirt is a linen "voyager"-style shirt from a commercial pattern, using a cloth appropriate to the period. His brain-tanned breechcloth is the same as that of the contact period hunter. The leggings are an actual pair of eighteenth-century winter leggings found in a barn in north-central Vermont. The moccasins are a modern Abenaki-Iroquois hybrid style. Accessories include a wool hunter's pouch with beaded designs derived from historic Lake Champlain Valley pouches found in European museum collections; the powderhorn and musket are those shown in figure 26. *The Cornplanter:* She wears a blouse and skirt copied from a 1788 painting of a Wabanaki woman on the southern shore of the St. Lawrence near Quebec City. Her jewelry includes bugle and candy-stripe beads, both old and new, as well as a silver brooch copied from one on display at the Chimney Point Museum, Addison, Vermont. The eighteenth- or early-nineteenth-century corn mortar and pestle is from Phillipsburg, Quebec.

28. "Kwai." Abenaki warriors return home with materiel captured from the British. They are giving the "common signal" from the woodsedge as they near Missisquoi or Winooski. Note the use of horses. Oil on board (unsigned, 1997).

29. Representation of Abenaki delegate from the Seven Nations to Vermont legislature and wampum custodian in 1799. I believe that this is the most elegant period for eastern First Nations clothing. *Delegate:* The tricorn hat is known to have been used by both Native and Euro-American people. There exists an ambiguous tricorn sold in 1999 from central New Hampshire that may have had a First Nations provenance. It

had a trade-silver medallion and the remains of what I believe was a hawk feather affixed to it. The coat is a modern copy of a French trade coat that was excavated in the Great Lakes area, so it was conceivably available here as well. It is adapted from a commercial eighteenth-century coat pattern. The leggings are simple red wool leggings of a generalized style with no geographic origin, since we do not have good evidence of Wabanaki cloth leggings from this time. Moccasins are the same as in figure 27. His accessories are an Assumption sash, probably a bit out of period since this particular variant seems to begin around 1810 or later. *Custodian:* She wears the woman's hood of a more western Wabanaki style than the common Micmac hood. Her blouse is a caped blouse worn by almost all First Nations women during the late eighteenth and early nineteenth centuries; this variety also may be a bit out of period, since we see a similar one in a painting of a Lorette Huron woman of about 1830. Her skirt is a timeless blue wool wraparound with horizontal red bands. This skirt is seen in numerous paintings of people from the Maritimes to the Great Lakes in the late eighteenth and early nineteenth centuries. The solid trade-silver bosses, not brooches, are derived from an unclear print of an 1810 painting of a woman with one of these in southern Ontario. She holds a quahog wampum (strung on brain-tanned deer hide) peace belt.

30. Representation of wampum custodian and Abenaki delegate to the Great Council Fire at Kahnawake in 1840. I couldn't resist being in the posed photographs with my wife Anna. *Custodian:* She wears another of the classic woman's hoods. Her satin caped dress and skirt are derived from an old nineteenth-century photograph from Odanak, Quebec. She wears a bias-woven quahog wampum choker and necklace. She holds a bentwood box with the remains of black pigment double-scroll designs (southern Quebec, ca. 1840) and a modern quahog wampum treaty belt. *Delegate:* He wears an original man's top hat with silver heart and ring brooch embellishments (southern Quebec, ca. 1840), a white linen shirt, and grosgrain ribbon tie. The navy and red wool "Sagamore's coat" is based on a widespread style used by the Wabanakis, Lorette Huron, and Canadian Mission Mohawks. The collar scrolls are based on one of the few documented Western Abenaki double-scroll designs known, while the epaulets are more Micmac-inspired. The marginal zigzag beading is from a nineteenth-century man's collar found in New Hampshire. Pants are of a style known in the 1840s, as are the moccasins. He wears a Treaty of Greenville Medal, one of seven known (dated 1795).

31. Birch-bark canoe. This is a curator's dilemma: to leave the 1960s fiberglas patch seen below the gunwale, so as to document its persistence, or to remove it to restore the canoe to its early 1900s form. I have not been able to decide, so have left it untouched. Odanak, Quebec, ca. 1900; used until the 1970s.

32. Missisquoi Abenaki guides and camp cooks with their clients. This was taken by my grandfather on the Missisquoi River in 1910. Other than the most important presence of the Abenaki guides, note the white shirts and ties used by their clients. I have fished the river right by that family campsite, and it is a muddy, mosquito-infested tract. I couldn't imagine using a white shirt, much less a tie!

33. Monkey Drew with my father's trophy muskellunge, 1957. Unfortunately, this is the only photograph that I have of Monkey Drew.

34. Crooked knife with "Fred W. Wiseman, June 1913" inscribed on blade. Extremely curved "drop" antler handle. This is an interesting blade. After my grandfather gave me the knife when I was only seven years old I couldn't figure out how to use it. The handle was extremely uncomfortable to hold, and I couldn't exert any cutting force with it. It sat in my bureau drawer until I read about crooked knives for the first time while a student in Arizona. Although the blade is wider than most crooked knives

I have seen, it worked fine as a *left-handed* crooked knife. My father was left-handed, I wonder if my grandfather was?

35. Abenaque Indians, Sebago Lake. Tourist camp art with views of an Abenaki man wearing a cut-cloth fringe tunic (?) and carrying muzzle-loading firearms. The "Um-ha," "Caramb-ha," and "Lung-ha" labels are stereotypic pseudo-Indian words not in the Abenaki language. This obviously was designed to reinforce stereotypes about Indians. The clothing is problematic: the man wears common trousers and shoes and a white "athletic shirt." The only "Indian" wear is the feather headdress and the loose tunic carelessly slung over his shoulder (western Maine, ca. 1900).

36. Abenaki basketmaker and baskets. This is a wonderful photograph that shows several types of baskets that we can compare to museum examples, as well as the piles of various kinds of raw materials on the ground. It is dated 1927 on the back of the image, which seems a bit late for the style of dress. (Wiseman collection)

37. Tourist trade articles. *Top row:* Cowwiss basket with distinctive loop secondary weave seen in figure 37 (southern Quebec, ca. 1920). Tiny Odanak-style bark teepee, not inscribed "Made in Canada" as required after the McKinley Tariff Act of the early 1890s, may be Missisquoi Abenaki; sweetgrass basket with lid (bought in Johnson, Vermont, in 1922 from a "Gypsy" family). *Bottom row:* Abenaki canoe (although made in Swanton, Vermont, in the 1950s, the style developed in the 1800s); miniature bow and "bird arrow," not made by Abenakis but sold by them (Quebec, ca. 1900); miniature maple paddle (central New Hampshire, ca. 1900); miniature wooden snowshoes with string webbing (bought in Underhill, Vermont, in 1925 from an itinerant "Gypsy" family); moccasins, not made by Abenakis but obtained from Attikameks to sell in New England (Quebec, ca. 1900).

38. Pan-Indian "cut-cloth fringe" clothing, ca. 1900. *Woman:* Red velvet "princess crown" with tubular clear glass beads. Cotton "cut-cloth fringe" dress with appliqué decoration and applied Victorian-style buttons. Both found together (and sharing the same applied buttons) in the upper Connecticut River Valley. An Eastern Township–style habitant chair, made by Burlington Gypsy Abenakis and sold in Jefferson-ville, Vermont, holds a *cowwiss* and sweetgrass basket made in Odanak in 1997. *Man:* Turkey feather Plains-style headdress (western Maine, ca. 1900). Man's outfit embellished with Niagara-style beadwork. Style influenced by Anglo Order of Red Men secret society clothing (found in Essex Junction, Vermont, believed originally from South Hero, Vermont, ca. 1900). He holds a gray birch "root club" of a style somewhat different from the Penobscot root clubs of the era, may be a western form. Abenaki and other basket makers discovered that if they adopted Pan-Indian–style clothing they would be more identified with "Indiannness," perhaps inviting more sales. Traditional Abenaki clothing would probably not have been recognized as being "Indian." This style, which has more to do with Anglo perception than First Nations culture, persists at Dawnland pow-wows even today. However, there is a movement abroad to resurrect more traditional styles.

39. Abenaki hunter with .303-caliber Savage Model 1903 rifle. Canvas tent and paddle made by Abenaki people from the Phillipsburg, Quebec, area. Photographed by my grandfather on the Missisquoi River in 1907.

40. Recent Abenaki snowshoes and snowshoe mold. This mold, which came on the market in Swanton, Vermont, in the 1980s was used until the early 1950s. The snowshoes, also of that era, came from Swanton as well.

41. Henry Perkins. This is a copy of an often published old photograph of Perkins. He seems a bit younger in the painting.

42. Artifacts of the early Missisquoi Abenaki Renaissance. Man's loom-beaded

headband on leather (St. Albans, Vermont, ca. 1968). Woman's beaded necklace (Swanton Abenaki, ca. 1970).

43. Swanton Abenaki license plate. Issued to the author, June 1989.

44. Homer St. Francis in 1995. This is a copy of a photograph published in a newspaper in 1995.

45. First Abenaki Heritage Celebration poster. Announcing Cultural Heritage Week in May 1993. Offset print.

46. Women at the May 1999 Abenaki Heritage Day celebration. Note that the regalia is heavily influenced by Pan-Indian or western First Nations styles. (See the comment on figure 38.)

47. "The Future Abenaki Reservation according to the Burlington Free Press." This is an original interpretation, done in a political cartoon style to illustrate how ludicrous the position taken by the media can be.

48. Abenaki Tribal Headquarters in 1998. Tribal Museum is to the right.

49. Inside the Abenaki Tribal Museum and Heritage Center in May 1999. The author and Governor Howard Dean examine the exhibits. Governor Dean holds a check for $25,000 for a future Tribal Museum expansion.

Bibliography

Abenaki Nation of Vermont. 1982. *A Petition for Federal Recognition as an American Indian Tribe by the Abenaki Nation of Vermont*. Swanton.

Adney, Edwin T., and Howard I. Chapelle. 1964. *The Bark Canoes and Skin Boats of North America*. Washington, D.C.: Smithsonian Institution.

———. n.d. "The Calender of Months at St. Francis, the inhabitants of which were mainly refugees from the Kennebec after the destruction of Norridgwock, 1742." Maine Historical Society Collections.

———. n.d. "Astronomy and diagrams and notes, positions of the Big Dipper, the months of Kennebec-Abenaki (Rasles 1717)." Papers of E. T. Adney. Library of Peabody Museum, Salem, Mass.

———. n.d. "The Astronomy of the Malecite Indians of New Brunswick." Papers of E. T. Adney. Library of Peabody Museum, Salem, Mass.

Alger, Abby L. 1897. *In Indian Tents: Stories Told by Penobscot, Passamaquoddy and Micmac Indians to Abby L. Alger*. Boston: Roberts Bothing.

Allen, Ira. 1969. *The Natural and Political History of the State of Vermont*. Reprint, Rutland, Vt.: Charles E. Tuttle Co.

Allen, R., L. Feaster, A. Myers, and M. Woodruff. 1989. *The Vermont Geography Book*. 2nd ed. Burlington, Vt.: Northern Cartographic.

"Amucalu." n.d. Indian Township, Maine: Wabanaki Bilingual Education Program.

Anastas, Peter. 1973. *Glooskap's Children: Encounters with the Penobscot Indians of Maine*. Boston: Beacon Press.

Anderson, J. K. 1973. "Fisheries." Pp. 5–1, 5–2 in Winooski River Basin Water Quality Management Plan. Agency of Environmental Conservation. Special Collections, Bailey Library, University of Vermont, Burlington. Manuscript.

Anderson, R. Scott, and Charles D. Race. 1982. "Evidence for Later Holocene and Recent Sea-Level Rise along Coastal Maine Utilizing Salt Marsh Data." Pp. 79–96 in: *New England Seismotectonic Study Activities in Maine during Fiscal Year 1981*. Augusta: Maine Geological Society.

"The Annals of the St. Francis Indians," John B. Perry Papers, 24–46. "Lease of certain lands on the Missisquoi River by Abenakis of Missisquoi to James Robertson." Stevens Family Papers, g: 1 (copy from Public Archives of Canada).

Archambault, Marie-France. 1987. "L'Archaique sur la Haute Cote du Nord su Saint-Laurent." *Recherches Amerindiennes au Quebec* 17, no. 1–2, 101–4.

Aroostook Indian Resource Center. n.d. "Indian Medicine." Caribou, Maine: The Center.

Attean, Rene. 1983. "Penobscot Life: A Curriculum Guide." Old Town, Maine: Penobscot Nation.

Auger, Leonard, A. 1959. "St. Francis through the Years." *Vermont History* 27, no. 4 (October): 287–304.

Axtell, James. 1981. *The European and the Indian: Essays in the Ethnohistory of Colonial North America*. New York: Oxford University Press.

Bailey, Alfred Goldsworth. 1969. *The Conflict of European and Eastern Algonquian Cultures, 1504–1700*. 2d ed. Toronto: University of Toronto Press.

Bailey, J. H. 1939a. "Archaeology in Vermont 1938." Pp. 3–6 in *Archaeology in Vermont*, ed. J.C. Huden. Rutland, Vt.: Charles Tuttle.

——. 1993b. "A Ground Slate Producing Site near Vergennes, Vermont." *Bulletin of the Champlain Valley Archaeological Society* 1, no. 2, 1–29.

——. 1940. "A Stratified Rock Shelter in Vermont." *Proceedings of the Vermont Historical Society* 8, no. 1, 3–30.

Baker, E. W., et al. 1994. *American Beginnings: Exploration, Culture and Cartography in the Land of Norumbega*. Lincoln: University of Nebraska Press.

Baker, C. 1990. "Radiocarbon Dates in the State of Vermont." Montpelier: Vermont Division for Historic Preservation. Typescript.

Baker, C. Alice. 1897. *True Stories of New England Captives Carried to Canada during the Old French and Indian Wars*. Cambridge: E. A. Hall and Co.

Baker, J. S. 1976. *Report to Governor Thomas R. Salmon of the State of Vermont Regarding Claims Presented by the Abenaki Nation*. Montpelier, Vt.: Office of the Governor.

Ballard, Edward. 1866. "Character of the Penacooks." *Collections of the New Hampshire Historical Society* 8:428–45.

Barber, R. J. 1972. "Analysis of Manufacture and Use Reconstruction for Lithic Artifacts." University of Vermont, Department of Anthropology. Typescript.

——. 1980. "Archaeological Evidence Suggesting Communal Deer Hunting in Vermont." *Man in the Northeast* 19:66–71.

——. 1982. "The Wheeler's Site: A Specialized Shellfish Processing Station on the Merrimack River." *Peabody Museum Monographs*, no. 7. Cambridge, Mass.: Peabody Museum.

Barre, G., and L. Girouard. 1978. "Les Iroquois: premiers agriculteurs." Pp. 43–54 in *Images de la Prehistoire du Quebec*, ed. C. Chapdelaine. Montreal: Recherches Amerindiennes au Quebec.

Basa, L. 1971. "Vt-Ch-3; Progress Report." *VAS Newsletter* 5 (Summer): 4–5.

——. 1974. "Report on the Boucher Site (Vt-Fr-26), Highgate, Vermont." *VAS Newsletter* (Special Number), 5–6.

——. 1975. "The Boucher Site: A Progress Report." *VAS Newsletter*, pp. 1–6.

Bassett, T. D. S. 1976. *Outsiders inside Vermont: Three Centuries of Visitor's Viewpoints on the Green Mountain State*. Canaan, N.H.: Phoenix Publishing.

Bates, Oric, and Herbert E. Winlock. 1912. "Archaeological Material from the Maine Littoral." Bachelor's thesis, Department of Anthropology, Harvard University.

Baxter, James Phinney, 1894. *The Pioneers of New France in New England*. Albany, N.Y.: Joel Munsell's Sons.

Bayreuther, William A. 1980. "Environmental Diversity as a Factor in Modeling Prehistoric Settlement Patterns: Southeast Vermont's Black River Valley." *Man in the Northeast* 19 (Spring): 83–93.

Bear, Andrea Jeanne. 1966. "The Concept of Unity among Indian Tribes of Maine, New Hampshire and New Brunswick: An Ethnohistory." Senior Scholars Program study, Colby College.

Beecher, Catherine. 1868. *Miss Beecher's Domestic Receipt Book*. New York: Harper.

Beecher, Catherine, and Harriet B. Stowe. 1869. *American Woman's Home*. New York: Ford.

Belcher, William R. 1989. "Prehistoric Fish Exploitation in East Penobscot Bay, Maine: The Know Site and Sea-Level Rise. *Archaeology of Eastern North America* 17 (Fall): 175–91.

Belknap, Daniel F. 1986. "Addison Marsh; Damariscotta River; Glidden Point Shell
Middens; Sherman Lake; Cod Cove, North Edgecomb." Pp. 46–49, 59–67 in
*Coastal Processes and Quarternary Stratigraphy in Northern and Central Coastal
Maine*, ed. Joseph T. Kelley and Alice R. Kelley. Orono, Maine: Society of Eco-
nomic Peleontologists and Mineralogists (Eastern Section Field Trip Guidebook).

Bennett, Dean B., ed. 1980. *Maine Dirigo: "I Lead."* Camden, Maine: Down East
Books.

Bennett, M. K. 1955. "The Food Economy of the New England Indians." *Journal of Political Economy* 63, no. 3, 369–97.

Berkhofer, Robert. 1979. *White Man's Indian.* New York: Vintage Books.

Berry, George. 1989–99. "The Great Shell Mounds of Damariscotta." *New England
Magazine*, n.s., vol. 19, 178–88.

Biggar, H. P. 1922. *The Works of Samuel de Champlain.* Toronto: The Champlain
Society.

"Biography of Kancamagus." 1853. *The Farmer's Monthly Visitor* (Manchester, N.H.),
13, no. 5 (May): 129–38.

"Biography of Wanalancet." 1852. *The Farmer's Monthly Visitor* 12, no. 9 (September):
259–65.

Bird, S. E., ed. 1996. *Dressing in Feathers.* Boulder, Colo.: Westview Press.

Bolian, C. E., and J. B. Gengras. 1989. "Report on Phase II Archaeological Evaluation
of VT-ES-2 at the Stewartstown-Canaan Bridge Replacement BRZ-277(5), S-4159."
Submitted to the New Hampshire Department of Transportation, Concord,.

———. 1990. "Archaeological Excavation at the Canaan Bridge Site VT-ES-2 Canaan,
Essex County, Vermont: Early and Middle Woodlands Occupation in the Upper
Connecticut Valley. Report on Phase III Data Recovery of VT-ES-2 at the
Stewartstown-Canaan Bridge Replacement at BRZ-277(5), S-4159." Submitted to
New Hampshire Department of Transportation, Concord.

Bolton, R. P. 1930. "Indian Remains in Northern Vermont." *Indian Notes* 7, no. 1,
57–69.

Borns, H. W., Jr. 1973. "Possible Paleoindian Migration Routes in the Northeast." *Bulletin of the Massachusetts Archaeological Society* 34, no. 1–2, 13–15.

Borstel, Christopher L. 1982. "Archaeology Investigations at the Young Site, Alton,
Maine." *Occasional Publications in Maine Archaeology*, no. 2, Augusta: Maine Historic Preservation Commission.

Bostok, A. K. 1955. "Searching for Indian Relics in Vermont." *Vermont History* 23, no.
3, 233–40; no. 4, 327–32.

Boston Indian Council, 1982. *Wabanaki Curriculum Development Project. A Teacher-
Training Manual.* Boston: The Council.

Bourque, Bruce. 1975. "Comments on the Late Archaic Population of Central Maine:
The View from Turner Farm." *Arctic Anthropology* 12, no. 2, 35–45.

———. 1976. "The Turner Farm Site: A Preliminary Report." *Man in the Northeast* 2:
21–30.

Bourque, Bruce J. 1973. "Aboriginal Settlement and Subsistence on Maine Coast."
Man in the Northeast 6 (Fall): 3–20.

———. 1975. "Comments on the Late Archaic Populations of Central Maine: The
View from the Turner Farm." *Arctic Anthropology* 12, no. 2, 35–45.

———. 1989. "Ethnicity on the Maritime Peninsula, 1600–1759." *Ethnohistory* 36
(Summer): 257–84.

———. 1995. *Diversity and Complexity in Prehistoric Maritime Studies: A Gulf of Maine
Perspective.* New York: Plenum Press.

Bourque, Bruce J., and Ruth Holmes Whitehead. 1985. "Tarrantines and the Introduction of European Trade Goods in the Gulf of Maine." *Ethnohistory* 32: 327–41.

Bourque, Bruce J., and Harold W. Kruger. 1991. "Dietary Reconstruction of Prehistoric Maritime Peoples of North-eastern North America: Faunal vs. Stable Isotopic Approaches." Paper presented at the 24th annual meeting of the Canadian Archaeological Association, St. John's Newfoundland.

———. 1994. "Dietary Reconstruction from Human Bone Isotopes for Five Coastal New England Populations, in: Paleonutrition: The Diet and Health of Prehistoric Americans," ed. Kristen D. Sobolik. *Southern Illinois University Center for Archaeological Investigations Occasional Paper*, no. 22, 195–209.

Bradstreet, T. E., and R. B. Davis. 1975. "Mid-Postglacial Environments in New England with Emphasis on Maine. *Arctic Anthropology* 12, no. 2, 7–22.

Brasser, Ted J. 1968. "Group Identification along a Moving Frontier." *Proceedings of the 38th International Congress of Americanists* 2: 261–65.

———. 1974. *Riding on the Frontier's Crest: Mahican Indian Culture and Culture Change*. Publications in Ethnology, no. 13. Ottawa: National Museum of Man.

———. 1978. "Early Indian-European Contacts." Pp. 78–88 in *Northeast*, vol. 15 of *Handbook of North American Indians*, ed. B. G. Trigger. Washington, D.C.: Smithsonian Institution.

Brennan, Louis. 1976. "Coastal Adaptation in Prehistoric New England." *American Antiquity* 41, no.1 (January): 112–13.

Brightstar, D. 1992. "Abenaki Research Project." *VAS Newsletter* 86: 6.

Brink, J. A., and G. M. Day. 1991. *Alnobaodwa: A Western Abenaki Language Guide No. 1*. Swanton, Vt.: Franklin Northwest Supervisory Union, Title V Indian Education Office.

Brinton, Daniel G. 1898. "Note on the Criteria of Wampum." *Bulletin* no. 4, Free Museum of Science and Art, University of Pennsylvania, pp. 177–78.

Brooks, E. 1971. "A Laurentian Site in Addison County, Vermont." Pp. 24–32 in *Archaeology in Vermont*, ed. J. C. Huden. Rutland, Vt.: Charles Tuttle.

Brown, W. W. 1889. "Some Indoor Games of the Wabanaki Indians." *Transactions of the Royal Society of Canada*, vol. 6, sec. 2: Montreal.

———. 1890. "Wa-ba-ba-nal, or Northern Lights: A Wabanaki Legend." *Journal of American Folklore* 3: 231–34.

Bruchac, Joseph. 1985. *The Wind Eagle and Other Abenaki Stories as Told by Joseph Bruchac*. Illustrated by Kahionhes. Greenfield Center, N.Y.: Bowman Books.

———. 1988. *The Faithful Hunter: Abenaki Stories*. Greenfield Center, N.Y.: Greenfield Review Press.

Bruchac, Joseph, and M. Caduto. 1991. *Keepers of the Animals*. Golden, Colo.: Fulcrum.

Brumbach, H. J. 1975. "'Iroquoian' Ceramics in 'Algonkian' Territory." *Man in the Northeast* 10: 17–28.

———. 1977. "Report of Excavations at the Archaeological Site in the Village of Schuylerville, New York." Manuscript, Department of Anthropology, SUNY, Albany, N.Y.

Buchdahl, D. 1986. *Finding One's Way: The Story of an Abenaki Child*. Swanton, Vt.: Franklin Supervisory Union Title IV, Indian Education Program and the Abenaki Self-Help Association.

Bumstead, M. P. 1980. "VT-CH-94: Vermont's Earliest Known Agricultural Experiment Station." *Man in the Northeast* 19: 73–82.

Burns, Brian. 1977. "Massacre or Muster? Burgoyne's Indians and the Militia at Bennington." *Vermont History* 45, no. 3 (Summer): 133–44.

Burrage, H. S., ed. 1966. *Early English and French Voyages*. New York: Charles Scribner's Sons.

Butler, Eva L., and Wendell S. Hadlock. 1957. *Use of Birch-Bark in the Northeast*. Bulletin no. 7, Robert Abbe Museum, Bar Harbor, Maine.

Byers, D. S. 1954. "Bull Brook—A Fluted Point in Ipswich, Massachusetts." *American Antiquity* 19: 343–51.

Calloway, Colin G. 1983. "An Uncertain Destiny: Indian Captives on the Upper Connecticut River." *Journal of American Studies* 17 (August): 189–210.

——. 1984. "The Conquest of Vermont: Vermont's Indian Troubles in Context." *Vermont History* 52 (Summer): 161–79.

——. 1986. "Green Mountain Diaspora: Indian Population Movements in Vermont, c. 1600–1800." *Vermont History* 54 (Fall): 197–228.

——. 1987a. "Gray Lock's War." *Vermont History* 55 (Fall): 212–27.

——. 1988. "Wanalancet and Kancamagus: Indian Strategy and Leadership on the New Hampshire Frontier." *Historical New Hampshire* 43 (Winter): 264–90.

——. 1989. *The Abenaki*. New York: Chelsea House.

——. 1990. *The Western Abenakis of Vermont, 1600–1800: War, Migration, and the Survival of an Indian People*. Norman: University of Oklahoma Press.

——. 1991. *Dawnland Encounters: Indians and Europeans in Northern New England*. Hanover, N.H.: University Press of New England.

Campbell, Joseph. 1989. *Historical Atlas of World Mythology*. Vol 2, *The Way of the Seeded Earth*. Part 2, *Mythologies of the Primitive Planters: The Northern Americas*. New York: Harper & Row.

Carr, P. G., I. A. Worley, and M. W. Davis. 1977. "Post-Lake Vermont History of a Pond and Wetland in the Champlain Basin." Pp. 71–112 in *Proceedings of the 4th Annual Lake Champlain Basin Environmental Conference*. Plattsburgh, N.Y.: SUNY, Institute for Man and Environment.

Carter, Samuel. 1898. "The Route of the French and Indian Army That Sacked Deerfield Feb. 29th, 1703–4 [O.S.], on Their Return to Canada with the Captives." *History and Proceedings of the Pocumtuck Valley Memorial Association* 2: 126–51.

Cartier, Jacques. 1924. *The Voyages of Jacques Cartier*, ed. H. P. Biggar. Ottawa: Publications of the Public Archives of Canada.

Cassedy, D. F. 1978. "A Prehistoric Inventory of the Upper Connecticut River Valley." Raleigh: Garrow and Associates. Vermont Division for Historic Preservation, Montpelier. Manuscript.

Catania, V. A. 1991. "Flotation and Analysis of Ewing (VT-CH-5) and Winooski (VT-CH-46) Soils. Department of Anthropology, University of Vermont, Burlington. Typescript.

Chamberlain, Montague. 1904. "Indians of New Brunswick in Champlain's Time." *Acadiensis*, o.s. 4, nos. 3–4 (July-October): 280–95.

Champlain, Samuel. 1971. *The Works of Samuel de Champlain*. 2d ed. Edited by H. H. Langton and W. F. Ganong. Toronto: Champlain Society.

Chapedelaine, Claude. 1992. "The Iroquois of the St. Lawrence Valley." Pp. 53–64 in *Wrapped in the Colors of the Earth: Cultural Heritage of the First Nations*. Montreal: McCord Museum.

Chapman, D. H. 1937. "Late Glacial and Postglacial History of the Champlain Valley." *American Journal of Science* 34: 89–124.

Charland, Thomas M. 1960. "The Lake Champlain Army and the Fall of Montreal." *Vermont History* 28: 293–301.

———. 1961. "Un Village d'Abenaquis sur la Riviere Mississquoi," *Revue d'Historique de l'Amerique Francais* 15, no. 3, 319–22. (Translation by Grace Huden in Vermont Historical Society Library)

———. 1964. *Les Abenakis d'Odanak: Histoire des Abenakis d'Odanak, 1675–1937.* Montreal: Editions du Levrier.

———. "Atecuando (Jerome)." *Dictionary of Canadian Biography*, 3: 20–21. Toronto: University of Toronto Press.

———. "Joseph Louis Gill." *Dictionary of Canadian Biography*, 4: 293–94.

Charlevoix, Rev. Pierre F. X. de. 1962. *History and General Description of New France by the Reverend P.F.X. de Charlevoix, S. J.* Edited and translated by John Gilmeary Shea. 6 vols. Reprint, Chicago: Loyola University Press.

Chase, Francis, ed. 1986. *Gathered Sketches from the Early History of New Hampshire and Vermont.* Claremont, N.H.: Tracy, Kenney and Co.

Church, Benjamin. 1897. *The History of the Eastern Expeditions of 1689, 1690, 1692, 1696 and 1704 against the Indians and French.* Boston: J.K. Wiggin and Wm. Parsons Lunt.

Clark, Charles E. 1970. *The Eastern Frontier: The Settlement of Northern New England, 1610–1763.* New York: Alfred A. Knopf.

Clermont, N. 1978. "Le Sylvicole Initial." Pp. 31–42 in *Images de la prehistoire du Quebec*, ed. C. Chapdelaine. Montreal: Recherches Amerindiennes au Quebec.

Coleman, Emma L. 1925. *New England Captives Carried Away to Canada between 1670 and 1760 during the French and Indian Wars.* 2 vols. Portland, Maine: Southwourth Press.

Collins, R. 1991. *The Native Americans.* New York: Smithmark.

Conkling, Robert. 1974. "Legitimacy and Conversion in Social Change: The Case of French Missionaries and the Northern Algonkian." *Ethnohistory* 21, no. 1 (Winter): 1–24.

Cook, Sherburne F. 1973a. "Interracial Warfare and Population Decline among the New England Indians." *Ethnohistory* 20, no. 1 (Winter): 1–24.

———. 1973b. "The Significance of Disease in the Extinction of the New England Indian." *Human Biology* 45: 485–508.

———. 1976. *The Indian Population of New England in the Seventeenth Century.* Berkeley: University of California Press.

Cook Lynn, Elizabeth. 1998. "American Indian Intellectuals and the New Indian Story." Pp. 111–34 in *Natives and Academics*, ed. Devon Mehesuah. Lincoln: University of Nebraska Press.

Coolidge, Guy Omeron. 1938/1979. "The French Occupation of the Champlain Valley from 1609 to 1759." *Proceedings of the Vermont Historical Society*, n.s., 6, no. 3 (September): 143–313. Reprint, Harrison, N.Y.: Harbor Hill Books.

Cooper, J. M. 1938. *Snares, Deadfalls and Other Traps of the Northern Algonquians and Northern Athapaskans.* Anthropological Series, no. 5. Washington, D.C.: Catholic University of America.

Crisman, K. J. 1981. "The Lower Missisquoi River Region: An Archaeological Investigation." College honors thesis, Department of Anthropology, University of Vermont, Burlington. Typescript.

Crockett, Walter Hill. 1921. *Vermont: The Green Mountain State.* 5 vols. New York: Century History Co.

Cronon, William. 1983. *Changes in the Land: Indians, Colonists, and the Ecology of New England.* New York: Hill and Wang.

Culin, Stewart. 1907. "Games of the North American Indians." *Bureau of Ethnology, 24th Annual Report.* Washington, D.C.: Government Printing Office.

Cuneo, John R. 1959. *Robert Rogers of the Rangers*. New York: Oxford University Press.

Cunningham, W. M. 1948. "A Study of the Glacial Kame Culture in Michigan, Ohio and Indiana." *Occasional Contributions from the Museum of Anthropology of the University of Michigan*, no. 12. Ann Arbor: University of Michigan.

Curran, M. L. 1977. "Early Man in the Connecticut River Drainage: An Archaeological Test Case in Southern New Hampshire." Department of Anthropology, University of Massachusetts. Manuscript.

———. 1979. "Studying Human Adaptation at a Paleo-Indian Site: A Preliminary Report." Pp. 14–26 in *Ecological Anthropology of the Middle Connecticut River Valley*, ed. R. Paynter. Amherst: University of Massachusetts.

Daniels, Thomas E. 1963. *Vermont Indians*. Poultney, Vt.: Journal Press.

Davies, C. P. 1992. "Estuarine Preservation Potential Model for Archaelological Sites in Coastal Maine." Master's thesis, Institute of Quarternary Studies, University of Maine, Orono.

Davis, Margaret B. 1965. "Phytogeography and Palynology of Northeastern United States." *The Quaternary of the United States*, ed. H. E. Wright and D. G. Frey. Princeton, N.J.: Princeton University Press.

Davis, Mary. 1996. *Encyclopedia of Native Americans in the Twentieth Century*. New York: Garland Publishing.

Day, Gordon M. 1953. "The Indian as an Ecological Factor in the Northeastern Forest." *Ecology* 34, no. 2, 329–46.

———. 1959. "Dartmouth and St. Francis." *Dartmouth Alumni Magazine* 52 (November): 28–30.

———. 1962a. "English-Indian Contacts in New England." *Ethnohistory* 9, no. 1 (Winter): 24–40.

———. 1962b. "Rogers' Raid in Indian Tradition." *Historical New Hampshire* 17 (June): 3–17.

———. 1965a. "The Identity of the Sokokis." *Ethnohistory* 12, no. 3 (Summer): 237–49.

———. 1965b. "The Indian Occupation of Vermont." *Vermont History* 33 (July): 365–74.

———. 1971. "The Eastern Boundary of Iroquois: Abenaki Evidence." *Man in the Northeast* 1 (March): 7–13.

———. 1973a. "Greylock and the Missisquoi Settlement." Paper presented at the Spring 1973 meeting of the Vermont Archaeological Society, Burlington.

———. 1973b. "Mississquoi: A New Look at an Old Village." *Man in the Northeast* 6: 51–57.

———. 1974. "Henry Tufts as a Source on the Eighteenth Century Abenakis." *Ethnohistory* 21, no. 3 (Summer): 189–97.

———. 1975. *The Mots Loups of Father Mathevet*. Publications in Ethnology, no. 8. Ottawa: National Museums of Canada.

———. 1976. "The Western Abenaki Transformer." *Journal of the Folklore Institute* 13, no. 1, 75–89.

———. 1977a. "Indian Place Names as Ethnohistoric Data." Pp. 26–31 in *Actes du Huitieme Congres des Algonquianistes*, ed. William Cowan. Ottawa:.Carleton University.

———. 1977b. "The Western Abenaki of Quebec and Vermont." Paper presented at the Spring 1977 meeting of the Vermont Archaeological Society, Waterbury.

———. 1978. "Western Abenaki." Pp. 145–59 in *Northeast*, ed. B. G. Trigger. Vol. 15 of *Handbook of North American Indians*. Washington, D.C.: Smithsonian Institution.

———. 1979. "Arosagunticook and Androscoggin." Pp. 10–15 in *Papers of the 10th Algonquin Conference*, ed. William Cowan. Ottawa: Carleton University Press.

——. 1981a. "Abenaki Place-Names in the Champlain Valley." *International Journal of Applied Linguistics* 47, no. 2, 143–71.

——. 1981b. *The Identity of the St. Francis Indians.* Canadian Ethnology Service Paper, no. 71. Ottawa: National Museums of Canada.

——. 1984. "The Ouragie War: A Case History in Iroquois—New England Indian Relations." *Extending the Rafters: Interdisciplinary Approaches to Iriquoian Studies,* ed. Michael K. Foster, Jack Campisi, Marianne Mithun. Albany: State University of New York Press.

——. 1987. "Abenakis in the Lake Champlain Valley." Pp. 277–88 in *Lake Champlain: Reflections in Our Past,* ed. Jennie G. Versteeg. Burlington: University of Vermont, Center for Research on Vermont.

——. 1994. *A Western Abenaki Dictionary.* Vol. 1. Mercury Series Paper 128. Hull, Quebec: Canadian Museum of Civilization.

Decher, L. 1991. "Figures Show Indians Have Toughest Time in Vermont." *Burlington Free Press,* July 7.

Deloria, Philip. 1998. *Playing Indian.* New Haven, Conn.: Yale University Press.

Deloria, Vine. 1997. *Red Earth, White Lies.* Golden, Colo.: Fulcrum.

——. 1998. "Comfortable Fictions and the Struggle for Turf: An Essay Review of *The Invented Indian.*" P. 72 in *Natives and Academics,* ed. Devon Mihesuah. Lincoln: University of Nebraska Press.

Denys, Nicholas. 1908. *The Description and Natural History of the Coasts of North America (Acadia).* Toronto: Champlain Society.

Dexter, Warren, and Donna Martin. 1995. *America's Ancient Stone Relics: Vermont's Link to Bronze Age Mariners.* Rutland, Vt.: Academy Books.

Dincauze, D. F. 1971. "An Archaic Sequence for Southern New England." *American Antiquity* 36: 194–98.

——. 1972. "The Atlantic Phase: A Late Archaic Culture in Massachusetts." *Man in the Northeast* 4: 40–61.

——. 1975. "The Late Archaic Period in Southern New England." *Arctic Anthropology* 12, no.2, 23–34.

——. 1976. "The Neville Site: 8000 Years at Amoskeag, Manchester, New Hampshire." *Peabody Museum Monographs,* 4.

Dincauze, D. F., and M. T. Mulholland. 1977. "Early and Middle Archaic Site Distributions and Habitats in Southern New England." *Annals of the New York Academy of Sciences* 288: 439–56.

Dixon, James. 2000. "Coastal Navigators." *Discovering Archaeology* 2, no. 1, 34–35

Dixon, R. B. 1914. "The Early Migration of the Indians of New England and the Maritime Provinces." *Proceedings of the American Antiquarian Society,* n.s. 24, pt. 1, 65–76.

Dobyns, Henry. 1966. "Estimating Aboriginal American Population: An Appraisal of Techniques with a New Hemispheric Estimate." *Current Anthropology* 7, no. 4, 359–416.

——. 1976. *Native American Historical Demography.* Bloomington: Indiana University Press.

——. 1983. *Their Number Become Thinned: Native American Population Dynamics in Eastern North America.* Knoxville: University of Tennessee Press.

Dodson, James. 1991. "Nobody's Laughing at Chief Homer Now." *Yankee Magazine* (January): 60–67, 108–12.

Doolittle, Rev. Benjamin. 1909. "A Short Narrative of Mischief Done by the French and Indian Enemy on the Western Frontiers of the Province of the Massachusetts Bay,"with Notes and Queries. *Magazine of History* 7, no. 2.

Doremus, Christine A. 1985. "Jurisdiction over Adjudications Involving the Abenaki Indian of Vermont." *Vermont Law Review* 10: 417–35.

Doyle, Richard. 1985. "Late Paleo-Indians Remains from Maine and Their Correlations in Noertheastern Prehistory." *Archaeology of North America* 13: 1–34.

Drake, Samuel. 1852. *Indian Captivities, or Life in the Wigwam; Being true narratives of captives who have been carried away by Indians, from the frontier settlements of the United States, from the earliest period to present time.* Auburn, N.Y.: Derby and Miller.

——. 1897. *The Border Wars of New England Commonly Called King William's and Queen Anne's Wars.* New York: Charles Scribner's Sons.

——. 1970. *A Particular History of the Five Years French and Indian Wars in New England and Parts Adjacent.* Reprint, Freeport, N.Y.: Books for Libraries Press.

——. 1971. *The History of the Indian Wars in New England from the First Settlement to the Termination of the War with King Phillip in 1677, from the Original Work by Rev. William Hubbard.* 2 vols. Reprint, New York: Burt Franklin.

Driver, H. E., and W. C. Massey. 1957. "Comparative Studies of North American Indians." *Transactions of the American Philosophical Society* 47: 165–465.

Eccles, William J. 1969. *The Canadian Frontier, 1534–1760.* New York: Holt, Rinehart, and Winston.

Eckstorm, Fannie Hardy. 1932. *The Handicrafts of the Modern Indians of Maine.* (Bulletin 3). Bar Harbor, Maine: Abbe Museum.

——. 1934. "The Attack on Norridgewock." *New England Quarterly* (September): 541–78.

——. 1941/1978. *Indian Place Names of the Penobscot Valley and the Maine Coast* 1941: reprint, Orono: University of Maine at Orono Press.

——. 1945. *Old John Neptune and Other Maine Indian Shamans.* Portland, Maine: The Southworth-Anthoenson Press.

English, John Stephen. 1915. *Indian Legends of the White Mountains.* Boston: Rand Avery.

Fagan, L. A. 1978. "A Vegetational and Cultural Sequence for Southern New England, 15,000 BP to 7,000 BP." *Man in the Northeast* 15–16: 70–92.

Favour, Edith. 1974. "Indian Games, Toys and Pastimes of Maine and the Maritimes." (Bulletin No. 10). Bar Harbor, Maine: Robert Abbe Museum.

——. 1975. "First Families: Woodland People of Maine and the Canadian Maritimes." Augusta: Maine Department of Educational and Cultural Services, Division of Curriculum.

Fell, Barry. 1989. *America B.C.* New York: Pocket Books.

Fiedel, S. J. 1991. "Correlating Archaeology and Linguistics: The Algonquian Case." *Man in the Northeast* 41: 9–32.

Fisher, Margaret W. 1946. "The Mythology of the Northern and Northeastern Algonkians in Reference to Algonkian Mythology as a Whole." P. 229 in *Man in Northeastern North American*, ed. Frederick Johnson. Andover, Mass.: Robert S. Peabody Foundation for Archeology.

Fitzhugh, William W. 1975a. "A Comparative Approach to Northern Maritime Adaptations." Pp. 337–86 in *Prehistoric Maritime Adaptations of the Circumpolar Zone.* The Hague: Mouton; reprint, Chicago: Aldine.

——. 1975b. "A Maritime Archaic Sequence from Hamilton Inlet, Labrador." *Arctic Anthropology* 12, no. 2, 117–38.

——. 1975c. *Prehistoric Maritime Adaptations of the Circumpolar Zone.* The Hague: Mouton.

——. 1978. "Population Movement and Cultural Change on the Central Labrador Coast." In "Amerindians and Their Paleoenvironments in Northeastern North America," ed. Walter S. Newman and Bert Salwen. *Annals of the New York Academy of Sciences*, 288: 481–97.

——. ed. 1985. *Cultures in Contact: The European Impact on Native Cultural Institutions in Eastern North America, A.D. 1000–1800*. Washington, D.C.: Smithsonian Institution Press.

——. 1987. "Archaeological Ethnicity and the Prehistory of Labrador." Pp. 141–53 in *Ethnicity and Culture*, ed. Reginald Auger, Margaret Glass, Scott MacEachern, and Peter H. McCartney. Calgary: University of Calgary Archaeological Association.

Fixico, Don L. 1998. "Ethics and Responsibility in Writing American Indian History." Pp. 85–99 in *Natives and Academics*, ed. Devon Mihesuah. Lincoln: University of Nebraska Press.

Follette, Clara E. 1955. "The Iroquoian Claim on Vermont." *Vermont History* 23 (January): 54–55.

Foster, M. K., J. Campisi, and M. M. Thum, eds. 1984. *Extending the Rafters: Interdisciplinary Approaches to Iroquoian Studies*. Albany: State University of New York Press.

Foster, Michael K., and William Cowan, eds. 1998. *In Search for New England's Past: Selected Essays by Gordon M. Day*. Amherst: University of Massachusetts Press.

Frink, D. 1989. *The Blue Heron Site-VT-CH-36: An Early Archaic Food Processing Site*. Essex Junction, Vt.: Archaeology Consulting Team.

Frink, D. C. Baker, and K. Knoblock. 1992. *Petty Brook Estates, Milton, Vermont, Phase I Archaeological Site Identification and Phase II Site Evaluation Study*. Essex Junction, Vt.: Archaeology Consulting Team.

Frisch, Jack A. 1976. "The Abenakis among the St. Regis Mohawks." *Indian Historian* 4 (Spring): 27–79.

——. 1977. "Cognatic Kinship Organization among the Northeast Algonkians." *Occasional Papers in Anthropology*, no. 2. St. Mary's University, Department of Anthropology.

Funk, Robert E. 1972. "Early Man in the Northeast and the Late Glacial Environment." *Man in the Northeast* 4: 7–39.

——. 1976. "Recent Contributions to Hudson Valley Prehistory." *New York State Museum Memoir* 22.

——. 1977. "Early to Middle Archaic Occupations in Upstate New York." Pp. 21–29 in *Current Perspectives in Northeastern Archaeology: Essays in Honor of William A. Richie*, ed. R. E. Funk and C. F. Hayes. Albany, N.Y.: New York Archaeological Association.

——. 1978. "Post-Pleistocene Adaptations." Pp. 16–27 in *Northeast*, ed. B.G. Trigger. Vol. 15 of *Handbook of North American Indians*. Washington, D.C.: Smithsonian Institution.

——. 1988. "The Laurentian Concept: A Review." *Archaeology of Eastern North America* 16: 1–42.

Funk, R. E., and C. F. Hayes, III, eds. 1977. *Current Perspectives in Northeastern Archaeology: Essays in Honor of William A. Ritchie*. Albany, N.Y.: New York State Archaeological Association.

Funk, R. E., P. Weinman, and T. Weinman. 1966. "The Burnt Hill Phase: Regional Middle Woodland at Lake George." *Bulletin of the New York State Archaeological Association* 37: 1–20.

Gale, John E. 1939. "Northern Neighbors of the Pocumtucks." *History and Proceedings of the Pocumtuck Valley Memorial Association* 9: 22–30.

Gallagher, Nancy. 1999. *Breeding Better Vermonters: The Eugenics Project in the Green Mountain State.* Hanover, N.H.: University Press of New England.

Ghere, David Lynn. 1980. " The Twilight of Abenaki Independence: The Maine Abenaki during the 1750's." M.A. thesis, University of Maine.

——. 1988. "Abenaki Factionalism, Emigration, and Social Continuity: Indian Society in Northern New England, 1725 to 1760." Ph.D. diss., University of Maine.

Gifford, S. M. 1948. "A Brief Summary of Three Years' Digging on the Orwell Site." *Bulletin of the Fort Ticonderoga Museum* 8, no. 1, 26–28.

Gill, Sam D. 1982. *"Native American Religions: An Introduction.* Belmont, Calif.: Wadsworth.

Gilman, Carolyn. 1982. *Where Two Worlds Meet: The Great Lakes Fur Trade.* St. Paul: Minnesota Historical Society.

Goddard, I. 1978. "Central Algonquian Languages." Pp. 583–87 in *Northeast,* ed. B.G. Trigger. Vol. 15 of *Handbook of North American Indians.* Washington, D.C.: Smithsonian Institution.

Godfrey, John E. 1876a. "Ancient Penobscot." Pp. 3–22 in *Maine Historical Society Collections,* vol. 7, series 1. Bath, Maine: E. Upton and Son.

——. 1876b. "Bashaba and the Tarratines." Pp. 93–102 in *Maine Historical Society Collections,* vol. 7, series 1. Bath, Maine: E. Upton and Son.

Gonyea, R. 1988. *The Original People.* Plattsburgh, N.Y.: Clinton County Historical Association.

Gookin, Daniel. 1970. *Historical Collections of the Indians In New England.* Collections of the Massachusetts Historical Society.

Graff, N. P., ed. 1991. *Celebrating Vermont: Myths and Realities.* Hanover, N.H.: University Press of New England.

Graff, N. P., and W. Hosley. 1991. "Celebrating Vermont: Myths and Realities of the First Sixty Years of Statehood." Pp. 19–43 in *Celebrating Vermont: Myths and Realities,* ed. N. P. Graff. Hanover, N.H.: University Press of New England.

Graff, W. M., W. A. Haviland, and P. R. Mills. 1989. *Tools of Stone.* Burlington: University of Vermont, Video Production Unit.

Graffagnino, J. Kevin. 1983. *The Shaping of Vermont: From the Wilderness to the Centennial, 1749–1887.* Rutland and Bennington: Vermont Heritage Press and Bennington Museum.

Gramly, R. M. 1997. "Deerskins and Hunting Territories: Competition for a Scarce Resource of the Northeastern Woodlands." *American Antiquity* 42 : 601–5.

——. 1982. "The Vail Site: A Paleo-Indian Encampment in Maine." *Bulletin of the Buffalo Society of Natural Sciences* 30.

——. 1984. "Kill Sites, Killing Grounds and Fluted Points at the Vail Site." *Archaeology of Eastern North America* 12: 110–21.

——. 1988. *The Adkins Site: A Paleoindian Habitation and Associated Stone Structure.* Buffalo, N.Y.: Persimmon Press.

Grant, John Webster. 1984. *Moon of Wintertime: Missionaries and the Indians of Canada in Encounter since 1534.* Toronto: University of Toronto Press.

Greening, W. 1966. "Historic Odanak and the Abenaki Nation." *Canadian Geographic Journal* 73: 92–97.

Griffin, J. B. 1948. "An Interpretation of the Glacial Kame Culture." Pp. 46–51 in *A Study of the Glacial Kame in Michigan, Ohio and Indiana,* ed. W. M. Cunningham.

(Occasional Contributions from the Museum of Anthropology of the University of Michigan 12)

Griffin, J. R. 1979. "A New Look at Bull Brook." *Anthropology* 3, no. 1–2, 109–30.

Grimes, J. R., W. Eldridge, B. G. Grimes, A. Vaccaro, F. Vaccaro, J. Vaccaro, N. Vaccaro, and A. Orisimi. 1984. "Bull Brook II." *Archaeology of Eastern North America* 13: 35–57.

Grossinger, R. 1975. Interview with Louise Basa in Burlington, Vermont. In *Vermont* no. 21, 211–18.

Grumet, Robert S. 1995. *Historic Contact*. Norman: University of Oklahoma Press.

Guidmark, David. 1989. *The Birchbark Canoe*. Burnstown, Ontario: General Store Publishing House.

Hadlock, Wendell S. 1947. "War among the Northeastern Woodland Indians." *American Anthropologist*, n.s., 49: 204–21.

Hadlock, Wendell S., and Ernest Dodge. 1948. *A Canoe from the Penobscot River*. Salem, Mass.: Peabody Museum.

Hagar, Stanley. 1896. "Micmac Magic and Medicine." *Journal of American Folklore* 9, no. 34, 170–77.

———. 1897. "Weather and the Seasons in Micmac Mythology." *Journal of American Folklore* 10, no. 37, 101–5.

Hall, Benjamin H. 1858/1865. *History of Eastern Vermont from the Earliest Settlement to the Close of the Eighteenth Century*. New York: D. Appleton and Co.; reprint, Albany, N.Y.: J. Munsell.

Hall, Hiland. 1868. *The History of Vermont*. Albany, N.Y.: Joel Munsell.

Hall, R. L. 1977. "An Anthropocentric Perspective for Eastern European United States Prehistory." *American Antiquity* 42: 499–518.

Haller, P. 1991. "Long Before There Was Vermont . . . Settler's Arrival Spells Doom for Abenakis." *Burlington Free Press*, February 27.

Hallowell, A. I. 1928. "Recent Historical Changes in the Kinship Terminology of the St. Francis Abenaki." *Proceedings of the Twenty-Second International Congress of Americanists*, 519–44.

———. 1949. "The Size of the Algonkian Hunting Territories, A Function of Ecological Adjustment." *American Anthropologist* 51: 35–45.

Hamell, George R. 1983. "Trading in Metaphors: The Magic of Beads." Pp. 5–28 in *Proceedings of the 1982 Glass Trade Bead Conference*, ed. C. F. Hayes. Rochester, N.Y.: Rochester Museum and Science Center.

———. 1987a. "Mythical Realities and European Contact in the Northeast during the Sixteenth and Seventeenth Centuries." *Man in the Northeast* 33 (Spring): 63–87.

———. 1987b. "Strawberries, Floating Islands and Rabbit Captains: Mythical Realities and European Contact in the Northeast during the Sixteenth and Seventeenth Centuries." *Journal of Canadian Studies* 21, no. 4, 72–94.

Hamilton, Nathan. 1984. "Aboriginal Cultural Resources of Greater Moosehead Lake Region." *Maine Archeological Society Bulletin* 24, no. 1, 1–45.

Hancock, W., P. Lane, L. Huntington, and J. E. Kelley. 1978. *The Vermont Atlas and Gazetteer*. Yarmouth, Maine: David De Lorme and Co.

Hanson, James. 1981. *Voyagers' Sketchbook*. Chadron, Nebr.: The Fur Press.

Harp, Elmer Jr. 1964. "Evidence of Boreal Archaic Culture in Southern Labrador and Newfoundland." *National Museums of Canada Bulletin* 193, pt. 1, pp. 184–261.

Harp, Elmer, Jr., and David Hughes. 1968. "Five Prehistoric Burials from Port au Choix, Newfoundland." *Polar Notes* 8.

Harrington, C. R. 1977. "Maritime Mammals in the Champlain Sea and the Great Lakes." *Annals of the New York Academy of Sciences* 288: 508–37.

Harrington, Raymond. 1901. "An Abenaki Witch-Story." *Journal of American Folklore* 14: 160.

Harringon, Walter L. 1977. "Fort Dummer: An Archaeological Investigation of the First Permanent English Settlement in Vermont." Pp. 86–94 in *New England Archaeology: Dublin Seminar for New England Folklife, Annual Proceedings.*

Hartshorn, J. H. 1969. "Geography and Geology of Glacial Lake Hitchcock." Pp. 19–27 in *An Introduction to the Archaeology and History of the Connecticut Valley Indian,* ed. W. R. Young. Springfield, Mass.: Museum of Sciences.

Hasenstab, R. J., D. R. Gumar, A. H. McArdle, and M. T. Mulholland. 1988. *Archaeological Location Survey and Site Evaluation at the Dewey's Mill Complex and Mill Pond; and Data Recovery of the Hydro Energies Site, Quechee George, Hartford, Vermont: UM-12, a Survey for the Proposed Dewey's Mills Hydroelectric Project.* Amherst: University of Massachusetts Archaeological Services Environmental Institute.

Hauptman, Laurence M. 1978. "The Dispersal of the River Indians: Frontier Expansion and Indian Dispossession in the Hudson Valley." Pp. 244–60 in *Neighbors and Intruders: An Ethnohistorical Exploration of the Indian of the Hudson's River,* ed. L. M. Hauptman and J. Campisi. Ottawa: National Museum of Man Mercury Series.

———. 1980. "Refugee Havens: The Iroquois Villages of the Eighteenth Century." Pp. 128–39 in *American Indian Environments: Ecological Issues in Native American History,* ed. Christopher Vecsey and Robert W. Venables. Syracuse, N.Y.: Syracuse University Press.

Hauptman, Laurence M., and Jack Campisi, eds. 1978. *Neighbors and Intruders: An Ethnohistorical Exploration of the Indian of the Hudson's River.* Ottawa: National Museum of Man Mercury Series.

Haviland, William A. 1969a. "Excavations at Pine Island." *VAS Newsletter* 2: 3–4.

———. 1969b. "Men Hunted in Vermont in 7000 B.C." *Vermont Life* 24, no. 2, 53–55.

———. 1970. "Archaeological Sites of the Champlain Valley." *Lake Champlain Basin Studies,* 8. Burlington: University of Vermont, Department of Resource Economics.

———. 1973. "Mounds in Vermont: Prehistoric or Historic?" *VAS Monograph,* 2.

———. 1975. *Vermont Indians and Prehistory for Schools: A Selected Annotated List of Sources for Teachers.* Montpelier: Vermont Historical Society.

Haviland, William A., and Marjory W. Power. 1981. *The Original Vermonters: Native Inhabitants, Past and Present.* Hanover, N.H.: University Press of New England.

———. 1994. *The Original Vermonters: Native Inhabitants, Past and Present,* revised and expanded edition. Hanover, N.H.: University Press of New England.

Hayes, Lyman S. 1929. *The Connecticut River Valley in Southern Vermont and New Hampshire: Historical Sketches.* Rutland, Vt.: Charles E. Tuttle Co.

Heckenberger, M., and J. B. Petersen. 1988. *Archaeological Investigations at the Skitchewaug Site: A Multicomponent Stratified Site in Springfield, Windsor County, Vermont.* Report submitted to the Vermont Division for Historic Preservation. Farmington: University of Maine at Farmington, Archaeology Research Center.

———. 1990. "Considerations of Status, Role and Gender Differences in the Middlesex Mortuary Complex." Paper presented at the 57th annual meeting of the Eastern States Archaeological Federation, Columbus, Ohio.

Heckenberger, M. J., J. B. Petersen, and L. A. Basa. 1989. "The Boucher Site: Implications for Mortuary Variability during the Early Woodland Period in Northeastern North America." Paper presented at the 21st annual meeting of the Canadian Archaeological Association, Fredericton, N.B.

———. 1990. "Early Woodland Period Ritual Usage of Personal Adornment at the Boucher Site." *Annals of Carnegie Museum* 59, no. 3, 173–217.

Heckenberger, M. J., J. B. Petersen, E. R. Cowie, A. E. Spiess, L. A. Basa, and R. E. Stuckenrath. 1990. "Early Woodland Period Mortuary Ceremonialism in the Far Northeast: A View from the Boucher Cemetary." *Archaeology of Eastern North America* 18: 109–44.

Heckenberger, M. J., J. B. Petersen, and N. Asch Sidell. 1992. "Early Evidence of Maize Agriculture in the Connecticut River Valley of Vermont." *Archaeology of Eastern North America* 20: 125–49.

Herwig, Wes. 1964. "Indian Raid on Royalton." *Vermont Life* (Autumn): 16–21.

Hibbard, C. W., D. E. Ray, D. E. Savage, D. W. Taylor, J. E. Guilday. 1965. "Quaternary Mammals of North America." *The Quaternary of the United States*, ed. H. E. Wright and D. G. Frey. Princeton, N.J.: Princeton University Press.

Hill, Kay. 1963. *Glooscap and His Magic: Legends of the Wabanaki Indians*. New York: Dodd, Mead and Co.

———. 1978. *More Glooscap Stories: Legends of the Wobanaki Indians*. Toronto: McClelland and Stewart.

Hirsch, Adam J. 1988. "The Collision of Military Cultures in Seventeenth Century New England." *Journal of American History* 74 (March): 1187–212.

Hobart, Francis L. n.d. "The Early Indian Tribes of Vermont and Their Relics." Vermont Historical Society. Manuscript.

Hoffman, Bernard Gilbert. 1955. "Souriquois, Etchemin, and Kwedech: A Lost Chapter in American Ethnography." *Ethnohistory* 2: 65–85.

———. 1961. *Cabot to Cartier: Sources for a Historical Ethnography of Northeastern North America, 1497–1550*. Toronto: University of Toronto Press.

Holzer, Hans. 1992. *Long before Columbus*. Santa Fe, N. Mex.: Bear and Company.

Hoornbeck, Billie. 1976–77. "An Investigation into the Cause or Causes of the Epidemic Which Decimated the Indian Population of New England, 1616–1619." *New England Archaeologist* 19: 35–46.

Huden, John C. 1955. "Indians in Vermont—Present and Past." *Vermont History* 23 (January): 25–28.

———. 1956a. "The Abenakis, the Iroquoians, and Vermont." *Vermont History* 24 (January): 21–25.

———. 1956b. "The Problem: Indians and White Men in Vermont—When and Where (1500–?)." *Vermont History* 24 (April): 110–20.

———. 1956c. "The White Chief of the St. Francis Abenakis: Some Aspects of Border Warfare, 1690–1790." *Vermont History* 24 (July): 199–219; 24 (October): 337–55.

———. 1957a. "Adventures in Abenakiland." *Vermont History* 25, no. 3, 185–93.

———. 1957b. *Indian Place Names in Vermont*. Burlington, Vt.: Privately published.

———. 1957c. "Indian Troubles in Early Vermont." *Vermont History* 25, no. 3, 206–7.

———. 1957d. "Iroquois Place Names in Vermont." *Vermont History* 25 (January): 66–80.

———. 1957–58. "Indian Troubles in Vermont." *Vermont History* 25 (October): 288–91; 26 (January): 38–41; 26 (July): 206–7.

———. 1958. "Indian Groups in Vermont." *Vermont History* 26 (April); 112–15.

———. 1959–60. "Frontier Dangers, 1781–1784." *Vermont History* 27 (October): 352–53; 28 (January): 81–91.

———. 1962. *Indian Place Names of New England*. New York: Museum of the American Indian, Heye Foundation.

———. 1971. *Archaeology in Vermont*. Rev. ed. Rutland, Vt.: Charles Tuttle.

Hunt, George T. 1940–72. *The Wars of the Iroquois: A Study in Intertribal Trade Relations*. Madison: University of Wisconsin Press.

Innis, H. A. 1930. *The Fur Trade in Canada*. New Haven, Conn.: Yale University Press.

Jack, Edward. 1891–92. "The Abenakis of Saint John River." *Transactions of the Canadian Institute* 3: 195–205.

Jackson, Eric P. 1931. "Indian Occupation and Use of the Champlain Lowland." *Papers of the Michigan Academy of Science, Arts, and Letters* 14: 113–60.

Jaenen, Cornelius. 1976. *Friend and Foe: Aspects of French-Amerindian Cultural Contact in the Sixteenth and Seventeenth Centuries*. New York: Columbia University Press.

———. 1984. *The French Relationship with the Native Peoples of New France and Acadia*. Ottawa: Indian and Northern Affairs Canada, Research Branch.

———. 1986. "French Sovereignty and Native Nationhood during the French Regime." *Native Studies Review* 2: 83–113.

Jameson, J. Franklin, ed. 1959. *Narratives of New Netherland, 1609–1664*. New York: Barnes & Noble.

Jellison, Charles A. 1969. *Ethan Allen, Frontier Rebel*. Taftsville, Vt.: Countryman Press.

Jennings, Francis. 1984. *The Ambiguous Iroquois Empire: The Covenant Chain Confederation of Indian Tribes with English Colonies from Its Beginnings to the Lancaster Treaty of 1744*. New York: W.W. Norton.

———. 1988. *Empires of Fortune: Crowns, Colonies, and Tribes in the Seven Years War*. New York: W.W. Norton.

Jennings, J. 1989. *Prehistory of North America*. Mt. View, California: Mayfield.

Johansson, S. Ryan. 1982. "The Demographic History of the Native Peoples of North America: A Selective Bibliography." *Yearbook of Physical Anthropology* 25: 133–52.

Johnson, F., ed. 1946. *Man in Northeastern North America*. Papers of the R. S. Peabody Foundation for Anthropology 3, Andover, Mass.: The Foundation.

Johnson, Richard R. 1977. "The Search for a Usable Indian: An Aspect of the Defense of Colonial New England." *Journal of American History* 64: 623–51.

Johnson, Sir William. 1921–1965. *The Papers of Sir William Johnson*. Edited by James Sullivan et al. 15 vols. Albany: University of the State of New York.

Johnson, Susanna Willard. 1854. "A Narrative of the Captivity of Mrs. Johnson." Pp. 128–82 in *Indian Narratives*. Claremont, N.H.: Tracy and Brothers.

Judd, Sylvester. 1857. "The Fur Trade on the Connecticut River in the Seventeenth Century." *New England Historical and Genealogical Register* 11: 217–19.

Kelly, Eric P. 1929. "The Dartmouth Indians." *Dartmouth Alumni Magazine* 22 (December): 122–25.

Kendall, Edward Augustus. 1809. *Travels though the Northern Parts of the United States in the Years 1807 and 1808*. 3 vols. New York: I. Riley.

Kidder, Frederic. 1859. "The Abenaki Indians: Their Treaties of 1713 and 1717, and a Vocabulary, with a Historical Introduction." *Collections of the Maine Historical Society* 6: 250–62.

———. 1865/1909. *The Expeditions of Capt. John Lovewell and His Encounters with the Indians*. Boston: Bartlett and Halliday. Reprinted in *The Magazine of History with Notes and Queries*, no. 5.

King Titus. 1938. *Narrative of the King of Northampton, Mass.: A Prisoner of the Indians in Canada, 1775–1758*. Hartford: Connecticut Historical Society.

Klein, J. L. 1977. "Current Research: Northeast". *American Antiquity* 42: 643–47.

Kochan, G. P. 1988. "Aboriginal and Historic Euro-american Faunal Remains." Pp. 120–24 in *Archaeological Investigations at the Pearl Street Park Sites in Essex,*

Chittenden County, Vermont, ed. J. B. Petersen, M. J. Heckenberger, and P. A. Thomas. Burlington: University of Vermont, Department of Anthropology Report No. 95.

Konrad, Lee-Ann, and Christine Nicholas. 1987. *Artist of the Dawn: Christine Nicholas and Senabeh*. Orono, Maine: Northeast Folklore Society.

Krech, Shepard. 1981. *Indians, Animals, and the Fur Trade: A Critique of Keepers of the Game*. Athens: University of Georgia Press.

Krigbaum, J. S. 1989a. "Dietary Adaptation in an Early Woodland Skeletal Population from the Champlain Valley of Vermont." Master's thesis, Department of Anthropology, New York University.

———. 1989b. "Subsistence and Health in an Early Woodland Skeletal Population from Vermont." Paper presented at the 54th annual meeting of the Society for American Archaeology, Atlanta, Ga.

Lacy, David. 1992. "Green Mountain National Forest News." *VAS Newsletter* 86: 2–3.

Lampee, Thomas C. 1938. "The Missisquoi Loyalists." *Proceedings of the Vermont Historical Society*, n.s., 6 (June): 80–140.

Lape, Jane M. 1966. "Pere Roubaud, Missionary Extraordinary." *Bulletin of the Fort Ticonderoga Museum* 12, no. 1 (March): 63–71.

Larsen, Frederick D. 1972. "Glacial History of Central Vermont." Pp. 296–316 in *Guidebook for Field Trips in Vermont*. New England Intercollegiate Conference, Burlington, Vt.

"The Last of the Pennacooks." 1853. *The Farmer's Monthly Visitor* 13, no. 9 (September): 257–67; 13, no. 10 (October): 289–99.

Laurent, Joseph. 1884. *New Familiar Abenakis and English Dialogues, the First Ever Published on the Grammatical System by J. Laurent, Abenakis Chief*. Quebec: L. Brousseau.

Laurent, S. 1955. "The Abenakis: Aborigines of Vermont." *Vermont History* 23: 286–95, 24: 3–11.

Leach, Douglas Edward. 1961. "The 'Whens' of Mary Rowlandsons's Captivity." *New England Quarterly* 34: 352–63.

———. 1966. *Flintlock and Tomahawk: New England in King Phillip's War*. New York: W. W. Norton.

———. 1966–1974. *The Northern Colonial Frontier, 1607–1763*. New York: Holt, Rinehart and Winston; reprint, Albuquerque: University of New Mexico Press.

———. 1973. *Arms for Empire: A Military History of the British Colonies in North America, 1607–1763*. New York: Macmillan.

Leavitt, Robert M., and David A. Francis, eds. 1990. *Wapapi Akonutomakonal—The Wampum Records: Wabanaki Traditional Law*. Fredericton, N.B.: Micmac Maliseet Institute.

LeClercq, Chrestien. 1910. *New Relations of Gaspesia, with the customs and religion of the Gaspesian Indians*. Translated and edited by William F. Ganong. Toronto: Champlain Society.

Leland, Charles Godfrey. 1884a. *The Algonquian Legends of New England*. New York: Houghton Mifflin and Co.

———. 1884b. *The Algonquian Legends of New England or Myths and Folk Lore of the Micmac, Passamaquoddy and Penobcot Tribes*. Boston: Houghton Mifflin and Co.

Leland, Charles Godfrey, and John Dyneley Prince. 1992. *Kuloskap the Maser and Other Algonkin Poems*. New York and London: Funk and Wagnalls Company.

Le'ry, Captain de. 1942. "Diary Kept by Captain de L'ery, 1756." *Bulletin of the Fort Ticonderoga Museum* 6, no. 4 (July): 128–44.

Lescarbot, Marc. 1907–14. *The History of New France*. Edited by H. P. Biggar. 3 vols. Toronto: Champlain Society.

———. 1974. "The Defeat of the Armouchiquois Savages by Chief Membertou and His Savage Allies, in New France, in the Month of July, 1607." Translated by Thomas H. Goetz. Pp. 159–62 in *Membertou's Raid on the Chouacoet "Almouchiquois," The Micmac Sack of Saco in 1607*, by Alvin H. Morrison. National Museum of Man Ethnology Service, Mercury Series Paper No. 23, Sixth Algonquian Conferance.

Lester, Joan. 1987. *We're Still Here: Art of Indian New England*. Boston: Children's Museum.

Letters from Mission (North America):—The Jesuit Relations and Allied Documents: Travels and Exploitations of the Jesuit Missionaries in New France, 1610–1791. 1959. Edited by Reuben Gold Thwaites. 73 vols. in 36. New York: Pageant Book Co.

"Letters relating to Mrs. Jemina How, who was taken by the Indians at Hinsdale, N.H., in July 1755." 1837. *Collections of the New Hampshire Historical Society* 5: 256–58.

Lewis, R. B. 1986. "Why Are Early Woodland Base Camps So Rare? Pp. 496–597 in *Early Woodland Archaeology*, ed. K. Farnsworth and T. Emerson. Kampsville, Illinois: Center for American Archaeology Press.

Lincoln, Charles H., ed. 1913. *Narratives of the Indian Wars, 1675–1699*. New York: Charles Scribner's Sons.

Loring, Stephen. 1972. "An Appraisal of Vermont Archaeology." Montpelier: Vermont Division for Historic Preservation, Office of the State Archaeologist. Manuscript.

———. 1973. *A Bibliography of Vermont Archaeology*. Burlington, Vt.: Vermont Archaeological Society.

———. 1978. Richard Watson Collection, Chimney Point. Typescript, Vermont Division for Historic Preservation, Montpelier.

———. 1980. "Paleoindian Hunters and the Champlain Sea: A Presumed Association." *Man in the Northeast* 19: 15–41.

———. 1984. "Some Observations and Comments at the Conclusion of the Analysis of the Richard and Sandy Felion Collections, Leicester, Vermont." Typescript, Vermont Division for Historic Preservation, Montpelier.

———. 1985. "Boundary Maintenance, Mortuary Ceremonialism and Resource Control in the Early Woodland: Three Cemetery Sites in Vermont. *Archaeology of Eastern North America* 13: 93–127.

Lounsbury, Floyd G. 1978. "Iroquois Place-Names in the Champlain Valley." Pp. 103–49 in *Neighbors and Intruders*, ed. L. Hauptman and J. Campisi. Ottawa: National Museum of Man Mercury Series.

———. 1978. "Iroquoian Languages." Pp. 334–43 in *Northeast*, ed. B.G. Trigger, vol. 15 of *Handbook of North American Indians*. Washington, D.C.: Smithsonian Institution.

Lowndes, John P. 1994. "When History Outweighs Law: Extinguishment of Abenaki Title." *Buffalo Law Review* 43, no. 1, 77–118.

Lunn, Jean. 1939. "The Illegal Fur Trade Out in New France, 1713–1760." *Canadian Historical Association Report*, pp. 61–76.

Lynch, James. 1985. "The Iroquois Confederacy and the Adoption and Administration of Non-Iroquoian Individuals and Groups prior to 1756." *Man in the Northeast* 30 (Fall): 83–99.

MacDonald, G. F. 1968. "Debert: A Paleo-Indian Site in Central Nova Scotia." *National Museum of Canada Anthropology Papers* 16.

Maillard, Pierre Antoine Simon. 1758. *An Account of the Customs and Manners of the Mikmakis and Maricheets, Savage Nations, Now Independent on the Government at Cape Breton*. London: S. Hooper & A. Marely.

Maine Basketry Past to Present. 1989. Lewiston, Maine: Penmor Lithographers.

Maine Studies Curriculum Project. 1980. *Maine Dirigo: "I Lead."* Produced by the

Maine Studies Curriculum Project; project staff; Dean B. Bennett et al. Camden, Maine: Down East Books.

Mallery, Garrick. 1890. "The Fight with Giant Witch: An Abanali Myth." *American Anthropologist* 3 (January): 62–70.

———. 1893. *Picture Witing of American Indians*. Tenth Annual Report. Washington, D.C.: U.S. Bureau of Ethnology.

Malone, Patrick M. 1971. "Indian and English Military Systems in New England in the Seventeenth Century." Ph.D. diss., Brown University.

———. 1973. "Changing Military Technology among the Indians of Southern New England, 1600–1677." *American Quarterly* 25: 48–63.

Man in the Northeast. 1980. Vol. 19 (Spring). Special issue of papers on Vermont archaeology.

Mariois, R. J. M. 1978. *Le Gisement Beaumier: essai sur l'evolution des decors de la ceramique*. Collection Mercure, No. 75. Ottawa: Commission Archaeologique du Canada, Musée National de l'Homme.

Martin, C. S. 1974. "The European Impact on the Culture of a Northeastern Algonquian Tribe: An Ecological Interpretation." *William and Mary Quarterly* 3rd ser., 31: 3–26.

Martin, Calvin. 1987. *Keeper of the Game: Indian-Animal Relationships and the Fur Trade*. Berkeley: University of California Press.

Martin, John Patrick. 1948. *Our Storied Harbor, the Haven of Halifax*. Halifax, N.S.: Department of Tourists and Travel.

Mary Ellery, the Indian Captive. n.d. Montpelier: Vermont Historical Society.

Mason, Bernard. 1974. *Woodcraft*. New York: Dover.

Mason, R. J. 1962. "The Paleo-Indian Tradition in Eastern North America." *Current Anthropology* 3: 227–78.

———. 1981. *Great Lakes Archaeology*. New York: Academic Press.

Masta, Henry Lorne. 1928–29. "When the Abenaki Came to Dartmouth," *Dartmouth Alumni* 21: 302–3.

———. 1932. *Abenaki Indian Legends, Grammar, and Place Names*. Victoriaville, P.Q.: La Voix des Bois-Francs.

Maurault, Joseph P. A. 1866. *Historique des Abenakis, depuis 1605 jusqu'a nos jours*. Sorel, Quebec: Gazette de Sorel.

Maxwell, J. 1992. *America's Fascinating Indian Heritage*. Pleasantville, N.Y.: Reader's Digest.

Mayhew, Edgar, and Minor Myers. 1980. *A Documentary History of American Interiors*. New York: Charles Scribners.

McAleer, George A. 1906. *A Study of the Etymology of the Indian Place Name Missisquoi*. Worcester, Mass.: Blanchard Press.

McBride, Bunny, and Herald Prins. 1982. "Micmac Redbook: Resource Manual for the Micmac Recognition Effort." Prepared for the Aroostook Micmac Council. Photocopy.

———. 1983. "A Special Kind of Freedom." *Down East Magazine*, June, pp. 88–93; 114–115.

———. 1984. "Genesis of a Micmac Community of Maine." Prepared for the Aroostook Micmac Council. Photocopy.

———. 1989. "A Penobsoct in Paris," *Down East Magazine*, August, pp. 62–64; 80–84.

———. 1990a. "Last of the Pequawkets" *Down East Magazine*, July, pp. 79–84.

———. 1990b. *Our Lives in Our Hands: Micmac Indian Basketmakers*. Gardiner, Maine: Tilbury House.

McCarthy, Jim. 1982. "The People of the Dawn." *Portland*, Fall, pp. 34–42.

McCord Museum. 1992. *Wrapped in the Colors of the Earth: Cultural Heritage of the First Nations*. Montreal: McCord Museum.

McEwan, Alice Clark. 1965. Excerpts from "The Burning of Royalton." Dartmouth College, MS 965900.

McGhee, Robert. 1976. *The Burial at L'Anse Amour*. Ottawa: National Museum.

———. 1989. *Ancient Canada*. Ottawa: Canadian Museum of Civilization

McGuire, Joseph. 1980. "Ethnological and Archaeological Notes on Moosehead Lake." *American Anthropoligist*, n.s., 10: 549–57.

McLaughlin, Robert. 1977. "Giving It Back to the Indian." *Atlantic Monthly*. February, p. 70.

MacLeod, Peter. 1996. *The Canadian Iroquois and the Seven Years War*. Toronto: Dundurn Press.

McMillan, Alan D. 1988. *Native People and Cultures of Canada: An Anthropological Overview*. Vancouver, B.C.: Douglas & McIntyre.

Melvin, Eleazar. 1837. "Journal of Capt. Eleazar Melvin, with eighteen men in his command, in the Wilderness towards Crown Point, 1748." *Collections of the New Hampshire Historical Society*, 5: 207–11.

Melvoin, Richard Irwin. 1983. "New England Outposts: War and Society in Colonial Frontier Deerfield, Massachusetts." Ph.D. diss., University of Michigan.

Merrell, James H. 1984. "The Indians' New World: The Catawba Experience." *William and Mary Quarterly*, 3d ser., 41 (October): 537–65.

Mihesuah, Devon A. 1998a. "Introduction," *Natives and Academics*. Lincoln: University of Nebraska Press.

———, ed. 1998b. *Natives and Academics*. Lincoln: University of Nebraska Press.

Mills, P. R. 1984. A Refinement of the Typologies of Vermont Projective Points and Other Chipped Stone Tools in the Champlain Valley. College honors thesis, Department of Anthropology, University of Vermont.

Mitchell, Lewis. 1990. "The Wampum Records." Pp. 38–49 in *Wapapi Akonutomakonal—The Wampum Records: Wabanaki Traditonal Law*, ed. Robert Leavitt and David A. Francis. Fredericton, N.B.: Micmac and Maliseet Institute.

Moody, John. 1978. "Missisquoi: Abenaki Survival in Their Ancient Homeland." Manuscript on file with the author, Sharon, Vt.

———. 1982. "The Native American Legacy." Pp. 54–65. *Always in Season: Folk Art and Traditional Culture in Vermont*, ed. Jane C. Beck. Montpelier: Vermont Council on the Arts.

Moorhead, W. K. 1922. *A Report on the Archaeology of Maine*. Andover, Mass.: Andover Press.

Morison, Samuel Eliot. 1971. *The European Discovery of America: The Northern Voyages*, A.D. 500–1600. New York: Oxford University Press.

Morrison, Alvin Hamblen. 1974. "Dawnland Decisions: Seventeenth-Century Wabanaki Leaders and Their Responses to the Differential Contact Stimuli in the Overlap Area of New France and New England." Ph.D. diss., University of New York at Buffalo.

———. 1975. "Membertou's Raid on the Chouacoet Almouchiquois: The Micmac Sack of Saco in 1607." Pp. 141–58, *Proceedings of the Sixth Algonkian Conference, 1974*, ed. William Cowan. Ottawa: Canadian Ethnology Service, Merchury Series.

———. 1976. "Dawnland Directors: Status and Role of Seventeenth Century Wabanaki Sagamores." *Papers of the Seventh Algonquian Conference*, ed. William Cowan. Ottawa: Carleton University Press.

———. 1977a. "Tricentennial, Too: King Philip's War Northern Front (Maine,

1675–1678).” Pp. 208–12 in *Actes du Huitieme Congres des Algonquianistes*, ed. William Cowan. Ottawa: Carleton University Press.

———. 1977b. “Western Wabanaki Studies: Some Comments.” Pp. 230–43 in *Actes du Huitieme Congres des Algonquianistes*, ed. William Cowan. Ottawa: Carleton University.

Morrison, Kenneth M. 1974. “Sebastien Racle and Norridgewock 1724: Eckstorm Conspiracy Thesis Reconsidered.” *Maine Historical Society* (Fall): 76–97.

———. 1975. “The People of the Dawn: The Abenaki and Their Relations with New England and New France, 1600–1727.” Ph.D. diss., University of Maine.

———. 1979. “Towards a History of Intimate Encounters: Algonkian Folklore, Jesuit Missionaries, and Kiwakwe, the Cannibal Giant.” *American Indian Culture and Research Journal* 3: 51–80.

———. 1980. “The Bias of Colonial Law: English Paranoia and the Abenaki Arena of King Phillip’s War, 1675–1678.” *New England Quarterly* 53 (September): 363–87.

———. 1981. “The Mythological Sources of Abenaki Catholicism: A Case Study of the Social History of Power.” *Religion* 11: 235–63.

———. 1984. *The Embattled Northeast: The Elusive Ideal of Alliance in Abenaki-Euroamerican Relations*. Berkeley: University of California Press.

Morse, Bradford. 1985. *Aboriginal Peoples and the Law: Indian, Metis and Inuit Rights in Canada*. Ottawa: Carleton University Press.

Muller, Henry N., III. 1969. “The Commercial History of the Lake Champlain–Richelieu River Route, 1760–1815.” Ph.D. diss., University of Rochester.

Murdock, G. P. 1965. “Algonkian Social Organization.” Pp. 24–35 in *Context and Meaning in Cultural Anthropology*, ed. M. E. Spiro. New York: Free Press.

Murrin, John M. 1984. “Colonial Government.” *Encyclopedia of American Political History*. Edited by Jack P. Greene. New York: Charles Scribner’s Sons.

Nelson, Eunice. 1982. *The Wabanaki: An Annotated Bibliography of Selected Books, Articles, Documents about Maliseet, Passamaquoddy, Penobscot Indians in Maine Annotated by Native Americans*. Cambridge, Mass.: American Friends Service Committee.

Newell, Cathrine. 1981. *Molly Ockett*. Bethel, Maine: Bethel Historical Society.

Newman, W. S., and B. Salwen, eds. 1977. “Amerindians and Their Paleoenvironments in Northeastern North America.” *Annals of the New York Academy of Sciences*. New York: New York Academy of Sciences.

Nicholas, Andrea Bear. 1986. “Maliseet Aboriginal Rights and Mascarene’s Treaty, Not Dummer’s Treaty.” Pp. 215–29 in *Actes du dix-septieme congres des Algonquinistes*, ed. William Cowan. Ottawa: Carleton University Press.

Nicolar, Joseph. 1893. *The Life and Traditions of the Red Man*. Bangor, Maine: C. H. Glass & Co.

———. 1941. “*Penobscot Place-Names*.” Orono: University of Maine Press.

Norman, Howard. 1989. *How Glooskap Outwits the Ice Giants and Other Tales of the Maritime Indians*. Toronto: Little, Brown and Co.

Norton, Thomas Elliott. 1974. *The Fur Trade in Colonial New York, 1686–1776*. Madison: University of Wisconsin Press.

O’Callaghan, E. B., ed. 1850. *The Documentary History of the State of New York*. 4 vols. Albany, N.Y.: Weed, Parsons and Co.

———. 1855–61. *Documents Relative to the History of New York*. 15 vols. Albany, N.Y.: Weed, Parsons.

Orchard, William C. 1909. “Notes on Penobscot Houses.” *American Anthropologist*, n.s. 2, no. 4, 601–6.

——. 1916. *The Technique of Porcupine-Quill Decoration among the North American Indians.* New York: Museum of the American Indian.

——. 1975. *Beads and Beadwork of the American Indians.* New York: Museum of the American Indian.

O'Toole, Francis J., and Thomas N. Tureen. 1971. "State Power and the Passamaquoddy Tribe: A Gross National Hypocrisy?" *Maine Law Review* 23, no. 1, 1–39.

Otterbein, Keith F. 1964. "Why the Iroquois Won: An Analysis of Iroquois Military Tactics." *Ethnohistory* 11: (Winter) 56–63.

Palmer, R. S. 1939, "Late Records of Caribou in Maine." *Journal of Mammalogy* 19 (February): 37–43.

"Papers Relating to Fort Dummer." *Collections of the New Hampshire Historical Society* 1: 143–47.

Parkman Francis. 1898a. *Count Frontenac and New France under Louis XIV.* Toronto: George N. Morang.

——. 1898b. *A Half-Century of Conflict.* 2 vols. Toronto: George N. Morang.

——. 1898c. *The Jesuits in North America in the Seventeenth Century.* Toronto: George N. Morang.

——. 1898d. *Pioneers of France in the New World.* Toronto: George N. Morang.

Paul, Daniel. 1993. *We Were Not the Savages: A Micmac Perspective on the Collision of European and Aboriginal Civilization.* Halifax, N.S.: Nimbus Publishing.

Paul, Stewart. 1986. *"As Long as the Sun and Moon Shall Endure": A Brief History of the Maritime First Nations Treaties, 1675 to 1783.* Big Cove Miigemagig Elsipogtog and Big Cove N.B. Education Program.

Pearo, Linda, Frederick Wiseman, Madeline Young, and Jeff Benay. 1996. *New Dawn: The Western Abenaki.* Swanton, Vt.: Franklin Northwest Supervisory Union Title IX Indian Education Program.

Pelletier, Gaby. 1977. *Micmac and Maliseet Decorative Traditions.* Saint John: New Brunswick Museum.

——. 1978. "From Animal Skin to Polyester: Four Hundred Years of Micmac and Maliseet Clothing Styles and Ornamentation." *Journal of the New Brunswick Museum* 2:118–30.

——. 1982. *Abenaki Basketry.* Canadian Ethnology Service Paper no. 85. Ottawa: National Museum of Man.

Pendergast, J. F. 1989. "Native Encounters with Europeans in the Region Now Known as Vermont in the 16th Century." Paper presented at the Vermont Historical Society Conference, Vermont and Canada: Regional Ties That Bind, Montpelier, Vt.

Penhallow, Samuel. 1971. *Penhallow's Indian Wars: A Facsimile Reprint of the First Edition, 1726.* Edited by Edward Wheelock. Freeport, N.Y.: Books for Libraries Press.

"Pennacook Papers." 1832. *Collections of the New Hampshire Historical Society* 3: 214–24.

Pennacook/Sokoki Inter-Tribal Nation, comps. 1977. *Historical Indian-Colonial Relations of New Hampshire.* Manchester: Pennacook/Sokoki Inter-Tribal Nation, New Hampshire Indian Council.

Pennell, Elizabeth Robins. 1906. *Charles Godfrey Leland: A Biography.*Vol. 2. New York: Houghton, Mifflin and Co.

"People of the First Light: A Television Series about Native Americans in Southern New England." 1979. Viewer's guide. Produced by WGBY-TV public television, Springfield, Mass., project staff: Joanne G. Linowes et al.; New York: TLC-TV Project; Lincoln, Neb.: Great Plains National Instructional Television Library, distributor.

Perkins, G. H. 1873. "On an Ancient Burial Ground in Swanton, Vermont." *Proceedings of the American Association for the Advancement of Science* 22: 76–100.

Perry, J. B. 1868. "On the Swanton Site." *Proceedings of the Boston Society of Natural History* 23, no. 3, 247–54.

Petersen, James B. 1977. "A Study of the Prehistoric Ceramics of VT-CH-5, the Ewing Site." University of Vermont, Department of Anthropology. Typescript.

——. 1978a. "Aboriginal Ceramics in the Connecticut River Valley." University of Vermont, Department of Anthropology. Typescript.

——. 1978b. "A History of Archaeological Research in Vermont." University of Vermont, Department of Anthropology. Typescript.

——. 1978c. "Prehistoric Ceramics from the Ewing Site." *VAS Newsletter* 26: 6.

——. 1979. "Prehistoric Pottery in Vermont." *VAS Newsletter* 27: 1–4.

——. 1980. *The Middle Woodland Ceramics of the Winooski Site A.D. 1–1000.* Vermont Archaeological Society, Monograph I.

——, ed. 1985. *Ceramic Analysis in the Northeast: Contributions to Methodology and Culture History.* George's Mills, N.H.: Man in the Northeast, Occasional Publications in Northeastern Anthropology, 9, no. 2.

——. 1985. "Ceramic Analysis in the Northeast: Resumé and Prospect." Pp. 1–25 in *Ceramic Analysis in the Northeast: Contributions to Methodology and Culture History.* George's Mills, N.H.: Man in the Northeast, Occasional Publications in Northeastern Anthropology.

——. 1986. "The Piscataquis Archaeological Project: A Late Pleistocene and Holocene Occupational Sequence in Northern New England." *Archaeology of Eastern North America* 14 (Fall): 1–18.

——. 1988. "An Overview of Early Woodland Period Ceramic and Fiber Industries from the Northeast." Paper presented at the 55th annual meeting of the Eastern States Archaeological Federation, Toronto.

——. 1990. "Evidence of the Saint Lawrence Iroquoians in Northern New England: Population Movement, Trade, or Stylistic Borrowing?" *Man in the Northeast* 40: 31–39.

——. 1991. "Archaeological Testing at the Sharrow Site: A Deeply Stratified Early to Late Holocene Cultural Sequence in Central Maine." *Occasional Publications in Maine Archaeology* 8: 1–164.

——. 1992. "'Iroquoian' Ceramics in New England: A Reconsideration of Ethnicity, Evolution and Interaction." Paper presented at the 57th annual meeting of the Society for American Archaeology, Pittsburgh.

Petersen, James B., and N. D. Hamilton. 1984. "Early Woodland Ceramic and Perishable Fiber Industries from the Northeast: A Summary and Interpretation." *Annals of the Carnegie Museum* 53: 413–45.

Petersen, James B., and M. J. Heckenberger. 1990. "The Boucher Site and the Relationship of the Middlesex Complex in Eastern North America." Paper presented at the 57th annual meeting of the Eastern States Archaeological Federation, Columbus, Ohio.

Petersen, James B., M. J. Heckenberger, and L. A. Basa. 1989. "Lithic and Ceramic Artifacts from the Boucher Site: A Summary of Internal and External Correlations." Paper presented at the 54th annual meeting of the Society for American Archaeology, Atlanta, Ga.

Petersen, James B., M. J. Heckenberger, and P. A. Thomas. 1988. *Archaeological Investigations at the Pearl Street Park Sites in Essex, Chittenden County, Vermont.* Burlington: University of Vermont, Department of Anthropology. Report No. 95.

Petersen, James B. and M. W. Power. 1983a. "A Middle Woodland Exchange Network

in Northern New England." Paper presented at the 48th annual meeting of the Society for American Archaeology, Pittsburgh.
———. 1983b. "The Winooski Site and the Middle Woodland Period in the Northeast."
Burlington: University of Vermont, Department of Anthropology.
Petersen, James B., J. A. Wolford, N. D. Hamilton, L. A. LaBar, and M. J. Heckenber-
ger. 1985. "Archaeological Investigations in the Shelburne Pond Locality, Chitten-
den County, Vermont." *Annals of the Carnegie Museum* 54: 23–76.
Peterson, Harold L. 1971. *American Interiors*. New York: Charles Scribner's.
Petrone, Penny, ed. 1983. *First People, First Voices*. Toronto, University of Toronto
Press.
Phillips, Ruth B. 1987. "Like a Star, I Shine: Northern Woodlands Artistic Traditions."
Pp. 53–92 in *The Spirit Sings, Artistic Traditions of Canada's First Peoples*, ed. Julia
D. Harrison. Toronto: McClelland and Stewart.
"Phineas Stevens Account Book kept at Fort #4, Charlestown, N.H., 17s2-lys6." Stevens
Family Papers (box I, folder 8). Microfilm copy at the Silsby Library, Charlestown,
N.H.
Pierce, Ken. 1977. *A History of the Abenaki People*. Burlington: University of Vermont,
Instructional Development Center.
Pike, John. 1832. "Journal of Rev. John Pike." *Collections of the New Hampshire Histor-
ical Society* 3.
Plaice, L., trans. 1984. *Native Peoples of Quebec*. Quebec: Secretariat des activities,
gouvernementales en milieu Amerindian et Inuit (SAGMAI).
Pohl, Frederick J. 1974. *Prince Henry Sinclair: His Expedition to the New World in 1398*.
New York: Clarkson N. Potter.
Porter, Frank W., III, ed. 1986. *Strategies for Survival: American Indians in the Eastern
United States*. Westport, Conn.: Greenwood Press.
Power, M. W. 1975. Archaeology in Vermont: A Summary of Information and Re-
sources for Teachers. Montpelier: Vermont Historical Society.
———. 1979a. "Middle Woodland Subsistence and Settlement: A Preliminary Model."
VAS Newsletter 28: 10–11.
———. 1979b. "The Winooski Site: A Test Case for a Middle Woodland Settlement and
Subsistence Model." Paper presented at the 44th annual meeting of the Society for
American Archaeology, Vancouver, B.C.
———. 1989. "The Isle La Motte Site: A Revisionist's look at Glacial Kame." Paper presented at the 54th annual meeting of the Society for American Archaeology, Atlanta, Ga.
Power, M. W., F. L. Cowan, and J. B. Petersen. 1980. "Artifact Variability at the Multi-
Component Winooski Site." *Man in the Northeast* 19: 43–55.
Power, Marjory, and James B. Petersen. 1981. "The Use of Ethnographic Analogy in Ar-
chaeology: A Case Study from Vermont." Paper presented at the annual meeting of
the Central States Anthropological Society, Cincinnati, Ohio.
———. 1984. *Seasons of Prehistory: 4000 Years at the Winooski Site*. Montpelier: Ver-
mont Division of Historic Preservation.
Powers, Grant. 1841. *Historical Sketches of the Discovery, Settlement, and Progress of
Events in the Coos Country*. Haverill, N.H.: J. F. C. Hayes.
Price, Chester B. 1956. "Historic Indian Trails of New Hampshire." *New Hampshire
Archaeologist* 8: 2–13.
Prince, John Dyneley. 1897. "The Passamaquoddy Wampum Records." *Proceedings of
the Philadelphia American Philosophical Society* 36, no. 154, 479–95.
———. 1921. "Passamaquaddy Texts." *Publications of the American Ethnological Society*.

Vol. 10. New York: G. E. Stechert & Co. (This volume contains the Wampum Records, a number of Koluscap and other legends, and Passamaquoddy songs.)

Prins, Herald E. L. 1986. "Micmacs and Maliseets in the St. Lawrence River Valley." Pp. 263–78 in *Actes du 17e Congres des Algonquinistes*, ed. W. Cowan. Ottawa: Carleton University.

——. 1987. "The Search For Cushnoc: A Seventeenth Century Pilgrim Trading Post in the Kennebec Valley of Maine." *Kennebec Proprietor* 1, no. 3, 8–13.

——. 1988. "Tribulations of a Border Tribe: The Case of the Aroostook Band of Micmacs in Maine." Ann Arbor, Mich. University Microfilms International, 152–202.

——. 1989. "Native Newcomers: Mount Desert in the Age of Exploration." Pp. 21–36 in *An Island in Time: Three Thousand Years of Cultural Exchange on Mount Desert Island*. Bar Harbor, Maine: Robert Abbe Museum.

——. 1990. "Indian Artifacts and Lost Identity." *Salt Magazine* 10, no. 3, 6–10.

——. 1992, "Cornplanters at Meductic: Ethnic and Territorial Reconfigurations in Colonial Acadia," *Man in the Northeast* no. 44, 55–72.

——. 1993. "To the Land of the Mistigoches: American Indian Traveling to Europe in the Age of Exploration." *American Indian Culture and Research Journal* 17, no. 1, 175–95.

Prins, Herald E. L., and Bruce J. Bourque. 1987. "Norridgewock: Village Translocation on the New England–Acadian Frontier." *Man in the Northeast* 33 (Spring): 137–58.

Purchas, Samuel. 1906. "The Description of the Country of Mawooshen." In *Hakluytus Posthumus or Purchas His Pilgrimes, Contayning a History of the World, in Sea Voyages, and Lande-Travells, by Englishmen and Others*, 20 vols. Glasgow: James MacLehose and Sons.

Pynchon, John. 1982. *The Pynchon Papers*, Vol. 1, *Letters of John Pynchon, 1654–1700*. Edited by Carl Bridenbaugh. Boston: Colonial Society of Massachusetts.

Rasle, Sebastien. 1833. "A Dictionary of the Abenaki Language in North America, [1690–1722]." In *Memoirs of the American Academy of Sciences*, n.s. Edited by John Pickering. Washington, D.C.: American Academy of Sciences.

——. 1893. "Letter from Norridgewock (October 12, 1723)," *Collections and Proceedings of the Maine Historical Society* 4: 267.

Ray, Roger B. 1983. "A Malecite Calender of the Pre-Contact Period." *Archaeoastronomy* 6, nos. 1–4, 81–85.

"Report on the First Archaeological Conference on the Woodland Pattern." 1943. *American Antiquity* 8, no. 4, 393–400.

Richter, Daniel K. 1982. "Rediscovered Links in the Covenant Chain: Previously Unpublished Transcripts of New York Indian Treaty Minutes, 1677–1691." *Proceedings of the American Antiquarian Society* 92, pt. 1.

——. 1983. "War and Culture: The Iroquois Experience." *William and Mary Quarterly*, 3d ser., 40 (October): 528–59.

——. 1984. "The Ordeal of the Longhouse: Change and Persistence on the Iroquois Frontier, 1609–1720." Ph.D. diss., Columbia University.

——. 1988. "Cultural Brokers and Intercultural Politics: New York-Iroquois Relations, 1664–1701." *Journal of American History* 75 (June): 40–67.

Richter, Daniel K., and James, H. Merrill, eds. 1987. *Beyond the Covenant Chain: The Iroquois and their Neighbors in Indian North America, 1600–1800*. Syracuse: Syracuse University Press.

Riley, T. J., R. Edging, and J. Rossen. 1990. "Cultigens in Prehistoric Eastern North America." *Current Anthropology* 31, no. 5, 525–41.

Rippeteau, B. 1973. "Late Archaic, Transitional and Early Woodland Tree Ring Corrected Dates in Northern United States." *Man in the Northeast* 6: 61–67.

Ritchie, William A. 1938. "A Perspective on Northeastern Archaeology." *American Antiquity* 4, no. 2, 94–112.
Ritchie, W. A. 1944. "The Pre-Iroquoian Occupations of New York State." *Rochester Museum of Arts and Sciences, Memoir,* no. 1.
———. 1949. "An Archaeological Survey of Trent Waterway in Ontario, Canada." In *Researches and Transactions of the New York State Archaeological Association.* Rochester, N.Y.: The Association.
———. 1953. "A Probable Paleo-Indian Site in Vermont," *American Antiquity* 18: 249–58.
———. 1955. "Recent Discoveries Suggesting an Early Woodland Burial Cult in the Northeast." *New York State Museum and Science Service,* Circular 40.
———. 1957. "Traces of Early Man in the Northeast." *New York State Museum and Science Service Bulletin,* 358.
———. 1958. "The Northeastern Archaic." A review. Albany, New York: New York State Museum. Manuscript.
———. 1968. "The KI Site, the Vergennes Phase and the Laurential Tradition." *New York State Archaeological Association Bulletin* 42: 1–5.
———. 1969. *The Archaeology of New York State.* Rev. ed. Garden City, N.Y.: Natural History Press.
———. 1971. "The Archaic in New York." *New York State Archaeological Association Bulletin* 52: 2–12.
———. 1979. "The Otter Creek No. 2 Site in Rutland County, Vermont." *The Bulletin and Journal of the Archaeology of New York State* 76: 1–21.
Ritchie, W. A., and D. W. Dragoo. 1960. "The Eastern Dispersal of Adena." *New York State Museum and Science Service Bulletin* 379.
Ritchie, W. A., and R. E. Funk. 1960. "Aboriginal Settlement Patterns in the Northeast." *New York State Museum and Science Service,* Memoir 20.
Robinson, B. S., E. R. Cowie, T. R. Buchanan, W. C. Crandall, R. P. Corey, and J. B. Petersen. 1991. *Archaeological Phase I Survey of Vermont's Segment of the Champlain Pipeline Project (FERC Docket No. CP98–656–000).* Vol. 1. Farmington: Archaeology Research Center, University of Maine at Farmington.
Robinson, B. S., T. R. Buchanan, E. R. Cowie, W. B. Dorshow, and C. A. Quinn. 1992. *Archaeological Phase I Survey of the Vermont Segment of the Champlain Pipeline Project (FERC Docket No. CP98–656–000).* Vol. 2. Farmington: Archaeology Research Center, University of Maine at Farmington.
Robinson, B. S., & A. K. eds. 1992. *Early Holocene Occupaton in Northern New England.* Occasional Publications of Maine Archeology 9. Augusta: Maine Historic Preservation Commission, Brown University.
Rogers, Robert. 1985. "The Machiasport Petroglyphs." *Maine Historical Society Quarterly* 25, no. 1, 22–39.
———. 1987. "The Embden, Maine Petroglyphs." *Maine Historical Society Quarterly* 27, no. 1, 14–23.
Ronda, James P. 1979. "The Sillery Experiment: A Jesuit Indian Village in New France, 1637–1663." *American Indian Culture and Research Journal* 3, no. 1, 1–8.
Rosier, James A. 1906. *True Relation of the Voyage of Captain George Waymouth, 1605: Early English and French Voyagers, 1534–1608.* Edited by H. S. Burrage. New York: Scribners.
Ross, I .B. 1935. "Remains of an Ancient People Found in Vermont." *Vermonter* 40, no. 12, 227–28.
Roy, Pierre-Georges. 1946. *Hommes et choses du Fort Saint-Frederic.* Montreal: Les Editions du Dix.

Russell, Howard S. 1980. *Indian New England before the Mayflower*. Hanover, N.H.: University Press of New England.

Salisbury, Neal. 1982. *Manitou and Providence: Indians, Europeans, and the Making of New England, 1500–1643*. New York: Oxford University Press.

———. 1987a. "Social Relationships on a Moving Frontier: Natives and Settlers in Southern New England, 1638–1675." *Man in the Northeast* 33 (Spring): 89–99.

———. 1987b. "Toward the Covenant Chain: Iroquois and Southern New England Algonquians, 1637–1684." Pp. 61–73 in *Beyond the Covenant Chain*.

Salwen, B. 1975. "Post-Glacial Environments and Cultural Change in the Hudson River Basin." *Man in the Northeast* 10: 43–70.

Sanders, David C. 1812. *A History of the Indian Wars with the First Settlers of the United States, Particularly in New England*. Montpelier, Vt.: Wright and Sibley.

Sanger, D. 1973. *Cow Point: An Archaic Cemetery in New Brunswick*. Ottawa: National Museum of Man, Archaeological Survey of Canada, Mercury Series 12.

———. 1975. "Culture Change as an Adaptive Process in the Maine-Maritimes Region." *Arctic Anthropology* 12, no. 2, 60–75.

———. 1979a. "The Ceramic Period in Maine." Pp. 99–115 in *Discovering Maine's Archaeological Heritage*. Augusta: Maine Historic Preservation Commission.

———. 1979b. *Discovering Maine's Archaeological Heritage*. Augusta: Maine Historic Preservation Commission.

———. 1986. "Boom and Bust on the River: The Story of the Damariscotta Shell Heaps." *Archaeology of Eastern North America* 14 (Fall) 65–79.

———. 1987. *The Carson Site and the Late Ceramic Period in Passamaquoddy Bay, New Brunswick*. Ottawa: Canadian Museum of Civilization, Mercury Series no. 135.

———. 1988. "Maritime Adaptation in the Gulf of Maine." *Archaeology of Eastern North America* 16: 81–100.

———. 1991. "Five Thousand Years of Contact between Maine and Nova Scotia." *Bulletin of the Maine Archaeology Society* 31, no. 2, 55–61.

Sanger, David, R. B. Davis, R. G. MacKay, and H. W. Borns, Jr. 1977. "The Hirundo Archaeological Project: An Interdisciplinary Approach to Central Maine Prehistory." *Annals of the New York Academy of Sciences* 288: 457–71.

Sanipass, Mary. 1990. *Baskadegan: Basket Making Step by Step*. Madawaska, Maine: The Saint John Valley Publishing Co.

Sargent, H. R. 1960. "The Summer Falls Site." *New Hampshire Archaeologist* 10: 7–12.

———. 1969. "Prehistory in the Upper Connecticut Valley." Pp. 28–32 in *An Introduction to the Archaeology and History of the Connecticut Valley Indian*, ed. W. R. Young. Springfield, Mass.: Museum of Science.

Sark, John. 1988. *Micmac Legends of Prince Edward Island*. Lennox Island and Charlottetown, P.E.I.: Lennox Island Band Council and Ragweed Press.

Sawaya, Jean-P. 1998. *La Federation des Sept Feux de la Valle du St. Laurent*. Sillery, Quebec: Septentrion.

Schleiser, K. H. 1976. "Epidemics and Indian Middlemen: Rethinking the Wars of the Iroquois, 1609–1653." *Ethnohistory* 23 (Spring): 129–45.

Schurr, T. 2000. "The Story in the Genes." *Discovering Archaeology* 2, no. 1, 59–60.

Seeber, Pauleena MacDougall. 1984. "The European Influence on Abenaki Economics before 1615." Pp. 201–14 in *Papers of the 15th Algonquian Conference*, ed. William Cowan. Ottawa: Carleton University Press.

Service, E. R. 1971. *Primitive Social Organization*. 2nd ed. New York: Random House.

Sevigny, P.-Andre. 1976. *Les Abenaquis: Habitat et Migrations (17e et 18e siècles)*. Montreal: Editions Bellarmin.

Seymour, E. C. 1969. *Flora of Vermont*. Burlington: University of Vermont, Agricultural Experiment Station Bulletin 660.

Shea, Peter. 1985. "A New and Accurate Map of Phillip's Grant." *Vermont History* 53 (Winter): 36–42.

Sheldon, George. 1895–96. *A History of Deerfield, Massachusetts . . . with a Special Study of the Indian Wars in the Connecticut Valley*. 2 vols. Deerfield, Mass.: E. A. Hall and Co.

Sheldon, Helen L. 1988. *The Late Prehistory of Nova Scotia as Viewed from the Brown Site*. Halifax: Nova Scotia Museum, Curatorial Report 61.

Sherman, T. H. 1941. "A Cave Habitation in Vermont." *American Antiquity* 2: 176–78.

Sherwood, Mary. 1970. "Thoreau's Penobscot Indians." *Thoreau Journal Quarterly* 2 (January): 1–13.

Shortt, Adam, and Arthur G. Doughty, eds. 1918. *Documents Relating to the Constitutional History of Canada, 1759–1791*. 2 vols. Ottawa: Historical Documents Publication Board.

Siccama, T. G. 1971. "Presettlement and Present Forest Vegetation in Northern Vermont with Special Reference to Chittenden County." *American Midland Naturalist* 85, no. 1, 153–72.

Siegel, J., A. R. Beals, and S. A. Tyler, eds. 1978. *Annual Review of Anthropology*. Palo Alto, Calif.: Annual Reviews.

Silman, Janet. 1987. *Enough Is Enough: Aboriginal Women Speak Out*. Toronto: Women's Press.

Silver, Arthur P. n.d. [1907]. *Farm, Cottage, Camp and Canoe in Maritime Canada*. London: G. Routledge & Sons.

Simmons, William S. 1981. "Cultural Bias in the New England Puritans' Perception of Indians." *William and Mary Quarterly*, 3d ser., 38 (January): 56–72.

———. 1986. *Spirit of the New England Tribes: Indian History and Folklore, 1620–1984*. Hanover, N.H.: University Press of New England.

Sioui, George. 1992. *For an Amerindian Autohistory: An Essay on the Foundations of a Social Ethic*. Montreal: McGill-Queens University Press.

Skinas, David. 1993. "Long Houses on the Upper Connecticut River?" *Vermont Archaeological Society Newsletter* 71 (March): 6–7.

Slotkin, J. S., and Karl Schmitt. 1949. "Studies of Wampum." *American Anthropologist*, 51, no. 1, 223–36.

Slotkin, Richard, and James K. Folsom, eds. 1978. *So Dreadful a Judgment: Puritan Responses to King Phillip's War, 1676–1677*. Middletown, Conn.: Wesleyan University Press.

Smalley, J. C. 1976. "Traces of an Indian Legend." *Catholic World* 22: 277–81.

Smethurst, Gamaliel. 1774. *A Narrative of an Extraordinary Escape out of the Hands of the Indians in the Gulph of St. Lawrence*. London: Privately printed.

Smith, B. D. 1989. "Origins of Agriculture in Eastern North America." *Science* 246: 1566–71.

Smith, Marion Whitney. 1962. *Algonquin and Abenaki Indian Myths and Legends*. Lewiston: Central Maine Press.

Smith, Nicholas N. 1955. "Wabanaki Dances." *Bulletin of the Massachusetts Archaeological Society* 16: 29–37.

———. 1977. "The Changing Role of the Wabanaki Chief and Shaman." Pp. 213–22 in *Actes du Huitieme Congres des Algonquianistes*, ed. William Cowan. Ottawa: Carleton University.

———. 1979. "The Adoption of Medicinal Plants by the Wabanaki." Pp. 167–72 in *Papers of the Tenth Algonquian Conference*, ed. William Cowan. Ottawa: Carleton University.

Smith, Robinson V. 1952. "New Hampshire Persons Taken Captive by the Indians." *Historical New Hampshire* 8 (October): 24–31.

Smith, Timothy J. 1983. "Wampum as Primitive Valuables." *Research in Economic Anthropology* 5: 225–46.

Smith, Walter B. 1926. *Indian Remains of the Penobscot Valley and Their Significance.* Orono: University of Maine Press.

Smyth, Egbert C., ed. 1891. "The construction and first occupancy of Fort Dummer and a conference with the Scatacook Indians held there." *Proceedings of the Massachusetts Historical Society*, 2d ser., 6 (March): 359–81.

Snow, Dean. 1968. "Wabanaki Family Hunting Territories." *American Anthropologist*, n.s., 70: 1143–51.

——. 1976a. "Abenaki Fur Trade in the Sixteenth Century." *Western Canadian Journal of Anthropology* 6, no. 1: 3–11.

——. 1976b. "The Archaeological Implications of the Proto-Algonquian Urheimat." Pp. 339–46 in *Papers of the Seventh Algonquian Conference*, ed. William Cowan. Ottawa: Carleton University Press.

——. 1976c. *The Archaeology of North America.* New York: Viking Press.

——. 1976d. "The Ethnohistoric Baseline of the Eastern Abanakis." *Ethnohistory* 23: 291–306.

——. 1976e. "The Solon Petroglyphs and Eastern Abenaki Shamanism." Pp. 281–88 in *Papers of the Seventh Algonquian Conference*, ed. William Cowan. Ottawa: Carleton University Press.

——. 1977a. "Archaeology and Ethnohistory in Eastern New York." Pp. 107–12 in *Current Perspectives in Northeastern Archaeology: Essays in Honor of William A. Ritchie*, ed. R. E. Funk and C. F. Hayes. Albany, N.Y.: New York State Archaeological Association.

——. 1977b. "The Archaic of the Lake George Region." *Annals of the New York Academy of Sciences* 288: 431–38.

——. 1977c. "Rock Art and the Power of Shamans." *Natural History* 86, no. 2, 42–49.

——. 1978a. "Late Prehistory of the East Coast." Pp. 58–69 in *Northeast*, ed. Bruce G. Trigger. Vol. 15 of *Handbook of North American Indians*. Washington, D.C.: Smithsonian Institution.

——. 1978b. "Eastern Abenaki." Pp. 137–47 in *Northeast*, ed. Bruce G. Trigger. Vol. 15 of *Handbook of North American Indians*. Washington, D.C.: Smithsonian Institution.

——. 1980. *The Archaeology of New England.* New York: Academic Press.

——. 1992. "L'Augmentation de la population chez les Groupes Iroquoiens et les Conséquences sur l'Edude de Leurs Origens:. *Recherches Amerindiens au Quebec* 22, no. 4, 5–36.

Snow, Dean R., and Kim M. Lamphear. 1988. "European Contact and Indian Depopulation in the Northeast: The Timing of the First Epidemics." *Ethnohistory* 35 (Winter): 15–33.

Socobasin, Mary Ellen. 1979. "Maliyan." Indian Township, Maine: Wabanaki Bilingual Education Program.

Speare, Elizabeth George. 1963. *Life in Colonial America.* New York: Random House.

Speck, Frank G. 1904. "A Modern Mohegan Pequot Text." *American Anthropologist*, n.s., vol. 6, no. 4.

——. 1909. "Notes on the Mohegan and Niantic Indians." *Anthropological Papers* 3: 183–200. New York: American Museum of Natural History.

——. 1914. "The Double Curve Motive in Northeastern Algonkian Art." *Memoirs* (Canada Department of Mines Geological Survey) 42: 1–17.

————. 1915a. "The Eastern Algonkian Wabanaki Confederacy." *American Anthropologist*, n.s., 17: 492–508.

————. 1915a. "Medicine Practices of the Northeastern Algonquians." Washington, D.C.: *International Congress of Americanists, Nineteenth Session, Proceedings* 19: 303–21.

————. 1915b. "Penobscot Tales." *Journal of American Folklore*, vol. 28, no. 107.

————. 1915c. "Some Micmac Tales from Cape Breton Island." *Journal of American Folklore* 28: 59–69.

————. 1917a. "Game Totems among the Northeastern Algonkians." *American Anthropologist*, 19, no. 1.

————. 1917b. "Malecite Tales." *Journal of American Folklore* 30: 479–85.

————. 1917c. "One of Caesar's Anecdotes among the Indians of Eastern North America." *The Alumni Register*, University of Pennsylvania, vol. 19, no. 9, 686–90.

————. 1917d. "The Social Structure of the Northern Algonkian." *Publications of the American Sociological Society*, vol. 12.

————. 1918. "Penobscot Transformer Texts." *International Journal of American Linguistics* 1, no. 3, 187–244.

————. 1920. "Penobscot Shamanism." *Memoirs of the American Anthropological Association* 6, no. 3, 239–88.

————. 1921. "Bird-Lore of the Northern Indians." *Public Lectures of the University of Pennsylvania*, vol. 7.

————. 1923. "Reptile-Lore of the Northern Indians." *Journal of American Folk-Lore*, vol. 36, no. 141, 273–290.

————. 1927. "Symbolism in Penobscot Art." *Anthropological Papers*, vol. 29, no. 2,. New York: American Museum of Natural History.

————. 1928. "Wawenock Myth Texts from Maine." *Forty-Third Annual Report*. Washington, D. C.: Bureau of American Ethnology.

————. 1935a. "Mammoth or 'Stiff-legged Bear.'" *American Anthropologist* 37, no. 1, 159–63.

————. 1935b. "Penobscot Tales and Religious Beliefs." *Journal of American Folklore* 48, no. 187, 1–107.

————. 1937a. Montagnais Art in Birch-Bark: A Circumpolar Trait." *Indian Notes and Monographs*, vol. 11, no. 2, 45–157. New York: Museum of the American Indian, Heye Foundation.

————. 1937b. "The Penobscot Indians of Maine." *The General Magazine and Historical Chronicle, University of Pennsylvania* 34, no. 4 (July): 396–405.

————. 1938. "Aboriginal Conservators," *Bird-Lore* 40: 259.

————. 1940. *Penobscot Man: The Life History of a Forest Tribe in Maine*. Philadelphia: University of Pennsylvania Press.

————. 1947. "The Eastern Algonkian Block-Stamp Decoration: A New World—Original or an Acculturated Art." Research Series 1. Trenton: Archeological Society of New Jersey, State Museum.

Speck, Frank G., and Ralph W. Dexter. 1951. "Utilization of Animals and Plants by the Micmac Indians of New Brunswick." *Journal* (Washington Academy of Sciences) 41, no. 8, 250–59.

————. 1952. "Utilization of Animals and Plants by the Maliceet Indians of New Brunswick." *Journal* (Washington, D.C.: Academy of Sciences) 42, no. 1, 1–7.

Spence, M. W., and W. A. Fox. 1986. "The Early Woodland Occupations of Southern Ontario." Pp. 4–46 in *Early Woodland Archaeology*, ed. K. Farnsworth and T. Emerson. Kampsville, Ill.: Center for American Archaeology Press.

Spiess, Arthur E. 1985. "The Michaud Site: A New Major Fluted-Point Paleoindian Site in Auburn Maine." *Maine Archaeological Society Bulletin* 25, no. 2, 38–41.

————. 1992. "A Hell Gap Point and Late Paleoindian Maine." *Maine Archaeological Society Bulletin* 32, no.2, 31–47.

————. 1993. "The Turner Farm Fauna: Five Thousand Years of Hinting and Fishing in Penobscot Bay, Maine." Manuscript on file at the Maine State Museum.

Spiess, Arthur E., and Bruce D. Spiess. 1987. "New England Pandemic of 1616–1622: Cause and Archaeological Implication." *Man in the Northeast* 34 (Fall): 71–83.

Spiess, Arthur E., and Deborah Wilson. Michaud: 1987. *A Paleoindian Site in the New England–Maritimes Region.* Occasional Publications in Maritime Archaeology 6. Augusta: Maine Historic Preservation Commission and Maine Archaeological Society.

Squire, Mariella. 1977a. "An Archaeological Survey of the Proposed Water Pollution Control Project for Proctor, Vermont." Report submitted to Division for Historic Preservation, Montpelier.

————. 1977b. "Classification of Projectile Points from the Champlain Valley in Vermont." Master's thesis, State University of New York, Buffalo.

————. 1996. *The Western Abenakis: Maintenance, Reclamation and Reconfiguration of an American Indian Ethnic Identity.* Ann Arbor, Mich.: University Microfilms.

Stachiw, Myro O. 1979. *Massachusetts Offices and Soldiers, 1723–1743: Dummer's War to the War of Jenkin's Ear.* Boston: New England Historic Genealogical Society.

Stanford, D., and B. Bradley. 2000. "The Soultrean Solution." *Discovering Archaeology* 2, no. 1, 54–55.

Starbird, Glenn. 1977. "Fraud Found in Sale of Townships." *Wabanaki Alliance*, October.

————. 1978. "Nicatow: A Lost Island." *Wabanaki Alliance*, December.

Starbuck, D. R., and C. E. Bolian, eds. 1980. *Early and Middle Archaic Culture in the Northeast.* George's Mills, N.H.: Man in the Northeast, Occasional Publications in Northeastern Anthropology.

Steele, Zadock. 1854. "Captivity of Zadock Steele." Pp. 209–76 in *Indian Narratives.* Claremont, N.H.: Tracy and Brothers.

Stevens, Paul Lawrence. 1984. "His Majesty's 'Savage' Allies: British Policy and the Northern Indians during the Revolutionary War: The Carleton Years, 1774–1778." Ph.D. diss., State University of New York at Buffalo.

Stevens, Phineas. 1837. "Journal of Capt. Phineas Stevens to and from Canada, 1749." *Collections of the New Hampshire Historical Society* 5: 199–205.

————. 1916. "Journal of Captain Phineas Stevens' Journey to Canada, 1752." In *Travels in the American Colonies*, ed. Newton D. Mereness. New York: Macmillan Co.

Stevens, Susan McCullough. 1978. "Passamaquoddy Economic Development in Cultural and Historical Perspective." In *American Indian Economic Development*, ed. Sam Stanley. The Hague: Mouton.

Stiles, Dr. Ezra. 1809. "Indians on Connecticut River." *Collections of the Massachusetts Historical Society*, 1st ser., 10: 104–5.

Stillinger, Elizabeth. 1980. *The Antiquers.* New York: Knopf.

Stockwell, John. 1928. *The Account of John Stockwell of Deerfield, Massachusetts: Being a Faithful Narrative of His Experiences in the Hands of the Wachusett Indians, 1677–1678.* Somerville, N.J.: Clark S. Yowell.

Strong, W. D. 1934. "North American Traditions Suggesting a Knowledge of the Mammoth." *American Anthropologist* 36, no. 1, 81–88.

Stoltman, J. B. 1978. "Temporal Models in Prehistory: An Example from Eastern North America." *Current Anthropology* 19: 703–46.

Stvan, E. R. "Analysis of the Ewing Site Ceramics." Burlington: University of Vermont, Department of Anthropology. Typescript.

Sullivan John. 1930–39. *Letters and Papers of Major-General John Sullivan*. Edited by Otis G. Hammond. 3 vols. Concord: New Hampshire Historical Society.

Swartz, B. K., Jr. 1971. *Adena: The Seeking of an Identity*. Muncie, Ind.: Ball State University.

Tallchief, A. 1980. "Money vs. Sovereignty: An Analysis of the Maine Settlement." *American Indian Journal* 7, no. 5, 19–22.

Tanguay, Cyprien. 1871–90. *Dictionnaire Genealogique des Familles Canadiennnes*. 7 vols. Montreal: Eusebe Senecal.

Tanner, Helen Hornbeck, ed. 1987. *Atlas of the Great Lakes Indian History*. Norman: University of Oklahoma Press.

Taylor, Colin 1991. "The Subarctic" Pp. 182–203 in *The Native Americans*, by R. Collins. New York: Smithmark.

Temple, Josiah, and George Sheldon. 1875. *History of the Town of Northfield, Massachusetts, for 150 Years, with an Account of the Prior Occupation of the Territory by the Squakheags*. Albany, N.Y.: Joel Munsell.

Thomas, Peter Allen. 1973. "Squakheag Ethnohistory: A Preliminary Study of Culture Conflict on the Seventeenth Century Frontier." *Man in the Northeast* 5 (Spring): 27–36.

———. 1976. "Contrastive Subsistence Strategies and Land Use as Factors for Understanding Indian-White Relations in New England." *Ethnohistory* 23 (Winter): 1–18.

———. 1979. "In the Maelstrom of Change: The Indian Trade and Cultural Process in the Middle Connecticut River Valley, 1635–1665." Ph.D. diss., University of Massachusetts.

———. 1980. "Comments on Recent Trends in Vermont Archaeology." *Man in the Northeast* 19 (Spring): 3–14.

———. 1981. "The Fur Trade, Indian Land, and the Need to Define Adequate 'Environmental Parameters.'" *Ethnohistory* 28: 359–79.

———. 1984. "Bridging the Cultural Gap: Indian/White Relations." In *Early Settlement in the Connecticut Valley*, ed. John W. Ifkovic and Martin Kaufman. Deerfield, Mass.: Westfield College, Institute for Massachusetts Studies.

Thomas, P. A., G. P. Kochan, and P. J. Doherty. 1992. *Windows to the Past: Archaeological Excavations at the Grand Isle Fish Hatchery, Grand Isle, Vermont*. Report No. 115. Burlington: University of Vermont, Department of Anthropology.

Thompson, S. 1966. *Tales of the North American Indians*. Bloomington: Indiana University Press.

Thompson, Zadock. 1842. *History of Vermont, Natural, Civil, and Statistical*. Burlington, Vt.: C. Goodrich.

Thoreau, Henry David. 1981. *The Maine Woods*. New York: Crowell.

Thornton, Russell. 1987. *American Indian Holocaust and Survival: A Population History since 1492*. Norman: University of Oklahoma Press.

Thwaites, Reuben Gold, ed. 1896–1901. *The Jesuit Relations and Allied Documents: Travels and Explorations of the Jesuit Missionaries in New France, 1610–1791*. 73 vols. Cleveland, Ohio: Burrows Brothers Co.

Timreck, T. W. 1987. "Search for the Lost Red Paint People." *Nova* Program. Boston: WGBH Educational Foundation.

Tokec, Katop Qenoq Sipkiw; For Now, but Not for Long. 1974. Indian Township, Maine: Wabanaki Bilingual Education Program.

Tooker, Elizabeth. 1979. *Native North American Spirituality of the Eastern Woodlands: Sacred Myths, Dreams, Healing Formulas, Rituals and Ceremonials*. New York, Paulist Press.

Trelease, Allen W. 1960. *Indian Affairs in Colonial New York: The Seventeenth Century.* Ithaca, N.Y.: Cornell University Press.

Tremblay, Roland 1999. "Culture et ethnicité en archéologie les Aléas de l'Identité conjuuée au passe." *Recherches Amerindiens au Quebec* 29, no. 1, 3–8.

Trigger, Bruce G. 1962. "Trade and Tribal Warfare on the St. Lawrence in the Sixteenth Century." *Ethnohistory* 9 (Summer): 240–56.

———. 1971a. "Champlain Judged by His Indian Policy: A Different View of Early Canadian History." *Anthropologia* n.s., 13: 85–114.

———. 1971b. "The Mohawk-Mahican War (1624–28): The Establishment of a Pattern." *Canadian Historical Review* 52: 276–86.

———. 1976. *The Children of Aataentsic: A History of Huron People to 1660.* 2 vols. Montreal: McGill-Queen's University Press.

———. 1978a. "Cultural Unity and Diversity." Pp. 798–804 in *Northeast*, ed. B. G. Trigger. Vol. 15 of *Handbook of North American Indians*. Washington, D.C.: Smithsonian Institution.

———, ed. 1978b. *Northeast*. Vol. 15 of *Handbook of North American Indians*, ed. William C. Sturtevant. Washington, D.C.: Smithsonian Institution.

———. 1985. *Natives and Newcomers: Canada's "Heroic Age" Reconsidered.* Kingston and Montreal: McGill-Queen's University Press.

Trigger, B. G., and J. F. Pendergast. 1978. "Saint Lawrence Iroquoians." Pp. 357–61 in *Northeast*, ed. B.G. Trigger. Vol. 15 of *Handbook of North American Indians*. Washington, D.C.: Smithsonian Institution.

Trottier, Maxine. 1995. *The Voyage of Wood Duck.* Sydney, N.S.: University College of Cape Breton Press.

Trumbull, James Russell. 1898–1902. *History of Northampton, Massachusetts, From Its Settlement in 1654.* 2 vols. Northampton.

Tsonakwa, and Yolaikia. 1986. *Legends in Stone, Bone and Wood.* Minneapolis: Arts and Learning Services Foundation.

Tuck, J. A. 1970a. "Port au Choix." *Scientific American*, 223(1): 112–14.

———. 1970b. "An Archaic Indian Cemetery in Newfoundland." *Scientific American* 222, no. 6, 112–21.

———. 1971. "An Archaic Cemetery in Port Au Choix, Newfoundland." *American Antiquity* 36: 343–58.

———. 1975a. "Maritime Adaptation on the Northeastern Atlantic Coast." Pp. 255–67 in *Prehistoric Maritime Adaptations of the Circumpolar Zone*, ed. W. Fitzhugh. The Hague: Mouton; reprint, Chicago: Aldine.

———. 1975b. "The Northeastern Maritime Continuum: 8000 Years of Cultural Development in the Far Northeast." *Arctic Anthropology* 12, no. 2, 139–47.

———. 1977. "A Look at Laurentian." Pp. 31–40 in *Current Perspectives in Northeastern Archaeology: Essays in Honor of William A. Ritchie*, ed. R. E. Funk and C. F. Hayes. Albany: New York State Archaeological Association.

———. 1978a. "Northern Iroquoian Prehistory." Pp. 322–33 in *Northeast*, ed. B. G. Trigger. Vol. 15 in *Handbook of North American Indians*. Washington, D.C.: Smithsonian Institution.

———. 1978b. "Regional Cultural Development 3000 to 300 B.C." Pp. 29–43 in *Northeast*, ed. B. G. Trigger. Vol. 15 in *Handbook of North American Indians*. Washington, D.C.: Smithsonian Institution.

———. 1981. *Visages de la prehistoire du Canada.* James Wright. Ottawa, Ont.

———. 1984. *A Maritime Provinces Prehistory.* Ottawa: National Museum of Man.

———. 1985. *La Prehistoire des Provinces Maritimes.* Montreal: Presses Elite, for Editions Fides.

Tufts, Henry. 1807. *A Narrative of the Life, Adventures, Travels and Sufferings of Henry Tufts*. Dover, N.H.: Samuel Bragg, Jr.

——. 1930. *Henry Tufts: The Autobiography of a Criminal*. Edited by Edmund Pearson. New York: Duffield and Co.

Turgeon, L. 1932. "Pecheurs Basques et Indiens des Cotes du Saint-Laurent au Xvie Siecle: Perspectives de Recherches." *Etudes Canadians: Le Canada Atlantique, Acts de Colloque de Nantes* 13: 11.

Ulrich, Laurel Thatcher. 1982. *Good Wives: Image and Reality in the Lives of Women in Northern New England, 1650–1750*. New York: Knopf.

Underwood, Wynn. 1947. "Indian and Tory Raids on the Otter Valley, 1777–1782." *Vermont Quarterly*, n.s., 15 (October): 195–221.

Upton, L. F. S. *Micmacs and Colonists: Indian-White Relations in the Maritimes*. Vancouver: University of British Columbia Press.

U.S. Commission on Civil Rights, Maine Advisory Committee. 1974. *Federal and State Services and the Maine Indian*. Washington: The Commission.

Van Wart, Arthur F. 1948. "Indians of the Maritimes: Their Diseases and Native Cures." *Canadian Medical Association Journal* 59: 573–77.

Varny, Lloyd H. 1971. "A Blue Hill Bay Coastal Midden Site." *Maine Archaeological Society Bulletin* 2, no. 1, 14–32.

Vastokas, Joan M., and R. K. Vastokas. 1973. *Sacred Art of Algonkians: A Study of the Peterborough Petroglyphs*. Peterborough, Ont.: Mansard Press.

Vaughan, Alden T. 1979. *New England Frontier: Puritans and Indians, 1620–1674/5*. Rev. ed. New York: W. W. Norton and Co.

Vaughan, Alden T., and Edward W. Clark, eds. 1981. *Puritans among the Indians: Accounts of Captivity and Redemption, 1676–1724*. Cambridge, Mass.: Belknap Press of Harvard University Press.

Vaughan, Alden T., and Daniel Richter. 1980. "Crossing the Cultural Divide: Indians and New Englanders, 1605–1763." *Proceedings of the American Antiquarian Society* 90, pt. 1 (October): 23–99.

Vecsey, Christopher. 1983. *Traditional Ojibwa Religion and Its Historical Changes*. Philadelphia: American Philosophical Society.

Vermont, Secretary of State. 1918–80. *State Papers of Vermont*. 17 vols. Montpelier, Vt.: Secretary of State's Office.

Vetromile, Rev. Eugene. 1859. "The Abnaki Indians." *Maine Historical Society Collections* 6, ser. 1, pp. 53–92. Portland, Maine: Brown Thruston.

——. 1866. *The Abenakis and their History*, New York: J. B. Kirker.

Vogel, V. J. 1970. *American Indian Medicine*. Norman: University of Oklahoma Press.

Vogelmann, T. C., et al. 1972. *Prehistoric Life in the Champlain Valley*. Film available from the University of Vermont Media Services, the Vermont Department of Libraries Audio-Visual Unit, and the Vermont Historical Society.

"VT-CH-3, Progress Report." 1970. *VAS Newsletter* 3:1–2.

Walker, Willard, Robert Conkling, and Gregory Buesing. 1980. "A Chronological Account of the Wabanaki Confederacy." In *Political Organization of Native North Americans*, ed. Ernest L. Schusky. Washington, D.C.: University Press of America.

——. 1984. "Wabanki Wampum Protocal." Pp. 107–22 in *Papers of the Fifteenth Algonquian Conference*, ed. William Cowan. Ottawa: Carleton University.

Wallace, Anthony. 1957. *Political Orginization and Lane Tenure Among the Northeastern Indians, 1600–1830*. *Journal of Anthropological Research* 13: 301–21.

Wallis, Wilson D., and Ruth Sawtell Wallis. 1955. *The Micmac Indians of Eastern Canada*. Minneapolis: University of Minnesota.

——. 1961. "The Maliecite Indians of New Brunswick." *National Museum of Canada Bulletin* 173: 42–63.

Walton, E. P., ed. 1813–80. *Records of the Governor and Council of the State of Vermont.* 8 vols. Montpelier, Vt.: J. M. Poland.

"Waltes, an Ancient Micmac Game." *Cape Breton's Magazine,* December 1973, no. 6, 9–12.

Washington, George. 1931–44. *The Writings of George Washington.* Edited by John C. Fitzpatrick. 39 vols. Washington, D.C.: Government Printing Office.

Washington, Ida H., and Paula A. Washington. 1977. *Carleton's Raid.* Canaan, N.H.: Phoenix Publishing.

Wells, Frederic P. 1902. *History of Newbury, Vermont, from the Discovery of the Coos Country to the Present Time.* St. Johnsbury, Vt.: Caledonian Co.

West, John. 1827. *A Journal of a Mission to the Indians of the British Provinces of New Brunswick and Nova Scotia, etc.* London: Seely.

Wheelwright, Nathaniel. 1960. "Nathaniel Wheelwright's Canadian Journey, 1753–4." Edited by Edward P. Hamilton. *Bulletin of Fort Ticonderoga Museum* 10 (February): 259–96.

Wherry, J. D. 1979. "Abenaki, Etchemin, and Malecite." Pp. 181–90 in *Papers of the Tenth Algonquian Conference,* ed. William Cowan. Ottawa: Carleton University Press.

White, Rev. Henry. 1843. *The Early History of New England.* 8th ed. Concord, N.H.: I. S. Boyd.

Whitehead, Ruth Holmes. 1980. *Elitekey: Micmac Material Culture from 1600 A.D. to the Present.* Halifax: Nova Scotia Museum.

——. 1982. *Micmac Quillwork: Micmac Indian Technique of Porcupine Quill Decoration 1600–1950.* Halifax: Nova Scotia Museum.

——. 1987. "I Have Lived Here since the World Began: Atlantic Coast Artistic Tradition." In *The Spirit Sings: Artistic Traditions of Canada's First People.* Calgary: McClellan and Stewarts and the Glenbow Museum.

——. 1988. *Stories from the Six Worlds,* Micmac Legends. Halifax, N.S.: Nimbus.

——. 1991. *The Old Man Told Us: Excerpts form Micmac History 1500–1950.* Halifax, N.S.: Nimbus Publishing.

——. n.d. "Every Thing They Make and Wear." Halifax: Provincial Museum of Nova Scotia. Unpublished manuscript.

Whitehead, Ruth Holmes, and Harold McGee. 1983. *The Micmac: How Their Ancestors Lived Five Hundred Years Ago.* Halifax, N.S.: Nimbus Publishing.

Whitt, Laurie A. 1998. "Cultural Imperialism and the Marketing of Native America" Pp. 135–71 in *Natives and Academics,* ed. Devon Mihesuah. Lincoln: University of Nebraska Press.

Wilbur, C. Keith. 1978. *The New England Indians.* Chester, Conn.: Globe Pequot Press.

Williams, Herbert U. 1919. "The Epidemic of the Indians of New England, 1616–1620." *Johns Hopkins Hospital Bulletin* 20: 340–49.

Williams, John. 1707/1966. *The Redeemed Captive Returning to Zion, or a Faithful History of Remarkable Occurrences in the Captivity and Deliverance of Mr. John Williams.* 1707; Ann Arbor, Mich.: University Microfilms.

Williams, Samuel. 1794. *The Natural and Civil History of Vermont.* Walpole, N.H.: Isaiah Thomas and David Carlisle.

Willoughby, Charles C. 1898. "Prehistoric Burial Places in Maine." *Archaeological and Ethnographical Papers of the Peabody Museum. Harvard University* 1, no. 6, 1–52.

——. 1905. "Dress and Ornaments of the New England Indians." *American Anthropologist*, n.s., 7(2): 409–508.

——. 1906. "Houses and Gardens of the New England Indians." *American Anthropologist*, n.s., 8(1): 115–32.

——. 1907. "The Adze and the Ungrooved Axe of the New England Indians." *American Anthropologist*, n.s., 9(2): 296–306.

——. 1935. *Antiquities of the New England Indians*. Cambridge, Mass.: Peabody Museum of American Archaeology and Ethnology.

Wiseman, F. M. 1986. "The Scientific Antiquary." *Maine Antiques Digest*. Edited by Samuel Pennington. Waldoboro, Maine: May C11–C13.

——. 1991a. "Colchester Jar." Pp. 98–99 in *Celebrating Vermont: Myths and Realities*, ed. Nancy P. Graff. Hanover, N.H.: University Press of New England.

——. 1991b. "Quillwork Trinket Box"; "Thimble Cover, Notions Basket, and Pincushion"; "Beaded Reticule." Pp. 178–83 in *Celebrating Vermont: Myths and Realities*, ed. Nancy P. Graff. Hanover, N.H.: University Press of New England.

——. 1991c. "Rectangular Bark Container." Pp. 204–5 in *Celebrating Vermont: Myths and Realities*, ed. Nancy P. Graff. Hanover, N.H.: University Press of New England.

——. 1991d. "Tipi and Canoe"; "Samoset." Pp. 216–19 in *Celebrating Vermont: Myths and Realities*, ed. Nancy P. Graff. Hanover, N.H.: University Press of New England.

——. 1995a. *The Abenaki People and the Bounty of the Land*. Ethan Allen Homestead Abenaki Education Series no. 3. Burlington Vt.: Lane Publications.

——. 1995b. *Gift of the Forest*. Ethan Allen Homestead Abenaki Education Series, no. 1. Burlington Vt.: Lane Publications.

——. 1995c. *Negwejigaden Alnôbaiwi: The Abenaki Calendar*. Poster. Underhill, Vt.: Cedarwood Press.

——. 1995d. *Wabanaki Games*. Underhill, Vt.: Cedarwood Press.

——. 1995e. *Western Abenaki Clothing*. Ethan Allen Homestead Abenaki Education Series no. 2. Burlington Vt.: Lane Publications.

——. 1997a. *The Great Council Fire*. Swanton, Vt.: Wôbanakik Heritage Center Publications.

——. 1997b. *Wabanaki Wampum*. Swanton, Vt.: Wôbanakik Heritage Center Publications.

——. 1999. "The Last Alliance: The Abenaki and the Great Council Fire." Paper presented at the "Revisiting the Original Vermonters" symposium, University of Vermont, Burlington. November.

Wiseman, Frederick M., and Laurence Hauptman. 1996. "The Western Abenaki." *Encyclopedia of Native Americans in the Twentieth Century*, ed. Mary Davis. New York: Garland Publishing.

Woodrow, Arthur D., ed. and comp. 1928. *Metallak: The Last of the Coonshaukes*. Rumford, Maine: Rumford Publishing Co.

Woodward, Arthur. 1970. *The Denominators of the Fur Trade*. Pasadena, Calif.: Western Lore Press.

Wright, H. E., and D. G. Frey. 1965. *The Quaternary of the United States*. Princeton, N.J.: Princeton University Press.

Index